YUGOSLAVIA:
Utopia or Inspiration?

From Exalting Vision
to Fractured Reality

YUGOSLAVIA:
Utopia or Inspiration?

From Exalting Vision to Fractured Reality

SRDJAN RISTIC

ISBN: 9798878919012

Published by:
Maverick
Belgrade, Serbia

For permissions, contact author:
yutopia.or.inspiration@gmail.com

First Edition in English: 2024

Disclaimer:
The information presented in this book is based on extensive research, historical records, and the author's interpretation of events. While every effort has been made to ensure accuracy, historical events, perspectives, and interpretations may vary. The author and publisher do not claim to present an exhaustive or definitive account of the subjects discussed. The views, interpretations, and con-clusions presented herein are those of the author and do not necessarily reflect the views of all scholars, institutions, or histori-cal experts. Readers are encouraged to consult a varie-ty of sources and experts to form a comprehensive understanding of the topics covered

Table of Contents

Foreword

Within the pages of this book lies a fascinating exploration of Yugoslavia's history—a story woven with the threads of diverse perspectives, geopolitical intricacies, and the aspirations that shaped a nation and its eventual dissolution.

Srdjan Ristić meticulously unravels the tale, chronicling the emergence of the pan-Slavic Yugoslav idea amidst the Balkan Peninsula's strategic significance. From the arrival of the South Slavs and the religious schisms that delineated their identities, to their struggles between Ottoman and Habsburg rule, each chapter unpacks the kaleidoscope of events that laid the foundation for Yugoslavia's birth.

The book navigates through the dawn of Yugoslavia, exploring the circumstances that gave rise to the state and the challenges faced in its recognition on the international stage. Ristić delves into lesser-known facts about Serbia in First World War and the internal strife within the Kingdom of Yugoslavia, capturing the complex essence of a nation grappling with its unity.

The Second Yugoslavia, under Josip Broz Tito's leadership, emerges vividly—a period marked by political dilemmas, internal shifts, and the country's golden age in the 1970s. Ristić then examines the twilight years, portraying the buildup to Yugoslavia's eventual demise and the emergence of figures like Slobodan Milošević, whose policies sparked seismic shifts in the region.

The final chapters document the disintegration of Yugoslavia, the Balkan wars of the 1990s, and the aftermath—a period marked by struggles for sovereignty, conflicts like the Kosovo War, and the post-Yugoslav reconciliation efforts.

In the concluding reflections, Ristić deftly explores the question: Was Yugoslavia a mistake? The differing views from Serbian, Croatian, Slovenian, Macedonian, Bosniak, and Montenegrin perspectives provide a nuanced range of opinions, painting a vivid picture of the complex legacy left behind.

The book also delves into the intriguing debate on whether the Yugoslav idea was a utopian dream or an enduring inspiration. It invites readers to contemplate the lasting impact of an idea that briefly unified a diverse array of people and ideologies in pursuit of a common identity.

Ristić's meticulous research and empathetic portrayal of divergent narratives offer readers not just a historical account but a reflection on the human spirit's resilience amid turbulent historical currents—a narrative that transcends borders and ideologies.

This book serves as an invitation—an invitation to journey through a tumultuous yet captivating history, to unravel the complexities of a nation born of aspirations, conflicts, and the perennial search for identity amidst diversity.

Dr. Rudy B. Baker
Austin Peay State University
Clarksville, TN
December 23, 2023

Acknowledgements

I extend my sincerest gratitude to the Museum of Yugoslavia in Belgrade and its Curator, Mr. Radovan Cukić. Over the years, their friendship, professional cooperation, and support have been invaluable. This generous assistance, particularly in drawing attention to and providing photographs from the museum fund, enriched this work, infusing it with depth and visual richness.

Furthermore, I express my immense gratitude to Professors Rudy and Olja Baker for their friendship, support, and contribution to refining this manuscript. Through many fruitful exchanges with Rudy over the years, delving into the historical and political processes in the former Yugoslavia, my understanding of this complex topic has significantly expanded. Rudy's insightful Foreword beautifully illuminates the material's essential strengths.

I also extend my heartfelt thanks to numerous colleagues, readers, and attendees at my lectures. Their willingness to share knowledge, insights, offer constructive criticism, and pose excellent questions has significantly contributed to my ongoing understanding.

Author's Preface

The birth, life, and disintegration of Yugoslavia continue to elude full comprehension, sparking enduring interest in the subject. Despite countless pieces of evidence presented in international and domestic courts for crimes committed in the former Yugoslavia, numerous books written, scientific papers published, and documentary and feature films made, it appears that the former Yugoslav state still harbors unexplored avenues of insight and knowledge.

When visiting countries that were formerly part of Yugoslavia, foreign visitors often pose the same questions:

"Why did Yugoslavia disintegrate?"

"Why did you kill each other so brutally?"

"Why didn't you stay together in the same state when it would have been better for everyone?"

"Why did you Yugoslavs divide—while Europe was unifying?"

"Did Slobodan Milošević instigate the breakup of Yugoslavia?"

However, a thorough and comprehensive understanding remains elusive, even for us, the former citizens of Yugoslavia. The reason is simple. Except for relatively rare individuals, most people are firmly anchored in the viewpoints of the nation they belong to, from which only very limited, partial truths can be seen. The lingering memories of the war inhibit efforts to view the conflicts and traumas from the perspective of the former adversaries. Yet, a fuller understanding requires viewing in a far broader frame than has been the case up until now.

Efforts to unravel the Yugoslav enigma only from the perspective of one's own nation, or by examining the last decade of the state's existence, are bound to fail. Such a narrow view reveals just a small portion of the full picture. The situation is further complicated by both global and local media's pronounced tendency to present events, actors, and processes in a simplified, black-and-white manner. This has led to the creation of a series of prejudices and entrenched semi-truthful narratives, which to this day maintain—or even deepen—existing divisions, as they are uncritically passed on to younger generations.

I developed an interest in Yugoslavia during my school days. Its complexity, avant-gardism, and unique spirit had already captivated my attention back then. However, the motivation to undertake the writing of this book came much later, at the end of the first decade of the 21st century. At that time I was intensely traveling the world, but I was also often meeting foreigners in Serbia. Almost as a rule, my interlocutors were genuinely interested in the country that had long ceased to exist and insisted on thorough explanations. Thus, the idea to transform these conversations into written material primarily intended for a foreign audience was born.

The object of observation—Yugoslavia—is multidimensional, multilayered, and extremely complex. This I affirm from my own conviction and experience. For more than thirty years, I have dedicated much thought to the country in which I was born, spent my carefree childhood, and later, as a young man, was witness to its tragic, painful, and relatively long descent from the historical scene. The book before you is the culmination of years of study, research, preparation, and lectures, as well as discussions with numerous contemporaries of Yugoslavia.

In writing, I was guided by the desire to present the material in a logical and chronological way so that it would be understandable to the widest possible audience, both domestic and foreign.

In order to achieve this goal, I endeavored to include the perspectives of all the relevant internal and external actors who wove the intricate dynamics of the Yugoslav drama. I described the events which I witnessed firsthand and presented my personal insights and conclusions. Additionally, I looked back into the past as far as I deemed necessary. I hope that most readers of this book will find information that will deepen and enrich their understanding of Yugoslavia. This thought gives me sparks of optimism regarding the future.

The country that no longer exists still offers a wealth of opportunities for learning and reflection—on vision, courage, sacrifice, love, honor, the play of great powers, delusions, low and high politics, hatred, blindness, and brutality. In the simplest terms—on the great takeoff and fatal fall.

I am particularly hopeful that this work will resonate with the younger generations born after the tragic dissolution of their parents' country. The future will bring them the challenge of reconciliation with their neighbors in the former Yugoslav space. My hope is that they will be wiser and correct the mistakes of our generation. I will be truly fulfilled if this book aids in this endeavor.

Introduction

In the spring of 2009, I was asked to explain the breakup of Yugoslavia to passengers on a river cruiser that had arrived in Belgrade. The company representative informed me that their guests were confused, and had many questions, but their intellectual hunger was still not satisfied.

"It's very complicated," he said to me with a sigh. "They have heard one side of the story in Croatia, another in Serbia today. They don't know what the truth is, but they are very interested." He then asked me, honestly, "Can you help us out, do a presentation, and explain it all?"

"All of it?" I asked with a broad smile. "It will take me about a week," I joked.

"No, no, you only have one hour," was the response. "Do you accept the challenge?"

That day my career as a guest lecturer began.

***

The tragic dissolution of Yugoslavia, which brought a series of wars, United Nations embargo, international sanctions, isolation, and ultimately NATO air strikes on the Serbs, has severely damaged the image of Serbia worldwide, especially in the West. Visitors often come with a preconceived image, which makes them approach exploration and investigation with a degree of hesitation and caution. However, their immediate experience is usually very positive. They feel safe in Serbia and describe its inhabitants as friendly and hospitable people, many of whom speak foreign languages, most commonly very decent English. They are impressed by the vivid atmosphere, cultural heritage, architecture, opulent history, excellent prices, first-class food and drinks, concerts, festivals, and music clubs at a world-class level.

Over time, I came to understand that many of the passengers boarding the cruise down the Lower Danube wanted to actually see and comprehend what is called Eastern Europe. I will never forget the baby-blue, childishly curious eyes of the elderly British lady who, sometime in the early 2000s, exclaimed to me with excitement, "For us in Britain, Eastern Europe is like a big gray zone. We know so little about it, and now, towards the end of my life, I have come to see it. I am eagerly looking forward to exploring Belgrade, knowing I'll learn a lot." I smiled kindly. I recalled how in Yugoslavia we had never classified ourselves as Eastern Europeans. In fact, it was offensive to us when Western tourists did so, and we were left surprised by their lack of awareness.

Indisputably, the Serbs, Serbia, and the ancient city of Belgrade are the keys to understanding the complex historical processes that have been unfolding in this part of the Balkans like a suspenseful thriller for centuries. The enigma called Yugoslavia, in which they have played a major role turns out to be the most fascinating episode yet.

I am particularly delighted that the world still remembers Yugoslavia vividly. Many prominent intellectuals have delved into writing about it. As if its emergence, persistence, and disappearance have extended far beyond the Balkans stage and left a tangled, yet still unsolved, knot in the collective consciousness of humanity, worth researching and pondering. How could the 'Little America', as some labeled the 'melting pot' of the South Slavic nations, not bring about the realization of peace, unity, and prosperity dreamt by the progressive Croatian, Serbian, and Slovenian intellectuals of the 19th and 20th centuries? Were these people just mere idealists? Will we ever get to the bottom of all the dimensions of the 'Yugoslav phenomenon', all its highs and lows?

Due to the undeniable collective traumas we have gone through while our country was painfully and slowly dying, due to the state in which we have entered, and how much damaged we have exited from this nightmare, a vast number of Yugoslavs are still rummaging through their common past trying to find definite answers.

We are not alone. Recently, while strolling down Knez Mihailova, the oldest street in Belgrade, I was pleasantly surprised to see a newly published book about my former country, written by one of the most influential thinkers of our time, Noam Chomsky[1] in the window of my favorite bookstore. I learned that his book had caused some stir and disapproval in certain Western circles as it exposed a critical analysis of the established views on the Yugoslav civil war and the role of the West in it. But that's the beauty of democracy. Let's hear every opinion, even the one that hurts our ears, and think about it soberly.

Although the history of Yugoslavia is burdened with dark pages, there are also those that are very bright. Yugoslavia carried within it ideals that resonated with people all over the world because they vibrated with freedom, justice, equality, brotherhood, and cooperation among nations.

The book before you is inspired by my lectures in English, "Serbia Explained: A Country at the Crossroads of Worlds" and "East Meets West: Our Oriental Heritage." It begins with historical and geopolitical processes that started long before the Yugoslav idea was born, follows its growth and maturation, realization, duration, and eventual dissolution, continuing its

---

[1] Chomsky, Noam. *Yugoslavia: Peace, War, and Dissolution*, edited by Davor Džalto. Oakland: PM Press, 2018.

analysis up to the present moment, and daring to cast restrained glances towards the future.

In a chronological and logical manner, a large number of historical facts have been arranged, many of which will be novel to audiences outside the Yugoslav space. This does not make them any less important, but quite the opposite. Some of them have had a key influence on the perception of the Serbs, as well as other local peoples, which is why their presentation in this work is necessary for a more comprehensive and deeper understanding of Yugoslavia.

I express my sincere gratitude for the opportunity to share with you the results of my long-term research. However, I must admit that this book would likely have never been created if I had not been persistently drawn to it by a particular feeling of love. Yugoslavs are well-acquainted with it, but they can't explain it. Not even to themselves.

"The Blind Men and the Elephant"

Once upon a time, a group of blind people came across an elephant.

"What is this?", asked the first one, touching the animal's side.

"It's an elephant," said the guide, who was standing beside it.

"Ah, so this is an elephant! I've always wondered what an elephant is like," said the blind man, stretching out his hands as far up and down the elephant as he could.

"An elephant is like a big, warm wall!" he said at last.

"What do you mean, wall?" said the second blind man, embracing the elephant's leg.

"This isn't like a wall. It's more like a pillar. Yes, that's it, an elephant is like a big, warm pillar!"

"Pillar? That's a strange kind of pillar!" said the third man, stroking the elephant's trunk. "It's too flexible, like a snake. See, it's winding around my arm. An elephant is like a snake!"

"No way!" said the fourth blind man, tugging at the elephant's tail. "This isn't a snake, it's a rope. Elephants are like ropes."

"Guys, what are you talking about?" shouted the fifth blind man, waving the elephant's ear back and forth. "It's big like a wall, okay, but thin like a sheet and flexible like a piece of cloth. An elephant is like a sail!"

The animal moved on, and the blind men kept arguing, each one of them insisting that he was right and all the others were wrong.

Indian story

Viewing From One Angle or Approaching the Whole From Multiple Perspectives?

There is an important principle that I have adopted over time while participating in numerous, often very intelligent and argumentative discussions on social issues, politics, or history. I will adhere to it while writing this book. In my experience, a successful way to achieve a qualitative shift in the understanding of a topic is to approach it from all relevant points of view.

As a rule, each of us has a unique way of looking at an object, phenomenon, or problem. We see our perspective as right and perceive it as true. We are often willing to fight for our point of view, expressing the intention to impose it or make it dominant within a group of people.

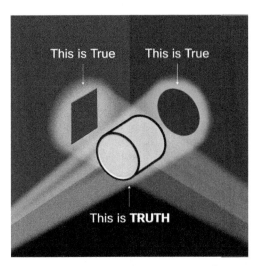

Partial truth emerges from one perspective,
the whole truth from many

But other people usually perceive the same thing quite differently. This is inevitable, expected, and completely natural. The formation of an individual's view is determined by acquired knowledge, mental images, culture, upbringing, previous experiences, but also by their position in space and time. Therefore, it is even theoretically impossible for two individuals to have an exactly identical view of something, although a great proximity is possible.

Is the whole truth then attainable at all? Not in absolute terms, but to a great extent it is. The truth is always multidimensional and the only way to it leads through the consideration and respect of all the essential perspectives that make up its entirety.

For such a task we must be willing to accept that our personal truth is only part of a much larger whole; that it is a partial truth arising from our own perspective and therefore is not superior or inferior to the partial truths of other people.

Moreover, we must include intellect and empathy and be willing to discard certain prejudices that have been taught to us or that we may have formed and carefully nurtured for years. However, as most of us know from personal experience, looking at a different perspective can often be an uncomfortable experience for our ego.

This principle is of course applicable to larger groups of people and even to entire nations. The willingness to look through the eyes of others when searching for a more complete truth can contribute to better mutual understanding and easing of tensions among individuals or groups caused by the breakdown of communication. Such breakdowns occur precisely due to the unwillingness to consider the "enemy's" perspective, as well as all the other ones present in a complex problem such as revolutions or wars.

So far, a large number of authors have dealt with the topic of Yugoslavia and I am sure there will be more in the future. My impression, however, is that too often attempts have been made that did not cover the full multidimensionality of this very complex and exciting story, nor a sufficiently wide temporal and spatial framework.

By traveling through the time and history that this book takes us on, we wish to gain a more comprehensive view of the phenomenon called Yugoslavia. To achieve such an ambitious goal, the reader is given an insight into a very long period of time that begins many centuries before the formation of the South Slav state. In addition, various cause-effect relationships that triggered processes, often in a hidden way, have been illuminated. Adhering to the commitment described above, we will change perspective and move from one corner to another in our observation of things, thus examining the partial truths of the main characters in our story.

I expect that such an approach, known in literature as "multiple viewpoint processing", will bring us to a better understanding of the Yugoslav state and motivate us to persistently reflect on the challenging question:

was it a utopia or an inspiration?

The Strategic Significance of the Balkan Peninsula

or: Life at an Eternal Crossroads

For most people in the modern world, the mere mention of the Balkans often evokes a range of unpleasant associations: mostly of war, violence, and inter-ethnic hatred. During the bloody dissolution of Yugoslavia in the 1990s, the pejorative term "Balkanization" was brought back into wide use, coined in the 19th and early 20th centuries. The renowned Merriam-Webster dictionary defines it as "to break up (a region, a group, etc.) into smaller and often hostile units".

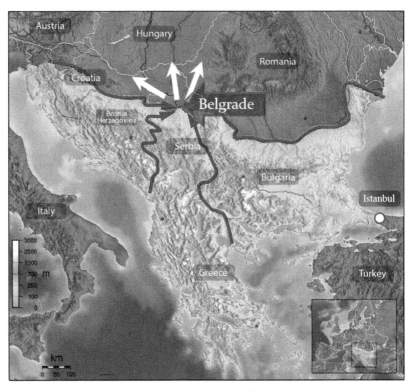

Physical map of the Balkan Peninsula

The Balkans is also commonly referred to as the "powder keg of Europe". Why is this such a turbulent region for thousands of years? This question does not have a simple answer. On the contrary, a deeper understanding will require consideration from different perspectives.

Let us begin with geography.

If we look at the attached physical map, we can see that the Balkan Peninsula has a triangle shape with the tip pointing downwards, filled with mountains. Its shape resembles a wedge inserted between East and West. The tip of the triangle is the southern end of the Peloponnese Peninsula in Greece. On the western side are the Alps and the states of Austria and Italy, thus the geographical beginning of Western civilization, and on the east, Istanbul, the point where the European continent touches Asia. The northern geographical border of the Balkans is formed by two large rivers, the Sava and the Danube, which stretch from west to east, from the Alps to the Black Sea. At the same time, they sharply separate the Balkan Mountains from the vast Pannonian Plain, which occupies a significant part of Central Europe. Within this plain are the territories of the following countries: Serbia, Croatia, Slovenia, Austria, Hungary, Slovakia, Romania, Poland, and Ukraine.

Once, an American group told me that the plains of Pannonia irresistibly reminded them of the state of Kansas in the US. It is a fertile plain where the inhabitants mostly engage in agriculture. Due to the lack of natural obstacles such as mountain ranges or hills, the Pannonian plain is difficult to defend militarily and this fact is important for understanding certain historical processes that preceded the creation of Yugoslavia. On the other hand, there are only a few natural paths that lead through the mountains of the Balkan Peninsula. They follow the valleys of larger rivers, which are mostly tributaries of either the Sava or the Danube. And thus we come to an interesting fact: all of the natural paths through the Balkans converge at the place where the Sava flows into the Danube. It is therefore quite logical that one of the oldest human settlements in the world was placed precisely at this strategic point.

Belgrade—the Crossroads of Worlds and the Key to the Balkans

Belgrade, the capital of Serbia and formerly of Yugoslavia, is an ancient city, having been around for thousands of years. It is situated on a natural elevation, like a watchtower, overlooking the Pannonian Plain. From this "hill for contemplation", as the Ottoman Turks called it, one can enjoy a fantastic view of the confluence of the Sava and Danube rivers, as well as the vast plain and the immense sky above it. As the point where all the most important roads through the Balkan Peninsula meet, the city is probably in the most important strategic position in the region. In other words, whoever holds Belgrade, in a certain sense holds the key to the whole of the Balkans.

The military-strategic position of the city is further enhanced by the fact that there are no natural obstacles to the north of it, which would impede the progress of an army through the Pannonian Plain, all the way to Budapest or Vienna. When you climb up to the Belgrade fortress and look out over the landscape and plain that lies before you, it becomes crystal clear why this place is called the "open gate to Europe". This geographical and strategic position was recognized by people in times that history has not recorded, but archaeology has. The settlement at the site of present-day Belgrade has endured for thousands of years, since pre-historic times.

The written history of Belgrade, however, describes events of the last approximately 2700 years. This chronicle reveals to the astonished reader a secret that is little known in the world. During the historically researched period, forty-four destructions of the city and a total of sixty changes of its rulers have been recorded. In the 20th century alone, Belgrade was bombed five times. It is a great question whether there is any other city in the world with such a turbulent history.

Somewhere in the whirlwinds of time, one name appeared for this unusual place that, it seems, best reflects the essence of its existence. That name is *Crossroads of Worlds*. Here the word "worlds" is deliberately used in the plural. We will see that at this so important strategic point, very different worlds of religions and empires, powerful and great, clashed in an incessant game for supremacy. It is then the right moment to change and broaden our perspective again and look at the whole Balkan from the point of view of a very important scientific discipline, which affects the making of strategic and political decisions in the world.

The Balkans in the Light of Geopolitics

Swedish scholar Rudolf Kjellén (1864–1922) was the first to introduce the term *geopolitics* in 1889 to describe one of the five important elements in his theory of the state, which he published in the work *State as a Life Form*[2]. Geopolitics provides a certain view of the world; it offers an interpretation of various terrestrial phenomena, including historical processes, and thus in many aspects it approaches philosophy, and in a certain sense, ideology. With its specific methods and approaches, it interprets the place of a particular state in the wider context of international political forces, based on its spatial characteristics (position, size, population, natural resources, etc.). The key question of geopolitics is the identification of the strategic interests of individual countries, as well as the selection of methods and means to promote these interests.

Geopolitics investigates the dynamism and relative strength of continental and maritime powers, among other things. "A maritime empire is undoubtedly a world empire,"[3] was the conclusion of an American admiral, historian, and strategist Alfred Mahan (1840-1914), who regarded access to the seas in general, and particularly to the warm seas, as the most important factor in the game for geopolitical supremacy. This is certainly the case with the Balkan Peninsula—it has access to the Adriatic, Ionian, and Aegean Seas, through which it accesses the Mediterranean Sea to the south, but also the Black Sea to the east.

Perhaps the most significant thinker, one of the founders of both geopolitics and geostrategy, was undoubtedly Sir Halford John Mackinder (1861-1947), a British geographer, professor, and politician. In his renowned work, *The Geographical Pivot of History*[4] presented to the Royal Geographical Society in 1904, Mackinder formulated the so-called Heartland Theory, an event which many take as the beginning of the scientific study of geopolitics.

At the heart of Mackinder's theory is the so-called *The World-Island*, a vast continuous expanse of connected continents of Africa, Europe and Asia which he refers to as *Afro-Eurasia*. It is the largest, most populated and wealthiest part of the planet in every respect. At the center of this vast expanse, according to Mackinder, lies the *Pivot area*, which he also calls

---

[2] Kjellén, Rudolf. *Staten som lifsform*. Stockholm, 1916.
[3] Mahan, Alfred Thayer. *The Influence of Sea Power upon History, 1660–1783*. Boston: Little, Brown and Company, 1890, 25.
[4] Mackinder, Halford John. "The Geographical Pivot of History." *The Geographical Journal 23, no. 4* (Apr. 1904): 421-437. Published by The Royal Geographical Society, UK.

the *Heartland*, geographically between the Volga River to the west, the Yangtze to the east, the Himalayas to the south and the Arctic to the north.

One of the main conclusions of Mackinder's theory is that the power that controls the World-Island simultaneously achieves control over more than fifty percent of the world's resources. According to Mackinder, to achieve this goal it is necessary to gain control over the Heartland, the central pivot area which is key to controlling the entire World-Island or Afro-Eurasia.

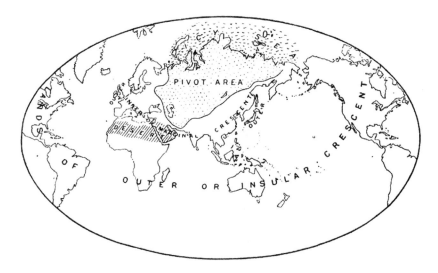

Mackinder's division of the world. The Heartland, or as he calls it the *Pivot area*, dominates the center of the map and covers most of Russia.

Such conclusions of the British professor, as well as of other geopolitical thinkers, inevitably attracted the attention of the centers of power in the West, since the largest part of the pivot area is occupied by Russia, then in its imperial, and later in its expanded Soviet form.

In his next work, which was significantly influenced by the First World War and the October Revolution, entitled *Democratic Ideals and Reality: A Study in the Politics of Reconstruction*[5], Mackinder reflected on the geopolitical aspects of the Versailles Peace Conference of 1919 and criticized the political visions of the US President Woodrow Wilson, perceiving them as idealistic. I quote in full a passage from this book which represents the essence of Mackinder's views. These words shed light on the geopolitical

[5] Mackinder, Halford John. *Democratic Ideals and Reality: A Study in the Politics of Reconstruction*. London, UK: Constable and Co. Ltd, 1919.

importance of the Balkans, where the newly formed Kingdom of Yugoslavia was located shortly after the Versailles Conference:

> "Whoever rules Eastern Europe commands the Heartland; whoever rules the Heartland commands the World-Island; whoever rules the World-Island commands the world".[6]

As early as 1919, such a strong and far-reaching conclusion thus pointed to the possibility of Germany and the Soviet Union clashing over supremacy in Eastern Europe, and thus also in the Balkans. Twenty years later, this would indeed come to pass. Mackinder went one step further, predicting that one of the possible scenarios for taking control of the Heartland would be *a successful invasion of Russia by the Western European nations—most likely Germany,* and concluded that the emergence of a ramified railway network in Eurasia had weakened the hitherto impregnability of the Heartland. However, it seems that in this last point he was mistaken.

Russians certainly read Mackinder's works. Whether for that reason or some other, they made their tracks non-standard by increasing the track gauge. Thus began the inconvenience later experienced by all those travelling to the countries of the Eastern Bloc by train—waiting for the exchange of the railway wagon's wheelset chassis to the Soviet standard at the borders of the Warsaw Pact.

At the beginning of the 20th century both Mackinder and Kjellén, contemporaries, considered that the time would bring a weakening of the power of naval forces (let us look at the case of Britain), and that the focus of the struggle for world domination would turn to the continental control of the world island, or Eurasia. In other words, that the significance of Eastern Europe as a passage to the Heartland would become of key interest. In light of these findings, it becomes much clearer why Yugoslavia, in the heart of the Balkans and partly in Eastern Europe, suffered almost constant pressure from Germany and the USSR. Both powerful forces opposed the creation and maintenance of an independent and sovereign state of the Slovenes in the Balkans, but each from their own interests, mutually opposed.

Nicholas John Spykman (1893–1943), an American journalist, diplomat, scholar and professor, was another very significant thinker in the field of geopolitics. He accepted a great deal of Mackinder's ideas, but opposed some of them. Spykman believed that the Rimland, the peripheral belt surrounding the Heartland, was much more significant than Hartland itself. Re-formulating his teacher's famous maxim, he expressed his own, different view in the following way:

---

[6] Ibid., p. 150.

"Who controls the Rimland rules Eurasia; who rules Eurasia controls the destinies of the world".

It is believed that such conclusions of Spykman had a significant influence on the formation of the American "containment policies" towards the Soviet Union, which began in the 1940s as The Truman Doctrine and continued during the Cold War through the Marshall Plan and NATO. This policy was particularly strongly expressed in the Rimland, that is, the belt around Hartland. Zbigniew Brzezinski, founder of the Trilateral Commission and a man with great influence on US policy from the Cold War to his death in 2017, is considered to be a descendant of the geopolitical school of thought to which Mackinder and Spykman belonged. One of his thoughts, derived from the presented geopolitical theories, reads: "Without Ukraine, Russia cannot be an Eurasian empire"[7]. However, Brzezinski wrote this statement as early as 1997 and, in a way, predicted the great escalation between the two countries. It will indeed start twenty years later with political changes, the change of the Ukrainian president, civil war, Russian annexation of the Crimean Peninsula, and finally, the large-scale Russian-Ukrainian war.

It is therefore of great importance to carefully study geopolitics. In this way, it is possible to understand the interests of the great powers and even be successful in predicting future movements, which is of exceptional importance for people in traditionally turbulent Balkans. There is no doubt that the Balkans is constantly in the focus of geopolitical confrontations because it is located within the thinnest part of Rimland, and where Heartland (Russia) naturally strives to break it.

The accompanying figure shows both Mackinder's and Spykman's geopolitical thoughts, as well as the fact that the peripheral belt in the Balkan Peninsula is vulnerable and thin. It is precisely this geopolitical "weakness" of the region that will have an exceptional impact on Yugoslavia and the processes that will take place there. It must be understood that the Balkans is a stage of fundamentally important geostrategic conflict of interests of the major powers. In terms of its importance, it far surpasses the interests and power of the local small nations and consequently, their political projects such as Yugoslavia.

Studying the Balkan situation, I have gradually come to recognize yet another secondary geopolitical game being played between Germany on one side and Turkey on the other. Germany naturally desires access to the warm Mediterranean through the Austria-Croatia line to the Adriatic Sea, while Turkey, its main opponent, also has its own geopolitical interests in

---

[7] Brzezinski, Zbigniew. *The Grand Chessboard: American Primacy and Its Geostrategic Imperatives*. New York: Basic Books, 1997, 36.

the Balkans and attempts to strengthen its influence. It does this primarily in Bosnia and Herzegovina, the region of Sandzak which spreads through present-day southern Serbia and northern Montenegro, Albania and disputed province of Kosovo and Metohija. We must remember that the Ottoman Empire was the military and political dominant force for nearly six centuries in this part of the region. Hence, the battle for influence in the Balkans between these two powers, nor the fact that Germany has for decades expressed mistrust in Turkey's progress toward Euro-integration, come as no surprise.

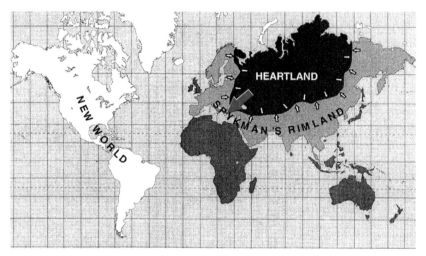

A map that simultaneously represents Mackinder's and Spykman's theories. Russia strives to break the Rimland belt where it is thinnest—in the Balkans (marked with a white arrow) and reach the warm Mediterranean Sea. The West has been trying to prevent this for centuries.

If we were to pictorially describe this scene for a continuous Balkan thriller, we could say that the creators of Yugoslavia had built their state house in the middle of an important and congested crossroads. This parallel to the crossroads was already mentioned by the esteemed Serbian scientist, geographer and ethnologist, Jovan Cvijić (1865–1927), who warned that the implementation of Yugoslav idea had to be done with caution. When you build a house at the crossroads, he said, you will often unavoidably receive uninvited guests. Unfortunately, not all of them will have good intentions.

In theory, the geopolitical importance of the Balkans could be undermined only if the borderline between the East and West, the Hartland and the Rimland – which crosses these territories – was displaced as far as possible. The point of contact between opposed geopolitical forces is a key factor that has generated strong tensions practically without interruption for centuries. Although creative things and cultural exchanges sometimes arise from this dynamism, it is nevertheless concluded that the Balkan peoples have been captives of these titanic processes for the vast majority of the time. Despite the fact that this dynamism sometimes results in creative appearances and cultural exchanges, the conclusion remains that Balkan peoples were captives of these titanic processes for most of the time.

But when did it all start? The answer to this question brings us to an unexpected change of perspective and a journey back in time, around 1700 years.

Primary Fissure:
East and West are Defined and Formed

Saint Bede, an English Benedictine monk from the 7th century, who was canonized by the Catholic Church, have said: "Rome will exist as long as the Colosseum stands. When the Colosseum falls, so will Rome, and when Rome falls, so will the world." In this statement, we find a timeless fascination with the Roman Empire, the greatest and most powerful state of the ancient world and the birthplace of European civilization. Ancient Rome incorporated the best elements of ancient Greek and other nearby cultures, and its influence can be clearly traced until today. A good example is the present superpower, the United States, with its senate, senators, political structure and symbols, which, although different, find some of their inspiration in the Roman model.

The Roman Empire reached its territorial peak in the 2nd century. Around that time, serious problems regarding the management of such a huge territory populated by numerous nations were observed. Communications at that time were much slower, thus it was not possible to respond quickly enough to changes in remote parts of the Empire. Rome then attempted to overcome this problem through experimenting with management models. For a while, the idea was to decentralize power and have more than one emperor at the same time. Thus, Emperor Diocletian (284–305) introduced what is known as the 'Tetrarchy' in 293. The Empire was divided in two halves, managed by the 'Augustus' as the higher Emperor and by the 'Caesar' as the lower emperor, totaling four Emperors.

It is interesting to mention that seventeen Roman Emperors were born on the territory of present-day Serbia, which makes it unique in the world. One of them, Constantine the Great, is of utmost relevance to our story. It seems that this visionary soon realized that his decaying Empire did not need new military legions, new conquests, more gladiators and coliseums for the masses, but rather a fundamental change in its political and societal paradigm, which also includes administrative reforms, i.e. *a change of the management model*.

A new ideology was, of course, necessary for such a change—a completely different outlook on life, and Constantine found it in Christianity, the religion of a determined and very persistent Jewish sect which was at that time in great expansion. Taking a new course, this visionary did everything to pave the way for the expansion of Christianity within the Roman Empire. In favor of such an endeavor are certain similarities between the teaching of Jesus and Mithraism—the most popular religion of the time in Rome, which was widely spread among the legionnaires.

Constantine was aware that with the new religion comes a new system of values, an entirely new set of standards, beliefs, and prohibitions, new words, symbols, and images. All of these were necessary elements as part of the planned reform. Naturally, such a fundamental intervention wasn't possible without changing the state's most important attributes, primarily the choice and location of the capital itself.

Thus, we come to the pivotal decision whose consequences are still felt today. Constantine had insulted and belittled the eternal city of Rome by making the decision to move the seat of the empire elsewhere. Old Byzantium, a city in an incredible location where the two continents of Europe and Asia meet, became the new imperial capital, and was renamed after its reformist emperor—Constantinople. At this point, a whole new era began, and the insulted Rome would never forgive Constantine for this act. By shifting the center of power to the East, Constantine had set in motion the future tensions between East and West. Here is a story which will provide us with a compelling affirmation of this conclusion.

Constantine the Great,
the first Christian emperor of Rome

In 2013, the Christian world celebrated the 1700th anniversary of the Edict of Milan (313 AD), a decree by which Emperor Constantine granted legitimacy and freedom to Christianity in the Roman Empire. The main celebration took place in Serbia since the emperor was born in its current territory, in the city of Niš. Many religious dignitaries from various parts of the world and from various Christian denominations were arriving in Belgrade. At that time, by a coincidence, I found myself involved in an interesting conversation taking place at the headquarters of the Archdiocese of Belgrade, between a group of journalists on one side, and His Eminence the Archbishop of Belgrade on the other.

A journalist from Slovenia was interested in why the Orthodox Church recognized Emperor Constantine as a saint, while the Roman Catholic Church did not. He considered it to be a strange phenomenon, stating that Christianity, as it is today, would certainly not exist without Constantine's historic decisions. As the archbishop hesitated slightly to answer the question, I jumped into the spontaneous conversation in an attempt to help. "Is it because the emperor was a soldier and warrior and killed many people?" I asked. "No" was the brief reply, and the gentle smile still lingered on the archbishop's face. "Does the Catholic Church not recognize Constantine as

33

a saint because he killed his wife and son?" I pursued persistently. "No, that is not the reason" was the brief reply from the now serious church dignitary. Silence descended on the room and the audience focused their attention on me, expecting me not to give up. "So what is the reason, Your Eminence?" I asked with respect. The answer we received surprised us all. With a determined and somewhat angry voice, the archbishop said: "We do not recognize him as a saint because he moved the capital of the Empire from Rome to Constantinople!"

From today's temporal distance, we can conclude that Constantine's reform was undoubtedly visionary and substantial. It was a kind of quantum leap that breathed new life into the Roman Empire. He managed to make a change that inexorably prepared the stage for an entirely new period of prosperity, founded on a different theological-political paradigm, that would last for the next one thousand years.

The Border Between East and West at the Place Where Yugoslavia Will be Born in a Distant Future.

Several decades later, however, something completely unexpected and even bewildering occurred. In 395 CE, Emperor Theodosius decided to divide the empire upon his death into two parts—the eastern and the western—to be governed by his sons, Arcadius and Honorius.

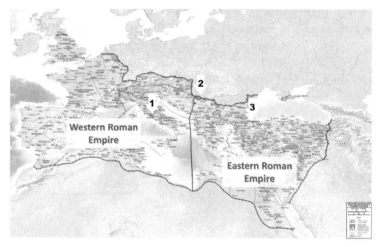

Theodosius's division of the Roman Empire; the respective positions of (1) Rome, (2) Singidunum (modern day Belgrade) and (3) Constantinople (modern day Istanbul)

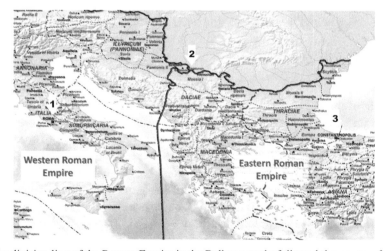

The division line of the Roman Empire in the Balkans partly followed the course of the rivers Sava and Drina; the positions of (1) Rome, (2) Singidunum (present-day Belgrade) and (3) Constantinople (present-day Istanbul) are represented by arrows

Constantine's brilliant effort to infuse a new paradigm and thereby save the integrity, power and strength of a crumbling empire was deeply threatened by Theodosius's move. The line of division was, in part, established on the rivers Danube, Sava and Drina, stretching through the central part of the Western Balkans—precisely the area in which Yugoslavia would form 1,600 years later.

This division constituted a kind of geopolitical tectonic shift, producing a split that would mark the history not only of the Balkans but of the entire world. From then onwards, the Roman Empire would never be reunited under the rule of one Emperor. This moment marks the birth of the tensions and rivalry between the West, with its center in Rome, and the East, whose capital would remain Constantinople. In the ensuing centuries, the Western center moved from Rome to Paris, London and eventually Washington, while the Eastern shifted away from Constantinople, settling firmly in Moscow.

Although still unified at the time of Theodosius' division, the Christian Church would suffer the consequences of the territorial split for all time.

Emperor Theodosius the Great

History will record the gradual estrangement between the church leaders in Constantinople and the Roman bishops, leading eventually to the Great Schism of 1054 and the division of Christianity into the Eastern and Western branches.

The decision of Theodosius to divide the empire was a moment of rupture in the cradle of European civilization. The East and the West were defined and formed within its framework and began their separation. This civilization includes the European peoples in both the east and the west of the continent, as well as other nations throughout the world that have originated from Europe but today mainly live in Canada, USA, Australia and New Zealand. Two clearly distinguished domains formed from it, recognized today as Western civilization and Orthodox civilization.

The dividing line between East and West has shown to be a tangible political, cultural and religious factor in all subsequent historical events and strongly influenced the fate of Balkan peoples. According to the prevailing opinion of historians, the South Slavs—Serbs, Croats and Slovenes—arrived in the Balkans more than two centuries after the division of the Roman Empire. Croats and Slovenes settled in territories west of the line of separation, whereas the situation was much more complicated with the Serbs. They populated mainly the eastern parts, but also some western parts, the fact that would later bring them numerous challenges. Thus, Serbs alone found themselves *on both sides of the border.*

It is interesting to observe that even today, fourteen hundred years after their arrival in the Balkans, Serbs are perceived as part of the East while Croatians and Slovenes are seen as part of the West. What is more remarkable is that the division line of the Roman Empire has lasted up to the present day and separates Serbia from Croatia and Serbia from Bosnia and Herzegovina. As Orthodox Christians, the Serbs settling on the Western side have been, and remain a kind of 'intruders', and were consequently exposed to displacement to the East. Such a tendency can be observed up to the present day.

Returning to geopolitics at the end of this chapter, taking into account what has been outlined so far, it seems that the future of the Balkans is not difficult to predict. The extremely turbulent historical and political movements of the last seventeen centuries show that the permanent displacement of the line of confrontation between the interests of the East and the West from the Balkan peninsula is an improbable future scenario. We can say that, in this sense, there is very little basis for optimism. It is much more likely that the tensions caused by geopolitics and other factors will be the eternal destiny of the Balkans and its inhabitants.

Warfare Using Intermediaries

What is to be a "Proxy" in Modern Political Terminology?

I had only a general understanding of the concept of proxy wars until I had a very interesting and insightful conversation with an American gentleman who had spent his working life in the military structures. After my lecture about Serbia and the former Yugoslavia, he approached me and asked for my opinion on certain specifics of the Yugoslav wars. At one point, making parallels with the then ongoing war in Syria, this gentleman resignedly and with a hint of concern said to me, "Things are no longer like they used to be" and that "the Russians have broken an unwritten rule that was always implied and strictly observed during the Cold War." As I showed no knowledge of this unwritten rule, my kind interlocutor, with some hesitation, told me: "We never confronted them directly, *but always using proxies.*"

Although the meaning of the term "proxy war" in the context of warfare had not been known to me at that moment, I instantly understood that it was significant information for my deeper understanding of relations between great powers. Simultaneously, it was unintentionally suggested to me that a direct armed conflict between Russian and US forces had taken place in Syria. This in itself was an exciting discovery. Slightly later, I came to the official confirmation of this acquired information.

According to the statement made by US diplomat James Jeffrey to Russian media in late 2018, Russian and US forces in Syria had clashed multiple times, sometimes with an exchange of fire and casualties. Thus, a new precedent had occurred with possible significant implications on the future and international relations. However, on my way home, it became clear to me that my interlocutor had inadvertently drawn my attention to one piece of my Balkan puzzle, the importance of which had escaped me until that moment.

The Cambridge Dictionary states that a proxy war is a term that denotes "hostilities between groups or smaller countries, each representing the interests of a larger power from which it can get support and assistance". The

Oxford Dictionary provides a simpler definition: "a war instigated by a major power which does not itself become involved".

Therefore, proxies in this context are small nations that are used by powerful forces to fight for their interests. These great powers in the past were usually empires or mighty kingdoms, although the actions of religious organizations can also be observed in this light, such as the launching of the Crusades by the Roman Catholic Church or the holy war, jihad, in Islam. Today it might be states, but we can assert with some certainty that multinational corporations managing billions of dollars of capital have the power to wage wars for their interests.

As already analyzed on the pages dedicated to geopolitics, the great powers and their interests have intertwined on the Balkans in a, from the average observer's viewpoint, hardly understandable Gordian knot.

From all that has been said so far it follows that the destiny of the small nations of the Balkans is to be pawns in the complex dynamism of the interests of the big powers in the long term: East and West Roman Empires, Roman Catholicism and Orthodoxy, Christianity and Islam, Habsburg Monarchy and Ottoman Empire, Germany and Turkey... In the last centuries we see that the far strongest confrontation in the Balkans is between Russia and the West. Russia seeks to penetrate this strategic territory in order to occupy the natural crossroads, revive its presence on the western coast of the Black Sea and emerge into the Mediterranean's warm seas. Western powers, in different eras and in different organizational forms, have tried to prevent it. Today (2022), the presence of Russia in the Balkans is impeded by the NATO military alliance which has significantly moved its boundaries eastwards and included all countries of the region except Serbia and Bosnia and Herzegovina.

It can be seen, then, that the great powers' proxy strategy has been ever-present in the turbulent Balkans, and can be traced backward in time all the way back to the primary split—the division of the Roman Empire into East and West. Whoever studies Yugoslav affairs must always bear this state of affairs in mind and include it in their reasoning and conclusions. It is only in this way that a more comprehensive and deeper understanding of the processes that led to the formation of Yugoslavia, as well as the many problems this creation had to face during its lifetime, can be attained.

The proxy role is unfavorable for any nation as it brings about an uncertain future, tensions, conflict, war, and above all, human loss. It is logical and expected that the geopolitical games played and the constant confrontation of the interests of powerful forces in the Balkans have led to attempts by the local smaller nations to break away from this unfortunate fate. The Yugoslav idea was born from the resistance to this "proxy state of affairs." It was a possible solution that would make this unfortunate situation a permanent past. The scenario of achieving the visions of Yugoslavism foresaw the national liberation, followed by the unification of the South Slavs into a new nation and state on a unified territory. Such a state would be more powerful in any respect than the situation of sad fragmentation and lack of liberty which had been a centuries-long reality for all Yugoslav nations.

And as would later be shown, this new state was indeed created, but was internally burdened from the start with essential disagreements regarding its structure and the unwillingness of the constituent nations to form a unified supra-nation similar to the American 'melting pot' model.

What about the external factors? Taking into account the understanding of geopolitics and proxy strategies in the Balkan Peninsula, it is clearly evident that the creation of a single and powerful Yugoslavia was not in line with the interests of either the major powers or formidable religious centers.

But could Yugoslavia still survive and somehow slip through the needle's eye under such unfavorable conditions? Was it merely an illusory vision doomed to fail, David surrounded by Goliaths? Or was the South Slav state a project that might bring inspiration to social thinkers of the future when studied? It is these very questions that this book delves into.

PREHISTORY

The Arrival of South Slavs to the Balkan Peninsula

Reflection on the Origin, Duration, and Disappearance of Their States in the Middle Ages

According to the prevailing opinion within historiography, the Slavs had lived in distant past in the northeastern part of Europe and had subsequently spread to the east, west, and south. Although science has not accurately located their original homeland, it is usually assumed that it encompassed the territories of present-day Ukraine, Poland and Belarus. In the

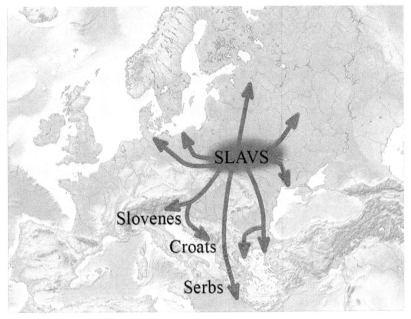

Illustration of the hypothesized routes of Serbs, Croats and Slovenes to the Balkans as part of the Great Migration of the Slavs (6th-7th century).

times before the migrations, Slavic tribes lived together. One interpretation holds that this led to a significant population increase in a relatively small area they inhabited, eventually resulting in food shortage and mutual hostility and territorial struggles. In order to solve this problem, tribal elders gathered and made a decision to part and leave their homeland. Tribes migrated in three directions: eastward, westward, and southward. Thus, until present day, we can identify three main groups of Slavs divided according to the direction of their migration from their original homeland in the following way: Eastern Slavs are Russians, Belarusians and Ukrainians; Western Slavs are Czechs, Slovaks and Poles.

For the analysis of Yugoslavia, the most important are the South Slavs: Serbs, Croats and Slovenes. Not less important are Bosniaks, Montenegrins and Macedonians who later differentiated themselves from the original three South Slavic tribes. The arrival of the Serbs, Croats and Slovenes to the territory of the Western Balkans is placed in the second half of the 6th and the beginning of the 7th centuries CE. According to historiography, the Serbs were the largest and most numerous of the three tribes and in their migration to the south they arrived as far as the Peloponnese Peninsula in present-day Greece, or the then Eastern Roman Empire—Byzantium. The most detailed and probably best known record of the settlement of the Serbs and Croats in the Balkan Peninsula is the work 'On the Governance of the Empire' (De Administrando Imperio) by the Byzantine Emperor Constantine VII Porphyrogenitus, who ruled in the 10th century CE. This document has served as a kind of collection of information and instructions, which the Emperor addressed to his son and successor of the throne Roman. The highly educated man and historian Constantine wrote, among other things, about the peoples with whom Eastern Roman Empire was in contact, and at this point he quite exhaustively spoke about the origin and settlement of the Serbs and Croats.

Serbs

According to Porphyrogenitus' account, the original homeland of the Serbs was referred to as White Serbia or Bojka (pronounced [boyka]). Its exact location has not been determined, and there are multiple hypotheses about where it could have been located. According to the most popular one, it was situated in the north of Europe, in present-day Poland and eastern Germany. Porphyrogenitus' opus states that after the death of the Serbian ruler, the throne was inherited by two sons. One of them decided to lead half of the people southward, towards the Byzantine lands, and the Serbs arrived as far as Thessaloniki, where the emperor Iraklios allocated them territories around the city in 626. In fact, there is still a place there called Servia (Greek Τά Σέρβλια). The legend goes further by saying that they did not remain in this region for a long time, but instead set off back to White Serbia. Nevertheless, they soon changed their minds and returned, crossing the Danube near the city of Singidon—present-day Belgrade— and, through the Byzantine commander of the city, they sent a petition to the emperor to assign them different lands. Iraklios acceded to their request and gave them the "Avar-ravaged territories" extending from the Sava and the Danube in the north to the Dinaric Mountains and the Adriatic coast in the south, for their use and protection. Thus the Serbs settled in the Balkans and became Byzantine subjects in the first half of the 7th century CE. Probably, the other half of the people stayed in their original homeland, finally assimilating with other peoples over time. The fact that in the German provinces of Saxony and Brandenburg there is still a Slavic minority known as Lusatian Serbs (also 'Sorbi') speaks in favour of this theory.

Emperor Constantine VII Porphyrogenitus narrates further about how the rulers of the Serbs in the 7th and 8th centuries were descendants of an unnamed tribal leader who had brought them to the Balkan region. History in this period recorded the existence of five interrelated Serbian principalities. Four of them were located on the Adriatic coast, in the territories of today's Croatia and Montenegro, while the fifth one was continental, mostly in today's southern and central Serbia and Bosnia and Herzegovina. All these countries went through periods of internal dynastic disputes, mutual quarrels and conflicts, as well as tests posed by powerful neighbors—

Constantine VII Porphyrogenitus (left), Emperor of the Eastern Roman Empire in the 10th century and author of the treatise "On the Administration of the Empire" (*De Administrando Imperio*).

Byzantium, Bulgaria, the Venetian Republic, and sometimes the Crusaders. They managed to survive, often through the wise coquetry with both East and West, which was the imperative of survival and prosperity. They sometimes succeeded to achieve a certain degree of state or church autonomy, mostly in relation to Byzantium. It influenced them with its developed culture, art, and religion, but also continued to ignite their desire for independence, which, inadvertently, strengthened and solidified the sense of Serbian national identity.

At the end of the twelfth century, the Serbs gave rise to a powerful leader. He was wise and ambitious, ruthless and strict, gifted in politics. Partly by fire and sword, partly by political and diplomatic efforts, he extended his power to all Serbian lands and formed a strong and centralized principality. His name was Stefan Nemanja (pronounced [Nemanya]). He was the progenitor of the historically most important Serbian ruling family named after him: the Nemanjić dynasty. For more than two hundred years, Nemanja's descendants would raise the Serbian state, both culturally and territorially, until its historical maximum in the 14th century.

His descendant, King Dušan 'the Mighty', doubled the territory of the Serbian kingdom through conquests, mostly at the expense of Byzantium. In 1346, he was crowned "Emperor of Serbs and Greeks" in the city of Skopje which was then roughly located in the geographical center of his state. Not long afterwards, Emperor Dušan moved the capital of the Serbian Empire to Kosovo, a hundred kilometers to the northwest, in the city of Prizren. Since the first half of the 13th century, the region of Kosovo already housed the seat of the Serbian Orthodox Church, in the Patriarchal Monastery of Peć. Thus Kosovo became the seat of both ecclesiastical and secular power during the height of the Serbian medieval state.

After Dušan's conquests, the Byzantine Empire was reduced to a small territory of only about a hundred kilometers in diameter, but Constantinople remained an unfulfilled dream. By meddling in the internal Byzantine struggle for the throne, the Serbian ruler sought to impose himself as the co-ruler, with the prospect of making his Kingdom the heir of the Eastern Roman Empire. However, at the peak of his strength, at the age of 46 or 47, Dušan suddenly died on December 20th, 1355. The cause of death remains unknown to this day. According to one hypothesis, the Serbian ruler was poisoned to prevent him from taking Constantinople and crumbling Byzantium. If Dušan was indeed killed, who could have been behind this act? It would not be a surprise if future historical research comes to the conclusion that the death of the most powerful South Slavic medieval ruler was merely one of the episodes in the backstage games of the great powers in the Balkans.

Discovered recently, after 1000 years, the seal of Prince Strojimir Vlastimirović attests to the existence of a Serbian state administration in the 9th century. (Historical Museum of Serbia, Belgrade)

After the death of Dušan the Mighty in 1355, clouds of greed and conflict among the nobility rose over the Serbian Empire. Civil unrest ravaged the state, which the Ottoman Turks skillfully capitalized upon by launching their attacks. Just thirty-four years after having experienced its golden period, the medieval Serbian state began its gradual decline under Turkish rule following the titanic battle at the Field of Kosovo on June 28th, 1389. In this epic struggle, deeply entrenched in the collective awareness of the Serbs and immortalized in numerous poems, most of the Serbian lords perished, but also the Turkish Sultan Murat, which is the only known case of a Sultan of the Ottoman Empire to have fallen in battle.

The consequences for the Serbs will be dramatic: within 70 years, the Turks will completely conquer all Serbian lands. The most powerful Balkan state and a kind of successor to Byzantium will disappear from the historical scene, and will not return until the second half of the 19th century. After two uprisings against the Ottoman rule, Serbia first became a principality in 1830; under the rule of Prince Mihailo in 1867, the Turks withdraw from Serbia. At the Congress of Berlin of 1878, Serbia was finally recognized as an independent sovereign state.

A map of the Serbian Empire, circa 1350, published by German historian Johann Gustav Droysen in 1886. While modern historiography has a somewhat different view regarding its eastern boundaries, the extent of the then-current Serbian state was observed to stretch much further to the south than what is the case today. The seat of the Serbian Orthodox Church and Empire's capital city were located in Kosovo, in towns Peć and Prizren, marked with numbers 1 and 2, respectively, while the original capital of the empire in Skopje, today the capital of Serbia's southern neighbour North Macedonia, is marked with number 3. Belgrade can be seen in the far north of the map, on the border with Hungary. The once powerful Byzantine Empire occupies a very small area west of Constantinople, marked with the words 'Byzantisches Reich'.

The belonging of the Serbs to the Byzantine culture is undeniable. Although some historians will blame Dušan for the fall of Byzantium, such a thesis is deeply inaccurate. Byzantium had been attacked long before the Serbian tsar by Arabs, crusaders, Turks and many others. Dušan wanted to restore Byzantium, not to destroy it. It can be rightfully said that his state was the last great upsurge of the so-called Byzantine commonwealth, after which the Ottoman-Islamic culture quickly conquered the Balkans.

In order to gain a more thorough comprehension of the complex relationships in Yugoslavia, it is important to note that the former medieval capital of the Serbian Empire—the city of Skopje—is today the capital of Serbia's neighboring country of North Macedonia. It is even more significant to emphasize that in the Middle Ages in the contested and sensitive region of Kosovo and Metohija the seats

Map showing the Serbian lands in the 9th century (814). It reveals a very long presence of Serbs in the territories of modern day Croatia, Bosnia and Herzegovina, Montenegro, Albania, Northern Macedonia, Greece, region of Kosovo, and Serbia.

of the Serbian state and church power during were located. Moreover, the second part of the name of this area comes from the word 'metoh', which denotes a church or a monastery estate. From these facts, Serbian claims of historical belonging of the region of Kosovo to the Serbian state can be seen in a clearer light. It is also important to recognize that, after the Second Balkan War and the expulsion of the Turks from the Balkans, the region of today's North Macedonia was ceded to the Kingdom of Serbia according to the terms of the 1913 Bucharest peace treaty. In the internal structure of the modern Serbian kingdom after 1913, Macedonia, together with the regions of Kosovo and Raška, became part of a wider area known as Old Serbia, a term which implies the historical center of the former Serbian medieval empire.

Likewise, it seems that now is a good time for an important insight arising from all of the above. The Serbs not only established the present-day Serbia, nor do they live exclusively in its territory. They settled in numerous Balkan regions which were part of Serbian medieval states. Today, some of these regions belong to independent and internationally recognized countries, but this by no means implies that the Serbs have disappeared from them. On the contrary. The existence of Serbs in the present-day countries of Bosnia and Herzegovina, Croatia, Montenegro, Macedonia or the disputed province of Kosovo is not a consequence of the conquests during the Yugoslav civil war at the end of the 20th century, as is often wrongly assumed in the world. Serbs in the aforementioned countries have in fact existed for a very long time—around 1400 years, from the original settlement in the Balkans, until today.

As the most numerous of the arriving Slavic tribes, the Serbs consequently settled and inhabited the most territories. They continue to live on them, together with other peoples.

Croats

In the treatise "On the Governance of the Empire" it is stated that both Croat and Serb primordial homes were referred to as "white". Hence the terms White Croatia and White Croats—Belohrobatoi.

According to Emperor Constantine VII Porphyrogenitus, one of the five brothers separated from the motherland and with his people from the ancient homeland which was "behind Bagibareia", probably north or northeast of Bavaria, came to present-day Dalmatia, on the shores of the Adriatic Sea. These newly arrived Croats eventually overpowered and subdued the Avars they found there.

Later, according to this testimony, part of the people separated and went north, through the territory of present-day Bosnia and Herzegovina, reaching Pannonia. This account seems feasible as it is precisely in the territories inhabited by the Croats today. Another interesting detail we learn from the imperial record is that already in the 7th century Croats established a connection with the Roman Church, from where the bishops came to convert them to Christianity. Historical research suggests that the connection between Croats and Rome has persisted for many centuries, and is still very strong today. The Vatican sees the Croats as their protectors of Roman Catholicism in the Balkans from Orthodox or Islamic influences.

However, it is not all so simple. The treatise On the Governance of the Empire was written about three centuries after the settlement of Serbs and Croats on the Balkans, which is one of the reasons why opinions arose among some historians that it is not realistic to fully trust it. They believe that other data had to be sought that could tell us more about this important topic. However, the factual lack of written sources about the origin and migration of Serbs and Croats created space for many, often very loose theories.

It has been speculated for example that the name Croat could be of Iranian origin and that the Croats could be a Sarmatian people who were part of another great wave of the migration that was happening concurrently with the Slavic one. One of the main advocates of this theory was the Jesuit priest Stefan Kazimir Sakač. The Catholic Church has had a natural interest in distancing Croat Catholics ethnically from Orthodox Serbs as much as possible. There is also a theory that the Ancient Croats were of Eastern Gothic—Ostrogothic origin, one of the most powerful Germanic tribes, which is based on the claim of the widespread use of the name Croat on territories inhabited by Gothic tribes. If we add to this list the theory of Croatian archaeologist Dr. Vladimir Sokol, who claims that the Croats are actually Czechs with origins traced back to the Laba River area, whose Celtic name Alba (i.e. white) is inaccurately responsible for the 10th century term 'White Croatia,' we can say that currently there are at least four theories on the ethnogenesis of Croats: Slavic, Iranian, Gothic, and Czech. However, these theories can be easily just a product of the political factor of their time of development. Leading up to the final dissolution of Yugoslavia, there were expressed tendencies in Croatia to establish ethnic and historical distinctiveness in contrast to Serbs, from whom they were to separate at that time by withdrawing from the common state.

However, anthropological study of human skeletons from several archaeological sites using the method of craniometric[8] analysis conducted by Croatian scientist Mario Šlaus[9] appears to confirm the prevailing opinion in historical science about the Slavic origin of Croats, as well as the relative accuracy of the data from the Byzantine document of Emperor Porphyrogenitus. In this paper, he concludes that Croatian populations descended to the eastern coast of the Adriatic Sea and its hinterland "most likely from the territory of present-day Poland", and that they later, around the 10th century, expanded north, to the territory of present-day Bosnia and Herzegovina and to the region of the Sava and Drava rivers. A number of historical sources record that in the 9th century there were two Croatian principalities: Dalmatian, in the hinterland of the Adriatic Sea, and Pannonian, between the rivers Sava and Drava. Both were vassals of the Francian state. However, within the scientific community there are different opinions about which ethnic group—Croats, Serbs, or some other Slovenian tribe—inhabited the Pannonian principality. Some researchers, among

---

[8] Craniometry is a method within anthropometry (the measurement of the human body) and specifically refers to the study of the shape and dimensions of the cranium, i.e. the main portion of the skull.
[9] Slaus, Mario, et al. "Craniometric relationships among medieval Central European populations: implications for Croat migration and expansion." *Croatian Medical Journal 45, no. 4* (2004): 434-444.

which there are a few Croats, dispute the thesis about Pannonian Croatia, and maintain that it is more accurate to say that this area was inhabited by Pannonian Slavs. There are opinions that its population was a mixture of Serb, Croat and even Slovene tribes. In 879, while Duke Branimir was in power, Dalmatian Croatia received acknowledgement of principality status from Pope John VIII. By the beginning of the 10th century, in 910, the Croatian ruler had become prince Tomislav. Fifteen years later, and with a blessing from Pope John X, Tomislav became the first king of Croats, and the principality was elevated to the status of a kingdom.

Croatian Kingdom reached its peak in the 11th century, when the region of Pannonian Croatia, as well as parts of present-day Bosnia and Herzegovina, entered its territory. This zenith occurred during the reign of King Zvonimir Trpimirović, who ruled from 1075 to 1089. However, after Zvonimir's death there was no successor to the throne, so Queen Helena, of Hungarian origin, transferred the royal rights to her brother—Hungarian King Ladislaus I—and invited him to unite Croatia to Hungary by force. This led to a revolt of Croatian nobility, who from the monastery pulled out previously exiled Stephen II Trpimirović, the last descendant of the most successful line of Croatian kings, and proclaimed him the new king. After two years, 1091, the aged Stephen II passed away without appointing an heir.

The last Croatian king chosen by the people but never formally crowned, was called Petar Snačić. He led the Croats in the fateful battle against the Hungarians in 1097. The Croats lost the battle, and Petar perished. In 1102, Hungarian pretensions towards Croatia were formally realized with the forced agreement of a so-called "personal union", which effectively placed the Croatian lands and people under the authority of Hungarian kings. The subordinate status of Croats with respect to Hungarians lasted until 1918 and the collapse of the Austro-Hungarian Empire after the First World War. The confluence of historical circumstances led the Croats at that time to form a new kingdom in union with the Slovenes and Serbs, to be called Yugoslavia.

At the moment of falling under Hungarian domination in the early 12th century, a strong centennial aspiration of Croats to regain their statehood and kingdom was born. This aspiration would be called "millennial dream" in Yugoslavia in the 20th century. However, this term would become a synonym for Croatian secessionism, a phenomenon that would shake Yugoslavia throughout its existence.

Slovenes

The smallest ethnic group included in the South Slavic family are the Slovenes. I deliberately use the word included because new data seems to suggest that this definition may have been—or still is—incorrect. The people who today identify themselves as Slovenes have inhabited an area ranging from the North Adriatic Sea to North East Italy (Tyrol) and to Julian (or Eastern) Alps, to today's Southern Austria and Western Hungary. Sources about their settling consist of historical written data, archaeological remains, ethnographical traces as well as linguistic research on toponyms.

Available information suggests that the settlement of the Slovene ethnic space probably occurred in two migratory waves, very likely constituted of two distinct groups of Slavs.

The first wave took place in the mid-6th century, when the Slavic tribes from Moravia settled in the Eastern Alps region. Moravia is part of the Czech Republic and, according to the prevailing division, the local people belong to the group of Western Slavs, which is the first reason to potentially challenge the thesis that the Slovenes are part of the South Slav family along with the Serbs and Croats.

The second migratory wave originated from the southeast, from the Pannonian plain. In the second half of the 6th century, the Slavic tribes, along with their rulers, the Avars, expanded towards the Eastern Alps, pushing out the Lombards and the Bavarians. By the end of the 6th century, they had settled the upper reaches of the rivers Sava and Drava. Most likely, the second wave was made up of the South Slavs from the Pannonian plain, probably the tribes which gave rise to the modern-day Croats.

In 623, several Slavic tribes revolted against the Avars and placed themselves under the leadership of Duke Samo, who created the first Slavic political-territorial entity, the forerunner of a state, known as Samo's Tribal Union. It existed until Samo's death in 658. Two years after its dissolution, a smaller principality was formed in the territory of present-day Austria, called Carantania. This state did not exist autonomously for long, but was partially the origin of what we today recognize as the Slovene ethnic corpus. Indeed, the Slovenes can still be found there, mostly in the region dominated by the city of Klagenfurt in Austria (Slovene name Celovec). When forced in the 8th century to ask for the assistance of the Bavarians in defense against the Avar counterattack, the Carantanians had to accept union with Bavaria, and by the mid-8th century they were absorbed by the Frankish State.

Within the Holy Roman Empire, which was established in 800 AD with the coronation of Frankish King Charlemagne (Charles the Great) as the first emperor, another principality populated by Alpine Slavs was formed, called Carniola It was mainly ruled by Bavarian and Frankish nobles, and by the Habsburgs from the mid-14th century until the dissolution of the Austro-Hungarian Empire in 1918. This brings us to the important fact: ruling classes in the Slovenian ethnic space spoke German for approximately a thousand years. This long exposure to Austrian-German administration might lead to the understanding of a German-influenced attitude towards work and life, which significantly distinguished Slovenes from other Yugoslavs during the existence of the common state.

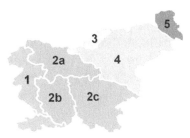

Boundaries of historical Habsburg regions in present-day Republic of Slovenia:

1. Slovene Littoral
2. Carniola
   (2a Upper, 2b Inner, 2c Lower)
3. Carinthia
4. Styria
5. Prekmurje

Although Slovenian is commonly classified as a South Slavic language today, modern DNA analysis suggests that the first migratory wave from Moravia was dominant, while the second one from Pannonia was less extensive and significant. It appears that the modern Slovenian language has been influenced by the South Slavic newcomers and neighbors, but originally it probably belonged to the West Slavic language group. A recent analysis[10] conducted by scientists from the University of Ljubljana concluded that "Slovene population shows close genetic connection with the West Slavic populations" and points to the genetic similarity with the Slavs in the Central European region.

Although these new data suggest that the Slovenes might not be Southern Slavs after all, they were one of the three nations, along with Croats and Serbs, that created Yugoslavia—a common state of the Southern Slavs, after the First World War. Such a shift in perspective in the light of new findings can help us better understand one phenomenon. It is the persistent

---

[10] Zupan, Andrej, et al. "The paternal perspective of the Slovenian population and its relationship with other populations." *Annals of Human Biology* 40, no. 6 (2013): 515-526.

feeling of distinctiveness and incompatibility that the Slovenes have always had towards other nations in Yugoslavia, although at that time they could not have been rationally aware of being less genetically related to the others.

On the other hand, the relatively short existence of independent Slovenian principalities in the Middle Ages explains the strong determinant of this nation to finally create its own sovereign national state after the definitive collapse of the Habsburg Empire in 1918. This makes clearer a part of the reasons as to why Slovenes have always seen Yugoslavia as a temporary, transitional solution—a topic which will be dealt with in much greater detail later on in this book.

Second Fissure:
Religious Schisms and Their Consequences

The South Slavs Between Eastern and Western Christianity,
Gnosticism and Islam

When they migrated to the Balkans, Serbs, Croats and Slovenes were not Christians. Like their ancestors, they practiced a polytheistic religion close to Scandinavian or Nordic religions in its roots, which is now experiencing a renewed affirmation among pan-Slavic or nationalist-oriented circles. Through their "return to Slavic roots", they express a certain cultural revolt and resistance to the encroaching and prevailing Western cultural model.

The acceptance of Christianity first began amongst the Slovenes in the 7th century. There are historical indications that, approximately at the same time, a smaller number of Serbs and Croats adopted Christianity, soon after their migration to the Balkans. However, the definitive transition to Christianity among the South Slavic peoples took place in the second half of 9th century, largely due to the enlightening work of Saints Cyril and Methodius—Christian missionaries and founders of the literacy among the Slovenes.

It was a time when neighboring Byzantium wanted to expand its influence, religion and culture among the Slavs and thus integrate them into its world. The most effective way to integrate the Slavic tribes into Byzantium's paradigm, system of values, symbols and beliefs, was to spread Orthodox Christianity. As the Slavs were mostly pagan and illiterate, an alphabet had to be invented for them and the holy books had to be translated into their language. At that time the influence of the Roman Church in the north and west of Europe was already very significant and Byzantium wanted to prevail in this game of power. So it was decided for Cyril and Methodius to be dispatched on a mission of spreading Christianity. Their work proved to be more than successful. This led to the establishment of a significant influence of the Eastern Roman Empire and the Eastern Church on many Slavic peoples, of which the Serbs are being the most important for our analysis of the future complex phenomenon of Yugoslavia.

It is interesting to note that Saint Cyril himself was not the creator of the Cyrillic script. It was his disciples and pupils who continued his work after his death, eventually compiling the basis of an alphabet that is still used by many Slavic peoples in various forms. Out of respect to Saint Cyril, the alphabet was named Cyrillic. Serbs adopted the script early on, evidenced by inscriptions and hand-written gospels from the 10th and 11th centuries A.D.

In the Middle Ages the strong influences of political and increasingly religious rivalry between Byzantium, i.e. the Eastern Roman Empire, and Rome, or the West, (where the Holy Roman Empire would later be established as a counterbalance to Byzantium), can clearly be seen. This conflict of interests is reflected on the Slavic peoples of the Balkan region. As it has been demonstrated, the border between East and West crosses through their countries. Over time, the Serbs, geographically closer to Byzantium, will succumb to the influence of the Eastern Church and Constantinople, while Slovenes and Croatians, for mostly the same reasons, will mostly accept the influences of the West and the Roman bishops.

As if the painful fissure of the once unified Roman Empire, geographically following the Sava and Drina rivers, had somehow shifted to the invisible realms. This state-political and ideological-theological division placed the Serbs in the East and the Croats and Slovenians in the West.

However, nothing in the Balkans is simple, particularly when it comes to the Serbs. It is important to note that only the Serbs inhabited the territories on both sides of this civilization border, which will significantly affect their fate up to the present day. Although the majority of Serbs today live to the east of this ancient border between the two halves of the Roman Empire, there are still some that live to the west of it. For them in Serbian language there is a term "Serbs of Beyond" ("Srbi prečani"), which translates to "those on the other side of the border". These are the Serbs from Bosnia, Herzegovina, Dalmatia, Slavonia, and Vojvodina, i.e. those who were predominantly under the Habsburg rule and in the sphere of Western cultural influence.

Let us now turn our attention to the divided Roman Empire. In a certain sense, the only "glue" that still somehow kept the opposing interest spheres of the former empire in some kind of unity was religion – Christianity. However, after the Great Schism and the definitive division between the Orthodox and Roman Catholic Churches in 1054, mutual connections weakened further and two civilizations moved increasingly farther apart. This spiritual-ideological rift would inevitably be reflected in the fate of the peoples who lived on either side of the boundary, and would play its role both in the processes of creation and the processes of disappearance of the later common state project – Yugoslavia. The main actors of these processes will be Serbs and Croats.

In times of distancing between East and West, the Serbs, inhabiting both sides of the civilizational divide, found themselves in a very delicate position. It was a difficult decision with far-reaching consequences for Stefan Nemanja, the powerful leader and unifier of Serbian lands. Should

Serbia and its people – partly in the East, partly in the West – turn to the embrace of the Catholic or Orthodox Church? Which one would be better in the long run? Was this determination an inevitability of the moment or could it have been postponed by political maneuvering between Rome and Constantinople? And ultimately, was the decision made by Nemanja at the end of the 12th century the best one?

Serbs in the East, Croats in the West

There are various interesting theories and debates concerning the adherence of Serbs to Eastern Christianity, focusing primarily on the figure of Grand Prince (in Serbian: Veliki župan) Stefan Nemanja, the creator of a strong medieval Serbian state and pro-genitor of the Nemanjić dynasty—the most successful Serbian dynasty ever.

During the internal conflict within the ruling family to which he belonged, Ne-manja's father was forced to flee with his family from Raška, the future heart of the unified Serbian state, to the coastal region of Duklja, on the southern Adriatic. Around 1113, during their exile, Nemanja's young-

Grand Prince Stefan Nemanja

est son was born, likely near Podgorica, the capital of modern-day Monte-negro. According to the record of Nemanja's son and biographer Stefan, the child was soon baptized "by Latin priests" according to the Western rite. After the civil war had ended and the family returned to Raška, Nemanja was baptized a second time, this time according to the Orthodox rite.

This very fact—that the one who would eventually unite Serbian re-gions into a singular powerful state was baptized both in Latin and Ortho-dox ceremonies—may enable us to understand today his later political be-havior, characterized by oscillation between the East and the West. At times, he would make an alliance with Byzantium, and, at other times, he would join forces with the Western powers of the time in order to attack it.

It is certain that Stefan Nemanja was concerned about the peculiarity of Serbia's position between East and West. He wanted the state to be recog-nized by both powerful forces—Byzantium and Rome—between which Serbia was fatefully located. His vision was a difficult-to-achieve new quality, which I see as the beginning of a school of thought in Serbian poli-tics that inclines towards achieving political neutrality between the two eternally opposed poles. In this light, the deep roots of the constant ambition of the Serbs to achieve and preserve autonomy and independence can be better understood. This can be observed during the existence of Yugoslavia, as well as in the politics of modern Serbia. In the second half of the 20th century, the significant role of socialist Yugoslavia as the founder and leader of the Non-Aligned Movement was witnessed. In present times (2022), the Republic of Serbia is expressing its allegiance to being a militarily neutral country, even though it is almost completely surrounded by NATO member states.

Let us now return to Stefan Nemanja and his difficult dilemma. Due to frequent changes in the political course, it is not the clearest how he made the final decision, but his abrupt change in behavior is seen after a lost war against the Byzantine Empire in the seventh decade of the 12th century.

The Eastern Roman Empire was a source of inspiration and authority, a hegemon to be freed from, and a powerful neighbor for Serbia to compare and compete with during this time period. Serbia was like an adolescent son growing up in conflict with a powerful father. It is not surprising, therefore, that Nemanja even attacked Byzantium, though he lost and was captured and taken to Constantinople. He was publicly humiliated and paraded with a rope around his neck, barefooted and bareheaded, through the streets of the imperial city. Surprisingly, Emperor Manuel I Komnenos gave him a second chance, granting him the title of Grand Prince. This was a crucial moment in the life of the man who is now considered one of the most important rulers of Serbia ever. Stefan Nemanja returned home changed, indoctrinated by Byzantium and determined to bring their values and models to his country. He swore to the emperor to remain a loyal vassal until the end of his life.

The most significant and far-reaching change was Nemanja's implementation of the Roman model of state governance, which is still strongly felt in Serbia today.

At this point, it is appropriate to make a small digression and go back to the fourth century AD. Constantine the Great, the Roman emperor, is best remembered for setting Christianity on the path to becoming the official religion of the Empire. Implementing a new religion was not Constantine's goal; it was a necessary means of saving the most powerful state in the world at that time from unavoidable decline and disappearance. Experimenting with the Roman Empire having multiple emperors (tetrarchy) had not given the desired results, and Constantine knew that the path to the survival of the state did not lie in more legions, wars, conquered territories, or war booty. It was apparent that Rome was rotten from the inside, and Constantine knew it. The Empire needed an all-encompassing change of paradigm. A new capital, a new religion, new standards, a value system, beliefs, symbols, words... The essence of this profound reform, which would breathe another thousand years of life into the Roman Empire, was simple. It was represented by a *new model of governing the Empire* embodied by the symbol of the *two-headed eagle*.

Two heads represent a model of a state structure whose key characteristic is the unity of church and state in one body. This involves governing through the simultaneous use of the state apparatus, characterized by force and power, and the ecclesiastical, which manages a system of values, beliefs, and morals. This structure is in the Roman-Byzantine political model described by the principle of symphony or *synallelia*, which represents a harmonious cooperation of civil and ecclesiastical functions of Christian society. In other words, the ruler, through these two key institutions, governs people who are at the same time members of the church and subjects of the state.

After the Cross, the two-headed eagle is the most recognizable symbol of the Late Roman Empire, which became the official symbol of both the Byzantine Empire in the East and the Holy Roman Empire in the West.

In addition to the coat of arms of Serbia, the double-headed eagle adorns the coats of arms of the Russian Federation, Montenegro, Albania, the Greek Orthodox Church, and the Patriarchate of Constantinople. In recent history, it was also featured on the coats of arms of the Habsburgs, the Austro-Hungarian Monarchy, and the Kingdom of Yugoslavia. Today, it can also be found on the coats of arms of some cities, such as Perth in Scotland. It is interesting to note that the two-headed eagle is also the symbol of the highest, 33rd degree of the Scottish Rite of Freemasonry.

To establish a state government model in Serbia symbolized by a two-headed eagle, Nemanja had to carry out the religious unification of the population, imposing Orthodox Christianity upon all of his subjects. This led to a harsh confrontation with Christian Gnostics starting from the 12th century, with consequences that have yet to be healed, even to this day. This important subject will be discussed in more detail in later chapters.

| The Imperial Seal of Byzantium | Tetragrammatic Cross[11] The symbol of Byzantine Emperors from the Palaiologos Dynasty (14th-15th century) | The Coat of Arms of the Medieval Serbian Kingdom | Coat of Arms of the present-day Republic of Serbia |

The Heraldic Connection Between Serbia and Byzantium

In order to achieve a model of unity between the Church and the State, Nemanja forcefully set the path towards Orthodoxy as the only religion of the Serbs in the mid-12th century. This had far-reaching consequences, firmly allocating the Serbs to the East in the eyes of the Western world. His youngest son and favorite, Prince Rastko, played an important role a decade later. Very young, he went to a monastery, became a monk, and took on the name Sava. He had a decisive influence on the formation of the religious and national identity of the Serbs as Orthodox Christians, which strengthened his father's decision that the Serbian people and state should be aligned with Constantinople and the Eastern Church. After a rich life described by several of his contemporaries and biographers, he is now venerated as the most important Serbian saint—Saint Sava, the founder of the autocephalous[12] Serbian Orthodox Church and its first archbishop, theologian, and enlightener, protector of Serbian schools, and according to folk tradition, a miracle worker.

It is little-known today in Serbia that a dramatic shift in Stefan Nemanja's political course, and his last attempt to switch to the Western side, took place in 1189. At a meeting on Serbian territory, in the city of Niš, he offered the Holy Roman Emperor Frederick Barbarossa an alliance against Byzantium, twenty thousand soldiers, a political marriage, and a vassal

---

[11] Four "B"s (pronounced as "V"s in Greek) represent the motto *Βασιλεὺς βασιλέων βασιλεύων βασιλεύουσιν* meaning "King of Kings ruling over the kings/rulers".

[12] Autocephalous status of an Eastern Christian Church means that it is governed by its own national synod and appoints its own patriarch or archbishop.

status of his state to the Western, Roman Catholic, Holy Roman Empire. This offer was not accepted, perhaps because Eastern Christianity had already been established as the state religion in Serbia at that time.

By deciding to turn Serbia towards Orthodoxy and Constantinople, Stefan Nemanja and Saint Sava made an exceptionally important geopolitical decision whose effects have endured for about eight hundred years. It crucially influenced the way the West viewed Serbia and the Serbs: as a part of the East pushed onto the strategically important Balkan peninsula, and a potential satellite (or a 'proxy') for promoting Eastern interests.

The Crusaders conquered Constantinople in 1204

However, fifteen years after Serbia had affiliated with the spiritual and political realm of Orthodox civilization, the West dealt a fatal blow to Constantinople. During the Fourth Crusade in 1204, the city was captured, plundered, and burned; this marked the start of a process of Western geopolitical superiority over the East on the Balkan peninsula, which continues to this day. In this light, it can be argued that Nemanja and Sava's decision effectively placed the Serbs on the side of the geopolitical loser: first it was the Byzantine Empire until its collapse in 1453, then Russia, attempting to become the leading power of the Orthodox world, yet failed to gain dominion over the Balkan Orthodox Slavs.

Therefore, it comes as no surprise that, due to the affiliation of Serbs to the East, the Vatican gave a very important role to Croats as border guards and defenders of Roman Catholicism from Orthodox and, later, Islamic influences. This religious division set the scene for many future dramas: Serbs and Croats became proxies of the Eastern and Western Church, and, through them, of East and West in general. Two key South Slavic tribes, which settled in the Balkans from Northern Europe, were given roles in a much bigger geopolitical game against their will. By settling strategically important regions, they found themselves caught up in an already existing geopolitical antagonism, dividing them and causing to fight for many centuries—until the present time. The effects of these processes weighed heavily on the attempt of Serbs, Croats and Slovenes to create a unified state and nation; however, it was a noble effort to escape the matrix of East-West tensions and the roles of proxies, which we will discuss in more detail later. Now, let us return to Nemanja and Saint Sava and investigate the series of tragic events remaining a suppressed trauma in the collective memory of the Serbian people, which is rarely and unwillingly spoken about.

The Tragic Fate of Serb Bogomils
Little-Known Root of Bosnian Traumas

The following story is particularly interesting because many details related to it are unknown to general public, both domestically and internationally. It is a story of the Bogomils, derogatorily known as 'Babuni' in Medieval Serbia, an insufficiently known Christian religious community. They had a strong foothold across the Balkans, even to the point of having their own medieval state in what is present-day Bosnia and Herzegovina, the only Bogomil state in Europe ever. Explorations of the Bogomils have been clouded by prejudices, which prevents the public from getting a full, accurate, and objective picture of their history, doctrine, and influence.

Furthermore, it seems that the trauma inflicted on the Bogomils had an effect on the collective subconscious and directed the behavior of ethnic groups in the war in Bosnia and Herzegovina (1992-1995). While this thesis may be surprising and confusing to many, it is worth being considered.

It is believed that Bogomilism emerged in the 10th century, in present-day North Macedonia, in the vicinity of Prilep and Veles. It is not entirely certain whether the name comes from priest Bogomil, a Christian theologian from Macedonia who is considered the founder of this teaching, or if they called themselves that because they were "worthy of God" ("bogu mili"), given the belief in the truthfulness of their teaching and their humble, righteous way of life. Bogomils were Christians, but independent from both the Eastern and Western Churches. According to some views, Bogomilism essentially represented a precursor to the Christian Reformation, advocating for a return to Jesus of Nazareth's original principles and teachings.

According to the theory, the Bogomils are successors of the original Gnostic line which dates back to the Essenes, a small Jewish community that practiced a very pious and esoteric form of Judaism. Some authors believe that the founder of Christianity Yeshua ben Yosef—Jesus of Nazareth, also belonged to this community[13]. A common characteristic of Gnostics throughout all eras, including the Bogomils, is their striving for a *direct connection* with the Creator, typically achieved through personal dedi-

---

[13] This opinion can be found in the works of Holgen Kersten, Nicholas Roerich, Nicholas Notovich, and others.

cation and devoted spiritual practice such as meditation, prayer, and living by certain guidelines. It is important to note that Gnosticism encourages an active and direct approach and rejects relying on intermediaries between man and God, as well as their interpretations of God's teaching. Gnostics believe that they are children of God and that they have every right to independently establish contact with their Creator.

In any case, historiography has recorded the belief of the Bogomils that their teaching conveyed the original Christian doctrine. If this was true, then it follows that Bogomilism represented an internal, spiritual Christianity as opposed to the worldly and political one, which was formed in the 4th century by Emperor Constantine in order to breathe new life into the decaying Roman Empire through a new paradigm and synergy of theological and political power. Contrary to the efforts of the state, the Bogomils opposed the established churches and did not accept the authority of Church elders nor the decisions of the Church councils. They considered all of this to be imposed dogmas that had nothing to do with the original Christianity. Thus they opposed the Byzantine rule and hellenization and lived a very simple and humble life. They did not construct churches; rather, they believed that if ten of them gathered in any given building, they could hold a service, thus temporarily consecrating the area.

What is particularly interesting to us is that the Bogomils preached brotherhood, harmony, equality, and freedom among people—politically "dangerous" ideas that echoed in the French Revolution's iconic slogan *Liberté, Égalité, Fraternité* seven hundred years later and have since become part of our civilizational heritage. The Bogomils considered the state as some kind of devil's creation, limiting these fundamental values. For such beliefs, they refused to go to wars, especially those that were fought in pursuit of foreign interests. To use modern terminology—these people refused to be "proxies".

It is clear that any authority wishing to control its subjects considered the doctrines and beliefs of the Bogomils to be sinful. To make matters worse, they threatened the feudal system of the time by calling on peasants to no longer serve their lords and to become emancipated, which, taking into account the then structure of social relations, was equivalent to calling for a revolution. The principle of "evangelical equality" they advocated, was a central motivator of the Bogomils not only in a theological but also in a social context.

Reports from history show that Bogomil teachings spread significantly among the Serbs, especially in the Raška region, the heart of the Serbian state, and not only among the common people but also among the nobility. The local Bogomils referred to themselves as Christians.

Based on the relatively limited historical records that remain of Bogomilism, we know that they would be baptized with prayer, fasting, and the laying of John's gospel on the head. Additionally, many of them were said to have known the entire gospel by heart. The Old Testament was rejected, except for the Psalms, and Moses and the other prophets were not accepted. One of the most notable Bogomils, presbyter Vasilije (also known as Priest Dragolj), left behind an anthology of apocryphal books. Bogomils also made a noteworthy contribution to Serbian medieval translation literature.

In the time of Nemanja, during the second half of the 12th century, the Serbs had not yet made a definite decision about the branch of Christianity to which they belonged. It is possible that the spirit of the natural crossroads which they occupied also contributed to their religious openness. To be fair, such phenomena were present in Europe at the time among other peoples as well.

Some Serbs were Roman Catholic, some Orthodox, and there was also a third group: the Bogomils, a thorn in the side of the ecclesiastical powers in Rome and Constantinople as well as all the rulers.

From the Balkans, Bogomilism spread to other parts of Europe, resulting in related religious movements known as Paulicians, Cathars, and Patarenes. One of the main tendencies of Bogomilism was resistance to Byzantine Hellenization, the state structure, and church dogma, so it is unsurprising that it appealed to the Slavs of the Balkans, whose memories of pre-Christian Slavic faith and customs were still alive. When we add independence of thought, righteousness, and resistance to authority—characteristics known to be inherent in the Serbian people—it is no surprise that the Bogomil view of the world appealed to many and experienced a long-lasting, deeply-rooted expansion.

At that time, Grand Prince Stefan Nemanja of the Serbs was in a situation similar to that of the "prodigal son" who had unsuccessfully challenged the powerful Byzantine "father", who then gave him life and allowed him to reign. Nemanja, a vassal who had pledged lifelong loyalty to the emperor, had no other option but to strengthen the state and church authority among the Serbs according to the Byzantine model. As we shall see, this was a violent precedent and the beginning of a split in the Serbian national being, the effects of which are still strongly felt today.

At the end of the 12th century, around 1180, we observe Nemanja's decisive turn to Orthodoxy and the beginning of the unification of the Serbian religious identity, which was undoubtedly motivated by the strengthening of the state and its structure. The path to achieving this goal was, from today's perspective, extremely difficult and painful. At the request of Byzantium, it was necessary to solve the problem of Bogomilism among the Serbs. And the Bogomils were numerous and deeply rooted, not only among the ordinary population but also among a number of noble families. The course of historical events, unfortunately, led to the Church-State Council against the Bogomils, which was con-

Fresco depicting Bogomils (detail). Church of Saint Ahilius in Arilje, Serbia, circa 1290.

vened by Stefan Nemanja in 1186 in the then capital, the city of Ras. The course of the Council showed the full extent of the problem. Contemporaries speak of great disagreements and resistance of some magnates to the proposed clash with the Bogomils, and that they did not even try to hide their beliefs. In the end, the ruler's stream prevailed, and the army was sent to fiercely persecute the heretical Serbs. Many people perished, some were forcibly converted to Orthodoxy and a large number were expelled. There were also survivors who retreated to mountainous regions and hid from persecution.

We could call this pogrom, according to all modern standards, anti-civilizational, considering the fact that, according to contemporary accounts and biographers of Nemanja, mass crimes were committed against Bogomils: they were mutilated, tortured, killed and their property was confiscated. It is important to note that all of these atrocities were carried out by the Nemanjić elite against members of their own people.

As the medieval Serbian state dealt with the Serb-Bogomils, so were their apocryphal books burned. In the Synodikon of Orthodoxy, the Bogomils—the "babuni"—are cursed with these words:

"Evil heretics, wicked babuni, who falsely call themselves Christians, and who mock our true faith, omitting words from the holy books and turning them to heresy, and who are torn away from the holy and orthodox Church, and who mock the holy and honorable cross, and who mock the holy icons and do not bow down to them—let them be cursed!"

These lines leave no doubt about the determination of the Orthodox elite at the time to eliminate any competition that had different thoughts and beliefs.

It appears that Bogomilism was so deeply rooted among the people that this religious confrontation could not completely eradicate it. One hundred and sixty years later, we find it again in the provisions of the famous Dušan's Code, where the Serbian emperor labels Bogomilism as a heresy and sets penalties for those who belong to it or preach this teaching. Most of the Bogomils who were expelled from Nemanja's state went to the neighboring Serbian ruler in Bosnia, the "Good Ban Kulin", who was married to Vojislava; Nemanja's sister. At the same time, Kulin's sister was married to Nemanja's brother Miroslav, so these two states were also firmly connected by marriages. To this day, the saying is known in the people that speaks of the prosperity of Bosnia in Kulin's time: "From Ban Kulin and good days". But to complete the stage of the drama we are describing with the famous Balkan complexity—both Kulin and his wife Vojislava were Bogomils. It is believed that it was probably during Kulin's time that the formation of the autochthonous Bosnian Church, which was Bogomil in its doctrine, took place.

It happened so that the Bosnian ruling pair warmly welcomed their countrymen—Serb refugees fleeing Nemanja's pogrom. At the time, there were Serb Bogomils who inhabited territories south of Bosnia, predominantly Roman Catholic region of Dalmatia. They, too, were systematically persecuted—but by the Roman Church, which had jurisdiction over that territory. These people were also forced to flee to Bosnia under the protection of the good Ban Kulin and the shelter of the Bosnian Church. Due to these processes, it seems that Bosnia in the 12th century, under Ban Kulin, became an ethnically mostly Serbian, Bogomil state—and the only Bogomil state ever. It lasted, with great impediments from Catholic and Orthodox kings and church leaders, until the Ottoman invasion of the Balkans in the 15th century, when the trace of the Bogomil church suddenly disappeared.

The fact that Bosnian Ban Kulin was receiving Bogomils in his state was sharply condemned by both Roman Catholic and Orthodox centers of power, and the pressure on him did not diminish. Interestingly, even though they mutually despised each other and called each other schismatics, both Eastern and Western Christians weren't opposed to cooperating when it was necessary to persecute the Bogomils, who were bearers of a kind of early Reformation in Christianity. For example, Nemanja's brother

Vukan, who was then the Orthodox King of Serbian maritime lands, addressed the Vatican in a letter in which he said:

> "In the land of the Hungarian king[14], in Bosnia, a heresy of no small proportion is developing, and to such an extent that Kulin himself, having been seduced with his wife and his sister, the widow of Miroslav Humski, and several of his relatives, converted to that heresy more than ten thousand Christians."[15]

This Serbian-Orthodox denunciation of the Bogomils to the Roman Catholic Church, in the hope of provoking a military intervention, can be seen as both sad and tragic. The response was not long in coming. Pope Innocent III, the founder of the Inquisition, put pressure on his ally, the Hungarian king Emeric, to immediately take military action against the heretic Kulin in Bosnia.

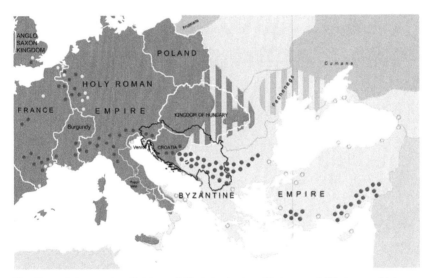

The Great Schism—the division of Christianity into Eastern and Western, which occurred in 1054—runs through the middle of the future Yugoslav space (marked by a black line). Dark dots represent the Bogomils, who were called different names in different parts of Europe: Paulicians, Patarenes, Cathars.

---

[14] At that time, Bosnia was a vassal of Hungary.
[15] Imamović, Mustafa. *Historija Bošnjaka*. Sarajevo, Bosnia and Herzegovina: BZK "Preporod", 1997.

Serbia of the Nemanjićs was not an isolated case in this matter. A similar fate befell the spiritual brotherhood of Bogomils—Cathars, Patarenes, and Paulicians—in other parts of Europe. In northern Italy and southern France, they suffered crusades from Roman Catholic kings. Interestingly, there are records of a Bogomil theological or spiritual university near today's town of Visoko, in Bosnia and Herzegovina, which was attended by Patarene and Cathar teachers from Italy and France. It was in Bosnia that they were educated in their spiritual science and then returned back to their countries to continue teaching to church and secular authorities.

Given that pogroms of Bogomils, persecutions, physical punishments, and confiscation of property have been continued in Serbian states for at least two centuries after these first tragic events, we can conclude that the uniformization of faith among the Serbs was one of the constant high priorities of the Serbian rulers from the Nemanjić dynasty. It seems that it was considered a necessity for the homogenization of the state and strengthening of its structure. Otherwise, the persecution of one's own people for different religious affiliations is hard to explain.

The Ethnogenesis of the Bosniaks

The moment has come for a new perspective to progress in gathering the pieces of the Yugoslav puzzle. The processes that will be presented are very important for a deeper understanding of the relations in Bosnia and Herzegovina, as well as the complex civil war that recently took place in this Yugoslav republic from 1992 to 1995.

During those years, we witnessed bloody ethnic conflicts between Christian Orthodox Bosnian Serbs, Roman Catholic Bosnian Croats, and Muslim Bosniaks. The world was confused by the sudden eruption of the darkest emotions and brutality that had struck the area, where those same nations had lived peacefully under the shelter of the Yugoslav state for decades. To a careful eye, some epic, deep, and inexplicable force was not overlooked, which, acting from the collective consciousness, was driving people from all the conflicting sides to do each other terribly incomprehensible things. What repressed distant trauma released the spirit from the bottle in Bosnia and Herzegovina in 1992? In order to answer this question, it is necessary to pay attention to the ethnogenesis of the Bosniaks, the people of the Islamic faith who inhabit the territories of today's Bosnia and Herzegovina, northeastern Montenegro, and southwestern Serbia.

Today, all the nations in Bosnia and Herzegovina, as well as others in former Yugoslavia, have their own views on the ethnic identity of Bosniaks. The reasoning presented in this book is supported by the study of historical sources and the results of recent analyses of Balkan nations' genetics. However, I wish to emphasize that this is a complex and very sensitive issue, full of heavy emotions. Many different opinions on the origin of Bosniaks arise due to the still-present nationalisms, propagandist pseudohistories that stem from conflicting interests, as well as unresolved conflicts, and traumas from the past. Bosniaks suffered the most in the Yugoslav wars. They endured around 60,000 casualties or roughly 46% of the total death toll on all sides. Therefore, I present my conclusions on the ethnogenesis of Bosniaks as a sincere attempt to approach the ultimate truth on this highly important subject for understanding the painful emotions in Yugoslavia and, especially, the exceptionally complex war in Bosnia and Herzegovina.

Who are Bosniaks? Are they Turks, remaining after the fall of the Ottoman Empire? No. These people are of Slavic origin. If they are Slavs, then the conclusion is that they must be either Serbs or Croats, since, according to the prevailing opinion, there were no other Slavs in this area. Some, mostly Bosniak authors, put forward the thesis that Bosniaks originated from the indigenous people of the Balkan Peninsula—Illyrians, who populated it before the arrival of the Slavs. However, this view does not have majority support in the scientific community.

To go one step further in the conclusion, Bosniaks are therefore people of Serbian or Croatian origin who at some point changed their faith and converted from Christianity to Islam. For certain reasons, which we will devote more attention to on the pages that follow, the converts began to perceive themselves, over time, as a newly formed and distinct *ethnic* and not just religious community.

Chronologically, the process of the creation of the Bosniak ethnic community proceeded briefly as follows:

The Ottoman Empire conquered regions of Bosnia and Herzegovina in the 15ᵗʰ century. At the time, it was inhabited by members of three Christian denominations, three groups of people with smoldering religious conflicts: Bogomil Serbs, about whom we wrote in detail in the previous chapter, Orthodox Serbs, and Roman Catholic Croats. However, under the Ottoman rule Islam was the state religion, and so, only Muslims could be first-class citizens, enjoying full rights regardless of their ethnic origin. On the other hand Christians were condemned to suffering, as they were designated as "raja" or second-class citizens. They were deprived of their rights, exposed to mistreatment, persecution, forcible abduction of children also known as the notorious "tax in blood", and other high impositions of the Ottoman government.

What was the way out, then? Conversion to Islam. Such a change of religion meant the end of suffering and the opportunity to have a normal life. Unsurprisingly, the Turkish government viewed this process very favorably and actively encouraged it. Despite this, however, many proud Orthodox Serbs and Roman Catholic Croats in Bosnia stubbornly held on to their faiths, national homelands in the neighborhood, and religious identity. To avoid persecution, many fled to the mountains and organized armed resistance against the powerful empire.

Bogomils took a different path. After centuries of being killed, crippled, oppressed, and persecuted—first by their Orthodox co-nationals and then by Catholic Croats and Hungarians—the Serbs of the Bogomil faith saw the new Turkish rule as an escape, a relief, and a chance for a long-dreamed-of normal life. In accepting the Ottoman offer to convert to Islam, these people were finally given the opportunity to be protected, accepted, and to become equal citizens of the most powerful empire of the time. And not only that, they suddenly became privileged in relation to their former oppressors.

That is how the massive conversion of Serbs of the Bogomil branch of Christianity to Islam in the fifteenth century occurred in Bosnia. This process, according to the opinion of a number of authors, among whom I include myself, was the beginning of the ethnogenesis of contemporary Bosniaks.

In relation to this, it is worth mentioning a quote from the work *Serbs in Dalmatia* (1938) by Dr. Lujo Bakotić, a Yugoslav diplomat and writer, who wrote:

> "As it is known, in Bosnia and Herzegovina the majority of the former Bogomils passed to the Muslim faith, who were nothing but *Orthodox* Protestants who had passed from Orthodoxy to Bogomilism."

As previously shown, Orthodox were the Serbs, while the Croats were of Roman Catholic faith.

In short, Grand Prince Stefan Nemanja inflicted a deep wound in the Serbian collective being in 1186 with the brutal pogrom, expulsion and forced Christianization of his Bogomil compatriots. The Bogomils experienced a change in their fortune when the Turks arrived and they converted to Islam. Consequently, the antagonism between Orthodox and Bogomils reached a new level, as the Orthodox held even greater contempt for the Islamized Bogomils, branding them traitors with the pejorative term *poturica* ("one who became a Turk").

Additional reasons for the mass conversion of Bogomils to Islam can be found in theology. There are obvious similarities between the two religions, such as prayer multiple times a day, fasting, rejection of religious symbols, modest places for religious ceremonies, and prohibition of icons. Moreover, Muslims can perform their religious service at home without the need for clergy, which corresponded to the Bogomil religious mentality, since their rituals were also held in private homes. Islamic Imams or teachers are not equivalent to Christian priests, as there is no theological "mystery of the sacraments" in Islam. In sacramental churches, only a priest can be a bearer of theological mysteries, a dogma that Protestantism later rejected. In Islam, it is believed that the relationship between God and man is direct, thus eliminating the need for mediation. This same direct relationship with God was advocated by the Bogomils, which is seen in their resistance to church authorities and imposed dogmas. However, sacramental versions of Christianity were imposed on them by force, resulting in harsh persecutions and abuse. Refusing religious assimilation, Bogomils stayed true to their theological and moral convictions and refused to return to the "Holy Church".

Expectantly, the Serbian Orthodox Church did not fight against this Serbo-Serbian schism. On the contrary, the fight against heresy was deemed more important to them than the fact that the heretics were also

Serbs. Thus, Bogomils—or "Serb heretics"—welcomed Ottoman rule and often became devoted supporters of its institutions.

The calculating Ottoman administration took full advantage of this Serbian internal conflict, deepening it for their own needs. The principle of "divide and rule" was applied treacherously and brutally; newly converted Muslim Serbs were often delegated with the job of controlling and punishing stubborn and rebellious Orthodox Serbs, reversing the roles of oppressor and victim. The three-century-long Serbian schism was further compounded and deepened by these events, now within a completely new Ottoman context, only adding more salt to the long-open wounds.

In the times from the Nemanjić persecution of the Bogomils in the 12th century until their mass conversion to Islam after the 15th century, a hard-set attitude was established that a Serb could only be of the Orthodox faith. This attitude persists in large measure today as an integral part of the national identity of Serbs and is officially supported by the Serbian Orthodox Church. However, one must ask: did those who perpetrated the pogrom against the Bogomil Serbs—the Church and state authorities—promote such exclusivism in the nation for centuries in order to justify and hide their actions? We can also see the persistence of this point of view in more recent times. During Socialist Yugoslavia, the Serbian Orthodox Church was much more accepting of a Serb being an atheist and a Communist Party member than if they had changed to another faith—the latter was simply unimaginable.

From everything presented, it is easy to understand that the Bogomil Serbs, when they became Muslim Serbs, knew that their motherland would never recognize them as part of the same Serbian nation. The separation was complete and the rejection was definite. Therefore, they had no other choice but to embrace the culture and customs of the Ottoman state and Islam, retain some of their old traditions, and form a new ethnic group—to become a new nation, today called Bosniaks.

Foundation for this view of the ethnogenesis of Bosniaks is provided by modern genetics. Recent scientific DNA research has shown an extraordinary similarity and common origin of Serbs, Croats, and Bosniaks. Additionally, in a 2005 research (with the caveat that it was conducted on a relatively small sample of 256 men), the authors came to the conclusion which supports the theory of the mostly Serb-Bogomil ethnic origin of modern Bosniaks:

"Analysis of the frequency of the main components of the Y-chromosomal haplogroups among three ethnic groups in Bosnia and Herzegovina—Serbs, Croats, and Bosniaks—showed that

Bosnian Serbs and Bosniaks were closer to each other in Y-DNA than either group was to Bosnian Croats."[16]

Looking at these intra-Serbian processes from a historical distance, it seems that the religious uniformity imposed by Stefan Nemanja and his successors has led to a significant erosion of the Serbian national corpus. Those Serbs who, through contacts and life with other peoples, switched to other faiths—Catholicism or Islam—were predominantly rejected by the Orthodox national matrix, and they usually became ethnic Croats or Bosniaks over time. It is therefore interesting to think in the direction of the thesis that Yugoslavia may never have existed if the Serbs had adopted religious pluralism in the 12th century. In such a scenario, it is quite possible to envision the formation of a much larger Serbian state across the entire Serbian ethnic space—both East and West, Orthodox and Catholic, as well as Islamic—after liberation from foreign, colonial rule. Such an integrated, multi-confessional Serbian state, with its existence and size, would greatly reduce the chances of Yugoslavia even appearing on the historical stage.

On the other hand, it is possible that some wise head in the Serbian elite of the 19th or 20th century saw in the Yugoslav idea the possibility of reversing the erosive process. By uniting all Serbs within one state and using the Yugoslav supra-nation as a kind of catalyst, eventually, there would be a gradual reintegration of parts of the Serbian national corpus that had been rejected and separated earlier due to not belonging to Orthodox faith.

There are few Bosniaks and Serbs today who are aware of these historical events as a whole, as they have long since faded from most people's consciousness with the passage of centuries. All that remains are crude fragments of memories and deeply buried negative emotions in the collective unconsciousness of both groups. But we shall see that the proper trigger could bring them to the surface with all their might.

It is not possible to heal the trauma by either suppressing or forgetting it, even after centuries have passed. The genie came out of the bottle in 1992, and now we are getting a glimpse of what set it free. The brutal conflict between Serbs and Bosniaks in the Bosnian War can also be seen as the last episode in the intra-Serbian spiral of violence that began in 1186, when Great Prince Stefan Nemanja, intending to establish a state based on the Byzantine model, ordered a brutal purge of the Bogomils.

---

[16] Marjanović, Damir, S. Fornarino, S. Montagna, et al. "The peopling of modern Bosnia-Herzegovina: Y-chromosome haplogroups in the three main ethnic groups." *Annals of Human Genetics 69*, no. 6 (2005): 757-763.

South Slavs Between Ottomans and Habsburgs

The Ottoman Conquest of the Balkans and its Influence on the South Slavs

Battle of Kosovo, by Adam Stefanović (1870).

After the death of Serbian Emperor Dušan the Mighty in 1355, his son Uroš the Weak ascended to the throne. Uroš's inability to govern the state led to the strengthening of local magnates, resulting in the fragmentation of the empire into independent fiefdoms. The Ottoman Empire recognized and exploited this situation, launching a series of attacks on the weakened Serbian lands. These attacks culminated in the Battle of Kosovo on June 28th, 1389, which is deeply imprinted in the collective consciousness of the Serbian people to this day. In the battle, the Serbian prince Lazar, the Turkish sultan Murat, and most of the soldiers on both sides perished. Serbia suffered heavy losses and was unable to resist the new Ottoman attacks that followed the next year. By the end of the 14th century, the period of disintegration of the medieval Serbian state began and the gradual transition of Serbian lands under Ottoman rule. This period lasted for seventy years, until 1459, when the Ottomans conquered the last Serbian stronghold, the fortified city of Smederevo. Most of the Balkans passed into the hands of the Ottoman Empire, where Islam was the state religion. Christians became second-class citizens, exposed to heavy taxes and assimilation pressure. All the lands inhabited by Serbs, as well as some Croatian lands, fell under Ottoman rule.

Most of the occupied Serbs persisted in maintaining their roots, traditions, and Christian faith. They frequently rebelled, resisting the conquerors in various ways. The Ottoman policy of establishing control over the conquered peoples sought to incorporate local collaborators into its structure. As a rule, this was an ethnic group of Islamic faith to whom a privileged status was granted and the task of enforcing the Empire's laws over their Christian neighbors. Of course, this also entailed the implementation of punishments and other forms of repression. Whenever possible, the Ottomans sought to avoid direct involvement. They had learned from the ancient Romans a very important principle: *divide et impera* ("Divide and Rule").

In Bosnia and Herzegovina, Turkish auxiliaries became Bosniaks, as detailed in the previous chapter. In Kosovo and Metohija, a region that represented the spiritual and state center of the Nemanjić kingdom and empire, local Turkish auxiliaries eventually became Albanians, specifically that part of this nation that inhabited the inaccessible mountain areas in present-day northern Albania. To better control the rebellious Serbs, the Turks repeatedly, from the 15th century onwards, encouraged the settlement of Albanian Muslims primarily in Kosovo, the region where the capital of the Serbian Empire and the seat of the Serbian Orthodox Church were located. The Turks realized that they had to make the Serbs a minority in their holy land in order to break their resistance. Consequently, the efforts of the Ottomans in the following centuries would reduce the number of Serbs in Kosovo and increase the number of Albanians. The Serbs would indeed become a minority there, and this Ottoman policy caused the beginning of the centuries-long hostility between the Serbs and the Albanians. This would turn into a sinister spiral of violence that, unfortunately, continues to this day. We shall return to this very complex relationship in later chapters.

The Point of Contact Between Two Very Different Worlds

Over time, small states in the Balkans disappeared, and two regional powers took their place: Habsburg Austria and the Ottoman Empire. By the 15th century, they had conquered all the Balkan peoples, including the South Slavs.

The Balkans in 1815

Belgrade, a city at the 'crossroads of worlds', has been a witness to the titanic clash of the Orient and Europe, the Ottomans and the Habsburgs, Islam and Christianity for centuries.

The border between the Ottomans and the Habsburgs in the Balkans and Central Europe often changed, but stabilized for long periods on the rivers Sava and Danube. Belgrade, dominating the vast Pannonian lowlands, became the most important Ottoman stronghold and a strategic point from which numerous attempts to conquer the Habsburg lands of Central Europe were launched. Vienna and Budapest were within reach of the Turkish troops and thus under constant threat.

Serbs were under Ottoman rule, while the Habsburgs ruled the Croats and Slovenes. This led to further division among the South Slavs. It was no longer just a matter of belonging to the Western or Eastern Christianity, but they found themselves under the rule and influence of two very different, conflicting empires with completely different cultures, religions and value systems.

Croats and Slovenes enjoyed greater rights and freedoms in the Roman Catholic environment of German rulers than Serbs, who were oppressed and deprived under the Islamic rule of the Ottomans. As a border nation, Croats became a Roman Catholic shield against the spread of Islam and Orthodoxy, while Serbs, on the other side of the border, firmly held on to Orthodox Christianity, believing it was the only thing that could save them from Islamization and assimilation.

Habsburg Response:
Creation of the Military Frontier

How Were the Serbs Called Upon to Become Defenders of the Habsburg Monarchy?

The story that follows will be one of the key points in understanding the roots of animosity between Croats and Serbs. This is an important piece of the puzzle in striving to provide a comprehensive insight into the genesis of future Yugoslav turbulences.

In order to prevent further Ottoman expansion, Habsburg Austria created a special military border region in the 16th century, with the role of a buffer zone between the two empires. This region stretched along the difficult-to-defend river valleys of the Sava and Danube, which flow from the Alps in the west to the Black Sea in the east, forming the northern geographical border of the Balkan Peninsula.

The Military Frontier zone (blue) existed between the Habsburg
and Ottoman Empires from the 16th to the 19th centuries.
The migration of Serbs is indicated by red arrows.

At the same time, the rivers Sava and Danube sharply divide the mountain ranges of the Balkans on one side, from the fertile plains of Pannonia on the other. The newly formed military district, called the *Military Frontier*[17], was initially populated mostly by Croatian and Hungarian peoples. In Slavonia, one of the areas that became part of the Frontier, there were also Orthodox Serbs who had settled there in previous centuries.

In order to increase the population density in this dangerous border area, the authorities in Vienna promised better status to all those who would voluntarily settle and take on the role of border guards. It is very likely that they had in mind primarily the disenfranchised Serbs under the Ottomans, whom they saw as ideal candidates. Why? Under the Ottoman Empire, the Serbs had:

- deep animosity towards the Turks
- experience in fighting them
- been existentially threatened
- paid high taxes and
- been victims of religious and social oppression.

In accordance with Austria's expectations, the Serbs, who were dissatisfied and oppressed under the Ottomans, readily accepted the offer and began a mass migration to the newly formed Military Frontier. For them, crossing the river and arriving in the border zone meant freedom and a new life, an escape from Ottoman repression. Serbian settlers were grateful and loyal to the Crown and, as skilled warriors, were successful in warfare. Vienna saw this policy as its own great success and later further encouraged the arrival of Serbian settlers by increased privileges and tax exemptions. The Serbs were given the right to freely practice their Orthodox faith, and over time they were given the possibility to *acquire ownership of land in exchange for military service*. And they used this right to build houses and cultivate the land in times of peace. Additionally, these people knew that a potential return to the occupied Serbian lands would likely mean death at the hands of the Ottomans, so they had no choice but to stay where they were and put down roots in the new land.

For the sake of objectivity, it is now time to change perspective and look at the above-described process of Serbian migration from the point of view of the native Croatian population in the Military Frontier. Many of them, as subjects of Austria, also fought against the Turks. Understandably, the Serbian settlers were perceived as competition and a threat, and their settlement as unacceptable and threatening. The Croats were deeply concerned that Austria would change the demographic structure by settling

---

[17] In Serbo-Croatian: *Vojna krajina*

tens of thousands of Serbs in their Croatian homeland. In addition, it seems that the authorities offended the Croats, who were mostly in a vassal relationship to the local nobility (serfs), by granting the Serbs the status of free citizens and privileged warriors. In this way, Croatian suspicion and deep animosity towards the Serbian settlers were aroused. But by far the biggest problem in the Croatian eye had to be that the authorities were giving the Serbs the right to acquire *ownership of the land*. From their perspective, the Habsburg authorities were giving Croatian land to Serbian settlers, and the Croats could not prevent this process. The frustration must have been immense. The closest brethren in Slavic blood, Orthodox neighbors and local competitors had now transformed into intruders. Was Vienna, in this way, also applying the ancient doctrine of "divide and rule" to promote Serbian-Croatian animosity and more easily govern its subjects? It is possible. However, it looks more likely that it was just a pragmatic solution to the Ottoman threat, without delving too much into what inter-ethnic problems might arise from these policies.

The described processes likely represent a key moment for the emergence of intolerance between Croats and Serbs. However, we should also consider the pre-existing factors that, like fertile soil, were already in place. Serbs, as Orthodox Christians, and Croats as Roman Catholics, have often been pawns in the fierce battles for influence between the two conflicting branches of the church throughout history. From a cultural perspective, there are also significant differences. After their migration in the 7th century, both Serbs and Croats were exposed to the influence of the Eastern Roman Empire—Byzantium, but Croats later turned strongly towards the West and Rome. In contrast, Serbs were deeply rooted in the political, cultural, and religious influence of the East and Constantinople. Consequently, the closest relatives of the same Slavic origin, two tribes of the same language and first neighbors, Serbs and Croats, found themselves on different sides and were too often drawn, as proxies, into the disputes between the East and the West at the ever turbulent Balkan crossroads of worlds.

It is useful to cite here the British political activist and historian R.W. Seton-Watson (1879–1951), the protagonist of the idea of South Slavic unification into one nation, who believed that the differences between Serbs and Croats come from outside rather than from within:

> *"The differences between Serb and Croat are above all psychological. They go back for many centuries, and are due to their very different history, the Serb having been under the influence of Byzantium, of the Eastern Church and Empire; the Croat under that of the West, of Rome, of Vienna, of Budapest.*

The difference is not one of race—Serb and Croat are as near to each other as Wessex to Mercia—of a language, which is of course identical, though two scripts are used; or, again, of religion, since the three religions live amicably side by side. [...] Foolish phrases have sometimes been uttered as to the unbridgeable gulf between Eastern and Western culture, as an explanation of Serbo-Croat divergence; but this is a preposterous exaggeration of a real factor. The existence of two currents loosely called Rome and Byzantium must always be borne in mind, but while it retards the process of fusion, it ought in the end to enrich and strengthen the common stock."[18]

Based on church censuses, censuses of non-noble populations, and other censuses from the era, a group of authors[19] presented an estimate of the ethnic structure of the Military Frontier around 1790, which showed the extent of Serbian migrations and that Serbs outnumbered Croats in this territory at that time. According to these sources, there were 388,000 Serbs (42.4%) and 325,000 Croats (35.5%).

Half a century later, in 1846, the Austrian Statistical Yearbook reported that the Military Frontier had 1,226,408 inhabitants, of whom 598,603 were Orthodox (48.82%) and 514,545 were Roman Catholics (41.96%).[20]

***

It is important to note that some of the prominent scientists and artists born in the Military Frontier were of Serbian descent. The most notable of them was the genius scientist and inventor Nikola Tesla.

He was born in the village of Smiljan, located in the Lika region of the Austro-Hungarian Empire, on July 10th, 1856. This region was once part of the Military Frontier and is today in the Republic of Croatia. Tesla's father, Milutin, was a Serbian Orthodox Church priest and a parish priest in the village, while his mother descended from a renowned Serbian priestly and monastic family Mandić. The rest of his family and ancestors were mostly Austrian border guards and officers, some of whom were decorated for

---

[18] Seton-Watson, R. W. "Jugoslavia and Croatia." *Journal of the Royal Institute of International Affairs 8*, no. 2 (1929): 117–33.

[19] Rokai, Petar, Zoltan Djere, Tibor Pal, and Aleksandar Kasaš. *Istorija Madjara*. Beograd: IP CLIO, 2002, 214.

[20] Uebersichts-Tafeln zur Statistik der österreichischen Monarchie: besonderer Abdruck des X. und XI. Heftes der "Statistischen Mittheilungen". 1850, p. 2

their military service. Tesla's ancestors had moved to the Military Frontier from the Herzegovina region, which was then under Ottoman rule.

Nikola Tesla
(1856-1943)
Father of alternating current, induction
motor and wireless transfer of
energy and information

Turmoil Among the South Slavs From the Beginning of the 19ᵗʰ Century to the Outbreak of the First World War

Serbian National Liberation in the 19ᵗʰ Century and Its Consequences

Let us now focus on the Serbs who lived under Ottoman rule, in the lands south of the Sava and Danube rivers. The centuries-long Turkish occupation failed to extinguish their dreams of freedom and state restoration. History has recorded numerous uprisings that were suppressed, followed by exoduses or retaliations by Ottoman authorities against the rebellious people.

The two most striking examples of these migratory processes are the migrations of Serbs that took place in the late 17ᵗʰ and early 18ᵗʰ centuries. During the Great Turkish War (1683-1699) and the Russo-Austro-Turkish War (1735-1739), the Serbs, at the invitation of the Serbian Church, massively joined the Austrian army, fighting against Turkey and hoping for the liberation of their territories. However, Austria suffered

Djordje Petrović Karadjordje
Leader of the First Serbian Uprising and founder of the dynasty of Karadjordjević

defeats in both wars, and the consequences for the Serbs were severe. In fear of Turkish retaliation, tens of thousands of Serbian families fled from Kosovo, Metohija, and other southern regions to the north, to southern Hungary and the Austrian Military Frontier. Ottoman authorities filled the newly created vacuum with Albanian Muslim population. This will lead to demographic advantage of Albanians over Serbs in these areas and affect the complexity of the Kosovo issue, whose quality resolution is still not apparent.

At the beginning of the 19ᵗʰ century, after extremely repressive measures against the Serbian people implemented by the *Dahije*—Turkish rebels from the central government in Istanbul—a wave of intolerable dissatisfaction gave rise to the great leader Djordje Petrović, who in 1804 took the lead of a general uprising that history remembers as the First Serbian Uprising. Military leaders and insurgents gave him the title of *Vožd*, meaning Supreme leader. He was strong and very tall, with a sharp character, black hair, eyes, and mustache. Because of these traits, he was nicknamed Karadjordje, which means Black Djordje in Turkish. After several years of successful warfare, the central Serbian lands and Belgrade were liberated, dealing a fatal blow to the centuries-old Ottoman occupation. From that moment on, the wheel of history would turn in favor of the Serbs. Karadjordje himself would later experience a tragic fate in the internal Serbian turmoil—he was brutally killed in his sleep in 1817. However, his descendants would become princes and kings of Serbia, and then of Yugoslavia, playing a key role in its creation.

Sweet freedom lasted almost a decade, and then Serbia fell into Turkish hands once again. Napoleon attacked Russia, and while Europeans were busy fighting each other, the Turks regained their possessions in the Balkans. Karadjordje had to flee Serbia and seek safety in Austria. Soon after that, his best commander and right-hand man Miloš Obrenović led the people in 1815 in a new uprising—the Second Serbian Uprising. Apparently, the Sultan realized then that the Serbs had no intention of calming down. After years of negotiation and haggling with the Turks, Miloš managed to secure recognition of Serbian autonomy within the Ottoman Empire. By the Sultan's document, the so-called Hatt-i-Sharif from 1830, Serbia gained the status of a principality, and Miloš himself the hereditary title of Prince of Serbia.

Miloš Obrenović,
Leader of the Second Serbian Uprising, Prince of Serbia and founder of the dynasty of Obrenović

Today, Serbia regards these two heroes as the founders of the modern Serbian state. Their descendants were bitter rivals throughout the 19th century, taking turns on the throne and exiling each other from the country. History remembers them as the Obrenović and Karadjordjević dynasties. At the beginning of the 20th century, in 1903, an officer conspiracy against the Obrenovićs resulted in the brutal murder of King Alexander and Queen Draga, and the extinguishing of the dynasty. Although they tragically and in an unacceptable manner disappeared from the historical scene, the Obrenović dynasty undoubtedly made a crucial contribution to the establishment and full international recognition of the restored Serbia in the 19th century.

The Return of the Kingdom of Serbia and the Principality of Montenegro to the Family of Sovereign Nations in 1878

The Principality of Serbia after the Congress of Berlin of 1878, squeezed between the Austro-Hungarian and Ottoman Empires
(the borders of Serbia are outlined with a black line)

The Congress of Berlin of 1878 was an important international conference hosted by the renowned German Chancellor Otto von Bismarck. The conference aimed to stabilize the situation in the Balkans after the Russo-Turkish War, which ended with the Treaty of San Stefano. The provisions of this treaty granted independence to Serbia and Montenegro, but Russia's intention to create Greater Bulgaria contrary to the vital interests of Serbia and Greece led to great dissatisfaction and instability. For these and other reasons, it was necessary to revise the Treaty of San Stefano. Perceiving the Russian

Milan Obrenović,
the first modern king of
Serbia (1882-1889)

initiative as a kind of betrayal, Serbia changed its foreign policy orientation from pro-Russian to pro-Western.

The Congress of Berlin was attended by the six major European powers of that time: Russia, Great Britain, France, Austria-Hungary, Italy, and Germany. Four interested Balkan states were also present: Greece, Serbia, Romania, and Montenegro. On the other side was the lonely, defeated, and declining Ottoman Empire.

Serbia finally gained full international recognition, independence, and sovereignty under the name of the Kingdom of Serbia at this conference. Although it had many reasons to celebrate, there was a painful awareness that many territories were still not liberated. The state territory of the Kingdom of Serbia was far smaller than the one it had in the Middle Ages, squeezed between the declining Turkey and still strong Austria. The task of national liberation and state consolidation was not yet completed. Many Serbs in the north and west were under Austrian rule, while others in the south were under Turkish rule. After the Congress of Berlin, the desire of all Serbs, everywhere in the Balkans, to liberate themselves from Austrian and Turkish rule and join their regions to the Kingdom of Serbia grew stronger.

A Few Words About Montenegro

At the Congress of Berlin, the Ottoman Empire and all other great powers *de jure* recognized the independence of another state that would play an important role in the story of Yugoslavia—the Principality of Montenegro. This small mountainous state on the southern Adriatic coast has existed under various names (Duklja, Zeta) since the original arrival of the Serbs in the Balkans in the 7th century. Today's Montenegrins are overwhelmingly of Serbian ethnic origin. This people is characterized by courage, pride, and a devotion to authentic tradition. The Montenegrins gained freedom from the Turks much earlier than the other Serbs and established theocracy first, then a principality, and finally a kingdom under the

Nikola I Petrović, Prince of Montenegro from 1860-1910, and King from 1910-1918

Petrović dynasty. Therefore, among the Montenegrins, over time, a sense of a special identity was formed, which is a kind of enhancement of the basic Serbian identity. Although modern Serbs and Montenegrins share the same language, script, names, religion, and common historical roots, they differ in their opinions on identity. A large number of people in Montenegro still identify themselves as Serbs. However, in recent decades, there has been a noticeable shift in sentiment, and today, more than half of the population identify themselves as Montenegrins. This process has been particularly pronounced since Montenegro decided to become an independent nation in 2006. In the Montenegrin ethnic definition, there is a full awareness of Serbian ethnic origin, but also a recognition of qualitative enhancement, a kind of transformation that has evolved over centuries.

It is very interesting for uncovering subtle movements within the Serbian nation that many of its leaders came from Montenegro: in the Middle Ages, Stefan Nemanja, undoubtedly one of the most important Serbs ever and the father of the founder of the Serbian Orthodox Church, St. Sava. The Nemanjić dynasty, of which he was the progenitor, ruled Serbia for two centuries, until 1371. The parents of Karadjordje Petrović, the leader of the First Serbian Uprising and the founder of the royal dynasty that ruled Serbia and Yugoslavia, were of Montenegrin origin. Yugoslav King Alexander I Karadjordjević was born and spent his childhood in Montenegro, and his maternal grandfather was Montenegrin King Nikola I Petrović. In times of Yugoslav turbulence and the bloody civil war of the 1990s, several people who were born there or have Montenegrin origins played a significant role. Above all, political leader of the Bosnian Serbs during the Bosnian War, Radovan Karadžić and Slobodan Milošević, the infamous president of Serbia, whose parents were born in northern Montenegro.

The Situation in Austria-Hungary

The re-establishment of Serbian statehood strongly resonated among other Southern Slavs, especially those under the rule of Austria-Hungary. The aspirations of Slovenes and Croats for freedom and independence gained momentum during this period. Serbs in these areas, mostly in the region of Vojvodina, strongly yearned for unity with Serbia. Many intellectuals from all three nations were captivated by a sense of romantic enthusiasm, and they wholeheartedly promoted ideas of Pan-Slavism and unity of Slavic nations. It was entirely clear to everyone that together they had much better prospects of freeing themselves from Habsburg rule.

The decisions of the Congress of Berlin assigned the region of Bosnia and Herzegovina, although formally still part of the Ottoman Empire, to be administered by Austria-Hungary. In addition to Serbs and Croats, Bosniaks who perceive themselves as a separate and distinct ethnic group also lived there. Their sense of a different identity is rooted in their centuries-long affiliation with the Ottoman-Islamic religious, cultural, and customary milieu.

After the Congress of Berlin and the establishment of the Kingdom of Serbia and the Principality of Montenegro in the immediate neighborhood of Austria-Hungary, a new sense of unease gripped the hearts of Slovenes, Croats, Serbs, and Bosniaks in its southern provinces. They all shared a common aspiration for liberation from foreign rule and living in their own country. It was an excellent idea and a logical goal, but the question remained: how could they achieve it?

It was actually a much more complex task than it seemed at first glance. What kind of state would it be? A unitary one or not? A monarchy, perhaps? A republic? Should it be structured as a federation or confederation? Is it better to unite or to establish several small national states that would again be an easy prey for powerful neighbors in the future? Moreover, would the diverse mix of peoples even allow for the creation of several smaller states without triggering mutual disputes and even wars over territory?

How do Balkan Peoples Define Their Identity?

One Perspective That Confuses Many, Especially in the West

To be honest, for years I couldn't understand what it was that prevented many foreigners, especially Westerners, from fully understanding us. It wasn't until I traveled extensively around the world, learning about different cultures, customs, and beliefs, that I began to find a place for the Balkans in the broader picture of the world. Now I realize why this realization was out of reach for me for so long. There is a mentality among the people here that is foreign to the modern Western way of thinking about the structure of human society. That paradigm is firmly rooted in the reasoning of the Balkan peoples and represents a completely natural state of awareness for them. It pertains to defining identity and a sense of national belonging that are taken for granted here and are not proven, akin to an axiom in mathematics. In the Balkans, we grow up and shape ourselves within that paradigm, unaware that some other people on the other side of the planet think that such a mentality is a remnant of the past from which their societies, they hope, have long since moved past. I fear that they are not right and that history, unfortunately, will prove them wrong.

My "aha moment" about this important topic happened during a conversation I had with an American tourist in Belgrade about the Bosnian War of the '90s. The man, from his point of view, asked a completely logical question: "Bosnia has Bosniaks living there. That means that Serbs and Croats who fought in this war came from Serbia and Croatia, attacked Bosniaks to conquer parts of their land and join these territories with their own countries. Is that correct?"

For a moment, I was stunned, but then it became clear. I understood why many foreigners, especially Westerners, have difficulty understanding the Yugoslav wars. They try to understand this complex matter from the perspective of their own definition of national identity, which is completely opposite to ours.

The gentleman said something quite simple, which is actually untranslatable in our language. That is where the essence of this misunderstanding lies. He used the word "Serbians" instead of "Serbs" and "Croatians" instead of "Croats." In his world, that meant the same thing as "Americans." In other words, "Serbians" for him does not mean "ethnic Serbs" but "citizens of Serbia." In his understanding, the name of the nation comes from the name of the state with which the nation is identified, and ethnic groups living in that state are subgroups of one and unique nation. In America, ethnic identity at the national level does not exist, and they therefore cannot understand that we identify ourselves according to ethnic principles, not with a cumulative multiethnic supra-nation ("melting pot") that arises from the state and is linked to its name.

How could I explain to this gentleman, who has shown a sincere desire to understand us, that this assumption, which is completely natural and logical for him and from which his question arises, is actually completely wrong from the perspective of the people of the former Yugoslavia?

"No, sir. You see, there are no Bosnians in Bosnia in the same way that there are Americans in America." "What do you mean?" he asked, surprised. "In Bosnia, there are Bosnian Croats, Bosnian Serbs, and Bosniaks. Nobody would declare themselves as 'Bosnian' on a census in that country, but rather as 'Croat,' 'Serb,' or 'Bosniak.' Similarly, there is nobody in Serbia who would identify themselves solely as 'Serbian.' Here, the vast majority are Serbs, along with Hungarians, Croats, Slovaks, and others, totaling over twenty different ethnic groups. We draw our national identity exclusively from our ethnic background, not from the name of the state in which we live. Citizenship in our part of the world is not synonymous with nationality. What is written on our passports does not define our sense of identity. In contrast to America, identity is almost exclusively defined by ethnic background, regardless of which country you were born and live in."

The gentleman stared at me, trying to understand what I had just said. I looked at his surprised face, feeling excited that I had finally grasped the essence of this civilization misunderstanding.

Europeans, and people in the Balkans in particular, often derive their national identity from their ethnic affiliation. This is true not only for Slavs but also for other peoples, such as Romanians, Hungarians, Greeks, or Turks. However, they do it in a completely different way than people in the US or Australia, for example. In America, most people define themselves as Americans of English, Irish, German, Jewish, Mexican, or often mixed ancestry. A different paradigm applies to people in the Balkans. A Serb is always a Serb, whether they live in Serbia, Bosnia, or Croatia. A Croat is always a Croat: in Croatia, Herzegovina, Hungary, or Serbia. For example, there is a large Hungarian community in northern Serbia. No Hungarian there would define themselves as a "Serbian of Hungarian origin," but exclusively as a "Hungarian (from Serbia)." However, the same Hungarian, if living in America, would probably define themselves as an "American of Hungarian origin"—a phrase that hardly exists in local languages.

So, the essence of the misunderstanding lies in diametrically opposed ways of defining national identity between modern Westerners and the peoples of the former Yugoslavia. This initially prevents the former from understanding who fought with whom in Yugoslavia and why. Guided by their own mental matrix, they usually draw simplified and wrong conclusions about the wars here.

The way the Balkan peoples define national identity largely has the characteristics of a tribal mentality. For the mental makeup we are talking about, the modern word "tribalism" can be used. Generally, in the West, this phenomenon is viewed negatively as socially backward and culturally retrograde. Although this prevailing view is entirely understandable, it should be said that there are other opinions that prove how the tribal mentality is naturally inherent in *Homo sapiens* and the way it makes connections with other members of its species.

In my opinion, tribalism in the Balkans manifests itself as a very strong sense of belonging to one's own ethnic group, which is made up of not only genetic but also cultural, mythical, and religious heritage. These characteristics form an identity rooted in the paradigm of "blood and soil"—a connection to ancestors and territory. An ethnic group calls itself a nation and describes itself with synonyms such as Serbs or the Serbian people, Croats or the Croatian people, and so on. In other words, according to this paradigm, a nation is composed of ancestors—that is, blood—and territory—that is, the territories where they lived in the past or live today—as well as a common religion, history, and mythology. Therefore, all Balkan people have feelings of pride and unshakable loyalty to all elements of this identity. Changing religion, for example, is usually perceived as leaving the nation or tribe and is considered a serious offense equal to betrayal, which leads to partial or complete rejection.

As a rule, Balkan people idealize their own history while downplaying the history of their neighbors or other South Slavic brethren. A tendency toward mythomania is present in everyone. One of the most widespread negative human programs—the "us versus them" mentality—is always present in the Balkans. Generally, it smolders beneath the surface and is fueled by fears and traumas from the past. Sometimes, as we have witnessed not too long ago, it takes on its brutal form in which ethnic determinants override humanity in people. We can call this phenomenon toxic tribalism. It is characterized by dogmatism and losing touch with reality, closing oneself off from others, and sliding into chauvinism. In its extreme form, toxic tribalism usually arouses exclusivity and hatred, leading to interethnic tensions, conflicts, and ultimately, war.

The mental framework described here illustrates how the mechanism of identity formation in the Balkans differs from the Western model, which is primarily civic and political. Local people strongly resist creating a supranational identity based on the American "melting pot" model because it is unfamiliar and difficult to understand. Mixed marriages were rare before the creation of Yugoslavia, and even during its existence, this idea was only supported by ruling structures for relatively short periods. Inter-religious and inter-ethnic marriages were almost always condemned by all three major religions: Catholic and Orthodox Christianity on one side, and Islam on the other. Religious leaders actively opposed mixed marriages. Despite the difficult circumstances, mixed marriages were quite common in Yugoslavia, especially in the period after World War II. This fact strongly suggests the natural and evolutionary nature of the Yugoslav idea.

There is another important difference in the mental framework between Balkan people and Westerners, especially Americans. Moving, which happens relatively easily and frequently in America, is much rarer in the Balkans and is usually limited to the ethnic territory of their own people. Although most former Yugoslavs speak the same language, tribalism prevented the promotion of interculturality and a change in the way of looking at the differences of others.

And yet, there came a time when many Serbs, Croats, Slovenes[21], Bosniaks, Montenegrins, and Macedonians believed in the vision of a better and more prosperous future that a new Yugoslav nation would bring them. They embarked on an adventure of creating it, led by people who were carried away by a favorable historical moment, the nobility of the idea, and personal royal ambition.

By the end of this book, we will show that the idealists of Yugoslavism never prevailed. The critical mass needed for a permanent change in the tribal paradigm was never reached. The nation in formation failed to truly form. It experienced two strong surges, but the old mentality overpowered it both times. Gradually, it disappeared from the historical scene and today lives only in the hearts of a few.

Will it ever reappear and mobilize the South Slavs towards unification?

---

[21] It is important to acknowledge that, during this period, many Slovenes and Croats prioritized their desire to avoid being on the losing side in the Great War and being assimilated by larger, more powerful neighbors over their commitment to Yugoslav ideals. This complex issue will be analyzed in greater detail in subsequent chapters.

BIRTH OF AN IDEA

The Dawn of Yugoslavia

Ethnic Distribution of the Southern Slavs
Just Before the Great War

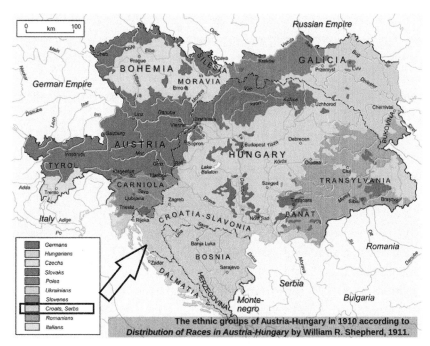

Ethnic groups in Austria-Hungary in 1911, according to American cartographer W. R. Shepherd.

Serbs and Croats are marked as the *same nation*, represented by the same color. They inhabit the regions of Bosnia, Herzegovina, Croatia-Slavonia, and Dalmatia, which are currently part of present-day Croatia and Bosnia and Herzegovina. At that time, Bosniaks were not yet recognized as a distinct nation.

To understand the historical stage and processes that preceded the creation of Yugoslavia, it is necessary to first consider the ethnic structure of the southern provinces of the Austro-Hungarian Empire at the beginning of the twentieth century, a few years before the outbreak of the First World War. For this purpose, we will use a map published by the American cartographer and historian William Robert Shepherd in his famous Historical

95

Atlas in 1911, which shows the ethnic groups in Austria-Hungary. We will focus exclusively on the southern provinces—the territory on which a large part of the future Yugoslavia will be located, and which today consists of three states that emerged after its dissolution: Slovenia, Bosnia and Herzegovina, and Croatia.

As we can see, in the province of Carniola—the old German name for part of present-day Slovenia—there were mainly Slovenes, and in much smaller numbers, Germans and Italians. To the southeast, in the provinces of Croatia-Slavonia, Dalmatia, Herzegovina, and Bosnia, Croats and Serbs lived. On the eastern border of Austria-Hungary, we see two small sovereign states, Serbia and Montenegro, where also the vast majority of people are ethnically Serbs. So far, everything is correct.

However, a careful eye will not miss the fact that someone is missing from Mr. Shepherd's map. Why are there no Bosniaks in Bosnia, the ethnic group that gained the status of a constituent people under the name Muslims for the first time in Tito's socialist Yugoslavia in 1971? Why did these people have to declare themselves either as Serbs or Croats on the censuses before that? With around two million members, Bosniaks are a large nation by South Slavic standards, who today live not only in Bosnia and Herzegovina but also in all former Yugoslav republics, and most notably in Serbia and Montenegro. They currently make up about half of the population of the Republic of Bosnia and Herzegovina, yet they are missing from Shepherd's map. Did the American cartographer make a mistake in his work? From the perspective of the time he lived in—no. He made a map of the *ethnic*, not the *religious* distribution of the population. For this reason, he could not represent Muslims as an ethnic group. But why was this religious group later given the status of a nation, which was a kind of precedent?

On the previous pages, we have discussed the thesis of the religious split between the Bogomils on the one hand, and the Orthodox and Catholics on the other side, which began the process of Bosniak ethnogenesis. I see this religious and then ethnic split as a key part of the puzzle that has not been sufficiently illuminated so far, and because of its lack, it is difficult to understand all the complexity and brutality of the Bosnian war of the 1990s as well as the current situation. And without understanding on all sides, both domestic and foreign, the future, I'm afraid, will continue to be just a repetition of the past.

It is almost unknown in the world today that the Bosniak population of former Yugoslavia consists mainly of ethnic Serbs and a small percentage of ethnic Croats who converted to Islam during Ottoman rule between the 15th and 19th centuries. These people, after conversion, accepted completely different cultural and religious standards, beliefs, and customs and consciously approached the Turks. Over time, they developed a sense of identity that is different from their ethnic roots. However, their former ethnic communities saw them as estrangers, traitors, and collaborators.

Were only the "accursed" Bogomils, those non-Orthodox Serbs subjected to pogroms by their Orthodox compatriots, converted to Islam? Did even the "regular" Christians—Orthodox and Catholic inhabitants of Bosnia sometimes do the same? Yes. But why? Let us remember, in the Ottoman Empire, Islam was the state religion and only Muslims could be first-class citizens. Christians had limited freedoms and rights and paid higher taxes. They were often subjected to corporal punishment and violence, and the rape of women was also a regular occurrence. The worst thing, which people still recall with a special emotional charge, was the infamous "blood tax"—the practice of forcibly taking boys aged eight to eighteen from their families and taking them to Turkey. Their lives took a dramatic turn from that moment on: they were converted to Islam, and then sent for harsh training and indoctrination with the aim of forgetting their origins and becoming fiercely loyal military or state officials of the empire. The fate of the most capable boys was to become Janissaries—members of elite units of the Turkish army.

The only way to ward off these dangers and ensure the safety of their families was Islamization, or "Turkification," as this phenomenon was pejoratively called. To save their property, rescue their male children, or sometimes even their own lives after unsuccessful uprisings against the authorities, some Christians opted for this difficult step. Even today, we have a situation where many modern Serb and Bosniak families share the same surnames. Of course, the Ottoman authorities supported this process with certain concessions and privileges. Turkification began in the 15th century and was mainly observed in Bosnia and Herzegovina, and to a lesser extent in all other Balkan territories under Ottoman rule. This phenomenon was present until the mid-19th century.

Taking into account everything that has been stated so far about the scenario of the ethnic origin of Bosniaks, the thesis I advocate is that the core of today's Bosniak people originated from the Bogomil Serbs. In later periods, Orthodox Serbs and, to a lesser extent, Catholic Croats joined this group, motivated by existential reasons such as improving living conditions, preserving family, life, or property during the Ottoman period.

As previously shown, Serbs and Croats are exponents or proxies in the eternal conflict of interests between East and West in the Balkans. Bosnia and Herzegovina has always been a space where these two peoples have coexisted, fighting for dominance. Therefore, their "historical" claims to the right to this territory can be viewed from the perspective of a geopolitical rift, a boundary between worlds that forms the basis for our analysis.

In essence, the power that controls Bosnia has an advantage in controlling the Western Balkans. The power that controls the Western Balkans also controls access to the warm sea and a natural passage to Eastern and Central Europe, which is geopolitically extremely significant.

Looking at it in a simplistic manner, Bosniak converts to Islam have always been perceived as an obstacle in the Orthodox-Catholic or East-West power struggle for dominance over Bosnia. They were considered an unfortunate "excess" through the eyes of the major players, and always of the "wrong" faith: initially Bogomils—"heretics", and then Muslims—"Turks" and traitors.

Serbs and Croats, who were often unaware of their role as East and West proxies, viewed Bosniaks as a persistent Bosnian problem that stubbornly refused to disappear. They seemed to be uncertain about what to do with them and how to solve this "troublesome issue". Consequently, history has documented their attempts to assimilate or eliminate Bosniaks. Unfortunately, during the Bosnian War from 1992 to 1995, such intentions resurfaced and resulted in severe crimes.

On the other hand, there have been periods in history more favorable to Bosniaks, particularly during the Ottoman period when the violence pendulum turned against the Serbs and Croats. However, in the post-war, post-Dayton Bosnia and Herzegovina after 1995, there have been active efforts by Christians to resist the majority Bosniak people's intention to impose a unitary state structure instead of a federal one. Serbs and Croats fear Bosniak majoritization and Islamization, partly due to recent memories of the civil war, historical memory, and current tendencies towards "harder" Islam and even fundamentalism. These factors indicate that centuries-old internal tensions are still present, and that the current peace in Bosnia and Herzegovina can be easily disturbed.

Considering the events of the past eight hundred years, including those in the 20th century, there are weak reasons for optimism unless a new unifying paradigm emerges that is stronger than the Yugoslav idea. At this moment, only the European perspective is offered, but it seems to be out of reach, and its attractive power has weakened over time.

Yugoslav Dream

Based on our analysis so far, it is apparent that the South Slavs are hopelessly entangled in an inextricable web of mutual conflicts that has been constantly present on a small territory for many centuries. We see that the primary forces causing friction are located outside the Balkans, while local hatreds are the result of long-term repetitive cycles of violence that have produced deep traumas. Pain narrows people's awareness and prevents progress. They live their lives in the present, in a state of tension. Taught by historical memory, they believe that a new trauma will surely come, as has always happened in the past. The people in the Balkans always hope for a brighter future and strive for it, but it only comes briefly. No one believes any longer that long-lasting peace accompanied by prosperity and well-being in the Balkans is actually possible, and this is one of the reasons for the large outflow of young people, mostly to Western countries. Like Sisyphus, who was condemned to roll a boulder up a hill only to see it roll back down and repeat the task for eternity, ex-Yugoslavs push their boulder and await the moment of disappointment. Despite this, these people are strong and creative, resourceful and resilient, with an enormous will to live and an incredible sense of humor.

In the notable book "The Clash of Civilizations and the Remaking of World Order"[22] (1997), American political scientist Samuel Huntington put forward a theory that after the Cold War, some future wars would be fought between world civilizations rather than between great powers, and that Islamic extremism would be a source of world destabilization in the immediate future. He identifies nine civilizations that define human cultur-

---

[22] Huntington, Samuel P. *The Clash of Civilizations and the Remaking of World Order.*
New York: Simon & Schuster, 1997.

al and religious identities: Western, Orthodox, Islamic, Buddhist, Hindu, African, Latin American, Chinese, and Japanese. In the proposed map of civilizations published in the book, the contact line between Western and Orthodox runs through the Balkans and the area of former Yugoslavia. It partly follows the division line of the Roman Empire into East and West, established by Emperor Theodosius in the distant year of 395 AD. While I partly agree with the esteemed professor's thinking, I disagree with the presented timeframe. After the Cold War? No. The clash of civilizations has been going on much longer here in the Balkans. It has its permanent arena here, with always new generations of gladiators.

Even today, many people say that the Yugoslav dream was a great idea. Was its greatness in the brave attempt of gladiators to turn their backs on the powerful audience and refuse to fight?

Social and Historical Circumstances That Led to the Emergence of the Yugoslav Idea

The liberation of a part of the Serbian people from Ottoman rule at the beginning of the 19th century and the creation of a small but independent Serbian state triggered strong feelings of freedom among Serbs who lived under the rule of Austria-Hungary. At the same time, the desire for liberation also emerged among Croats and Slovenes.

It was clear that the Ottoman Empire was approaching its inevitable end, and there was a fear that its Balkan possessions would be divided between Austria and Russia. Polish political emigration strongly advocated pan-Slavism and the idea of creating a common South Slavic state that would later help, in cooperation with Britain and France, to liberate Poles from the grip of Russia. Similar ideas emerged among a smaller number of Croatian intellectuals around 1830. In the years that followed, their aspirations gradually gained support among influential figures from the higher echelons of the Slovenian and Serbian peoples. Therefore, it was a pan-Slavic concept that implied that the South Slavs were essentially one people of common origin, who spoke the same or almost the same language, and that it was necessary and natural to unite them into a common state. Contrary to the fragmentation caused by religious divisions or the colonialism of powerful empires in their vicinity, these visionaries understood that the principle of "together we are stronger" was the way to break free from centuries of subordination. South Slavic pan-Slavism was called Yugoslavism.

The attention of political circles in Europe during those decades was directed towards the Principality of Serbia and the Serbs as the only South Slavic nation that managed to independently liberate itself from colonial rule and create some kind of state. There was hope that Serbia could serve as a kind of nucleus for future pan-South Slavic unity, which would weaken the aspirations of Austria and Russia regarding their expansion in the Balkans after the departure of the Ottoman Empire.

The political elite of Serbia, on the other hand, had a plan for the restoration of the Serbian Empire from the 14th century, referring to it as a 'sacred historical right.' As early as 1844, the Serbian Minister of Foreign Affairs, Ilija Garašanin, composed "The Draft of the Foreign and National Policy of Serbia, known as *Načertanije* ("The Draft"). The program was based on a document presented to Garašanin by František Zah, a Czech emissary of Polish political emigration, which proposed the idea of creating a Yugoslav state. However, initially skeptical of this idea, Garašanin systematically removed all references to South Slavs from the text, replacing them with ideas about the unification of 'all Serbian nations'. According to "The Draft," Serbia was supposed to work towards liberating the Serbs and other Slavs under Austrian and Turkish rule, and annex Bosnia and Herzegovina, Montenegro, northern Albania and Kosovo, as well as the regions of Srem, Bačka, and Banat, which make up present-day Autonomous Province of Vojvodina. It was a secret document, but it seems that all Serbian political elites adhered to it throughout the 19th century. Although Garašanin himself evolved his political stance towards Yugoslavism in later decades, many in former Yugoslavia and today view his *Načertanije* as the first political program of 'Greater-Serbianism', or the imposition of Serbian domination over other South Slavs.

At the beginning of the 20th century, the Kingdom of Serbia and the Kingdom of Montenegro were independent and free. Together with Greece and Bulgaria, with the support of Russia, they waged the First Balkan War (1912-1913) with the aim of liberating their historical territories and completely expelling the dying Ottoman Empire from the Balkans. This process has many similarities to the better-known Reconquista, during which the Spanish and Portuguese expelled the Moors from the Iberian Peninsula several centuries earlier.

During the First Balkan War, the southern Austro-Hungarian provinces were inhabited by the entire population of Slovenes and Croats, as well as a large number of Serbs. In order to study the proto-Yugoslav processes, it is necessary to shift our focus to these three ethnic groups. They had lived mixed on the mentioned territories since the Middle Ages. Multiculturalism was usually very present in larger cities and towns. This factor significantly limited their opportunities in terms of acquiring national states after eventual liberation. Even if there was a liberation from Habsburg rule, separation on an ethnic basis would be practically impossible. The map of ethnic distribution resembled circles on a leopard's skin, and determining continuous ethnic boundaries was not possible. None of these peoples could achieve their national state without coming into conflict with their first neighbors over territory. And that is precisely the scenario that their rulers desired, so they encouraged mutual conflicts and intolerance in order to preserve their interests and rule more easily. This is a great moment to recall the ancient maxim that was so often applied in geopolitically complex Balkans: "Divide and conquer". Due to a combination of these circumstances, the intellectual elite of the Southern Slavs of the 19th century focused on finding an integrative solution. And that is what the Yugoslav idea offered.

Paradigm Shift?

In the second half of the 19th century, it became apparent that many South Slavs were embracing the vision of Yugoslavism with a great deal of idealism, enthusiasm, and even a kind of romantic fervor that is characteristic of the Slavic soul. This vision evolved into a political movement and ultimately led to the creation of a new state and nation, which this book analyzes. Among the Slovenes, Croats, and Serbs in Austria-Hungary, a new awareness slowly but surely emerged: it was much better and wiser to set aside their differences and disagreements and look at eventual unification as a light at the end of the tunnel. This path would be the means by which they would emerge from the darkness of servitude to foreign rulers.

The Yugoslav movement had a simple, emancipatory, progressive, natural, and logical tendency at its core, which manifested itself in the actions of the people and gained intensity. Freedom certainly had an intoxicating scent at that time. Only by being united could the South Slavic peoples achieve permanent and stable liberation from Austria-Hungary and Turkey. The state had to be as large, populous, and strong as possible, so all South Slavic territories had to be included, both those that were already states— Serbia and Montenegro—and those that were not. According to the vision of Yugoslav intellectuals, the new home for all, the common state, would give rise to a common supra-nationality. However, to achieve that essential goal, a price had to be paid, which consisted of renouncing their ethnic-tribal definitions in favor of a higher goal. For the first time, many Serbs, Croats, Slovenes, and Bosniaks would seriously consider inter-religious and inter-ethnic mixed marriages, from which offspring would be pan-South Slavic. The first generation of Yugoslavs would be created from such marriages, heralds of the creation of a new nation. It was a logical and achievable scenario in theory.

The South Slavs are genetically and ethnically extremely close, but tribalism and religion have strongly and systematically divided them over many centuries. The result of such a situation was that, until the appearance of Yugoslavia, people very rarely entered into mixed marriages. On the contrary, everyone held onto their ethnic and religious affiliations, which in the Balkans are inextricably linked as part of identity—Serbs are exclusively Orthodox, Croats and Slovenes are exclusively Catholic, and Bosniaks are exclusively Muslim. Changing one's religion meant changing one's ethnicity. Shared life in the same territories, the same language, and genetic kinship, surprisingly, could not overcome religious barriers.

It was quite unusual for, for example, a Christian man to marry a Muslim woman, or for a Catholic Croat to marry an Orthodox Serb woman.

Similarly, there was little mixing between Slovenes and Croats, although both peoples belong to the same Roman Catholic corpus. Such mixed marriages were always viewed as a problem and a kind of betrayal of the tribe, which often led to family condemnation and rejection.

At this point, an important question arises: Did the South Slavs in the majority show a genuine desire and readiness to create a new nation by mixing, in a way closest to the American model? However, events have shown that the integrative idea of Yugoslavism failed to produce the critical mass of Yugoslavs necessary for the complete formation of a nation and the longevity of a common state.

The translation is accurate and well-written. However, there are a few minor corrections and adjustments that could be made to improve the style and flow of the text:

The described socio-historical circumstances help us to better understand the birth and spread of a noble idea that brought unity, statehood, freedom, and moments of pride to the South Slavs. Its time was marked by periods of joy and love, but also of hatred and painful traumas that alternated for almost a whole century.

The Yugoslav nation emerged in the turbulent Balkans and brought with it a different paradigm of national sentiment. Today, it lives in the collective memory of all South Slavs. Many still stubbornly hold it in their hearts, believing that it carried wisdom, peace, and hope for stable prosperity. Others, who are now in the majority, think that it was all a great mistake and a delusion. At this moment, geopolitical processes have relegated the idea of Yugoslavism to the margins. What the future will bring remains to be seen.

I was born in Yugoslavia in 1968. My generation was raised on values different from those of today. We were taught that it was neither polite nor correct to divide people by nationality or religious affiliation. Only older people, those with memories of wars and times long before our birth, tended to suspiciously shake their heads and say that "history repeats itself" and that "those others" can never be trusted. As I listened to them, I felt the suppressed emotions of their past traumas. It disturbed me and produced a feeling of tightness in my chest. I turned away from their fear. I did not want to listen to them, telling myself that they were wrong and did not understand the present time. I wanted my future to be rosy, for carefree 1970s to extend into infinity. Unfortunately, today I know exactly what they meant, but I do not agree with them. I refuse to accept an "us vs. them" mentality. My choice is to remain faithful to an important humanistic principle that was taught to me in childhood:

"In the world, there are only two categories of people. The first is composed of those who are good, and the second consists of those who have room to improve. This means that we all belong to the second category."

Hidden Motives

Was the Yugoslav Movement, the political vision of creating a common state for all South Slavs, driven solely by noble and justice-seeking ideals of brotherhood and freedom? The answer is yes. However, some authors argue that the movement was also fueled by hidden, dark motives. If so, what were they?

According to some, the Yugoslav idea was simply a cover-up for Croatian intellectuals to collaborate with Austria and exploit local Serbs in order to obtain their own national and territorially enlarged state—what could be called Greater Croatia. Others argue that the Yugoslav idea concealed the hidden intention of dynastic Serbia to exploit Croats and Slovenes and create a kind of Greater Serbia, where all Serbs scattered across the vast Western Balkans would be united in one state. A third opinion suggests that the Slovenes sought to exploit the significantly more numerous Croats and Serbs to achieve liberation from Habsburg rule, after which they would turn to the creation of their own national and sovereign state of Slovenia.

Unfortunately, research on historical sources supports the thesis that these negative tendencies did indeed exist in all three nations. The ideals of Yugoslavism, accompanied by lofty sentiments, coexisted with opposing maximalist appetites that arose in nationalist circles. However, at its core, the Yugoslav idea represented a strong desire for national liberation and sovereignty for everyone.

Even today, after all the conflicts, mistakes, and bloodshed of the 1990s, it seems that the idea of Yugoslavism was a kind of a "light at the end of the tunnel" for the small, fragmented, and blood-related South Slavs. For them, it represented a way out of a long and tragic historical drama in which they were proxies of great powers, religions, and empires, torn apart by the constant tension of the eternal geopolitical border, the crossroads between East and West, where they settled in the 6th and 7th centuries. The Yugoslav idea was a quantum leap and a paradigm shift, a genuine attempt to finally take destiny into their own hands.

However, it is entirely justified to ask a completely different question: did centuries-old conflicts of geopolitical interests of great powers in the Balkans ever allow for the creation and longevity of the Yugoslav state? Did Yugoslavia ever have a chance, or was its collapse inevitable? Did the few South Slavs ever have significant prospects of breaking free from the role of proxies? Could the gladiators really turn their backs on the mighty audience?

Although many people, like the author of these lines, consider the study of the phenomenon called Yugoslavia to be a deep, important, and very inspiring topic, there will never be a definitive answer to these questions. However, what we *can* do to achieve a deeper understanding is to offer directions in this book that, if embraced by Yugoslavs, would significantly increase their chances of preserving the unity of their state.

The emergence of the idea of Yugoslavism and the creation of Yugoslavia have certain similarities with the American Revolution: fundamentally, it was the desire of the people to liberate themselves from foreign rule and control their own destiny, become independent and decide on their future. The Yugoslav idea aimed to create a new super-nation that would be the umbrella identity for Serbs, Croats, and Slovenes, as well as Bosniaks, Montenegrins, and other peoples. Similarly to the American model, the new identity would be a blend in which separated and often conflicting peoples of different religions, who had lived for centuries under different socio-political and cultural influences, would be united. The existing diversity was meant to enrich the new identity, instead of being a source of divisions. Using the example of the American Revolution, we see that it awakened in people a sense of national pride due to a great achievement and love for the newly formed nation. Something similar was done by the Yugoslavs, and the Americans will express great sympathy for their struggle after the First World War.

Simply put, the Yugoslav idea was a scenario in which all Serbs, Croats, and Slovenes would overcome religious, cultural, and historical differences accumulated over time and unite into a new Yugoslav supra-nation based on common origins and genetic relatedness.

The northern part of Serbia was once part of the Austrian Military Frontier, which was described in more detail on previous pages. About an hour's drive from Belgrade lies the town of Sremski Karlovci, a small Serbian Baroque gem that played an exceptionally important historical role and now serves as a kind of an open-air museum. It was the administrative and religious center of the Serbs in the Habsburg Monarchy, and it was there that the famous Karlowitz Peace Treaty between Turkey and the European Christian powers was signed in 1699.

In this picturesque place, I have friends who belong to one of the oldest local families. They are engaged in honey and wine production, have a private museum of beekeeping, a wine cellar that is three hundred years old, and rightfully boast of one of their ancestors, Jovan Živanović, a distinguished professor and intellectual who brought scientific methods of beekeeping and spread them among the local Serbs. Yugoslavia is our common favorite topic, so we have had many substantive conversations about it. On one occasion, they revealed to me that they possess letters from the late 19th and early 20th century in which their ancestor corresponded with Croatian professors and intellectuals of that period. The topic of their exchange of thoughts was the Yugoslav idea. Sending me a long, significant glance in an effort to get my attention and vividly convey the content and tone of their correspondence, my friend said, "Srdjan, their correspondence about the Yugoslav idea... those were essentially love letters!" He then described to me in detail how in the correspondence, they spoke deeply and philosophically about the sublime idea of unity, brotherhood, and ethnic closeness between Serbs, Croats, and Slovenes, as well as the need for a common state and liberation from colonial rule.

I am convinced that there were many such people among the South Slavs, I know that they are numerous today and will undoubtedly continue to exist in the future. The idealistic aspect of the Yugoslav idea is perhaps its most beautiful and enduring part. It was promoted by intellectuals who approached this noble vision with pure hearts and sincere conviction. If all of us ordinary people had been honest and devoted to this vision in mind, heart, and action until the end, Yugoslavia would probably exist today. However, as it often happens, the ideals that move the masses are later turned into their opposite, due to the inferior aspects of human nature, which ultimately lead to bitter disappointments.

Across the Balkan Rubicon to the Great War

Contrary to the provisions of the Congress of Berlin in 1878, Austria-Hungary annexed Bosnia and Herzegovina in 1908, which caused a crisis in the relations of the great powers and fierce protests from the local Slavic population. People had dreamed of freedom after the departure of the Ottoman Empire, but instead they got a new colonial master. Moreover, this region is located in the physical center of the South Slavic ethnic area, so the Austro-Hungarian annexation effectively made the dream of unifying all South Slavs unattainable. Such a demonstration of power and Vienna's expansionism led to strong anti-Austrian sentiment not only in Bosnia and Herzegovina but also in other provinces of Austria-Hungary where Serbs and Croats lived. Of course, it also provoked anger in neighboring Kingdom of Serbia, which sought maneuvering space to achieve a political project of unifying all Serbs within one state.

At this moment, I would like to clarify how the Serbian political elite viewed the solution to the Serbian national question after the Balkan Wars of 1912 and 1913. Although there were many different opinions, disagreements, and discordant tones, the prevailing belief was that unification with the Slovenes and Croats into Yugoslavia would still bring the best long-term solution. It would make all Serbs, scattered throughout the Western Balkans, live in one state, but it would also bring freedom and many other benefits for the other two co-founding nations of the new state.

Another option, with a large number of supporters, was the creation of an enlarged Serbian state that would include all historical territories that belonged to Serbia before falling under Ottoman rule, as well as areas in Austria-Hungary where Serbs constituted a majority of the population. However, such a project of an ethnically rounded enlarged Serbia had serious weaknesses: it would inevitably lead to conflicts between Serbs and other South Slavic brethren over territories where they lived mixed with each other, and the majority of territories were precisely of that kind. A fratricidal war would also greatly strengthen Vienna's chances of retaining control over these areas. Thus, the choice of the Yugoslav option prevailed and turned into the agenda of the Serbian state leadership, headed by the aging King Peter I Karadjordjević and his son and heir to the throne, Alexander.

However, more than a hundred years later, we get the impression that some circles within the Serbian elite were insincere towards the proclaimed humanistic goals of the Yugoslav idea. For these people, Yugoslavia was not the goal, but simply a means to place all Serbs under one state roof. For them, Croats, Slovenes, and other South Slavic ethnic groups in the process of formation and emancipation, such as Bosniaks and Macedonians, were a necessary evil. They were mainly nationalists and chauvinists who were carried away by Serbian military successes and territorial expansions in the Balkan Wars. Like hidden wolves wrapped in the Yugoslav idea, they were ready to show their true nature when the time came

By deciding to implement the agenda of liberating the South Slavs from Austria-Hungary and uniting these territories with the Kingdom of Serbia, the king counted on the fact that in the hypothetical new Yugoslav state, supreme authority would be in his hands. In this way, a favorable and secure status for Serbs in it would be ensured, and that was the argument used to silence advocates of creating an ethnically pure Greater Serbia.

Let's turn now to the events that followed after Austria-Hungary annexed Bosnia and Herzegovina. The great revolt and resistance to this act, supported by the "virus" of Yugoslavism that was spreading, led to the emer-

HM King Petar I Karadjordjević of Serbia

gence of a secret revolutionary organization of very young people on the historical stage. Their dream was freedom. They were determined to fight for their ideals by any means possible, including violence, and were willing to give their lives for the cause. Some of them were still minors, while others were in their early twenties. Although they didn't have a unified political platform—some were anarchists, others were communists—their common goal was the struggle for liberation. They came from all three ethnic groups, including Serbs, Croats, and Bosniaks. One of them would become a Nobel laureate much later. The organization was called *Young Bosnia.*

In the spring of 1914, news spread that the Austrian heir to the throne, Franz Ferdinand, would be visiting Sarajevo, the capital of annexed Bosnia and Herzegovina, with his wife. Members of Young Bosnia, who had already attempted to assassinate several high-ranking Austrian officials, decided to seize the opportunity. They wanted to kill the heir to the throne as a revenge for the annexation of their country.

For this act, they received ideological and logistical support, as well as training and weapons from a secret radical organization, "Unification or Death", which was hidden within the military counterintelligence service of the neighboring Kingdom of Serbia. Better known as the *Black Hand*, this organization had a reputation for being very violent and causing fear among the Serbian royal family and politicians. Its core was made up of a group of officers who brutally killed Serbian King Alexander Obrenović and Queen Draga in Belgrade in 1903. Petar Karadjordjević, from a rival dynasty who spent almost half a century in exile, was brought to power afterward. King Petar feared the Black Hand for the rest of his life, and its members exerted a strong influence on political movements in Serbia through intimidation and blackmail of politicians.

Colonel Dragutin Dimitrijević Apis, founder and leader of the secret organization *Unification or Death*, better known as the *Black Hand*.

The main political objective of this secret organization, which didn't hesitate to use extreme violence and even acts of terror, was the unification of all Serbian lands that were then under Austria-Hungary, and their annexation to the Kingdom of Serbia. On the other hand, Young Bosnia had pan-Slavic aspirations for the unification of all South Slavs, which included Bosniaks, Slovenes, and Croats. Although it is certain that the Black Hand instrumentalized Young Bosnia, it is evident that there was not complete ideological and political consensus among them.

As the centuries-old confrontation between East and West is the main theme of our analysis, we must draw the reader's attention to its appearance in this interesting episode. The Obrenović dynasty, which was dethroned by the Black Hand , was favorably disposed towards Austria-Hungary. In contrast, the Karadjordjević dynasty, which took power, initially found its support in Russia. Thus, a territorially expanded Serbia under the leadership of the Karadjordjevićs would have served the expansion of Russian presence and influence in the Balkans, which is why there are opinions that the Black Hand's actions were influenced by Russia. However, even if that was true in 1914, things would soon change drastically. By 1917, amidst the chaos of World War I, Regent Alexander Karadjordjević had dramatically shifted his stance. After a staged trial that has gone down in history as the Salonika Process, he executed the leaders of the Black Hand, and in the wake of the October Revolution, pursued a firm anti-Bolshevik course, turning instead towards France.

The Government of Serbia had certain information that indicated the possibility of an assassination of the Austrian Archduke Franz Ferdinand being planned, and tried to warn Vienna by urging the cancellation of the visit or, at the very least, increased security measures. However, due to the already disturbed political relations between the two states after the Annexation Crisis, Austria unfortunately decided to ignore this warning. The Archduke arrived in Sarajevo on the biggest Serbian holiday of Vidovdan, to walk around the city and then attend military maneuvers on the border between Bosnia and Serbia and Montenegro. These maneuvers greatly worried Colonel Apis, the leader of the Black Hand, the official chief of military intelligence. There was information that Austria was planning a war with Serbia and that the maneuvers on its border could easily escalate into a ground invasion. As early as 1912, the Italian General Staff had secretly provided Serbia with the Austro-Hungarian plan of attack. To make matters more complicated, in 1914, the Serbs were celebrating Vidovdan, June 28th, very intensively. On that day in 1389, the epic Battle of Kosovo took place, which Serbs see as the fall of their medieval state. With victories in the recently concluded Balkan Wars, Serbs expelled the Ottoman Empire and finally regained Kosovo after several centuries. Because of this exceptional event and military success, national pride and euphoria ran very high.

However, in light of the strained relations with Austria-Hungary, Serbs on all sides viewed the Archduke's visit to Sarajevo and the military maneuvers on the border with the Kingdom of Serbia on Vidovdan as a potential threat, provocation, and humiliation. This was recognized by the English historian Alan Taylor when he described the visit as "a folly that could be likened to the British monarch strolling the streets of Dublin on St. Patrick's Day".

The Trigger

On June 28th, 1914, in Sarajevo, the organization Young Bosnia assassinated Archduke Franz Ferdinand and his wife Sophie. This event served as a pretext for the outbreak of World War I. The following day, The New York Times published the headline: "Heir to Austria's Throne is Slain With His Wife by a Bosnian Youth to Avenge Seizure of His Country."[23] A brief but generally accurate description of the cause of this tragic event.

Although some other members of this secret group were designated as the immediate perpetrators of the murder, fate would have it that the killer

---

[23] *The New York Times*, June 29th, 1914.

was a 19-year-old Bosnian Serb student named Gavrilo Princip. Other attempts that day failed. One of them threw a bomb at the car, but it bounced off and exploded far from the target, injuring more innocent people on the street. The procession passed by too quickly for the other conspirators to react. All conspirators carried vials of cyanide given to them by the Black Hand to poison themselves in case of capture. However, nobody knew that the cyanide had expired. Instead of death, it only caused nausea and vomiting. Gavrilo Princip and some other members of Young Bosnia were immediately arrested and soon brought to trial. During their arrest, they expressed pride in their deed.

How should we define these young men? Are they terrorists, idealists, or freedom fighters? All of these qualifications are probably true to some extent. Even today, more than a century later, opinions are divided and the topic remains very sensitive. Let us therefore allow Gavrilo Princip himself to help us reach a conclusion. The trial transcripts have been published and allow interested parties to draw their own conclusions.

At one point during the trial, the presiding judge asked him:

"What is your political opinion?"

Gavrilo's answer represents a kind of definition of himself: f

"I am a nationalist, a **Yugoslav**. My aspiration is to unite all Yugoslavs in any form of state and to liberate them from Austria."

"How did you intend to achieve this?" the judge continued.

"Through terror," was the answer.

"Judge: What does that mean?"

"It means killing in general, removing those who hinder the unification and those who do evil. The main motive that drove me to this act was revenge for all the sufferings my people endure under Austria."[24]

"A nationalist, a Yugoslav"? The year was 1914 and at that time Yugoslavia did not exist. What was this young, fanatical, passionate and idealistic man talking about?

Until today, most textbooks in the West still persist in the narrative that defines Gavrilo Princip as a Serb nationalist. However, as it is unmistakably evident from the transcripts, he considered himself a *Yugoslav* nationalist. This distinction has far-reaching consequences for drawing conclusions about the processes and events that preceded the Great War. The attempt to attribute Greater Serbian nationalism to Princip is actually an effort to defend the thesis that is widely spread today: that the project of creating Yugoslavia was merely a hidden project of Greater Serbia. However, the facts

---

[24] The citation from the trial transcript was taken from: Bogićević, Vojislav. *Sarajevo Assassination.* Sarajevo: State Archives of Bosnia and Herzegovina, 1954, 58.

we present suggest that Yugoslavia was not merely a disguised Greater Serbia. Such a view is black and white, without recognition of the many nuanced aspects of the progressive and complex Yugoslav idea.

It's worth noting that simplistic, black-and-white narratives about the Serbian people are often shaped by the competing interests of Russia and the West. From the Western perspective on political developments in the Balkans, the Serbs are viewed as potential instruments of Russia, leading to a policy that obstructs the genuine aspirations of the Serbian people for unification and strength. This stance, which is usually at odds with Serbian goals, is often defended by the belief that the Serbs may be exploited as tools in Russia's expansionist designs on the Balkans.

Although the Black Hand de facto instrumentalized a group of young people for its own goals, and although both the Black Hand and Young Bosnia at the time saw Austria as their common enemy and occupier, it seems that Gavrilo Princip and his comrades fought for the so-called Great Solution—the formation of Yugoslavia, while the primary goal of the Black Hand was the unification of all Serbian lands into one state (the so-called Small Solution), and the formation of Yugoslavia—if it ever happened—was a desirable secondary gain for them.

The young men of Young Bosnia had a higher idealistic goal than just seeking liberation from Austria. They were willing to consciously sacrifice their lives to fulfill the dreams of their South Slavic compatriots for unification and create a new Yugoslav nation. However, at that time, it was just a dream, and the future was uncertain.

Although committing to revolutionary methods of struggle was a common occurrence in a significantly different time, it is unacceptable from a modern perspective. It is worth noting that there are different opinions on the issue. Some view Austria as an occupier and the Young Bosnia as freedom fighters and messengers of South Slavic unity who had the courage to fight against a powerful empire for their beliefs.

From a temporal distance of over a century, it appears that political processes could have and should have taken a different course, especially in the relations between Austria-Hungary and Serbia. However, history teaches us that the stage for the First World War had already been largely set, and it would not have been avoided even if the assassination had not occurred. Unfortunately, that tragic event served as an ideal pretext and triggered a domino effect that would lead to the most terrible war the world had ever seen.

About Franz Ferdinand

The tragically deceased Austro-Hungarian heir, warrants attention both for his political beliefs and personal character. His contemporaries described him as a dark figure prone to recklessness and violence. He often engaged in heated debates with his uncle, Emperor Franz Joseph, marked by raised voices and angry exchanges. Ferdinand was an unrestrained and surly character, attached to Catholic clericalism and absolutism. He harbored intolerance towards Protestants and Jews and viewed the dual monarchy in the empire as a great failure, intending to restore strong central authority upon ascending to the throne.

Archduke Franz Ferdinand, heir to the Austro-Hungarian throne

Despite his negative traits, Ferdinand held progressive ideas for the restructuring of Austria-Hungary's internal organization, advocating for federalization and broader rights for all ethnic groups.

Today there is extensive knowledge that debates about a potential confrontation with Serbia were taking place at the Viennese court long before the Sarajevo assassination. Intelligence activities were directed towards Serbia as part of the preparation for war, and the Serbian government knew about it. In a letter addressed to the Minister of Foreign Affairs, Berchtold, in 1913, Franz Ferdinand explained his opposition to a war with Serbia. His solution was to grant greater rights to the Slavs, which, he believed, would suppress the desires of the Serbs to join Serbia, or of the Croats and Slovenes to form independent states. He writes: "Irredentism in our country... would stop immediately if our Slavs were given a comfortable, fair, and good life."[25] These words can be seen as an acknowledgment from the highest level that the life of the Slavs in Austria-Hungary was not good and explain the reasons for the accumulated discontent that exploded tragically in 1914.

Hunting was the greatest passion of Franz Ferdinand. Even by the standards of his time, it was more than excessive. According to diary entries he kept, it seems he managed to kill around 300,000 animals. The figure seems unbelievable, but it is apparently accurate. I was also bewildered

---

[25] Valiani, Leo. *The End of Austria-Hungary*. New York: Alfred A. Knopf, 1973, 9-10.

and taken aback during my visit to Ferdinand's Konopiště Castle in the Czech Republic, where a collection of about one hundred thousand hunting trophies is on display. Walls throughout the castle are covered with numerous skulls and antlers of deer and antelopes. Many objects, such as chandeliers, chairs, beds, ashtrays, and even garbage cans, are made from parts of the bodies of killed animals. Glass eyes of prepared birds and mammals in various poses watch visitors from everywhere. During the tour, I noticed that even the people around me were uncomfortable, with a kind of resentment towards the unnecessary deaths that surrounded us. I remember an older lady, with a horrified expression on her face, telling a younger woman beside her, "This is the work of a disturbed mind. Poor animals. God sees everything, it's no wonder he was killed by a bullet." According to American historian Gary B. Cohen, professor of history and director of the Center for Austrian Studies at the University of Minnesota, "Emperor Franz Joseph described his nephew's hobby as mass murder, while others considered it a mania"[26]

`Aside from hunting, in which he narrowly avoided death at least once, Ferdinand was a passionate traveler. He traveled the whole world and left behind a two-volume diary of two thousand pages. From the diary, it can be learned that he had sympathies for Australian Aborigines or Native Americans, but he also disliked deforestation and democratic political systems. Clearly, he was a man of great, unrestrained energy and a stubborn, strong character.

Franz Ferdinand next to a killed elephant

We will never know how he would have fared as an emperor, which, in addition to energy and a firm hand, requires wisdom, tactfulness, and political balancing.

[26] PBS NewsHour. "8 things you didn't know about Franz Ferdinand." PBS NewsHour website, last modified June 28th, 2014. *https://www.pbs.org/newshour/world/8-things-didnt-know-franz-ferdinand* (accessed March 26th, 2023).

The Pogrom of Serbs After the Assassination

During his trial, Gavrilo Princip expressed regret for killing Archduke Franz Ferdinand's wife, Archduchess Sophie. He said that his real target was General Oskar Potiorek, the Governor of Bosnia and Herzegovina, who was also in the car with the imperial couple. The general was unhurt but felt a strong sense of guilt, considering himself partially responsible for the tragedy that happened right in front of him in the province he governed. He organized retaliation immediately. With the support of the central authorities, on June 28th and 29th, 1914, a pogrom against Serbs took place in Sarajevo and other places. The mob destroyed Serbian shops, burned and looted their property, beat people, and two people were killed. Serbian banks, the cultural society "Prosvjeta", newspapers, and even churches were attacked. According to one Russian report, there were about a thousand destroyed or damaged objects.

Potiorek did not stop there. He formed the infamous Shutzkor militia (Serbian Šuckor, German Schutzkorps), whose sole role was to persecute Serbs. Mostly Muslim people, today ethnic Bosniaks, were recruited into it, thus exploiting the centuries-long spiral of violence between these two ethnic groups and opening a new chapter of mutual killing. The balance sheet of the criminal formation Shutzkor was devastating: around 5,200 Serbian families were expelled from Bosnia and Herzegovina, 460 Serbs were sentenced to death, about 5,500 Serbs were arrested, several hundred of whom died in prisons.[27] Most Serbs were killed in Herzegovina and eastern Bosnia, usually without trial and in a summary procedure, while their homes were looted. Serbs suffered a form of ethnic cleansing, and unfortunately, future time will show that in Bosnia and Herzegovina Serbs and Bosniaks will ethnically cleanse each other several times during the 20th century.

This little-known event outside the Balkans is one of many examples that support the thesis that the world's attempt to understand the Yugoslav wars only from the perspective of the 1990s—was doomed to failure. Without serious analysis of even recent history, it was not possible to arrive at the correct conclusions. The international community was wandering in terms of political direction, and precious time was wasted to stop the bloodshed.

A month after the assassination, when the First World War broke out, Potiorek was appointed commander-in-chief of all Austro-Hungarian

---

[27] Velikonja, Mitja. *Religious Separation and Political Intolerance in Bosnia-Herzegovina.* College Station, Texas: Texas A&M University Press, 2003, p. 141.

troops in the Balkans. Although he desperately wanted to "avenge" and "punish Serbia," as he said, the numerically small Serbian army surprised the whole world with its brave resistance. It withstood the attacks of Potiorek's armies, inflicting heavy defeats and enormous losses on them in battles on Cer and Kolubara in 1914.

Imposing War on the Kingdom of Serbia

The cartoon by Nelson Harding, titled "A Threatening Situation," published in the American newspaper Brooklyn Daily Eagle on December 4th, 1912, vividly depicts the domino effect that would be triggered by the outbreak of World War I. The first domino is Serbia threatened by Austria-Hungary. It is noteworthy that the cartoon was created *two years before the assassination in Sarajevo*, which is one of the arguments showing that the event was used as a pretext for starting the war, but was by no means its cause.

The Real Reasons for World War I

World War I did not start because a teenager killed an Austrian prince. The facts indicate that there were at least two main groups of reasons:

- The great powers were dissatisfied and desired a change in borders and the redistribution of interests.
- Awakened nationalisms and anti-colonial aspirations caused tensions and instabilities in the Balkans and elsewhere in Europe.

– In addition, behind the scenes, there were secret interstate agreements and alliances that, after the assassination in Sarajevo, triggered a chain reaction.

The July Crisis and Austria's Ultimatum to the Kingdom of Serbia

After the assassination of Archduke Franz Ferdinand, Austria launched an extensive investigation. Several weeks later, an exhaustive intelligence report arrived in Vienna, which, among other things, stated that the government of neighboring Kingdom of Serbia was not behind the Sarajevo assassination. Such an outcome did not suit Austria, and the report was kept away from public view. Why?

Serbia did not want war, and it was perfectly clear. Exhausted from the battles in the First and Second Balkan Wars of 1912 and 1913, the small kingdom was not prepared for another war in 1914, especially not with such a powerful and large neighbor like Austria-Hungary. Serbia wanted a period of peace in which it could consolidate the areas that it had gained after the Balkan Wars. As an illustration of Austria's correct conclusion regarding the unpreparedness of the Kingdom of Serbia for war, we will quote Serbian Prime Minister Nikola Pasic, who expressed his cabinet's official position in an address to parliament in late 1913:

> "The Royal Serbian Government is convinced that the Serbian people need a long period of peace to cultivate the acquired territories and develop them comprehensively, and is therefore imbued with the desire to live in peace and friendship with all neighbors and other states, and to remove these obstacles that would weaken the policy of peace and good neighborliness."[28]

Such a situation created a conviction among the Austrian military and political leadership that Serbia would be an easy prey. On the other hand, Austria was under great pressure from Germany to launch a "punitive war" against Serbia in order to "justify her honor" in line with the narrative that "Serbs were guilty of the assassination of the Archduke." However, as will soon be shown, there were other strategic reasons behind the intention to start the war, not so visible at first glance.

Convinced that the invasion of Serbia would be a short and localized conflict, Austria decided on a move that would ultimately prove tragically wrong. The Emperor approved the sending of an impossible ultimatum to

---

[28] Stanković, Djordje. *Sto govora Nikole Pašića—Veština govorništva državnika*, knjiga 1. Belgrade: RAD, 2007, 359.

the Kingdom of Serbia —a political document that presented demands that would undermine the sovereignty of the state, in a commanding and humiliating tone. Contemporaries described it in the following words:

Sir Herbert Asquith, Prime Minister of the United Kingdom:

"...the situation is just about as bad as it can possibly be. Austria has sent a bullying and humiliating ultimatum to Serbia, who cannot possibly comply with it, and demanded an answer within forty-eight hours—failing which she will march."[29]

Winston Churchill, then First Lord of the Admiralty:

"Europe is trembling on the verge of a general war. The Austrian ultimatum to Serbia is the most insolent document of its kind ever devised."[30]

---

[29] Fromkin, David. *Europe's Last Summer: Why the World Went to War in 1914.* Random House, New York, 2004.
[30] Churchill, Winston. *The World Crisis: 1911-1918.* London: Thornton Butterworth Ltd, 1927, Vol. 1, p. 26.

Beginning of the Great War and the Strategic Reasons for Serbia to be the First Attacked

There are tactical and strategic reasons why the powerful Austro-Hungarian Empire and its even stronger ally, Germany, decided to attack the exhausted and impoverished Kingdom of Serbia. Looking at the map of Europe in 1914, just before the start of the war, things become quite obvious. In dark brown, we see the Central Powers, those who were dissatisfied with the borders, who started the war, and ultimately lost: primarily Germany and Austria-Hungary, and then Bulgaria and the Ottoman Empire who later joined them. The map clearly illustrates the position of Serbia as a small country, situated exactly between the Central Powers, and thus squeezed in the middle.

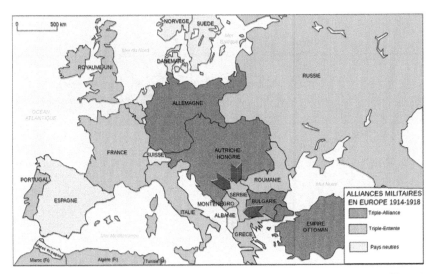

By initiating the war with an attack on Serbia, the Central Powers (Triple Alliance) aimed to gain territorial continuity, seize control of strategic crossroads like the cities of Belgrade and Niš, and secure unhindered access toward Greece, the Aegean, and Ionian seas.

It is clear that by invading the Kingdom of Serbia, the Central Powers would achieve at least four very important strategic and tactical objectives:

– All member states of that alliance would be territorially connected.

121

- Control over Belgrade—a key city at the strategic crossroads of the Balkans—would be gained. This would enable access to the valleys of Balkan rivers, which are the best and fastest travel routes between Europe and Asia Minor, all the way to the Middle East. The advance of armies through these valleys would lead to the rapid conquest of Greece, thus gaining complete control over the Mediterranean.
- The territorial aspirations of the Central Powers, primarily Bulgaria and Turkey, at the expense of Greece and Serbia, would be satisfied.
- Thus consolidated, territorially connected, and expanded, the Central Powers would be far more prepared for war with powerful members of the Entente, primarily France, Britain, and Russia.

Austrian war poster: "Serbia <u>must</u> die!"

From the perspective of the Central Powers, it was clear that any strategist would conclude that the war had to begin with Serbia. However, propaganda and information management with the aim of shaping public opinion were already integral to warfare at that time. Their purpose was to disguise the true motives for aggression and shift responsibility onto the enemy. In this case, a propaganda war with a false narrative had been waged against Serbia long before the outbreak of the war, since the Austro-

Hungarian annexation of Bosnia and Herzegovina in 1908. One should also view the German and Austro-Hungarian efforts to blame Serbia for causing the Great War in this light. These claims were repeated thousands of times and, unfortunately, have partially persisted until today in some environ ments, primarily as part of the beliefs of the general population. However, the uncritical adoption of these elements of the narrative in journalism and popular science has allowed them to find their way into historiography and official policy. This is certainly a worrying phenomenon that needs to be addressed.

Perhaps it was precisely in the propaganda campaign against Serbia before the First World War that the German doctrine of superiority over Slavic and other peoples, such as Jews and Roma, first manifested itself. Later, this doctrine became the infamous term "Untermensch," which means "inferior people" and was used to justify the state genocide in Hitler's Reich. An illustration of this thesis is the famous Austro-Hungarian propaganda poster that marked the beginning of the attack on Serbia with the title *Serbien muss sterbien!*—"Serbia must die!" The poster was a graphic representation of the narrative that Serbia had attacked Austria-Hungary with the treacherous assassination of Archduke Franz Ferdinand, thus causing the war, which was not the case—the opposite had happened. For the sake of objectivity, it should be noted that there was responsibility on the Serbian side as well. It consisted of encouraging Serbian and Yugoslav nationalism and secessionism in the southern provinces of Austria-Hungary, which Vienna understandably interpreted as interference in its internal affairs and territorial claims.

However, what is extremely controversial about this poster is its racism and chauvinism. The powerful imperial fist crushes and smashes the Serbian, who is depicted as a lower being with a chimpanzee-like face, an unintelligent and repulsive expression, a primitive peasant-terrorist with a bomb and a knife in his hands.

Later, after the Nazis came to power in Germany, a nearly identical style of insult based on national and racial grounds can be observed on posters directed against Jews, whose faces are depicted in an inappropriate manner, often with attributes of animals or insects. In the maelstrom of the First and Second World Wars, war posters were often used as a form of propaganda on all sides, so there were also examples of very ugly and caricatured depictions of opponents or ethnic groups in some other countries, both on the defeated and victorious sides, so this phenomenon is not exclusively related to Austria and Germany.

Serbia in World War I

The Point of No Return

At 11:10 a.m. on July 28th, 1914, Austria declared war on the Kingdom of Serbia by sending a telegram by regular mail and in the French language. It was only received at 12:30 p.m.

The text of the telegram reads:

"To the Royal Minister of Foreign Affairs in Niš,
The Royal Government of Serbia has not satisfactorily responded to the note dated July 23rd, 1914, delivered to it by the Austro-Hungarian envoy in Belgrade. Because of this, the Imperial and Royal Government finds itself compelled to resort to the use of force to safeguard its rights and interests. As of this moment, Austria-Hungary considers itself at war with Serbia.

The Minister of Foreign Affairs of Austria-Hungary, Count Berchtold"

The telegram in which Austria-Hungary declared war on the Kingdom of Serbia is kept in the State Archives of Serbia. This document marked the beginning of the First World War.

This act led to the activation of a series of secret alliances, and within a few weeks, all major European powers were at war. Soon after, the war spread throughout the world.

In this chapter, I would like to briefly draw attention to certain facts that are less known to the wider public today but are very important for understanding the role of the Kingdom of Serbia and its war aims in World War I. The way in which Serbia was brought into the war against its will, in combination with the Serbian character, influenced Serbian leadership to embark on an adventure to create Yugoslavia. A deeper insight into the character of the Serbian people, in which patriotism, idealism, a sense of justice, naivety, courage, and endurance are mixed on one side, with stubbornness, obstinacy, and self-sacrifice on the other, will be offered to the reader in the following part of this chapter.

On Serbia's Participation in World War I

- Serbia, along with Montenegro, fought on the victorious side of the Great War, alongside the Triple Entente states—the United Kingdom, France, and Russia—together with Belgium, Japan, Italy, the US, and other allies.
- Despite exhaustion caused by the Balkan Wars, the small Kingdom of Serbia was not an easy prey for Austria-Hungary—it repelled three invasion attempts in 1914, inflicting heavy losses on the enemy.
- Only six months after the start of the war, on December 7th, 1914, the Serbian government issued a historic declaration in the city of Niš, proclaiming the unification of the South Slavs into a joint state as Serbia's war aim, alongside the liberation of the country:

> "Convinced of the resolve of the entire Serbian people to persevere in the holy struggle for the defense of their hearths and freedom, the Government of the Kingdom considers as its foremost and in these decisive moments, the sole task to secure the successful completion of this great warfare which, at the moment of its inception, *has become, at the same time, the fight for the liberation and unification of all our unfree brothers, Serbs, Croats, and Slovenes.*"

Through this document, the Kingdom of Serbia not only declared its intention to defeat aggressors and reclaim its territory (which seemed like an impossible mission given the significantly greater numbers and better-equipped enemies), but also to *conquer Austro-Hungarian provinces in the Balkans inhabited by Serbs, Croats, and Slovenes in order to create Yugoslavia.* The government's declaration was supported by the Serbian National Assembly, clearly indicating a political consensus among all ruling structures of Serbia, including the king, the government, and the parliament, on this important matter.

- As the Central Powers were not succeeding in achieving their strategic-tactical goals in their initial attempts, they decided that the tough Balkan nut must be broken at all costs. In October 1915, the fourth offensive known as the Triple Invasion of Serbia began. It was a massive simultaneous attack by the German Empire, Austria-Hungary, and Bulgaria from three different directions. Serbia faced an enemy ten times stronger. The defense finally gave way and Belgrade was occupied.

- Despite being overwhelmed, Serbia refused to surrender. The entire remaining army, along with the king and government, as well as tens of thousands of civilians, embarked on a retreat across the snow-covered Albanian mountains toward the Adriatic Sea. During this horrific exodus, known as the Albanian Golgotha, a large number of people perished from freezing, starvation, typhus, and attacks by Albanian armed groups. The official report of the Minister of War to the President of the Serbian Government, Pasic, states that "243,877 people disappeared, died, were killed, or captured." Upon the arrival of the Serbian army on the Adriatic coast, allied ships, especially French ones, transported these defiant, proud, and exhausted people to Greek islands and other safe places, such as Bizerte in Tunisia. Around 150,000 Serbian soldiers recovered and were sent to the southern Salonika front. Two years later, they would play a key role in its breakthrough and significantly contribute to the faster end of the war.

- Contrary to the expectations of the Serbian War Command, political leadership, and allies from the Entente, Croats, Slovenes, and many Serbs from Austria-Hungary did not desert *en masse* to join the Serbian army and the victorious side. They mostly fought on the Serbian and other European fronts as Austro-Hungarian soldiers and officers, some with very notable military careers.

- Serbia suffered the highest percentage of human losses of all the countries that participated in World War I, which is a little-known fact in the world today.

What Sacrifices did the Kingdom of Serbia Make for the Liberation and Realization of the Yugoslav Dream?

According to data presented at the 1919 Paris Peace Conference, Serbia suffered 1,247,435 casualties, or 28% of the total population as per the 1914 census. Of this number, 402,435 soldiers were killed in action, died from wounds or typhus epidemic, while civilian casualties amounted to around 845,000. Looking at it from another perspective and translated into percentages, 53% of the male working population between the ages of 18 and 55 were killed, while 9% emerged from the war with permanent disabilities, resulting in a catastrophic total loss of 62% in this segment. About 500,000 children were left without one or both parents. The Serbian delegation estimated that the war damage reached about half of the total national property at that time, while approximately 70% of the industry was destroyed.

Poster calling for the collection of money for women and children in Serbia, 1918, New York. USA

Based on the presented indicators, experts agree that the First World War was the most devastating in the entire history of Serbia.

These horrific figures shed light on a very important perspective for understanding the later emotions and behaviors of Serbs in Yugoslavia. They have never shown a willingness to relinquish Yugoslavia, even when other nations desired to withdraw. This is quite understandable, considering the sacrifices made to achieve unification. A high price was paid for that state. However, this point of view is rarely taken into account when attempting to comprehend the Yugoslav crisis of the 1990s and the conduct of the Serbs within it. Instead, matters were viewed simplistically, lacking depth, and Serbs were accused of naked hegemonism. This approach has led to deep disappointment in Serbia with its former wartime allies, who were expected to appreciate the fact that Yugoslavia was established on the enormous sacrifices of the Serbian people and to take a completely different political course.

To be honest, such expectations in Serbia were entirely naive. They stemmed from a lack of comprehension of the historical moment, ignorance of the deeper geopolitical dynamics driving political processes, and a sort of unrealistic, romantic political-historical idealism that Serbs are prone to.

Several Lesser-Known Facts About Serbia and WWI

Ruth and Flora

Sergeant
Ruth Farnam

Sergeant Ruth Farnam (Ruth Stanley Farnam, 1873-1956) was the only American woman known to have served as a soldier in World War I. She joined the army of the Kingdom of Serbia as a volunteer and was decorated three times for bravery and service. In 1918, she published an autobiographical work in the United States[31] about her time spent with the Serbs during the war.

Flora Sandes (1876-1956) was the only British woman to officially serve as a soldier in World War I.

Captain Flora Sandes

She was an officer in the Serbian Royal Army and was severely wounded by a grenade in the battles near Bitola, for which Regent Alexander awarded her the Order of the Karadjordje's Star. She was decorated a total of seven times. After the war, she was demobilized from active service in the Serbian army with the rank of captain. She published two books about her war experience.[32] [33]

The Serbian Post issued
a postage stamp in honor
of Flora Sands in 2015

In her honor, the Serbian Post issued a postage stamp in 2015.

---

[31] Farnam, Ruth Stanley. *A Nation at Bay: What an American Woman Saw and Did in Suffering Serbia*. Bobbs-Merrill, 1918.
[32] Sandes, Flora. *An English Woman-Sergeant in the Serbian Army*. London: Hodder & Stoughton, 1916.
[33] Sandes, Flora. *The Autobiography of a Woman Soldier: A Brief Record of Adventure with the Serbian Army 1916–1919*. H. F. & G. Witherby, London, UK, 1927.

Serbia Day in the US

On July 28th, 1918, the United States officially celebrated *Serbia Day[34]*. The flag of Serbia was raised above the White House and other public buildings in Washington DC. This unique and memorable event was initiated by the American President Woodrow Wilson as a symbolic tribute to the Serbian people for their immense sacrifice in the Great War.

Illustration: Serbian and American flags waving together above the White House in Washington DC on July 28th, 1918.

Serbia Day was further enriched by the appeal to Americans to pray for the Serbs, issued by the US Secretary of State Robert Lansing. It was one of the most beautiful compliments Serbia has ever received in America, and is presented here in its entirety. It was published in an article titled "Call for Americans to Pray for the Serbs" in The New York Times on July 27th, 1918.

"On Sunday, 28th of this present month, will occur the fourth anniversary of the day when the gallant people of Serbia, rather than submit to the studied and ignoble exactions of a prearranged foe, were called upon by the war declaration of Austria-Hungry to defend their territory and their homes against an enemy bent on their destruction. Nobly did they respond.

So valiantly and courageously did they oppose the forces of a country ten times greater in population and resources that it was only after they had thrice driven the Austrians back and Germany and Bulgaria had come to the aid of Austria that they were compelled to retreat over the Albania. While their territory has been devastated and their homes despoiled, the spirit of the Serbian people has not been broken. Though overwhelmed by superior forces, their love of freedom remains unabated. Brutal force has left unaffected their firm determination to sacrifice everything for liberty and independence.

---

[34] *The Washington Post*, July 27th, 1918: "Washington, with the rest of the nation, will tomorrow observe "Serbia Day," the fourth anniversary of that nation's heroic refusal to submit to the arrogant demands of Austria-Hungary."

It s fitting that the people of the United Slates, dedicated to the self-evident truth that is the right of the people of all nations, small as well as great, to live their own lives and choose their own Government, and remembering that the principles for which Serbia has so nobly fought and suffered are those for which the United States is fighting, should on the occasion of this anniversary manifest in an appropriate manner their war sympathy with this oppressed people who have so heroically resisted the aims of the Germanic nations to master the world. At the same time, we should not forget the kindred people of the Great Slavic race—the Poles, the Czechs and Jugo-Slavs, who, now dominated and oppressed by alien races yearn for independence and national unity.

This can be done in a mariner no more appropriate than in our churches. I, therefore, appeal to the people of the United States of all faiths arid creeds to assemble in their several places of worship on Sunday July 28th, for the purpose of giving expression to their sympathy with this subjugated people and their oppressed and dominated kindred in other lands, and to invoke the blessings of Almighty God upon them and upon the cause to which they are pledged."

The Centennial of Serbia Day was ceremoniously celebrated in 2018 in Belgrade and Washington. In his congratulatory message on the occasion of Serbia's Statehood Day on February 15th, 2018, President Trump wrote:

"On behalf of the American people, I extend congratulations on your Statehood Day. Serbia has long been an important partner of the United States. This year marks the centennial of President Woodrow Wilson raising the Serbian flag over the White House, a good opportunity to reflect on our longstanding and fruitful bilateral relationship."

On the website of the US Embassy in Serbia, dedicated to the celebration of the centenary of Serbia Day[35], a comment can be found regarding the raising of the Serbian flag on the White House, indicating the great closeness of the Serbian and American people during the First World War: "Such a gesture marked the existence of friendly relations, as well as the sharing of the same values, key civilizational principles, and principles of freedom."

---

[35] U.S. Embassy in Serbia. "Day When the Serbian and U.S. Flags Flew Together Over the White House." Accessed March 30th, 2023. *https://rs.usembassy.gov/sr/day-when-the-serbian-and-u-s-flags-flew-together-over-the-white-house-sr/.*

THE FIRST YUGOSLAVIA

Who is Interested in Creating Yugoslavia and for What Reasons?

Political Interests of the Constituent Peoples in the Future State

In order to gain a comprehensive understanding of the factors that drove Serbs, Croats, and Slovenes to undertake the endeavor of establishing a shared state following the dissolution of the Austro-Hungarian Empire, it is necessary to illuminate certain lesser-known facts. Beside the lofty ideals of Yugoslavism, which are described in detail in the previous pages, very pragmatic political reasons also influenced the creation of a common state.

Among the Croats and Slovenes, there was a strong desire for the establishment of national states after their liberation from the Habsburgs. Therefore, as previously stated, it was neither logical nor desirable for them to form a union with Serbs and other South Slavs—Bosniaks, Montenegrins, and Macedonians. Instead, after centuries of foreign rule, the majority of Croats and Slovenes dreamed of being the "masters of their own house" by establishing independent national states. This was natural and completely understandable. Until this dream was realized, any other state arrangement with other nations would have been premature. Nevertheless, both of these peoples joined a state union with victorious Serbia, which represented the pivot of Yugoslav unification. Two reasons explain this outcome. The first is that they fought on losing side in the Great War that had just ended. Joining a common state project with the most important Balkan victor could bring them forgiveness and align them with the winners.

However, the second reason is much more concrete.

The Secret London Treaty of 1915

As the First World War was gaining momentum, an important diplomatic game was being played behind the scenes with the aim of securing Italy's entry into the war on the side of the Allied powers. The key Allied states—Britain, France, and Russia—promised Italy significant territories in northern Dalmatia, the Istrian Peninsula, most of the Adriatic islands, and approximately a quarter of today's Slovenia in return. This secret agreement was signed in London on April 26th, 1915.

The Allies also envisaged significant territorial expansions for Serbia, as communicated in an official note sent to her on August 4th. According to the plan, Serb-majority Croatian territories of central and southern Dalmatia and Slavonia were to be granted to Serbia. Additionally, the post-war Serbia was to include the whole of Bosnia and Herzegovina, Srem, and Bačka, as well as parts of northern Albania.

A map illustrating the hypothetical redrawing of borders in the Balkans based on the provisions of the London Treaty of 1915.

Montenegro was to receive a portion of southern Dalmatia, including the city of Dubrovnik, and a portion of Albania.

If the provisions of the London Agreement had been implemented, Croats would have lost the vast majority of the Adriatic coast and been reduced to less than half of the territory they inhabited, while Slovenians might have ended up with even less. Moreover, whether their national states would have been formed on such reduced territories and what their chances of survival as independent entities would be under these circumstances are questions that can only be speculated about today.

However, it is quite clear that an insight into the provisions of the London Agreement gives us a very clear picture of why Croats and Slovenes rushed into the winning camp by seeking an exit from this catastrophe through a marriage with the Kingdom of Serbia. It will prove to be the best possible decision for them, as they preserved their territories and entered a new state under excellent conditions. Seventy-four years later, they will realize their intentions to create independent sovereign states. The birth of those states will bring an end to the union and countless human tragedies.

On the other hand, from the Allies' point of view, Serbia made a surprising move. It rejected the territorial expansions offered to it by the London Treaty and persistently insisted on creating a joint Yugoslav state. An enlarged Serbia, which would finally bring under its roof the vast majority of Serbs and thereby permanently solve the Serbian national question, was within reach. Instead, the government, led by Prince Regent Alexander, opted for creating an even greater joint state with the Croatian and Slovenian brothers and other Southern Slavs.

How did this happen? A unified answer to this key question has not been provided to this day. Was it idealism, political thinking about the future, or sheer megalomania? I am optimistic that this book will facilitate a deeper comprehension of this highly significant subject and ultimately aid in discovering a conclusive response.

Today, many in Serbia consider the "Yugoslav project" to be the greatest mistake in modern Serbian history, which the nation paid for with the loss of territories, people, and reputation. Serbs feel betrayed, particularly by their Croatian and Slovenian brethren. They believe that it was the Serbs who saved Croats and Slovenes from the bitter fate intended for them by the London Agreement, a fate that those two nations further sealed by fighting to the end on the side of the defeated powers in World War I.

The decision of the Kingdom of Serbia to choose the much more difficult and uncertain path of creating Yugoslavia instead of simply accepting additional territories inhabited by Serbs was fateful. By choosing the harder path, the Serbs expected to have a sort of "credit" in the joint state, i.e. recognition and gratitude from their Slavic kin for saving them from disaster. However, as will be analyzed in detail on the following pages, events unfolded in a different direction.

In light of the facts we describe, it is possible to discern the reasons that led to the formation of the controversial narrative in the ruling circles in Serbia during the breakup of Yugoslavia in the 1990s. It was the conviction that it was perfectly acceptable to reach for a "Greater" or "London" Serbia when the joint state was disintegrating due to the departure of "ungrateful" Croats and Slovenes. Branded as unscrupulous, selfish, and insensitive, they had "trampled on Serbian generosity" that had brought them "forgiveness and salvation" after World War I.

This narrative was forcefully propagated to the public and gradually began to be accepted by the masses. Emboldened by it, some politicians at the time viewed these beliefs as entirely legitimate and even expected understanding, support, and agreement from the signatory states of the London Treaty. Support was found in the fact that in 1915, the key world powers officially promised the Kingdom of Serbia half of modern-day Croatia and the entire Bosnia and Herzegovina as a reward for participating in the war on the winning side.

Let us now redirect our attention towards the examination of the immediate interests of the three principal nations in establishing a joint state. In the most concise form, they can be presented as follows:

Kingdom of Serbia:

1. As a victorious power in the war, it wishes its heroic sacrifice to be adequately rewarded territorially;
2. It aims to gather all Serbs into one state under the rule of the Serbian dynasty of Karadjordjević;
3. It believes that territorial and demographic consolidation through the creation of a common state is the way for the Yugoslavs to emerge from a state of fragmentation, mutual conflict, and perpetual war for foreign interests.

Slovenes:

1. As a people who fought on the side of Austria-Hungary, they wanted to avoid territorial losses in favor of Italy under the London Treaty;
2. They fear that the victorious powers will deny them the possibility of forming any state, potential assimilation and fragmentation of the ethnic space, payment of war reparations, and therefore they opt for joining a common state with Serbia;
3. Part of the Slovenian intelligentsia sincerely promotes and supports the Yugoslav idea, seeing it as evolutionary, progressive and in line with national interests.

Croats:

1. As a people who fought on the side of Austria-Hungary, they wanted to avoid territorial losses in favor of Italy under the London Treaty;
2. They feared the loss of limited statehood they had within Austria-Hungary, fragmentation of ethnic space, assimilation, and payment of war reparations;

3. Part of the Croatian intelligentsia and people, especially in Dalmatia, supported the Yugoslav idea and unification with the Kingdom of Serbia, exerting pressure on politicians in Zagreb who hesitated to take concrete steps in that direction.

Creation of a Common State

To explain this complex series of parallel processes, their actors and events, we will start with perhaps the shortest possible explanation:

> The Austro-Hungarian Monarchy disappeared from the historical scene after its defeat in World War I. Representatives of the people from its southern provinces, populated by Slovenes, Croats, and Serbs, made decisions to leave the Austro-Hungarian Empire and unite with the Kingdom of Serbia and the Kingdom of Montenegro in a new joint state called the *Kingdom of Serbs, Croats, and Slovenes*. Ten years later, the name of the state would be changed to the *Kingdom of Yugoslavia*.

In this way, the newly formed state unified all Serbs, all Croats, and all Slovenes, (as well as other South Slavic peoples who would later define their national consciousness and their status in relation to the three original constituent peoples). The official state doctrine defined the emerging new nation as "one people with three names".

The name Yugoslavia is derived from a combination of two Serbo-Croatian words: "jug"[36] meaning "south" and "slavia" meaning "the land of Slavs". The name Yugoslavia literally translates to "the land of the South Slavs", i.e. the land of Serbs, Croats and Slovenes.

The creation of Yugoslavia was an interesting, intense, and complex process. It generated the first disagreements that are essential for a deeper understanding of the chronic problems that plagued the common state until its dissolution. Therefore, it needs to be presented in detail.

---

[36] In Serbo-Croatian language, letter "J" is pronounced like letter "Y" in English

Political Organization of Yugoslavs Abroad.
Signing of the Corfu Declaration

The 1915 London Treaty, which stipulated that Italy would receive a large portion of Dalmatia and Slovenia as a reward for joining the First World War on the side of the Allies, galvanized Yugoslavs against such an arrangement. Numerous Croatian politicians, who held Yugoslav-oriented views and had fled Austria-Hungary following the Sarajevo assassination, took the initiative to form a political interest body aimed at uniting all South Slavic countries into a single state. This effort aligned with the Kingdom of Serbia's declared war objective to "liberate all the unfree brethren—Serbs, Croats, and Slovenes." Consequently, the *Yugoslav Committee* was established in Paris on May 30th, 1915, shortly after news broke that Italy had allied with the Allies. Dr. Ante Trumbić, a distinguished Croatian politician from Dalmatia, was elected as the committee's president, while the exceptional Dalmatian sculptor and architect Ivan Meštrović emerged as a notable member. Meštrović is regarded as one of the 20th century's greatest artists, with the renowned Auguste Rodin deeming him "the greatest phenomenon among sculptors of his time."

The headquarters of the Yugoslav Committee was located in London, with additional offices in Paris, Geneva, Washington, and St. Petersburg. With the support of the Serbian government, the committee promoted the agenda of South Slavic unification after the war among the Allied powers and positioned itself as the political representative of the South Slavs from Austria-Hungary.

On the other hand, the Committee members assumed that the Central Powers would lose the war. Thus, this political body could serve as a bridge for Croats and Slovenes, enabling them to transition from the defeated camp to the victors' camp through unification with Serbia and Montenegro.

The relationship between the Serbian government, led by the highly skilled politician Nikola Pašić, and the Committee was strained due to differing views on the form of unification. The Serbian government insisted on the "liberation of the unfree brethren," while the Committee advocated for the "self-liberation" of Austrian-Hungarian Slovenes, Croats, and Serbs and their unification with the Kingdom of Serbia on equal terms. To this end, the Committee sought to form a Yugoslav Legion composed of young men from the diaspora, representing all three nations. This legion would join the Allies on the Thessaloniki front and participate in the final war actions. However, in an attempt to preserve its dominant position as the future liberator, the Serbian government successfully thwarted this political initiative by the Committee.

Yugoslav Committee

The positions of the two sides were largely reconciled when the Prime Minister of the Kingdom of Serbia, Nikola Pašić, and the President of the Yugoslav Committee, Dr. Ante Trumbić, signed the historic *Corfu Declaration* on July 20th, 1917. This was probably the most important document that definitively paved the way for the creation of the future state. The Declaration specified the following:

- The state will be called the Kingdom of Serbs, Croats, and Slovenes.
- It will be a constitutional, democratic, and parliamentary monarchy, led by the Serbian Karadjordjević dynasty.
- The territory of the future state will encompass the continuous territory inhabited by the "triple-named people," Serbs, Croats, and Slovenes, who are in fact one and the same nation.
- Both scripts, Cyrillic and Latin, will be equal.
- All religions will be completely equal.
- Equality of all citizens and the right to vote through secret ballot are guaranteed.

It was decided that the question of the internal organization of the new state would be finally defined by the constitution to be adopted by the constituent assembly after the war and with the king's consent. The Corfu Declaration envisages a decentralized model in which "the people will have the opportunity to develop their particular energies in self-governing units." However, there are indications that Nikola Pašić reluctantly put his signature on this text under pressure from the Allies. Subsequent political events showed that the Serbian political elite moved towards greater centralism than what was

Nikola Pašić, long-time Prime Minister of the Kingdom of Serbia and the Kingdom of Serbs, Croats, and Slovenes

agreed upon in the Declaration. As a result, some, mainly Croatian members of the Committee, later withdrew from it, expressing disappointment and protest. Pašić feared that Serbs could be outvoted in a decentralized state and that such a heterogeneous community of peoples would surely disintegrate if organized as a federation. Unfortunately, later times would prove that Pašić's reasoning on this issue was correct. It is clear that the deep conflict between the centralist and federalist concepts existed even before the state was formed. This conflict would never be resolved and would ultimately lead to the final demise of Yugoslavia in 1991.

In addition to the Yugoslav Committee, a group of younger intellectuals, mostly Croats, operated in the diaspora under the name *Yugoslav United (Nationalist) Youth*. Their political program was published in 1915. In it, we can see the complete agreement of their political vision with the doctrine of the "triple-named people" and South Slavic unification, as desired by the Serbian government and the Yugoslav Committee. Among other things, we find the following position in the program:

"Slovenes-Serbs-Croats—collectively referred to as Yugoslavs—are one nation. Therefore, they seek the liberation of all Yugoslavs and the unification of all Serbian, Croatian, and Slovenian lands with Serbia and Montenegro into a single, unique, free, and independent national state."

These young individuals were marked by their determination and enthusiasm, along with some radical viewpoints. This resulted in conflicts with the Yugoslav Committee, which aimed to exert control over them. Their

140

greatest political achievement is considered to be the organization of the Yugoslav emigrant movement in South America.

Chronology of the Domino Effect

During the First World War, and especially after its conclusion, the southern Austro-Hungarian provinces inhabited by Slovenes, Croats, and Serbs clearly expressed Pan-Slavic aspirations for unification with the neighboring kingdoms of Serbia and Montenegro in a common state. Some of these regions, such as Bačka, Banat, and Srem, directly united with the Kingdom of Serbia by the end of October 1918.

Events in the other former Austro-Hungarian southern provinces are more relevant to this part of our story. The people of Carniola, Slavonia, Croatia, Dalmatia, and Bosnia and Herzegovina formed the National Council of Slovenes, Croats, and Serbs in Zagreb, which declared itself the "political representative body of Slovenes, Croats, and Serbs." Fulfilling the people's wishes, this body proclaimed the creation of the *State of Slovenes, Croats, and Serbs* (SCS) on October 29th, 1918, in Zagreb. Although it was recognized only by the neighboring Kingdom of Serbia, this newly-formed state entity can be regarded as the first incarnation of what would become Yugoslavia in the near future.

Territory of the State of Slovenes, Croats, and Serbs (SCS) proclaimed in Zagreb on October 29th. 1918.

It is important to pause and reflect on this point. The initial *state* union of Serbs, Croats, and Slovenes was not established in Belgrade, but rather in Zagreb, the capital of present-day Croatia. The first president was a Slovene named Anton Korošec, while the two vice presidents were a Serb and a Croat. These developments highlight the dominance of pan-Slavic ideas of unification and cooperation over the many vocal proponents of separate national states. In pursuit of wider international recognition, which initially garnered little interest from the great powers, the National Council of the SCS State in Zagreb undertook several key political actions:

–   In a note dated October 31st, 1918, it informed the government of the Kingdom of Serbia, as well as key victorious countries in the war—Great Britain, France, Italy, and the United States—that the "State of Slovenes, Croats, and Serbs had been constituted in the South Slavic territories that were part of Austria-Hungary," and that the new state "expresses the intention to form a joint state with Serbia and Montenegro." The Serbian government responded positively to this note on November 8th, 1918, recognizing the National Council in Zagreb as the "legitimate government of Serbs, Croats, and Slovenes living in the territory of Austria-Hungary."

– In its next political declaration, on November 23rd and 24th, 1918, the National Council of SCS proclaimed the "unification of the State of Slovenes, Croats, and Serbs formed on the entire, continuous South Slavic territory of the former Austria-Hungary with the Kingdoms of Serbia and Montenegro into a single state of Slovenes, Croats, and Serbs." Immediately following this, a delegation was formed that traveled to Belgrade to negotiate the terms of unification with Prince Alexander Karadjordjević, the regent of the Kingdom of Serbia. These negotiations were successful.

Ultimately, the birth of the new state occurred on December 1st, 1918. On that day, Regent Alexander proclaimed the "unification of Serbia with the lands of the Independent State of Slovenes, Croats, and Serbs into a single *Kingdom of Serbs, Croats, and Slovenes.*"

The process of creating the new state highlights a crucial fact from an international law perspective: at the time of the Kingdom of SCS's formation, the Kingdom of Serbia and the considerably smaller Kingdom of Montenegro were the only internationally recognized states. Back then, Slovenia, Croatia, Bosnia and Herzegovina, and present-day North Macedonia did not exist as states. In other words, the former Austro-Hungarian provinces inhabited by South Slavic people joined Serbia and Montenegro, forming a sort of nucleus. The international community accepted and verified this state of affairs at the Paris Peace Conference of 1919–1920. The sequence of events described here explains why Serbia, along with Montenegro, saw itself as the founder of Yugoslavia and, much later, following the state's dissolution in the 1990s, as the successor to Yugoslavia.

However, the self-proclaimed unification of Serbs, Croats, and Slovenes was not immediately accepted by key players on the international scene.

Before the proclamation of the State of SCS, acting boldly and decisively to prevent the scenario of Italy seizing Dalmatia, Regent Alexander sent units of the Serbian Army to these areas, where they were warmly welcomed by the predominantly Croatian population. Dr. Josip Smodlaka, the mayor of Split, warmly welcomed the soldiers from the Kingdom of Serbia with gratitude and enthusiasm along the waterfront on November 20th,

1918. At that time, Serbs in Dalmatia were initially seen as champions of freedom and saviors from Italian threats. By the end of the 20th century, however, the perception had drastically changed. The Serbian population became unwelcome, and was even declared aggressors, eventually being forced out by Croatian forces. This shift in attitude and the reasons that led to it will be discussed in greater detail in later chapters.

"LONG LIVE FREEDOM! LONG LIVE KING ALEXANDER!
LONG LIVE YUGOSLAVIA"
Split, Dalmatia, November 20th, 1918.

Versailles Battles for International Recognition

The young kingdom faced a difficult path to achieve full international recognition. Britain and France did not support Serbia's war efforts to "liberate and unite all unfree brothers: Serbs, Croats, and Slovenes" from Austria-Hungary, considering them overly ambitious and unrealistic. Yet, Serbia proved that this war goal was achievable, albeit at great cost. Another reason for the lack of support from Britain and France was their obligations to Italy, having promised it large Yugoslav territories in the 1915 London Agreement. The third, less obvious reason, was the role British foreign policy had previously assigned to Austria-Hungary: to serve as a barrier against both Russia's penetration into the Balkans and German expansionism towards the same region. Therefore, Vienna and London maintained a close friendship, and Britain aimed to somehow preserve Austria-Hungary at the Paris Peace Conference in 1919. It seems that London's expectations for Austria-Hungary to be a successful barrier against Germany were based on incorrect assessments. Berlin's aggressive behavior before and during World War I disproved such predictions.

Finally, there is another very important reason for British animosity towards the idea of creating Yugoslavia, which requires more attention. For Britain, the fact that the Kingdom of Serbia was behind this political project was difficult to accept. Why was Serbia a problem?

Reasons for London's Skepticism; The Serbian-British Knot Issue

As demonstrated in the chapter on geopolitics, the Balkans are continuously caught in a struggle between Russia, which seeks to penetrate this strategically important peninsula, and the West, which opposes this while simultaneously striving for expansion to the east. In Britain, it was believed—and is still believed today—that Serbs are inclined towards Russia and, therefore, are potential Russian satellites in the Balkans. This was the crux of the problem. The possibility that an expanded Serbia, in the form of Yugoslavia, could become Russia's Trojan horse and enable its arrival in the Balkans and the Adriatic Sea, caused concern and skepticism in London. Truth be told, such a scenario never materialized in history. Yugoslavia played a political game that suited Western interests in the Balkans competition with Russia almost until its very end. Consistently refusing to belong to the Eastern military and political bloc, Yugoslavia acted as a barrier to Soviet expansionism and prevented the USSR from reaching the Adriatic.

Thus, as part of its long-standing global opposition to Russia, Britain, by default, expresses political reservations towards Serbia. This course can be traced back to the 19th century and continues to this day. The view that Serbs are a pro-Russian oriented nation with the potential to become a local hegemon in the Balkans has long been entrenched in London. Therefore, British efforts, particularly during and after the dissolution of Yugoslavia, were aimed at reducing Serbia's military and political strength and preventing the unification of former Yugoslav territories inhabited by Serbs into one state. Although certain connections, primarily religious, ethnic, and historical, between Russians and Serbs do indeed exist, as well as noticeable Russian influence, the British labeling of Serbs in the described manner still seems oversimplified, and even black-and-white.

Today, it is evident that this, I fear, short-sighted policy has caused the opposite effect for its creators. The constant pressure that Serbs were subjected to, with little or no positive tendencies, especially during and after the Yugoslav crisis, pushed this ancient and defiant European nation into the embrace of Russia, which presented itself as a protector. In this way, Russia has strengthened its influence in Serbia and elsewhere where Serbs live. Instead of being suppressed, Russia has gradually bolstered its presence in the Balkans over time, which Britain certainly did not want to happen. In other words, the policy of pressure and territorial fragmentation directed towards Serbs, as part of a broader anti-Russian policy, seems to have reinforced rather than weakened Russian influence within this nation.

As a man born in Belgrade, I can attest that independence and self-reliance are by far the most significant values on the Serbian list of values. Due to the severe trauma caused by centuries-long Ottoman occupation, freedom is the most sacred principle for Serbs. They have demonstrated this many times throughout their long history, in a particularly impressive manner during the First and Second World Wars, not hesitating to make great sacrifices for the sake of freedom. Knowing the character of the Serbian people, I am convinced that Serbia would never voluntarily submit to any occupation, including a Russian one. Any forced loss of political sovereignty imposed by another state would provoke a determined and immediate response from the Serbs. Studying history indicates that partnering with Serbs is a much better long-term plan.

However, whether it is possible to maintain an independent and self-reliant position as a small country at the strategic crossroads of the Balkans is an entirely different question.

So far, the West has not made the most of its potential to build strategic relationships with Serbia, opting for other allies in the Balkans instead. The foundation for building partnerships certainly includes the large Serbian diaspora in Western Europe, Canada, Australia, and, most notably, the United States. Additionally, Serbia takes pride in its liberating and anti-fascist wartime traditions and values its alliances in the world wars with key countries of today's Western world: America, Britain, and France. However, the relatively absent constructive engagement of the West, driven by its black-and-white policy towards the Serbs, has political consequences. The vacuum is filled by other interested parties, and today, Serbia is building partnerships with Russia and China. On the other hand, Serbia has placed membership in the European Union as its highest national priority and persists on that political course, which is an important fact that opens up space for a more balanced policy focused on a different future.

Within the Serbian nation, attention is modestly directed towards the possibility of the West approaching it with more understanding, respect, and acceptance than has been the case in the past, especially in recent decades. A misunderstanding between Serbia and the West exists, and the reasons behind it will be discussed later. Just as the West has room to better understand and respect Serbia, Serbian assessment of its own responsibility and the role that has influenced the creation of Western policies towards it is also incomplete and therefore cannot be objective. Serbian mistakes, delusions, and political failures are rarely discussed in the domestic public, which is not good and needs to change. The quality of great nations is their ability to honestly face their own mistakes. A cultural difference also complicates better understanding between Serbia and the West. Serbs are predominantly led by emotions in their reasoning, while Westerners are much more rational.

Disputes in Paris

Let's go back to the peace conference that brought international recognition to the Kingdom of Serbs, Croats and Slovenes. It was held in Paris in 1919-1920. At the beginning of the conference, Yugoslavs were represented as a delegation of the Kingdom of Serbia, not as the self-proclaimed Kingdom of Serbs, Croats, and Slovenes. Regent Alexander, a celebrated military commander in the Great War but also a ruler of an unrecognized new state, was not invited to the conference. However, Serbia persisted in presenting Croats and Slovenes as peoples who were not enemies of the Entente and who, together with Serbs, belonged to one and the same Yugoslav nation. And so, the delegation included Croats Ante Trumbić and Ivan Žogler, both former high-ranking officials of Austria-Hungary and great proponents of the idea of Yugoslav unification. This composition of the delegation caused a diplomatic knockout at the very beginning. Italian representative Vittorio Emanuele Orlando, pointing to where the Yugoslavs were sitting, demanded that "representatives of enemy states be removed from the hall," referring to Trumbić and Žogler

Indeed, with such a justified and understandable protest by Italy, which had made every effort not to be betrayed and to receive the territories of the Yugoslavs promised to it by the London Treaty, the Kingdom of Serbs, Croats and Slovenes had very little chance of being accepted and recognized. Yet, it happened.

The crucial help came from the United States of America, which was not a signatory to the London Treaty and therefore had no obligations to Italy. President Woodrow Wilson, whose political visions were ahead of his time, advocated for the people's right to self-determination. Despite facing great pressures, Wilson did not compromise on this issue, remaining unwaveringly consistent. His political platform, known as Wilson's Fourteen Points, brought a vision of a new world. Instead of the rule of the strongest, all states would be included in a global organization within which world policies and disputes would be resolved, and its decisions would be binding. This vision was embodied in the League of Nations, established after World War I as a precursor to today's United Nations organization.

In the tenth point of his program, Wilson guaranteed the right of all peoples in Austria-Hungary to decide their own fate. In the eleventh point, he explicitly mentioned Serbia, advocating for its freedom, independence, and access to the sea. Many authors today agree that without President Wilson, there would be no Yugoslavia. In the introduction of the 2004 *Bulletin of the Serbian Geographical Society*, authors M. Grčić and R. Gnjato expressed the following view:

> "The Kingdom of SHS (Kingdom of Serbs, Croats, and Slovenes) was created not only by the will, efforts, and sacrifices of the Serbian people, but also by the decision of the great powers, primarily influenced by one man. Neither the "struggle for liberation and unification," nor the enormous efforts, nor the bloody sacrifices of our people could have created a state of the South Slavs in the form in which it was created, even if they were ten times greater, without the will of one man—American President Wilson, winner of the Nobel Peace Prize."

Recognizing that the survival of Austria-Hungary was untenable due to both its peoples and America's opposition, the British abandoned their intention to preserve it. In this way, President Wilson, by affirming the right of peoples to self-determination, opened the door to international recognition of the Kingdom of Serbs, Croats, and Slovenes. The first recognition came from the Kingdom of Norway, followed by the United States, and then by France, Britain, and other countries. Understandably, Italy was the last victorious state to do so, only at the end of 1920.

U.S. President Woodrow Wilson provided crucial support for the international recognition of Yugoslavia at the Paris Peace Conference in 1919.

The Kingdom of Serbs, Croats, and Slovenes thus gained international recognition and an open adversary—Italy. The Vatican and the USSR immediately had motives for the new state to fail, and a decade later, they were actively joined by the recovering Austria, Hungary, and Germany. Not even ten years would pass before the Balkans would boil over again.

In a significant geopolitical shift, the newly recognized Kingdom of Serbs, Croats, and Slovenes (SHS) took on the role of a sanitary cordon against the Soviet Union, replacing Austria-Hungary. Prince Regent Alexander, who later became the king of Yugoslavia, maintained firm anti-communist stances. His animosity towards the Bolsheviks can be better understood through a personal detail. The prince cherished feelings for one of the daughters of Russian Tsar Nicholas II Romanov, most likely Olga. His father, King Peter I, sought to arrange this marriage with the Russian emperor before the outbreak of World War I. However, the war delayed these plans.

Contemporaries of Regent Alexander, who also served as the supreme commander of the Serbian army, recounted his deeply emotional moments when, at the front in July 1918, he received news of the tragic death of the Russian princess. The communists brutally executed the prince's unrequited love and the potential Yugoslav queen, along with the entire imperial family. The future king of Yugoslavia would never forget this atrocity.

Doctrine of Integral Yugoslavism

Following the creation of the Kingdom of Serbs, Croats, and Slovenes, King Alexander introduced the political-ideological doctrine of *Integral Yugoslavism*, driven by the need to nationally integrate, form, and consolidate the newly established state. According to this concept, Yugoslavs were defined as a *triune people*, distinguished only by their faith while being unhappily divided into three tribes due to historical challenges and foreign rule. Integral Yugoslavism aimed to reverse this process and reunite the tribes. Applying this principle, the state policy, from the time of unification, recognized only one nation—the Yugoslav nation—while the Serbian, Cro-atian, and Slovenian identities were reduced to subnational-tribal levels.

HM King Alexander I of Yugoslavia
"The Unifier"

Although the policy of Yugoslavism and a unified Yugoslav nation was strengthened and reaffirmed several times throughout Yugoslavia's existence through different political paradigms, it always lost the battle against the national-tribal sentiments of the Yugoslav peoples. These sentiments prevailed among the population and manifested through nationalism and separatism. Yugoslavism remained an elitist idea, primarily accepted, supported, and promoted by intellectual circles. Many inspired artistic works were created—from poetry and prose to film, painting, and sculpture—with the unity and mutual love of Yugoslavs as the main motif. However, most people on all sides criticized Yugoslavism as an idealism that did not align with their feelings and aspirations. Among ordinary people, there was always a certain fear of assimilating and blending with 'others.' Serbs, Croats, Slovenes, and other ethnicities resisted transforming into a Yugoslav supranation. Such a scenario was perceived as a loss of identity: faith, culture, tradition, and other characteristics. Clerical circles and external influences from those who did not have an interest in Yugoslavia's survival constantly reinforced these resistances, including resistance to mixed marriages.

It is worth mentioning that Yugoslavism was primarily adopted by Serbs, and this phenomenon was also notably evident in Bosnia and Herzegovina among Bosniaks. In Serbia, among all the former republics of the Socialist Federal Republic of Yugoslavia, there were the highest number of interethnic and interreligious mixed marriages. There were also many in Croatia, between Serbs and Croats. These facts lead to the possible insight that by accepting the Yugoslav paradigm, Serbs could elegantly reintegrate members of their own people who were pushed away and excluded from the core due to religion. In other words, through a unified Yugoslav nation, Catholic Serbs and Muslim Serbs would once again become one with Orthodox Serbs. This realization was never widely acknowledged, but it certainly affirmed Yugoslavism among Serbs, operating through their collective subconscious. It was an evolutionary and integrative process: reconciling and healing medieval religious traumas and schisms within one's own people through the acceptance of a unifying national paradigm. In this way, the Serbian national question would be resolved, and all Serbs, scattered across the vast territory of Central and Western Balkans, would be placed under one state roof. In such a state, they would constitute the most numerous people, which would be an added advantage and guarantee of survival. The price for such a result would be the voluntary merging of Serbdom into Yugoslavism.

The entire endeavor might have been successful if the Serbs had observed a similar willingness from other nations to embrace Yugoslavism. However, this sentiment was largely absent, leading to their disillusionment.

Croats, Slovenes, Bosniaks, Macedonians, and Montenegrins were supposed to gradually become Yugoslavs, but it didn't happen. If it had, within a hundred or a hundred and fifty years, everyone would have become solely and only Yugoslavs through mixed marriages, which would be an irreversible process. In such circumstances, a hypothetical but crucial question arises, which represents a strong argument in defense of the Yugoslavism concept: if everyone had become Yugoslavs, whom would they hate? With whom would they fight? How would they divide themselves?

Let's change the perspective to gain an even more comprehensive understanding. The reader will not miss the multiple foreign interests that were opposed to the existence of a unitary Yugoslav nation and state. If Serbs, Croats, Muslims, and others *indeed stopped fighting* and eventually became a united and mixed, thus a *single and stable nation on a large territory*, the great powers would lose their long-standing proxies in the form of small and quarrelsome South Slavic peoples. It would be much more challenging to create local hotspots. In such a scenario, successfully conducting power games with ever-active competition on the geopolitically significant Balkan stage would be difficult for them, if not impossible.

A very interesting scenario would occur if a significant geopolitical player managed to exclusively bring all Yugoslavs and their territory into their camp. We have witnessed such efforts in recent decades. The reaction of other strong players will inevitably lead to efforts to win over proxies and fragment the sensitive area.

Indeed, the task that destiny set before the protagonists of the Yugoslav idea was complex, difficult, and delicate. How were they supposed to accomplish it on such complicated ground? Perhaps that is precisely why the story about them has inspired and captivated the attention of many people worldwide, with an intensity that has not diminished over the years.

Freemasons and the First Yugoslavia

Freemasons played a significant role in the exciting events that led to the South Slavs creating their first joint state, after over thirteen hundred years of coexistence on the Balkan Peninsula.

Since the Austro-Hungarian annexation of Bosnia and Herzegovina in 1908, France had shown sympathies towards the unification of the Yugoslavs. At that time, its Freemasonry had a great influence on Yugoslav-oriented intellectuals who found inspiration for their pan-Slavic and emancipatory ideas in the ideals of the French Revolution—*Liberté, égalité, fraternité* (freedom, equality, brotherhood). Elevated emotions, idealism, and enthusiasm directed towards creating a freer, fairer, and more humane world were a strong leitmotif of that time.

Viewed from a different perspective, the Croats from Dalmatia were very concerned about Italian aspirations in that territory. Gentlemen who would later become the leaders of the Yugoslav Committee, Ante Trumbić and Frano Supilo, both Freemasons, lobbied Britain, France, and Russia to recognize the right of Yugoslavs to liberation and unification. All of these goals were in line with the aspirations of the Serbian bourgeoisie and elite, who wanted unification to solve the Serbian national question. Soon, with the blessing and support of the Serbian government, the Yugoslav Committee was formed in London, whose role was to have diplomatic and propaganda influence on the great powers and the entire world public opinion. Among the members of the Committee, a significant number were Freemasons, coming from all three constituent nations.

Through their international connections in French, British, and American Freemasonry, pro-Yugoslav Freemasons continuously lobbied the Allies during the First World War for the creation of Yugoslavia and to preclude Italian territorial aspirations. Their particular attention was directed towards the United States, where numerous immigrants from Yugoslav territories enthusiastically supported unification. Many of them sent monetary contributions, while a significant number volunteered to fight in order to help realize the centuries-old dream. The renowned scientist Nikola Tesla provided strong support to the Yugoslavs in his public appearances in America.

Serbian and Croatian Freemasons waged an extensive campaign during the war to win over French Freemasons for the Yugoslav cause, which provoked a sharp counterattack by Italian Freemasonry. This struggle was carried out at the time by Croatian Hinko Hinković and Serb Vasa Jovanović. The organized and fraternal work of Serbian and Croatian Freemasons through printed materials, conferences, and lectures yielded results behind the scenes. Jovanović's brochure "The Yugoslav Question," in which he presented counterarguments to Italian attacks, was considered at meetings of all 480 lodges of the Grand Orient of France.

In the midst of the war, in 1916, the Lodge *Unification*, led by Jovanović, sent a circular letter to all the Grand Lodges of the Allied countries. It detailed the reasons and goals for the creation of a united state of Serbs, Croats, and Slovenes. This letter significantly contributed to securing understanding and support for Yugoslav goals in key Masonic circles of the time.[37]

In the ceremonial hall of the Krsmanović Villa in the center of Belgrade, during the historic proclamation of the Kingdom of Serbs, Croats, and Slovenes on December 1st, 1918, many Freemasons were present, including some of the main actors. Among them was Ante Pavelić Sr.[38], a representative of the National Council from Zagreb and the State of Slovenes, Croats, and Serbs, which had self-proclaimed in October 1918 on former Austro-Hungarian territories. The Regent Alexander Karadjordjević signed the unification on behalf of the Kingdom of Serbia. Although there is no clear confirmation that he himself was a Freemason, the Regent was considered a great protector of Freemasonry and enjoyed a high level of respect in its circles.

Another great scientist and high-ranking Mason of Serbian origin, Mihajlo Idvorski Pupin—the president of the New York Academy of Sciences, a professor at Columbia University, an inventor, and a Pulitzer Prize winner—did a great deal to help the Serbian and Yugoslav struggles in World War I gain recognition and support in America. Between 1915 and 1920, Professor Pupin served as the honorary consul of the Kingdom of Serbia in the United States. His political influence later extended to the Paris Peace Conference, which he attended at the insistence of the Serbian government. Historiography has record-

Mihajlo Idvorski Pupin on a postage stamp of Serbia and Montenegro

ed his immense contribution to the Conference, ensuring that the future borders of the South Slavic state were settled favorably. He was a personal

[37] Nenezić, Zoran A. *Masoni u Jugoslaviji*. Belgrade: Narodna knjiga, 1984, p. 349.
[38] One should not confuse him with the leader of the infamous Independent State of Croatia during World War II, who shares the same name and surname.

friend of President Wilson, Secretary of State Lansing, and other officials of the American establishment at the time.

In this context, it is also noteworthy that among the delegates of the Kingdom of Serbs, Croats, and Slovenes at the Paris Peace Conference, there were as many as nine Freemasons besides Mihajlo Pupin. The delegation achieved almost complete success with relatively few concessions, and their most significant goal—full international recognition—was attained due to the strong lobbying by the United States and President Wilson personally.

Unfortunately, there was no unified stance on unification among the Freemasons. Before the end of World War I, there were serious disputes, mostly among the Croats, many of whom opposed the idea of a common state, and some even denied the Slavic origin of the Croatian people.

Emblem of the Grand Lodge of Serbs, Croats, and Slovenes "Yugoslavia"

Nevertheless, the unification of Yugoslav Freemasons took place in 1919 when, on July 9th, the Grand Lodge of Serbs, Croats, and Slovenes "Yugoslavia" was founded in Belgrade. It became the highest Masonic authority in the entire country. Initially, French Freemasonry had a significant influence on it, but later, before World War II, English influence would prevail. Interestingly, the Freemasons had always called the country Yugoslavia, even though it only became its official name in 1929. The Masonic motto during those years was: *A brother is dear, whatever faith he may have.*

The eternal conflict between East and West on Yugoslav territory, to which we often return, was also reflected among the Freemasons. In the 1920s and 1930s, Yugoslavia was torn between centrifugal and centripetal forces, with pro-Yugoslav unitarism opposing Croatian secessionism. Although the Freemasons were a unique glue of Yugoslav unity, even among them, there was a serious rift created by a number of Croatian Freemasons who did not believe in the common origin of Serbs and Croats nor wanted to participate in building a shared Yugoslav future. This rift was realized when the Symbolic Grand Lodge "Libertas" was founded in Zagreb in

154

1927, placing itself under the protection of the German Grand National Mother-Lodge.[39]

Unfortunately, some members of Libertas would later on become part of the Croatian ultranationalist Ustaša movement, which committed horrific crimes during World War II.

Among the Yugoslav peoples and Freemasons, there was a persistent fear influenced by the nearly archetypal conflict between East and West. This concern stemmed from the possibility that Yugoslavia—with Serbs playing the main role—would eventually turn towards the East and Russia. The same skepticism was projected by the Western sphere of influence onto Yugoslav unity. In the early 20th century, this primarily referred to Roman Catholic, German, and British circles. It could be argued that such views were unfair to the countless individuals who wholeheartedly supported the idea of unity among Serbs, Croats, and Slovenes and were willing to make sacrifices for these ideals. A prime example is Professor Mihajlo Pupin, who, despite being Serbian, identified himself as a "Yugoslav patriot and American citizen."

Milan Marjanović, one of the greatest Freemason advocates for Yugoslav unity, wrote the following words in the document *On the Goals of Yugoslav Freemasonry*:

"Our Yugoslav people and our state are a new creation, and thus Freemasonry could find a vast field of great possibilities here. It has enormous tasks and a significant responsibility towards its own people and the Freemasonry of the world.

Our people of Serbs, Croats, and Slovenes share a common root in their past, and only united can they flourish in the future. They are connected by blood and the most profound internal bonds, and they must be united due to the geographical location and distribution of their tribes. Our people are inevitably moving towards unification as a single Yugoslav nation. However, it is equally undeniable that they did not develop as one people in the past, nor do they feel like a unified nation today. Our people can only be accurately described when it is said: they are a nation in the process of unification, a nation that is emerging."[40]

In contrast, the thoughts of Frano Supilo, a Croatian politician, journalist, and Freemason who was one of the three founding and most prominent members of the Yugoslav Committee, have been documented. From his words, it is clear what troubles Croatians on a fundamental level and caus-

---

[39] Nenezić, Zoran A. *Masoni u Jugoslaviji*. Belgrade: Narodna knjiga, 1984, p. 407.
[40] Ibid., p. 407.

es the aforementioned skepticism. Mr. Supilo believed that the unification of Serbs and Croats *should happen*, but only with England's support and *if Serbia renounced the East*—that is, if it demonstrated "an evolution towards the West." In his opinion, "otherwise, the fusion of our nation [Serbs and Croats] would not be carried out."[41]

Clearly, the rift between Eastern and Western civilizations that we trace back to the division of the Roman Empire, resonates strongly in the early 20th century. Moreover, it represents one of the most significant reasons for the failure of the Yugoslav project thus far.

Under the patronage of the International Masonic Association, and hosted by the Grand Lodge "Yugoslavia", a Masonic congress was held in Belgrade from September 11th to 16th, 1926, under the slogan *In the Sign of Peace*. Representatives from 20 Grand Lodges of European countries and delegates from two overseas Grand Lodges attended the congress. The central figure in the photograph is Divisional General Petar Živković, the future President of the Council of Ministers of the Kingdom of Yugoslavia and a man who enjoyed the highest trust of King Alexander.

---

[41] Ibid., p. 395.

The Third Rift and Its Consequences

The Unequal Degree of National Development Among the Constituent Peoples of Yugoslavia at the Time of the Creation of the Common State in 1918

In the early Middle Ages, following their migration to the Balkans, Serbs, Croats, and Slovenes were differentiated tribes with an awareness of their mutual differences as well as their ethnic closeness. Over time, as described in earlier chapters, Serbs and Croats formed their own kingdoms, while the Slovenes had a short-lived principality. The Croatian kingdom fell under Hungarian domination in the 12th century, and the Serbian state ultimately vanished in the face of Ottoman conquests in the mid-15th century. The period of foreign rule lasted until modern times. The Serbs independently won their freedom in the first half of the 19th century and achieved full international recognition as the Kingdom of Serbia in 1878.

With the Turkish act of 1830, the formation of the Principality of Serbia was approved. This means that the Serbs lived freely in their own state for eighty-eight years until the creation of the Kingdom of Serbs, Croats, and Slovenes in 1918. In contrast, the Croats and Slovenes did not have such a path, and in this fact, we see a problem that would undermine the foundations of Yugoslavia from its very beginnings.

In the presented table, we can see the inequality in the national development of the constituent peoples of Yugoslavia shown in a clear and comparative manner. The small Slovenian people and slightly more numerous Croats did not independently achieve freedom from Habsburg rule, nor did they form their own national states. The long-dreamt-of freedom arrived, but self-determination and independence did not materialize. Instead of realizing an independent Croatia or an independent Slovenia, these two peoples found themselves in a state union with the Serbs in 1918. The union proclaimed the doctrine of a "triune people" and sought to merge everyone into a new Yugoslav nation. For the Croats and Slovenes, this was an unacceptable leap over the necessary phase in the process of national maturation—a path that ultimately leads to the establishment of independent, sovereign states.

	SERBS	CROATS	SLOVENES
Had an independent and sovereign state in the Middle Ages?	**YES**	**YES**	NO
Independently achieved national liberation by 1918?	**YES**	NO	NO
Independently achieved national liberation by 1918?	**YES**	NO	NO
Finished the process of nation-building and were prepared for unification into a new, "triune" supranational entity in line with the concept of integral Yugoslavism?	**PAR-TIALLY**	NO	NO

I call this imbalance the ***primary cause*** and see it as the most important of all the significant reasons why the "Yugoslav project" was burdened by the enduring conflict of interests between the main actors.

To further clarify and summarize:

– After the dissolution of Austria-Hungary, the majority of Croats and Slovenes felt an imperative need to create independent, territorially defined, and sovereign states. Essentially, this was an expression of their aspirations for freedom and taking responsibility for their own destiny. Such striving of peoples is not only understandable and justified but also leads to the conclusion that such a phase in national completion is *necessary* and therefore unavoidable.

– The *unfulfilled statehood aspirations* of the Croatian and Slovenian peoples created a fundamental fissure within the foundation of Yugoslavia. Following World War I, the great powers were not receptive to the idea of Croatian or Slovenian statehood. In 1918, Croats and Slovenes formed a union with the Serbs for misguided reasons, driven more by the war's loss and Italian territorial threats than by a genuine embrace of Yugoslavism. Neither nation was prepared for Yugoslavia, making it a premature endeavor for them. In reality, most Croats and Slovenes sought to establish their own independent, sovereign, and national states.

- The Kingdom of Serbia, leveraging its status as a victorious power in the war, persistently advocated for the creation of a Yugoslav state. A portion of the elite believed that, in time, everyone would come to understand and embrace the noble ideals of Yugoslav brotherhood, equality, and freedom. This misconception was primarily held by the Serbian prince, regent, and later Yugoslav king, Alexander, who ultimately paid for it with his life. As the old proverb says, "The road to hell is paved with good intentions." Many Croats, Slovenes, and members of other nations in Yugoslavia saw the King's promotion of these lofty ideals, at times enforced through repressive state measures, as oppressive and terrorizing, with Yugoslavism serving as a facade for Serbian hegemony. To some extent, they were right, as numerous members of the Serbian elite at the time indeed viewed Yugoslavia as an extension of Serbia.

- The Serbian comparative psychological advantage over Croats and Slovenes was that they had an independently created sovereign state, and after nearly nine decades of having that experience, they were much more prepared for a "marriage." Unifying with other, related peoples through the construction of a more complex state community was a logical next step in the development of state-building for them.

- Despite the strong commitment of a large number of intellectuals, artists, social, and, to some extent, political elites from *all peoples* to create and preserve a common state of the South Slavs, and despite the fact that Yugoslavism somewhat succeeded in penetrating broader social strata, the number of people who declared themselves as Yugoslavs in censuses never reached the critical mass necessary to form a nation.

- The inability to practically achieve the long-desired yet unfulfilled state-building aspirations of Croats and Slovenes within the framework of Yugoslavia would bring many misunderstandings, mutual grievances, and ultimately the painful breakup of the common state.

Internal Problems of the Kingdom of Yugoslavia

How the Yugoslavs Brought a Multitude of Problems Into Their Marriage

The United State of South Slavs was formed in 1918, during several tumultuous months following the end of World War I. In this process, opposing views and conflicting interests emerged, introducing the first instabilities. Like seeds of discord, these dichotomies were embedded in the roots of the state from the very beginning of its existence. To better understand why Yugoslavia was ultimately doomed to failure, let's take a look at the always fascinating Balkan historical stage and its main protagonists.

What mistakes were made? What pressures did the people face? Whose feelings were hurt, and whose expectations were betrayed?

Here are the perspectives of the main actors that form the most important elements of the overall picture at the moments of Yugoslavia's creation:

Serbian Perspective:

- The Kingdom of Serbia emerged as the winner of three consecutive wars in six years: the First Balkan War in 1912, the Second Balkan War in 1913, and World War I from 1914 to 1918. The country made significant territorial expansions in areas that were part of the former medieval Serbian state. Bearing the greatest sacrifices in World War I, Serbia enjoyed the favor and support of powerful allies—the Entente countries and the United States. As a result, the spirit of victory and confidence were exceptionally high.

- According to the secret London Agreement of 1915, the Allies promised Serbia a part of the territories with a predominantly Serbian population that are now part of modern Croatia, as well as the entire present-day Bosnia and Herzegovina. Thus, the key world powers offered Serbia almost the entire Serbian ethnic space in the form of territorial expansion.

- Serbs from the territories under the defeated Austro-Hungarian rule massively desired unity with the victorious homeland—the Kingdom of Serbia.

Croatian-Slovenian Perspective:

-   It is a fact that Croatian intellectuals were the first to give birth to, accept, and nurture the Yugoslav idea since the 17th century, but it experienced a particular upswing only in the late 19th and early 20th centuries. Although there were views advocating a completely unitary structure of the future Yugoslav state, the majority of the Croatian elite and politicians supported a federal arrangement and the necessary preservation of Croatian statehood within the new state.
-   In their efforts to find a solution to their national question, the Slovenes, as the smallest of the three South Slavic nations, mostly followed the more numerous Croats.
-   During the prolonged Habsburg rule, Croats and Slovenes had closer cultural connections and Roman Catholic religious affiliations with one another than with the Orthodox Serbs. Serbs displayed more pronounced elements of Oriental culture due to their extended exposure to Ottoman influence. Furthermore, Croats and Slovenes considered themselves to be more culturally advanced than the Serbs, a sentiment that had a realistic basis.
-   Both Croats and Slovenes, as citizens of Austria-Hungary, were mobilized and fought on its side during World War I. As a consequence, the victorious powers saw them as enemy nations and rejected the possibility of creating their independent national states after the end of the war.

Montenegrin Perspective:

After gaining internationally recognized status in the 19th century, the two Serbian states, Serbia and Montenegro, held formal talks on unification. Naturally, resistance to such a solution came from the Montenegrin royal family and its close circles. However, among the people of Montenegro, there was a strong desire for unification with Serbia. This desire was based on the prevailing feeling at the time that Montenegrins were an inseparable part of the Serbian ethnic corpus. The formal unification was realized through the decisions of the "Great National Assembly of the Serb People in Montenegro," or more briefly, the Podgorica Assembly, which took place in November 1918. This historically significant assembly was held amidst numerous controversies. To this day, there are viewpoints that challenge its legitimacy. According to them, there was military, political, and intelligence pressure from the Kingdom of Serbia that determined the decision-making process and the ultimate outcome—the unconditional unification of the Kingdom of Montenegro with the Kingdom of Serbia. The following are the two most important decisions:

- "To depose King Nikola I Petrović Njegoš and his dynasty from the Montenegrin throne".
- "To unite Montenegro with brotherly Serbia in a single state under the leadership of the Karadjordjević dynasty, and thus united, to enter the common homeland of our triune people: Serbs, Croats, and Slovenes".

***

From the details mentioned, it's undeniable that there's an underlying theme in the strategic actions of the Serbian state leadership: the joint South Slavic state was enabled by the Kingdom of Serbia's liberation efforts in World War I. This effort was driven by a key interest in *finding a lasting solution to the Serbian national question—through liberation, and then the unification of all Serbs, both from Serbia and Austria-Hungary, into one state led by the Serbian royal family Karadjordjević.* Those who truly advocated for the "grand solution" of Yugoslavism, most notably Regent Alexander, used this argument to obtain the hesitant backing of nationalists for their vision. Despite the fact that Yugoslavia would encompass all Serbs, they still preferred the "small solution" of Serbia's expansion based on *ethnic* principles, believing it to be a more advantageous long-term scenario.

On the other hand, the feelings of Croats and Slovenes were divided, and their maneuvering space was very limited. Some embraced the ideas of Yugoslavism, while others, leaning more towards nationalism, longed for the creation of national states. However, this was a scenario that the victorious powers didn't want to allow. To make matters worse, Italy intended to militarily seize the territories promised to them by the London Agreement. In these circumstances, it's evident that Croats and Slovenes had no other option but to seek protection from Serbian forces against the impending Italian annexation of their regions and to enter into a state union with the Kingdom of Serbia.

The second option was much less favorable for them. If the London Agreement had been realized, Serbia would have gained a large territorial expansion at the expense of Austro-Hungarian provinces where Serbs, Croats, and Bosniaks lived together, now encompassing the entirety of Bosnia and Herzegovina and parts of Croatia, while Italy would have gained Istria, parts of Dalmatia, and a significant portion of Slovenia. In this scenario, the territories of Slovenes and Croats would have been halved, and these peoples would have been fragmented and exposed to assimilation pressure from their neighbors.

Instead of pursuing its own territorial expansion, Serbia prioritized the higher objective of liberating and uniting all South Slavs. In doing so, Serbia politically and militarily opposed Italy, thereby protecting Croats and Slovenes from the catastrophic consequences of their civic loyalty to Austria-Hungary. Considering this, it's understandable that Serbs expected recognition and gratitude from their newly liberated South Slavic brethren in the new country.

Negative Emotions That South Slavs Brought Into Their New State Union

Every state "marriage" is created out of interest. Of course, emotions play an important part in the life of a shared country. So far, we have paid a lot of attention to those on the positive spectrum: pan-Slavism, the desire for unity and the creation of a new, strong nation, awareness of ethnic proximity, and a vision of a more prosperous and secure future. Consistently adhering to the methodology of examining different, often opposing perspectives, we will now examine several crucial negative emotions that existed at the beginning of Yugoslavia's life. We will see how destructive their influence was on the formation of the new nation in the first years of its existence.

Serbian Negative Emotions

Serbs were hurt and angry that their Slovenian and Croatian brothers, as well as many Muslims, as Austro-Hungarian soldiers, killed tens of thousands of Serbian soldiers and civilians during the war. Not only did they have to forgive them after the unification, but they also had to live with them in a common state. This was difficult. They did not trust them, did not love them, and were not willing to respect them as equals. From the point of view of many traumatized but victorious Serbian warriors, Croats, Slovenes, and Bosniaks deserved to be punished. The knowledge that, in addition to killing soldiers on the front, they also committed war crimes against the civilian population deeply hurt the Serbs. Consequently, there was mistrust and suppressed fear that, as a kind of security mechanism, manifested itself in a tendency to dominate in Yugoslavia.

Croatian Negative Emotions

Croats have dreamed for centuries of re-establishing their independent state. At the beginning of the 20th century, due to poor political judgment regarding Austria-Hungary, the attitude of the great powers after World War I, and the danger of losing large territories, the creation of an independent Croatia remained elusive. Instead of a millennia-long unrealized dream, Instead of achieving their millennial dream, the Croats found themselves in a state where they were forced to accept the assimilation of their own into the Yugoslav nation. This was a challenging process, especially in a state where Serbs had political and numerical dominance.

Croatian competitiveness towards Serbs, as well as animosity towards them, have existed for a long time and began in the Middle Ages on religious grounds due to the Catholic-Orthodox schism and resulting disputes. The creation of the Military Frontier in the 16th century, and the settlement of a large number of Serbs in the Habsburg lands inhabited by Croats, deepened this animosity. Croats saw Serbs as invaders and a more primitive people, culturally inferior and prone to militarism and autocracy. And then, in 1918, they were forced into a joint state with them as a defeated party. The fact that it was precisely those culturally inferior, militant Serbs who brought them the long-desired liberation from the Habsburgs made many Croats feel degraded and frustrated. These negative emotions were projected onto Yugoslavia, which in many heads began to be considered only a hidden project of Greater Serbia. Croatian resistance to the Habsburgs, caused by the dream of an independent Croatia, turned towards Belgrade and the Karadjordjević dynasty. Serbs were labeled as occupiers of Croatian lands, hegemonists, and treated as "default culprits".

Many Serbs were deeply offended by such a Croatian stance. Their perspective was completely different: they rejected the Allied offer to establish a territorially expanded Serbia; instead, they liberated all the South Slavs and created the common state of Yugoslavia. On the way to achieving their goal, they lost almost a third of the total population. They bled for everyone, and now they experience their brothers of the same language despising them, calling them occupiers and blaming them for hegemony.

Unresolved National Issues and Poor Interethnic Relations

The desire of Slovenes, Croats, and Serbs—"one nation with three names"—to create a common state and a new nation also dragged other ethnic groups from the same region into the vortex. Some still had unresolved national issues, while others were not interested in pan-Slavic ideas for simple ethnic reasons—because they were not Slavs. Albanians and Hungarians were the two largest non-Slavic national minorities in Yugoslavia. In addition, the relationship between Serbs and some of them was burdened by a history of conflict. Despite these objective problems, the state was created and political elites were left to address these significant issues as they emerged.

The Macedonian Question

In this text, we will refer to Macedonians as the South Slavic ethnic group originating from the region of Northern (or Vardar) Macedonia, which was part of Yugoslavia as one of its federal units called the Socialist Republic of Macedonia. After leaving Yugoslavia in 1991, a dispute with Greece arose over the name of the state, and until the resolution of this dispute in 2018, it was called the Former Yugoslav Republic of Macedonia. Today, this country is known as the Republic of North Macedonia. Its territory is located within a much larger area known since ancient times as Macedonia, which includes historical borders in Greece, Bulgaria, as well as smaller parts of Serbia, Albania, and Kosovo. In addition to Vardar Macedonia, we now distinguish two more regions with the name Macedonia. One is called Pirin Macedonia, in southwestern Bulgaria, and the other is Aegean Macedonia in northern Greece. The peoples in Pirin and Aegean Macedonia consider themselves Bulgarians and Greeks, respectively, rather than Macedonians, and are therefore not relevant to this analysis.

To distinguish themselves from Greeks, Bulgarians, or Serbs, north Macedonians were sometimes called Macedonian Slavs or Slavic Macedonians. Their language, called Macedonian, belongs to the South Slavic language family and is closely related to Bulgarian and Serbian.

There are varying opinions about the ethnic origins of present-day Macedonians. Scholars generally agree that they are of Slavic origin and arrived in the Balkans during the great migrations of Slavs in the 6th and 7th centuries. The official Macedonian stance is that modern Macedonians are a product of the mixing of Slavic tribes that settled in Macedonia in the 6th and 7th centuries with the existing local population (Thracians, Illyrians, ancient Greeks, ancient Macedonians, etc.). Their cultural character and heritage are Slavic, and their religion is Orthodox Christianity. Strong Byzantine and Ottoman influences are still very evident today.

After the arrival of the Slavs in the Middle Ages, this area was mostly under Byzantine, Bulgarian, and Serbian rule. Historiography has not reached a definitive conclusion about the existence of a Macedonian state during this period. According to some opinions, it was briefly established in the 10th century under the name of the Empire of Samuil and lasted until 1018, when it was destroyed by Byzantium.

Due to these historical circumstances, Macedonians suffered intense assimilation pressures from Greeks, Bulgarians, and Serbs over the centuries. Greek pressure was exerted through the church and Byzantine authorities, and Bulgarian thanks to the fact that their rule over Macedonians was the longest.

Serbia, like Bulgaria, ruled over the region of Northern Macedonia in the Middle Ages, as well as in modern times. Although today's Serbian state officially does not dispute the Macedonian nation, in the past, there was a different opinion prevailing in Serbian circles. The widely held belief was that Macedonians were actually Serbs who had been ruled by Bulgarians for too long, leading to their Bulgarianization due to assimilation pressure. This belief is based on several facts:

- According to Byzantine sources, the Serbian tribe settled the territory of present-day North Macedonia during the migration to the Balkans in the 6th and 7th centuries.
- North Macedonia was a part of the Serbian state in the 14th century, before the Ottoman conquest of the Balkans. Moreover, the capital of the Serbian Empire was established in Skopje, the present-day capital of this republic, in 1346.

If Macedonians are Slavs, then they cannot be Bulgarians, because the latter are not of Slavic ethnic origin. According to the *Encyclopedia Britannica*, modern Bulgarians are the result of the mixing of the early Bulgars, a nomadic tribe, with the Thracians and Slavs. These early Bulgars, also known as Proto-Bulgars, came to the Balkans in the 7th century under the leadership of Khan Asparukh. Over the centuries that followed, they gradually adopted the Slavic language, culture, customs, and religion.

In the fall of 1912, the First Balkan War began. The Kingdoms of Serbia, Montenegro, Greece, and Bulgaria formed the Balkan League and declared war on the Ottoman Empire with the goal of liberating their territories. It was a successful military effort that almost completely drove the Ottoman Empire out of Europe in just a few months.

Bulgaria was dissatisfied with the division of the spoils of war in Macedonia and attacked Serbia and Greece in the summer of 1913. This conflict is known as the Second Balkan War. Romania intervened on the side of Serbia and Greece, and even the Ottomans tried to take advantage of the situation. Bulgaria did not fare well in this war. Hostilities were ended by the treaties of Bucharest and Istanbul, under which Bulgaria lost significant territories. For our consideration, the most important fact is that the region of present-day North Macedonia then belonged to the Kingdom of Serbia, and dissatisfied Bulgaria became its covert enemy.

In the years that followed, there were visible efforts by the Serbian administration to weaken Bulgarian influence in Macedonia and subject the population to Serbianization. According to Serbian historians and geographers of that time, Macedonia was located in the region known as *Old Serbia*, which was the core of the medieval Serbian state prior to the arrival of the Ottoman Empire. The Macedonian people were considered southern Serbs; the Macedonian language was considered a dialect of the Serbian language, and the use of Bulgarian was forbidden.

Such a policy led to the exact opposite result of what Serbia wanted. Resistance to assimilation and pressure awakened and shaped Macedonian national consciousness and strengthened Macedonian separatism. Also, it opened up space for Bulgarian influences. The secret organization founded in the 19th century—the Internal Macedonian Revolutionary Organization (VMRO), whose initial goal was to liberate Macedonia from the Turks, turned into an instrument of pro-Bulgarian policy, and its operations took on a violent form. Several decades later, members of this organization, under the leadership of Croatian ultranationalists, will deal a tremendous blow to the Kingdom of Yugoslavia by assassinating King Alexander.

The Albanian Question in Yugoslavia

We have now come to the most complex, longest-lasting, and probably the worst of all problems that was imported into the newly created state of Serbs, Croats, and Slovenes. This concerns the unresolved Albanian national question. Like other Balkan peoples, Albanians also live mixed with other ethnic groups, over a relatively large territory. Since the mid-19th century, they have aspired to create their own national state that would encompass the entire Albanian ethnic space.

There are various opinions on the origins and migration of Albanians to the Balkans. One frequently encountered theory in encyclopedic literature claims that they already lived in the areas of the southern Balkans before the arrival of the Slavs. However, there are also historical data that suggest a possible ancestral homeland of today's Albanians in Azerbaijan, in an area called Caucasian Albania, and their arrival to the Balkans only in the first half of the 13th century. Their national state of Albania was created only in 1912, after being liberated from the Ottoman Empire during the Balkan Wars. However, it was not created large enough by the great powers to incorporate all ethnic Albanians into it. Apart from Albania, Albanians also live in Serbia, North Macedonia, Greece, and Montenegro.

And now we come to the problem at hand. A significant number of Albanians who had settled in the South Slavic territories found themselves within the newly formed Yugoslavia, deprived of the dream of a greater Albania where all Albanians would live together. To make matters worse, the position of Albanians in Yugoslavia was limited from the very beginning, as they were not ethnic Slavs and could only be recognized as a national minority at best.

But the demographic rights of the Albanian people in certain territories have clashed with the historical and demographic rights claimed by neighboring peoples on the same territories. This fact—a diametrically different view on the principle determining to whom a territory belongs—is at the root of the problem that exists today between the Albanian people on one side, and the peoples of Macedonia, Greece, Montenegro, and above all, the Serbian people on the other side. Why do I emphasize the Serbs? For the simple reason that the largest concentration of Albanian people outside of Albania is in Kosovo and Metohija—a region that Serbs consider their holy land, an inalienable part of their territory, and the cradle of their national identity.

I still vividly remember the political and historical conversations that grown men, with serious and worried expressions on their faces, often had during family gatherings. Although I was a child, I loved to listen to them carefully. My grandfathers were too young to participate in the Balkan Wars, but later they served as soldiers in the First and Second World Wars. Full of life wisdom, direct witnesses of many events and upheavals, they were contemporaries of key events both in the Balkans and worldwide at that time. I knew that their reasoning was based on vast personal experience and I am exceptionally grateful to them for having the privilege to absorb knowledge from their stories, anecdotes, insights, or advice.

I remember that in most of the adult conversations about Yugoslavia that I eavesdropped on as an interested boy in the 1970s, two topics prevailed: Serbian-Croatian and Serbian-Albanian relations. Most researchers and authorities who deal with this topic today will agree that we have just named the two most important political and historical knots in the Balkans. Very often, when it was mentioned about solving the problem in Kosovo and improving relations with Albanians, people would shake their heads hopelessly as if they were asked a million-dollar question. Almost half a century later, the questions are the same, people still shake their heads, and there is no real answer. If politicians capable of untying the knot between Albanians and Serbs around Kosovo appeared today, it is very likely that they would be awarded the Nobel Peace Prize.

Serbs and Albanians: From Friends to Sworn Enemies

Since the origin of Albanians has not been conclusively determined, there are several theories on this topic that have long been debated among scientists. If we start from the perspective that Albanians were indigenous inhabitants at the time of the migration of Slavs to the Balkans in the 7th century, it follows that the first contact between Albanians and Serbs occurred about fourteen hundred years ago. It is logical and quite possible that tensions arose between them over the territory at that time. However, I have not found historical sources that confirm such an assumption.

Later history records alliances and friendships between the two peoples who shared the Christian faith and were under the influence of powerful Byzantium. Unlike the Serbs, Albanians did not establish a lasting sovereign kingdom in the Middle Ages. They were mostly under the rule of Byzantium, Bulgaria, and, to the greatest extent, Serbia. Many Albanian nobles married Serbian princesses. There are several common heroes whose courage is inscribed in the epic poetry of both nations. The most significant of them is certainly Skanderbeg, the "Lord of Albania" and the leader of the Albanian uprising against the Ottoman authorities. He came from a Christian Kastriot family. His mother, Vojislava, was of Slavic, most likely Serbian origin, and of the Orthodox faith. Moreover, according to several authors, she came from the famous Serbian ruling house of Branković.

It was Skanderbeg's flag with the black Byzantine double-headed eagle on a red background that served as the basis for the current flag of Albania. In the late Middle Ages, Serbia also adopted the double-headed eagle as its symbol. However, the Serbian eagle is white, as opposed to the black Albanian one. This fact will surely attract the attention of symbolism enthusiasts. The Serbian Empire of Dušan the Mighty, proclaimed in 1346, contained all Albanian lands, and the ruler carried the title "Stefan, by the grace of God, faithful emperor and autocrat of the Serbs, Greeks, Bulgarians, and Albanians."[42] [43]

In the decisive battle against the advancing Turkish conquerors, which took place on the Kosovo field ('Blackbird's Field') on June 28th, 1389, the Serbs had the help of the Albanians. Several Albanian noblemen sent troops to fight on the Serbian side.

---

[42] Miklošič, Franc. *Monumenta Serbica Spectantia Historiam Serbiae, Bosnae, Ragusii.* Wien: Aus der kaiserlich-königlichen Hof- und Staatsdruckerei, 1858, p. 132.
[43] *Arbanassi* is an older name for the present-day Albanians that appears in South Slavic languages. The word "Albanian" came into wider use only after the establishment of Albania as a state in 1912.

In the late Middle Ages, Albanians were mostly Christians, partly Roman Catholics and partly Orthodox. As shown in earlier chapters, ever since the tectonic division of the Roman Empire into the East and West, a struggle for dominance and influence has been waged on the Balkans between Rome and Constantinople. This conflict certainly affected the internal divisions among Albanians, which their rulers, including the Serbs, always sought to exploit for their own interests. For example, there are well-founded assumptions that some of the anti-Latin provisions of the famous Dušan's Code ('Zakonik') were actually aimed at suppressing Catholicism among Albanians.

The separation of the two peoples begins with the Ottoman conquest of the Balkans in the 14th and 15th centuries. The Serbian Empire disappeared, as did some other smaller states. Islam strongly advanced, replacing Christianity. As explained earlier, in the Ottoman Empire only Muslims could be full-fledged citizens. This development motivated a significant number of Albanians to convert to Islam and align themselves with the Turks. In this way, they gained a more favorable status compared to Christians. Serbs, on the other hand, stubbornly clung to their national pride and Orthodox faith, hoping to restore their lost, powerful state.

Under pressure from the Ottomans, the Serbian population gradually moved north, leaving behind the southern regions, especially Kosovo and Metohija. This migration intensified after the unsuccessful Serbian uprisings against Ottoman rule. In response, the Ottoman Empire deliberately settled Albanian Muslims in Kosovo multiple times to create a demographic change in their favor, making it easier for them to control the rebellious Serbs by introducing a population loyal to their regime.

The most well-known historical examples of demographic changes in Kosovo occurred during the Great Turkish War (1683-1699) and after the Russo-Austro-Turkish War (1735-1739). In both conflicts, the Serbs took up arms and joined the enemies of the Ottoman Empire, hoping for liberation and the restoration of their statehood. However, the wars did not go in their favor, and the result was an exodus. In two large migrations, in 1690 and 1740, at least 250,000 Serbs left the territory of Kosovo and Metohija, fleeing from Turkish revenge. Led by church patriarchs, these people moved north to the territories of the Austrian Military Frontier, and smaller groups even arrived in the Russian Empire and settled in the area that is now Ukraine.

After the Serbian exodus, with the support of Ottoman authorities, Muslim Albanians from the mountainous areas of present-day northern Albania settled in the deserted villages and fertile plains of Kosovo and Metohija, filling the demographic vacuum. The Serbian ethnic center moved north, closer to Austria and Hungary.

Despite Kosovo and Metohija being regarded as the most significant region for the Serbs historically, as it was a religious and cultural center during the golden age of their medieval state, they were never able to regain demographic dominance over the Albanians on this territory, as a result of the aforementioned exoduses.

In the Ottoman doctrine of rule, converts to Islam held a significant place. They were expected to prove themselves both in faith and loyalty to the empire. The Turks themselves tried to avoid direct involvement in the implementation of unpopular measures, relying instead on local helpers. Therefore, tasks such as control, administration, or the enforcement of repressive measures against oppressed and often rebellious Christians were typically assigned to converts to Islam. As a result, Muslim Albanians became a privileged class in relation to the occupied and disenfranchised Serbs. Serbian folk tradition contains songs and stories passed down through generations about violence, murder, and the destruction of churches and monasteries committed by Albanians in the service of the Ottoman Empire.

One of the darkest events in Serbian oral tradition occurred in 1594, and it involved the Ottoman grand vizier Sinan Pasha, who was Albanian by birth. He ordered the exhumation of the relics of Saint Sava, the founder of the Serbian Orthodox Church, the most revered and beloved Serbian saint, and had them burned at the stake in Belgrade. This measure was a revenge for the Serbian uprising in Banat that occurred in the initial phase of the thirteen-year war between the Habsburg monarchy and the Ottoman Empire. In memory of this event and out of immense respect for Saint Sava, the Serbs started building a monumental memorial temple in 1935, one of the largest Orthodox churches in the world, which is nearing completion today in 2023.

On this graphic from the end of the 16th century, the nationality of the Grand Vizier Sinan Pasha is written as: *SINAN BASSA OF THE ALBANIAN NATION* ("SINAN BASSA NATIONE ALBANVS")

At the beginning of the 19th century, Serbs finally began to liberate their land from Ottoman rule. At the same time, a period of serious problems began for Albanians. They would soon lose their privileged status and be exposed to Serbian anger and revenge. The first Serbian uprising in 1804 resulted in the liberation of part of the country, pushing the Turks southward, along with the Albanians. Serbian insurgents treated Albanians the same way they treated Turks.

Opposite example occurred in 1901, when Albanians repeatedly massacred Serbs in the regions of today's Kosovo, Northern Macedonia, and Montenegro, then still part of the dying Ottoman Empire. On that occasion, cities and villages were burned, women were raped, mass killings, expulsions, and looting occurred. An international scandal erupted, and a diplomatic dispute between Austria and Russia emerged, showing how small Balkan nations were proxies for great powers in their fight for interests. Austria supported the Albanians and tried to cover up and minimize the crimes, while Russia was very vocal and put pressure on Istanbul to stop the massacres and protect the Serbs, which eventually happened.

The processes in which we see Serbian pressure towards Albanians, including their expulsion from liberated Serbian territories, lasted throughout the 19th century and culminated in 1912 during the First Balkan War. After it, the Ottoman Empire was almost entirely expelled from the European continent, and the Serbian army regained territories that were part of the medieval Serbian state, including parts of Macedonia and above all, Kosovo and Metohija. This war was seen as the most popular in Serbian history, with a huge response of volunteers who wanted to finally seek military revenge against the Turks for the defeat in the Battle of Kosovo in 1389 and centuries of occupation. "The revenge of Kosovo" was the popular name for Serbia's war goal in the First Balkan War.

The Carnegie Endowment for International Peace established an international commission to investigate the crimes committed during the First Balkan War. The commission was composed of distinguished experts from Austria, Germany, Russia, the United States, Great Britain, and France, including three Nobel Prize winners. Despite its significance, the report[44], published in Washington in 1914, remains largely unknown among the wider public in present-day Serbia. However, it is worthy of attention as it sheds light on the deep anti-Serb sentiments that were instilled among Kosovo Albanians and have been passed down from generation to generation. A better understanding of this report could provide insight into the root of these sentiments.

The document compiled by a group of international experts and philanthropists speaks of massive crimes committed by Serbian, Montenegrin, Greek, and Bulgarian forces against Muslims, as well as by Turkish forces against Christians. The report describes persecutions, mass murders, rapes,

---

[44] Carnegie Endowment for International Peace, Division of Intercourse and Education. *Report of the International Commission to inquire into the Causes and Conduct of the Balkan Wars*, Pub. No. 4. Washington D. C.: Carnegie Endowment for International Peace, 1914.

physical mutilations, denial of food and water, burning of entire villages and towns, looting, and forced conversion from Islam to Christianity or from one national church to another. The latter in the Balkans means a change of national affiliation. Certain church officials and dignitaries are characterized as mere exponents of nationalist policies and often as direct organizers of violent conversions or ethnic cleansing.

The described events are severe, distressing, and admonitory. Reading this document, we would like to believe, would evoke a reaction of conscience in a large number of honest people and patriots in the mentioned nations. However, overshadowed by the outbreak of World War I, the report was not properly received in the criticized states. Instead, it became a kind of herald for the terrifying crimes that would continue in World War II and during the Yugoslav wars at the end of the 20th century. In addition to numerous violations of international conventions, the report also provides a very sad characterization of the Balkan peoples, already in 1914:

> "The policy of ethnic cleansing is a normal and traditional occurrence in all Balkan wars and uprisings. [...] This is a custom among all these peoples. What they themselves suffered, they in turn do to others."

Later events will show that things have not changed. Therefore, the above statement is of great importance for our understanding of the brutality of the civil war during which Yugoslavia disintegrated and of the ethnic cleansing practiced by all warring parties.

The commission report summarizes the events in areas with predominantly Albanian population as follows:

> "Houses and entire villages have been turned to ashes, unarmed and innocent civilians have been massacred *en masse*, incredible acts of violence, looting, and brutality of all kinds—these are the means that the Serbian-Montenegrin army has applied and is still applying in order to completely transform the ethnic character of the areas populated exclusively by Albanians"

The famous Russian revolutionary, Leon Trotsky, was also a direct witness of these events, then as a Russian war correspondent in the Balkans. In his reports, he describes ethnic cleansing, and in one report explicitly says:

> "Serbs in Old Serbia, in their national endeavor to correct the data in ethnological statistics that are not in their favor, simply destroy the Muslim population in villages, towns, and entire districts."

Dimitrije Tucović, leader of the socialist movement in the Kingdom of Serbia, founder of the Social Democratic Party, and journalist, also criticized the events he witnessed as a Serbian soldier during the First Balkan War with extremely harsh words. He believed that Serbia had the opportunity to behave much more humanely and, as the conscience of the nation, disappointingly noted that:

> "Serbia did not enter Albania as a brother but as a conqueror, and with a bad policy that did not take into account people, it lost touch with representatives of the Albanian people and pushed them into hatred of everything Serbian."

We can see that the return of Serbs to their medieval holy land, Kosovo, during the times of the Turkish expulsion of everyone who served the Turks did not happen in a civilized manner. Unfortunately, Serbia missed the historic opportunity to rise above revenge and centuries-long conflict with Albanians and act in an integrative way. This mistake will bring much suffering to the people of both nations and have severe consequences for Serbia that continue to this day.

Emboldened by the victory in the war and the return of Kosovo, Serbia began implementing a suppressive policy towards the local Albanians, which would bring a long-term problem and loss of reputation. Oppressed and traumatized for centuries, Serbs could not resist the desire for revenge. The Serbian government, encouraged by the atmosphere in which Turkey and Greece successfully exchanged their population after the war, made similar plans for relocating Albanians to Turkey and Albania. Numerous reports describe the repressive measures, discrimination, and violent displacement that Serbian and later Yugoslav authorities carried out against Albanians from the end of the First Balkan War (1912) to Yugoslavia's entry into the Second World War (1941). At the same time, there was a planned colonization of Serbian, Montenegrin, and other Yugoslav peoples in Kosovo. Colonists were given the estates of displaced and relocated Albanians. Some of the land for colonization was obtained by buying up bey estates and clearing forests. An intergovernmental agreement between the Kingdom of Yugoslavia and the Republic of Turkey, which envisaged the relocation of even two hundred thousand Albanians from Kosovo to the Turkish province of Anatolia, was signed in 1938 but never ratified in the Turkish parliament, mainly due to the outbreak of the Second World War. With these measures, Serbia, and then the Kingdom of Yugoslavia, significantly re-drew the demographics of Kosovo and Metohija by 1941, in favor of the Slavic population, mostly Serbs and Montenegrins.

Albanian response to the weakening of the Ottoman Empire and pressure from Christians was to create a political program aimed at unifying all ethnic Albanians into one state, which was expressed as a demand at the Congress of Berlin in 1878. Since then, this aspiration has continued and enjoys majority support among the Albanian people. Given that territories populated by Albanians are not only in today's Albania but also in Greece, Montenegro, Serbia, and North Macedonia, the project of unifying the Albanian ethnic space into the so-called "Greater Albania"[45] is perceived as a terri-torial threat in the aforementioned neigh-boring countries. In the past, such territorial-political aspirations of Albanians

The borders of "ethnic" or "greater" Albania, as seen by the protagonists of maximalist Albanian territorial aspirations.

have led to their exposure to ethnic cleansing by Serbs, Montenegrins, and Greeks during the Balkan and First World Wars.

During World War II, when fascist Italy occupied Albania and Kosovo, Albanians carried out terror and ethnic cleansing against Serbs and Montenegrins, resulting in the killing or expulsion of tens of thousands of people. The Serbian-Albanian cycle of violence had repeated itself frequently and brutally since the early 19th century, with the pendulum of aggression swinging from one side to the other. However, there were also honorable exceptions, and my generation most vividly remembers national heroes Bora Vukmirović and Ramiz Sadiku, a Serb and an Albanian, respectively, who were both antifascists. They were arrested, tortured, and executed by fascist soldiers, but refused to be separated and died hugging each other.

In communist Yugoslavia after the Second World War, there was a change in attitude and policy in an attempt to solve the problems more permanently. Albanians were the largest national minority in the southern Slavic state, and although not Slavs themselves, the authorities made visible efforts to ensure their complete equality with others and correct the mistakes of the past. It all began with the decision of the new authorities in March 1945 to temporarily ban the return of colonists settled during the time of the Kingdom. These were mostly Serbs and Montenegrins who

---

[45] In Albanian nationalist circles, the term 'Ethnic Albania' is preferred.

managed to escape from Kosovo during the war, fleeing from Albanian terror and revenge. The decision was followed by a legal solution according to which those colonists whose land was forcibly taken from previous owners—lost the right to the land. However, these people were offered the estates of Germans expelled from Vojvodina.

The Kosovo and Metohija region gained the status of an autonomous province *within* Republic of Serbia—one of the constituent republics of the Yugoslav federation. But the old desire for the unification of all Albanians into one state—the Greater Albania project—and the intolerance towards Serbian and Montenegrin neighbors led to several waves of violent protests and attempts to secede Kosovo from Serbia and the rest of Yugoslavia.

The percentage of Serbs in Kosovo and Metohija was steadily declining during this period. According to the 1948 census, it was 23.62%. However, in 1991 it dropped to only 9.93%. Why? There are several reasons for this phenomenon. From 1945 to 1990, Serbs suffered various forms of pressure from the Albanian majority and, like during the Ottoman period, they were once again leaving Kosovo for central Serbia. The local provincial authorities, dominated by Albanians, enabled significant illegal immigration of ethnic Albanians from neighboring Albania to Kosovo, increasing the ethnic imbalance to the detriment of Serbs, in line with their policy of demographic takeover. At the same time, Albanian birth rates remained exceptionally high throughout the post-war period, among the highest in Europe. Exposed to these tendencies and feeling great insecurity about their future, many Serbs chose to sell their property to Albanians, often being offered substantial sums of money, with which they could buy land and property or start a business in central Serbia. The frustration caused by this situation had been accumulating for decades, during which the Yugoslav communist authorities turned a blind eye to the endangerment and emigration of Serbs from Kosovo, doing nothing to prevent it.

Everything pointed to the fact that the pendulum of violence was swinging again and that a new conflict between the two largest nations in the Western Balkans was inevitable. Suppressed problems first escalated in 1968 in the form of demands from Albanian students for Kosovo, an autonomous province within Serbia, to become an independent, seventh republic of the Yugoslav federation. Massive protests with the same demands from Albanians occurred in 1981 and were suppressed by the Yugoslav police and military. Dozens were killed, and thousands were arrested. The world didn't know much about this. What everyone remembers today is the Albanian guerrilla movement for the secession of Kosovo from Serbia and the truncated Yugoslavia in 1998 and 1999, which provoked a military and police intervention by the state. However, we can see that it was just the latest episode in a very long series of mutual clashes between Serbs and Albanians.

The last armed conflict, which is the subject of a separate chapter, was stopped by controversial NATO air strikes against the Federal Republic of Yugoslavia in the spring of 1999. UN Security Council Resolution 1244 placed Kosovo under temporary UN administration until political talks on the final status of the province were concluded. However, in 2008, local Albanian leaders unilaterally declared independence and the creation of an independent state. To this day, in 2023, they have not succeeded in becoming a member of the UN and many other international organizations. Kosovo and Metohija, like in previous centuries, remain a disputed land. However, the stage is much bigger now and the solution to this issue is no longer solely in the hands of Serbs and Albanians. Today, Kosovo is part of a global confrontation of interests of the world's major powers.

Now, it is time to return to the main chronological thread and analyze the period when the newly created South Slavic Kingdom was experiencing its first major challenges.

Separatism in the Kingdom of Serbs, Croats, and Slovenes: When did it Begin?

Thus far, we have focused on the intricate relationships between the South Slavs, whose coexistence in a small space was weighed down by territorial disputes, religious confrontations, and the interests of foreign powers. We have also detailed the battle for supremacy in the Balkans between the Roman Catholic and Orthodox churches, which often utilized small Balkan nations as marionettes. The arrival of Islam in the 14th century and the conversion of a substantial number of Christians to this religion further compounded relations and rendered the Balkans—fittingly referred to as a "powder keg"—even more intricate.

The belief is widespread worldwide that separatism in Yugoslavia started in 1980 following the demise of Marshal Josip Broz Tito, who governed the country with a firm hand and strong charisma for thirty-five years. Regrettably, this assumption is far from the truth.

Yugoslavia is a multi-layered and complicated phenomenon that rightfully garners attention today, decades after it disappeared from the historical stage. Therefore, it is logical that efforts have been made to simplify it for broader public understanding. Nevertheless, the facts, as this book gradually reveals, are fascinating and can serve as inspiration and a source of knowledge for other nations willing to learn from Yugoslav experiences and mistakes.

In the following paragraphs, we will provide a comprehensive portrayal of how nationalism and separatism disrupted Yugoslavia soon after its creation, with a significant surge occurring in the second and third decades of the twentieth century.

The Kingdom of Serbs, Croats, and Slovenes was a parliamentary monarchy in which the king, according to the constitution, held broad powers. He could dissolve the government and parliament and was also the supreme commander of the armed forces. Disputes and misunderstandings over the internal structure of the state began before unification and continued immediately after. The young and underdeveloped democracy could not cope with the entirely different strategic orientations of significant political parties that invariably had an ethnic-national prefix.

A number of Serbian politicians believed that the Yugoslav state was a natural continuation of the Kingdom of Serbia, relegating a progressive vision of the Yugoslav idea to the background. Similarly, some Croatian and Slovenian political parties considered the new state to be only a framework within which they could continue their national gathering and strengthen their national positions. Their ultimate goal was separation, or the extraction of their nations from Yugoslavia and the creation of independent, internationally recognized states. Thus, from the outset, advocates of the visionary ideas of Yugoslavism and Pan-Slavism faced two irreconcilable and community-destructive concepts as their political opposition:

– The first concept advocated a *unitary-centralist* Yugoslavia in which the Serbian people, as the most numerous and most deserving of the creation of the state, had a decisive role and responsibility.
– The second concept was declaratively *federalist* and advocated by Croats and Slovenes. It soon took clear separatist outlines. Macedonian, Bosniak, and Albanian separatism would join it, motivated by emancipation.

Both concepts are extreme and incompatible with the survival of the common state.

In the years following unification, the work of the Assembly was marred by constant conflicts among the deputies, including quarrels, insults, mutual accusations, and threats. Several governments resigned or were dismissed, and the king attempted to control the impossible political situation in the country by introducing reforms and making concessions to certain political demands.

By the end of the second decade of the 20th century, the political climate in the country had reached boiling point, and trouble was in the air. On June 20th, 1928, after a heated argument in the Assembly between Croatian and Serbian deputies, which was marked by mutual insults, slanders, mockery, and death threats, a great tragedy occurred. Puniša Račić, a Serbian deputy from Montenegro, provoked by the taunts of Croatian deputies, pulled out a pistol and fatally wounded the most prominent Croatian politician, the leader of the Croatian Peasant Party, Stjepan Radić. He killed two and injured several other Croatian deputies. Račić's last words before going to prison were: "I could no longer bear to watch how everything Serbian was being dragged through the mud. I'm here, I'm ready to be shot, I've done my duty."

Today, some historians believe that Račić did not act alone, and that there was a conspiracy to eliminate Radić, who was extremely popular among Croats, but whose politics did not suit the Crown. The charismatic Radić advocated federalism, was an opponent of the monarchy, and often changed his political rhetoric and coalition partners. The focus of his activities was directed towards the separation of Croats from Yugoslavia, and in achieving that goal, he did not hesitate to flirt with external enemies of the state, such as Austria, Italy, and the Soviet Union. The suspicion that it was a political assassination is supported by the fact that, after the trial and conviction for the multiple murders committed, the assassin enjoyed great privileges during his imprisonment.

This tragic event further worsened the already highly disrupted Serbian-Croatian relations in the newly formed kingdom. Large protests followed in Zagreb, and the entire Croatian opposition left the National Assembly. The unofficial leader of Croats in Yugoslavia, Mr. Stjepan Radić, died from his injuries a month later. Several hundred thousand angry Croats attended his funeral. The radical political faction gained momentum after this tragedy. Just a few months after Radić's death, on September 1ˢᵗ, 1928, the extremely right-wing Croatian Party of Rights issued a declaration in Zagreb calling for the secession of Croatia from Yugoslavia.

The state was in chaos and greatly shaken. Serbian nationalist political circles revived the beliefs expressed as early as the mid-1920s that "it was no longer possible to deal with Croats" and advocated the idea of a so-called amputation of Croatia, giving up on Yugoslavia, and creating Greater Serbia, roughly within the boundaries envisioned by the 1915 London Agreement. King Alexander himself, probably under great pressure from the new events, offered Croatia secession in July 1928. However, Dr. Vlatko Maček, the successor of the deceased Stjepan Radić at the helm of the Croatian Peasant Party, rejected the offer. Similarly, Svetozar Pribićević, the political leader of Serbs in Croatia, understandably did the same. Amputation would have separated many Serbs in Croatia from other Serbs in Yugoslavia. Both leaders advocated for efforts to overcome the crisis and work towards the survival of the common state.

As the country was in a deep political crisis with the possibility of outbreaks of unrest and bloodshed, the king consulted with the most prominent politicians and experts in an attempt to find a solution. An absolutist and soldier by character, he turned to a radical option. On January 6ᵗʰ, 1929, King Alexander I Karadjordjević introduced a dictatorship, abolished the Constitution, and dissolved the National Assembly. He decided to ban all political parties. A new government was appointed, headed by army general Petar Živković. Political rallies and trade unions were banned, and censorship was introduced in news reporting.

At that time, the king significantly changed the internal organization of the state. The name of the country, Kingdom of Serbs, Croats, and Slovenes, was changed to the Kingdom of Yugoslavia. The previous territorial and administrative division into 33 districts was abolished. Instead, "banovinas" were formed as administrative units, with a total of nine. The borders of these new units were defined in a way that avoided the application of any ethnic or religious principle.

It seems that this was a decisive political maneuver that was an "all or nothing" proposition. By making such radical decisions, the king reaffirmed the basic political vision that created Yugoslavia and sent a strong message to nationalists in all parts of the country. By introducing personal dictatorship, King Aleksandar was determined to break all forms of separatism and nationalism and to strongly support only one, unitary Yugoslav nation. The state came out with a strong official stance that Yugoslavs were "one nation with three names," or a "triune" nation of Serbs, Croats, and Slovenes. The solution to the deep crisis was seen by the king as a return to the original idea of South Slavic unity. He turned to the consistent application of the policy of Integral Yugoslavism, which he believed would eventually establish a Yugoslav nation.

If it had come to fruition on a scale that reached critical mass, and if the descendants of nationalist or separatist extremists had truly seen themselves one day not as Serbs, Croats, Slovenes, Montenegrins, Bosniaks, or Macedonians, but only and solely as Yugoslavs, such an outcome would have been a quantum leap and a total paradigm shift that would have truly brought Yugoslavia to life and ensured its survival. As we know today, critical mass was never reached, and the king's attempt to impose unity by force suffered a complete defeat. The ruler's "all or nothing" game would bring him a violent death a few years later.

The reaction was swift. Just one day after the introduction of dictatorship, the evil spirit emerged from the bottle. Croatian politician Dr. Ante Pavelić founded the ultra-nationalist organization *The Ustaša*[46] in Italy with the aim of establishing an independent and ethnically pure Croatian state by any means necessary, including terror and violence. Many sources describe this organization as one of the deadliest and most ruthless ever to have existed. Its fury would primarily be directed at Serbs, becoming the darkest stain on the collective conscience of the Croatian people. Members of this organization, which was active between 1929 and 1945, killed hundreds of thousands of people: Serbs, Jews, Roma, as well as political dissidents in Yugoslavia during World War II.

Symbol of Ustaša movement

Very quickly, Ante Pavelić connected with a similar separatist organization from Macedonia, which was under Bulgarian influence and fought

---

[46] Ustaša—Croatian Revolutionary Movement. The word "Ustaša" is often anglicized as Ustashas, and literally means "insurgents".

by any means, including terror, for the secession of Macedonia from Yugoslavia. The name of this organization was *VMRO* (Internal Macedonian Revolutionary Organization). As previously explained, Bulgaria's official stance at the time was that Macedonians were Bulgarians, so the true political goal of VMRO was to unite Macedonia with Bulgaria.

In an attempt to save Yugoslavia from chaos and disintegration by introducing dictatorship, King Alexander provoked massive resistance and signed his own death warrant. Two powerful terrorist organizations, backed by Italy and Bulgaria, joined forces to assassinate him.

The Assassination
of King Alexander I of Yugoslavia in 1934

A Brief Analysis of the Foreign Policy Challenges Faced by Yugoslavia in the Period Following World War I

Fascist Italy was dissatisfied with the outcome of World War I and the disregard for the Treaty of London by the Allies. Consequently, it had territorial claims against Yugoslavia, primarily in Dalmatia, an area encompassing most of the eastern coast of the Adriatic Sea. The annexation of Dalmatia by the Italian army at the end of World War I was prevented by the inhabitants of Dalmatia, mostly Croats, who called on the army of the Kingdom of Serbia for protection. Italy remembered this and was understandably angry.

Bulgaria suffered heavy defeats against Serbia in the Second Balkan War and World War I. On these occasions, it lost Macedonia, which first became part of Serbia, and then, as a region in Serbia, joined Yugoslavia. The Serbian army expelled the Bulgarian population from Macedonia during the aforementioned wars, and after their conclusion, the Serbian authorities carried out the Serbianization of the population in this area. All of this made Bulgaria very dissatisfied, hostile, and waiting for its opportunity.

The commander of the Serbian army that achieved the aforementioned war victories and was then the key armed force behind the process of establishing the Yugoslav state was Alexander I Karadjordjević, the Crown Prince and Regent of Serbia, and soon after, the King of Yugoslavia. The described animosities of Italy and Bulgaria motivated these countries to financially and organizationally support the Ustaša and VMRO: two separatist-terrorist organizations that joined forces to break up Yugoslavia and kill its king. Nonetheless, this did not mark the end of the extensive list of both his personal enemies and those of Yugoslavia; in fact, it was quite the opposite.

- Austria and Hungary, as defeated countries in World War I, were not friendly towards Yugoslavia, which partly emerged from their lost territories. Austria still painfully remembered the assassination of Archduke Franz Ferdinand in Sarajevo in 1914, carried out by a young man who described himself as a "Yugoslav nationalist" during his trial.

- Albania, then an Italian satellite in the Balkans, had its territorial claims on areas of Yugoslavia inhabited by Albanians—primarily on Kosovo and Metohija.
- A strong Yugoslavia was not in line with Germany's interests, which saw the areas inhabited by Slovenes and Croats as part of its sphere of interest and the shortest route to the geopolitically important access to the warm Adriatic Sea, and through it, the Mediterranean. Information published by East Germany in 1957 and 1958 accused Hitler and his spy network in Germany of secretly supporting the conspiracy that would lead to the assassination of King Alexander through an operation codenamed *Teutonic Sword.*
- Turkey hoped to restore its presence in the Balkans, with Yugoslavia being an obstacle, and did not look kindly upon the possible assimilation of Bosnian Muslims into the predominantly Christian kingdom.
- The Vatican was unhappy with the prospect of several million Croatian and Slovenian Roman Catholics merging into a single supranational entity with Orthodox Serbs. The Orthodox Church expressed similar resistance to the mixing of Serbs with Roman Catholics and Muslims.
- The Soviet Union, which traditionally needed access to a warm sea, was geopolitically opposed to the unequivocally anti-communist Yugoslavia and supported its internal separatist movements. The fourth, so-called Dresden Congress of the Communist Party of Yugoslavia in 1928 concluded that Yugoslavia was a "creation of the Greater Serbian bourgeoisie" and advocated for its disintegration into independent states. The Communists labeled the Serbs as an oppressive nation and blamed the Karadjordjević dynasty for turning Yugoslavia into a "prison of nations." All these qualifications were, of course, in full agreement with the position of Moscow and the Comintern. The Communist Party of Yugoslavia, working on the breakup of Yugoslavia, supported the Ustaša and VMRO during the 1930s, with whom it shared a common narrative about the "Greater Serbian dictatorship."

Preparations for the Assassination

Immediately after the introduction of the king's personal dictatorship, Ante Pavelić emigrated from Yugoslavia. He began working efficiently to mobilize Croatian extremists into the Ustaša organization. Training camps were established in Italy and Hungary. On April 29th, 1929, Pavelić signed a *Declaration of Mutual Assistance* between Macedonians and Croats with Vanča Mihajlov, the leader of the Macedonian extremist emigration, in their efforts to destroy Yugoslavia and create independent states of Croatia and Macedonia.

During 1933, Ante Pavelić made the definitive decision to assassinate King Alexander, who was seen as the cohesive element of the joint state of Serbs, Croats, and Slovenes. It was believed that the king's death would lead to unrest in the country and the possibility of achieving the goal—establishing an independent Croatian state. In the Ustaša camp in Hungary, volunteers were trained by Vlado Černozemski (pronounced *Chernozemsky*), a multiple murderer and VMRO executioner. The main purpose of this camp was to plan the assassination of the Yugoslav king and train the direct perpetrators.

As soon as they learned that the king would be making an official visit to France, the Ustaša began the final preparations for the assassination. Ante Pavelić himself oversaw the organization, and Vlado Černozemski was chosen to carry out the assassination.

Epilogue

At the very beginning of the state visit to France, in Marseille on October 9th, 1934, immediately after disembarking from the ship, riding in an open car and greeting thousands of French people who had come to welcome him, Alexander I, King of Yugoslavia, was killed along with French Foreign Minister Louis Barthou. The king was struck by three bullets and died in the car, while Minister Barthou passed away in the hospital from excessive blood loss less than an hour later.

Velichko Dimitrov Kerin a.k.a.
Vlado Černozemski, Assassin
of the Yugoslav King

The assassin, according to a previously established plan, was Vlado Černozemski (pronounced [Chernozemsky]). The real name of this Bulgarian citizen was Velichko Dimitrov Kerin[47]. To this day, he is described as a hero in the official Bulgarian and Macedonian historiography. He is seen as a fighter for Macedonian national liberation from Serbian and Yugoslav hegemony, who laid down his life for the creation of an independent Macedonian state.

---

[47] In Bulgarian: Величко Димитров Керин

The moment when the assassin Vlado Černozemski broke away from the crowd, leaping onto the King's car and firing fatal rounds at Yugoslav King Alexander I and French Minister of Foreign Affairs, Louis Barthou. October 9th, 1934. Marseille, France.

The world identified the Ustaša movement, led by Ante Pavelić, as the main organizer of this terrorist act, and its leaders were tried in absentia in France and Yugoslavia. They managed to avoid the most severe punishments to which they were sentenced, mainly by hiding in fascist countries.

Many European crowned heads, state and religious leaders, as well as about half a million deeply grieving Yugoslavs, attended the king's funeral. According to some testimonies that were later disputed as intentional state propaganda, the king's last words as he was dying were "Guard Yugoslavia." The assembly posthumously awarded him the title "The Unifier" in recognition of his historical achievements while expressing determination to continue with the king's political vision of a united, integral Yugoslavia.

The Yugoslav king passed away in the car, a few moments after the assassination.

Studying the facts related to the Marseille assassination leads to certain findings that suggest the possibility that the king consciously chose such a fate. Unlike the Yugoslav public at the time, he knew he was suffering from an advanced stage of stomach cancer and had little time left. This was kept as a top state secret. His son, the late Prince Tomislav, wrote about this in his memoirs:

"Little is known about the fact that my father was seriously ill. My mother later told me that he had cancer and that the doctors had predicted he had six more months to live. When he was killed, the pathological report confirmed that the diagnosis was accurate. He weighed only 50 kilograms[48] when he went to Marseille."

Although security services knew the king's life was in danger and warned him about it, he refused to wear body armor. Some conclude that he preferred to die as a soldier rather than in bed. It is possible. It can be assumed that Alexander hoped his death at the hands of Yugoslav separatists and ultra-nationalists would actually lead to outrage among the people, rallying the ranks, and consequently improving relations in his shaken kingdom.

The death of King Alexander stirred the entire Yugoslav public. He had three sons, but at the time of the tragedy, all of them were children. The solution to the sudden vacuum in leading Yugoslavia appeared in the provisions of the Constitution and the king's testament. This is an additional detail supporting the thesis that Alexander knew his end was near and that he was doing everything necessary to ensure a peaceful transfer of power after his departure. The Yugoslav Constitution provided for a three-member regency to govern the country instead of an underage king. In his will written in Bled on January 5th, 1934, the king defined that his cousin, a great art lover and former student at Oxford University, Prince Paul (Pavle) Karadjordjević, would govern the regency "in the event that the heir to the throne, for reasons listed in Article 41 of the Constitution, cannot exercise royal power." Crown Prince Peter II was just an eleven-year-old boy at the time of his father's demise.

It is interesting to quote here the words of the famous American scientist of Serbian origin, Nikola Tesla, who expressed a deep attachment to Yugoslavism and Yugoslavia. Shaken and outraged by the murder of the king, Tesla sent a response to the editor of *The New York Times* about ten days later under the title "A Tribute to King Alexander."[49] The article began with the following words:

"Much has been said about Yugoslavia and its people, but many Americans may be under a wrong impression for political enemies and agitators have spread the idea that its inhabitants belong to different nations animated by mutual hate and held together against their will, by a tyrannical power. The fact is that all Yugoslavs— Serbians, Slavonians, Bosnians, Herzegovinians, Dalmatians, Montenegrins, Croatians and Slovenes—are of the same race,

---

[48] 110 pounds
[49] Nikola Tesla, article "A Tribute to King Alexander," *The New York Times*, October 21st, 1934.

speak the same language and have common national ideals and traditions.

At the termination of the World War, Alexander brought about a political union creating a powerful and resourceful State. This was hailed with joy by all the Slavs of the Balkans, but it took time before the people found themselves in the new conditions.

Serbs Did the Fighting.

I was born in Croatia. The Croatians and Slovenes were never in a position to fight for their independence. It was the Serbians who fought the battles for freedom and the price of liberty was paid in Serbian blood. All true Croatians and Slovenes remember that gratefully. They also know that the Serbians have an unequalled aptitude and experience in warfare and are best qualified to direct the forces of the country in a crisis.

Ever since united Yugoslavia came into being through Alexander's efforts, political enemies have done all they could to disrupt it by sowing seeds of discord and disseminating malicious reports..."

At the end of the text, Tesla addresses the tragically killed king with expressions of deepest respect, words that certainly resonated loudly in America:

"The death of the King has shaken the country to its very foundations, but the enemies who say that it means the disruption of Yugoslavia will hope in vain, for the noble blood of the great man has only served to cement its parts more firmly and strengthen the national structure. Alexander will live long in the memory of his people, a heroic figure of imposing stature, both the Washington and Lincoln of the Yugoslavs; like Washington an able and intrepid general who freed his country from oppression; like Lincoln a wise and patriotic leader who suffered martyrdom."

World War II and Yugoslavia: A Feast for Beasts

Unfortunately, the political situation in the country only temporarily calmed down after the assassination of the king. Prince Pavle (Paul) Karadjordjević assumed the regency after the assassination of King Alexander I, as Alexander's son, King Peter II, was underage at the time. Prince regent tried to restore political balance and alleviate the increasingly strong demands of the Croatian people for an autonomous unit within Yugoslavia. After the German annexation of Austria in 1938 and the Italian occupation of Albania in 1939, it was clear that Yugoslavia would soon be drawn into the seemingly inevitable war. Realizing that the kingdom he governed was in extremely unfavorable circumstances, Prince Paul decided on a drastic measure to address Croatian de-

Regent of Yugoslavia, Prince Pavle Karadjordjević is seen wearing a black armband in a 1934 photograph as a sign of mourning for the assassination of his cousin, King Alexander.

mands, hoping that such a move would consolidate and stabilize the internal situation and strengthen the country in case of war.

As a result of such political endeavors, the Prime Minister of the Kingdom of Yugoslavia, Dragiša Cvetković, signed a direct agreement with the leader of the Croatian opposition, Vlatko Maček, on August 26th, 1939. Historically known as the Cvetković–Maček Agreement, this document defined the creation of the autonomous unit of Banovina Hrvatska within Yugoslavia. The new entity gained a *Sabor*, or parliament, with its seat in Zagreb, an independent budget, and other powers. The central government in Belgrade retained jurisdiction in foreign policy, defense, transportation, and a few other sectors. Through this agreement, Banovina Hrvatska expanded its territory beyond what is today's Republic of Croatia , and its political position within Yugoslavia significantly strengthened.

However, Regent Prince Paul's hopes for a final consensus and an end to the long-standing political instability did not materialize. A large number of Croats, politicians, and even Maček himself, saw the creation of Banovina Hrvatska as merely another step towards fulfilling the age-old dream of establishing a completely independent Croatian state. Unfortunately for the central government in Belgrade and to the anger and disappointment of Serbs, Croatian secessionist aspirations continued, and political tensions became even more acute.

This significant concession to the Croats, coupled with the abandonment of integral Yugoslavism—the basic principle upon which Yugoslavia was founded—gave rise to a plethora of new problems. Separatism now emerged among other nations and religious groups. Muslims called for an autonomous Bosnia, Macedonian separatism also flourished, and Slovenes increasingly demanded their own autonomous unit.

The Serbian political elite was angry with Prince Paul and highly dissatisfied with the fact that territories with hundreds of thousands of ethnic Serbs had now become part of the newly formed Banovina Hrvatska, which was persistently sliding towards secession. The hope that Croatian separatism would be satisfied by creating a special entity within Yugoslavia proved unrealistic. Serbs now firmly believed that Croatian politicians consistently lied to them, and that no further concessions would make Croats in Yugoslavia happy. Prince Paul and his Prime Minister Cvetković lost support among the Serbs.

Just a few days after the creation of Banovina Hrvatska, on September 1st, 1939, Germany invaded Poland, initiating the largest conflict in human history, for which Yugoslavia was unprepared. Prince Paul declared military neutrality and did everything in his power to preserve the country from war. His efforts would spark much resistance, controversy, internal and external political pressures, his removal from power, and expulsion from the country.

However, with today's hindsight, it seems that the Regent Prince sincerely tried to conscientiously fulfill the duty of head of state imposed on him by King Alexander's assassination. He did not want that duty at all. He was an art-loving, educated, and introverted man who, in his youth, hoped that one day he would manage a great museum. Instead, he bravely grappled with internal and external political challenges. Although primarily inclined towards Britain, he tried to preserve the neutral position of the state by striving to foster good relations with everyone: with Mussolini and Hitler, the Vatican, London, Paris, and Moscow. It seems that this was an overly ambitious task. King George VI made him a Knight of the Order of the Garter of the United Kingdom, France awarded him the Legion of Honor, and Italy the Order of the Crown of Italy.

Nonetheless, the maelstrom of historical events that destiny assigned to him led him into exile, and he would never return to his homeland. A life-long lover of art, he died in Paris in 1976. In 2011, the Higher Court in Belgrade corrected the historical injustice done to him and his family by deciding on their full rehabilitation.

Serbian "NO" to Adolf Hitler

It seems that Regent Paul found it extremely difficult to cope with the sudden burden of leading a country that was deeply divided and fraught with problems. Internal political disputes between Croats and Serbs were a reflection of the irreconcilable conflict between two diametrically opposed political concepts—unitarist and separatist. The strong Croatian desire for an independent state threatened the very foundations of Yugoslavia: with Croatia's secession, its existence in its original form would no longer be possible.

On the Serbian side, doubts grew about the validity of Yugoslav ideals and the justification of Serbia's war goal, the unification of all South Slavs, for which immense sacrifices had been made. Many believed that the Serbian state leadership, headed by Regent Aleksandar Karadjordjević, made a fatal mistake when they embarked on the adventure of creating Yugoslavia with Croats and Slovenes, instead of simply accepting the expanded Serbian borders that the Allies had envisioned for Serbia in the London Agreement of 1915.

By the spring of 1941, all neighboring countries had joined the Axis powers, and the political pressure Adolf Hitler exerted on Yugoslavia was immense. Although Yugoslavia's traditional friends, France, the United States, and the United Kingdom, were against signing a pact with Hitler, Prince Paul failed to obtain a promise from them that they would militarily protect Yugoslavia from a German attack. On the other hand, he knew that Croatian separatism, openly supported by fascist Italy, would significantly weaken the country's defensive capabilities. Yugoslavia faced two unfavorable options: to wage war against Germany, for which it was neither militarily nor politically prepared, or to enter into some alliance with it. Prince Paul attempted, and it seems, succeeded in finding the optimal solution that would give the country the best chance of survival and save it from war devastation and casualties.

After several secret meetings with Hitler, during which he managed to convince the Germans not to demand the transport of their troops through Yugoslav territory, Paul negotiated a privileged agreement for Yugoslavia with very clear and, for the Germans, extremely limited provisions. From these negotiations, it becomes clear that Hitler's main priority was to avoid opening a new front in Yugoslavia. Preparations for the attack on the Soviet Union were well advanced, and the operation was to begin as soon as possible. As a result, a very favorable agreement for Yugoslavia on joining the Tripartite Pact was signed on March 25th, 1941, in the Belvedere Palace in Vienna. The signing of the document was attended by the then-Yugoslav ambassador to Berlin, the future Nobel Prize laureate in literature (1961), Ivo Andrić.

The agreement granted Yugoslavia a special status compared to Romania, Bulgaria, Hungary, and Slovakia, which had previously joined. The text defines German and Italian recognition of the "sovereignty and territorial integrity of Yugoslavia," Italy and Germany's renunciation of requesting Yugoslav military assistance, except in cases where the "Yugoslav government decides it is in their interest to participate in military operations of the Axis powers." Member countries pledged not to demand the "passage or transportation of troops across Yugoslav state territory." Even the "expansion of Yugoslav sovereignty to the city and port of Thessaloniki" on the Aegean Sea in Greece was mentioned.

Distrusting Hitler and seeking additional security, Prince Paul requested that essential provisions of the agreement be made available to the German public, which was honored by reading the text on German state radio. Hitler later complained that the atmosphere at the banquet held after the official part of the meeting was like a funeral, clearly indicating the emotions with which the Yugoslav delegation approached the agreement.

This document can be briefly characterized as an agreement of friendship and non-aggression, along with inviolability of territory and non-participation of the Yugoslav army in the war. Seen from the perspective of politics as the "art of the possible," it is hard to imagine Prince Paul could have negotiated a better agreement for his country, especially in a year when the Nazis were rampaging through Europe virtually unopposed and had a non-aggression pact with the USSR. However, Serbian war veterans and patriots, who had bitter experiences with Germany in World War I, were appalled by the agreement with the Nazis. The negative sentiment was further spread by Radio Belgrade, which, in an act of sabotage against the government and the prince, broadcasted the pact's text accompanied by the sounds of a funeral march.

Such a reaction was not surprising. The cost of Yugoslavia joining the Axis powers existed, and it certainly damaged morale. The gradual concessions to Germany began in the mid-1930s and led not only to the rise of far-right forces within the country but also manifested concretely through the adoption of anti-Jewish laws in September 1940, a full six months before the signing of the Pact.

Anti-Semitism in the Kingdom of Yugoslavia was legalized and elevated to the state level: Jews were forbidden from engaging in the production and distribution of food for human consumption, and their enrollment in secondary and higher education institutions was severely restricted. Jews thus became biological enemies and were equated with communists, who were considered subversive ideological adversaries. It is interesting to note how right-wing propaganda in Yugoslavia blamed Jews for inventing communism and carrying out the revolution in Russia. The attitude towards Freemasonry also worsened under German pressure, and the Grand United Lodge "Yugoslavia", fearing for the safety of Freemasons, decided on self-suspension and complete cessation of activities on August 1st, 1940. This occurred a month before the adoption of the anti-Jewish ordinances, and it is an interesting fact considering that Prince Paul himself was a high-ranking Freemason. It leads to the assumption that he warned the Masons of what was to come.

These tendencies within the state caused disappointment and resistance among a large number of honorable people dedicated to freedom throughout Yugoslavia, who inclined towards civic and democratic values, human rights, and equality. The regime of Prince Paul became unacceptable to people of almost all political orientations: from ultra-nationalist-separatists, Serbian nationalists, to moderate democrats and socialists, and even the far-left dominated by the fairly numerous communists rooted in the young intelligentsia.

Both British and Soviet intelligence services decided to take action and try to prevent the implementation of the agreement for Yugoslavia's accession to the Tripartite Pact. The British wanted to open a new front to further preoccupy Hitler, while the Soviets knew that Germany was secretly preparing for Operation Barbarossa, which was the code name for the surprise attack on the USSR, and wanted to delay it as much as possible. The illegal Communist Party of Yugoslavia had its interests as well and would be used as assistance in inciting street rebellion against the government.

Through its intelligence organization, the Special Operations Executive (SOE), Britain had influence over a certain number of high-ranking aviation officers and several ministers in the government. The Soviet secret service NKVD (Russian: *Народный комиссариат внутренних дел, НКВД*) also had influence over some politicians and ministers, as well as the Communist Party.

The day after the signing of the pact, on March 26th, people began to spontaneously gather in the streets and protest. It was then that the famous slogan "Better the grave than a slave, better war than the pact" was coined, becoming the main message of the protests that spread virally in numerous Yugoslav cities.

A group of high-ranking officers of the Royal Yugoslav Air Force, led by Generals Simović and Mirković, with the support of Britain, decided to carry out a military coup in the early morning of March 27th, 1941. Regent Paul and the three-member Regency were removed from power, and the underage, seventeen-year-old King Peter II was declared of age and granted full powers, including command over the armed forces.

The Serbian Orthodox Church unanimously supported the coup at a Council held that morning, taking the position that, as in the case of the Battle of Kosovo in 1389, it was a choice for the "heavenly kingdom." Patriarch Gavrilo spoke of the "salvation of the nation's honor and state" and added, "If it is to live, let us live in sanctity and freedom; if it is to die, let us die for sanctity and freedom, as many millions of our glorious ancestors have."

Both the coup plotters and the Communist Party and the Serbian Orthodox Church called on the people for mass protests. It is estimated that there were about one hundred thousand demonstrators in Belgrade alone. Although there is clear evidence that foreign intelligence services were involved in the coup, the perspective of British diplomat and Emeritus Professor of History, Classics, and Archaeology at the University of Edinburgh, David A. Stafford, is interesting. He expressed the opinion that the greatest credit for the coup and the rejection of the pact must be attributed to ordinary people,

Tens of thousands of people protested on the streets of Belgrade on March 27th, 1941, against Yugoslavia's accession to the Tripartite Pact.

Yugoslavs, primarily Serbs. Without their quick, spontaneous, and strong reaction, such a development of events, Professor Stafford estimates, would have been completely impossible. "Initiative came from the Yugoslavs," he said, "and only by a stretch of the imagination can the British be said to have planned or directed the coup d'état."[50]

---

[50] Stafford, David A. T. "SOE and British Involvement in the Belgrade Coup d'état of March 1941." *Slavic Review 36*, no. 3 (September 1977): 399-419.

Führer's Reaction

Hitler was furious. It seemed as if he took the coup in Yugoslavia as a personal insult. During a meeting with military advisors called immediately upon receiving news from Belgrade, Hitler shouted. He demanded that Yugoslavia be declared an enemy state, punished, and completely destroyed. At the meeting, *Führer Directive No. 25* was drafted, which contained an order for an urgent and all-out attack on Yugoslavia. He instructed the military leadership to begin preparations for the attack immediately, not waiting for any potential positive political signal from the coup leaders. On April 2nd, the staff of the German embassy in Belgrade was ordered to evacuate, and a message in the same tone was sent to the embassies of "friendly countries." This was a clear signal that Yugoslavia would be attacked in the near future, perhaps in a few days or even hours. The ruthless German Blitzkrieg began with the infamous *Operation Punishment*, a brutal bombing of Belgrade in retaliation for Serbia's rejection of the Tripartite Pact.

In the early morning of April 6th, 1941, without any declaration of war or warning, the German Luftwaffe began an intensive bombing campaign against the Serbian capital, which lasted for two days and claimed between three and four thousand lives. On the same day, combined German, Italian, and Hungarian forces launched a ground invasion of Yugoslavia from all directions. The Germans entered first, followed by the Italians and Hungarians a few days later. The intentional destruction of the Serbian National Library, which burned to the ground, was particularly memorable. Thousands of medieval documents and manuscripts were irretrievably lost in addition to the books.

German troops entering the city of Maribor, Slovenia in April, 1941.

While German planes devastated Belgrade and other Serbian cities in retaliation, people's reactions in other parts of Yugoslavia were quite surprising. Nazi troops entered the city of Maribor in Slovenia without any resistance. Even Hitler himself came to Slovenia to express his satisfaction.

In Croatia, people took to the streets of their cities to welcome the German conquerors, seeing them as liberators. Many Croats hoped that the disappearance of Yugoslavia, which, in their view, had been dominated by Serbs, would pave the way for an independent Croatian state within the promised "New Order" (German: Neuordnung) imposed by the German Reich through the use of unprecedented brutality, fire, and sword. Before the invasion of Yugoslavia was over, Croatian ultranationalists led by Ante Pavelić—the same person who had organized and carried out the assassination of King Alexander I Karadjordjević a few years earlier—proclaimed the so-called *Independent State of Croatia*. This creation would go on to leave a dark and troubling legacy in Croatian history.

Citizens welcome German invasion forces in the Croatian capital of Zagreb. April 10th, 1941.

Fortunately, time would show that numerous Croats and Slovenes were deeply opposed to such developments in their communities and took swift and concrete actions. One of them would go on to become the leader of the largest liberation movement in Europe and the most significant Yugoslav figure of all time.

The Royal Yugoslav Army was unable to mount a serious resistance against a vastly superior enemy. Betrayals occurred everywhere, and the army was falling apart. Nearly all Croat soldiers abandoned their posts, and Croat officers handed over their units without engaging in combat. The situation was not much better in other parts of the country. Mostly, only Serbs attempted to resist the occupiers. After only eleven days, on April 17th, the country unconditionally capitulated, and the territory of Yugoslavia was divided between Germany, Italy, the newly created Independent State of Croatia, Bulgaria, and Hungary. Serbia was placed under direct German occupation, and the collaborationist regime of General Milan Nedić was brought to power, assisting the occupiers in locating, arresting, and executing thousands of Jews, Roma, and Serbian anti-fascists during the war. By his own account, Nedić wanted to save a large number of Serbian lives by collaborating with the Germans and "sacrificing his honor for the homeland." In the past two decades, there have been initiatives in Serbia by right-wing political parties and individuals to legally rehabilitate General Nedić, but all have been rejected.

King Leaves the Country

Seventeen-year-old King Peter II sincerely tried to cope with the challenging situation imposed by historical circumstances. He took responsibility and attempted to make the best decisions in circumstances that far exceeded the capabilities and experience of a teenager. When defeat seemed inevitable, on April 14th, 1941, he decided to leave the country and fly to Athens. The following day, members of the government followed him. Great Britain, the United States, and many other countries recognized the king and the government in exile as legitimate representatives of the country.

The young king did not surrender in his heart; he wanted to continue with the war efforts. His initial idea was to go to Canada and the United States, countries with great sympathy towards the Yugoslavs and a large Yugoslav community. He wanted to gather and organize volunteers there to join the Yugoslav army in exile and contribute to the Allied war efforts. However, after a call from the British government, the king and members of the government permanently settled in London. Queen Mother Maria of Yugoslavia had already been in Great Britain for some time due to illness, staying with Princes Tomislav and Andrew, so King

Marshal Montgomery, young King Peter II, and Winston Churchill in the summer of 1941.

Peter II's arrival in London also meant reuniting with the rest of the family. In London, he received a royal welcome with all honors. On that occasion, he met the British royal family and Prime Minister Winston Churchill. After consultations, it was decided that the young king would join the Royal Air Force (RAF) and continue his education at the University of Cambridge.

Independent State of Croatia (NDH) and the Rule of Croatian Fascists—Ustaša

While the Nazi attack on Yugoslavia was still ongoing, Croatian ultra-nationalists and fascists—the Ustašas—did not waste time. After a massive welcome prepared for German troops on the streets of the capital, Zagreb, and taking advantage of the prevailing sentiment of the masses towards secession, they declared the separation from Yugoslavia and the establishment of the so-called *Independent State of Croatia* (NDH) on April 10th, 1941.

Occupation and division of Yugoslavia in 1941.

This entity was created with the blessing and under the control of Germany and Italy, so its de facto independence cannot be discussed. It enjoyed great favor from the Vatican, and Croatian Catholic circles maintained exceptionally close ties with the Ustaša regime.

On the other hand, it is essential to note that its creation indeed reflected the majority desire of the Croatian people to gain their independent state. However, this strong desire overpowered the political reasoning of the people As in World War I, Croats once again found themselves in the same camp as Germany and Austria. In December 1941, the Independent State of Croatia declared war on the United States and the United Kingdom.

At the same time, a number of Croats did not reconcile with these developments. They defected to the partisans and offered organized resistance, initially in smaller numbers, and only from 1943 in more significant numbers. These people were a bright spot in the dark course of events in Croatia.

The territory of the puppet state of Croatian fascists was enormous by Yugoslav standards. It consisted of most of present-day Croatia, but without the Istrian peninsula and a large part of Dalmatia. The reason lies in one of Pavelić's first decisions after coming to power: he smoothly ceded these regions to Italy. What the Serbs—taking a considerable risk and at the cost of degraded relations or even war with Italy—had preserved for Croats after 1918, Croatian ultra-nationalists handed over to Mussolini on May 18th, 1941, by signing the *Rome Agreements*. On that occasion, Pope Pius XII received Pavelić in a half-hour private visit.[51] On the other hand, German occupation forces included all of Bosnia and Herzegovina and the Srem region in Serbia within the NDH, compensating for the Ustaša's concession to Italy. According to the official report of the German Ministry of Foreign Affairs from May 1941, published by Yugoslav-Croatian historian and professor, international expert on the history of the Independent State of Croatia (NDH) Bogdan Krizman, Serbs made up almost a third of the population of the Independent State of Croatia (30.62%), or 1,925,000 out of a total of 6,285,000 inhabitants.[52]

Genocide against Serbs, Jews, and Roma in Fascist Croatia

As has been demonstrated several times before, Serbs, especially those from the territories of the former Austro-Hungarian Empire, embraced the Yugoslav project and the creation of a new nation. As such, they represented an insurmountable obstacle for the Ustaša regime in establishing a stable, independent Croatian state. Almost two million people in the territory under their administration wanted Yugoslavia, not Croatia. The Ustaša au-

---

[51] Hebblethwaite, Peter. *Paul VI, the First Modern Pope*. Harper Collins Religious, 1993, pp. 153-57, 210-11.
[52] Krizman, Bogdan. *Ustaše i 3. Reich*, Vols. 1-2. Zagreb: Globus, 1983.

thorities quickly labeled Serbs as a hostile population. However, what would soon follow was something even the Germans could not have predicted. At this point, I would like to quote the Croatian Encyclopedia, which provides the following explanation:

> "The Ustaša ideology aimed to make the Independent State of Croatia (NDH) an exclusive state for the Croatian people. Some Serbs initially wanted to cooperate with the new authorities, but this quickly led to the exclusion of Serbs from public life, and the persecution and mass liquidation of the Serbian population. The Ustašas held Serbs collectively responsible for the suffering of Croats during the interwar period and considered them an obstacle to achieving a free Croatian state."[53]

The hostility of Croats towards Serbs was certainly partly caused by the difference in religion. After the division of the Christian Church into Eastern and Western branches, the two nations eventually found themselves on different sides. The Catholic Church has historically demonstrated a tendency towards religious confrontation with "Orthodox schismatics." Religious animosity was later exacerbated by the settlement of Serbs in the territory of the Military Frontier, traditionally inhabited by Croats. All of this has been extensively discussed in previous chapters. However, it was only in the Independent State of Croatia (NDH), influenced by Nazi ideology and methods, that the state "final solution" for the elimination of the Serbian population emerged. Ustaša regime Minister Milovan Žanić said the following at a public gathering in 1941:

> "Ustašas! You should know, I speak openly: this state, our homeland, must be Croatian and no one else's. And that is why those who came here [Serbs] should leave... This must be the land of Croats and no one else, and there is no method that we, as Ustašas, will not use to truly make it Croatian and cleanse it of Serbs, who have threatened us for centuries and would threaten us at the first opportunity. We do not hide this; it is the policy of this state, and when we accomplish it, we will only be fulfilling what is written in the Ustaša principles."[54]

---

[53] *Hrvatska enciklopedija, vol. 7*, Leksikografski zavod Miroslav Krleža, Zagreb, Croatia, 2005.

[54] *"Novi list"* Newspaper, June 3rd, 1941, Rijeka, Independent State of Croatia (NDH).

As a result of publicly proclaimed genocidal intentions, the Ustaša authorities established a series of camps in the summer of 1941, where the systematic killing of Serbian, Jewish, and Roma populations began. In the Independent State of Croatia, there were about fifteen concentration camps, with the largest and most horrifying death camp being Jasenovac. According to some sources, these camps for the systematic extermination of people were chronologically established before the Nazi camps in Auschwitz and Treblinka. Perhaps to prove themselves, the Ustašas competed in cruelty with German and other Nazis and fascists. They were the only ones to have concentration camps for children. These were mostly orphaned children of Serbian nationality, numbering in the thousands. Through the actions of Croatian women and humanitarians, these children were sometimes illegally removed from the camps and placed in Croatian families. In this way, many were saved from disease, hunger, and al-

The Ustaša militia utilized a knife, which they called "Srbosjek" (translated as 'Serb-cutter' in English), fastened to their hand, to carry out the mass murder of prisoners at Jasenovac concentration camp.

most certain death. At the Pula Film Festival in 2019, the absolute winner was the film "The Diary of Diana Budisavljević" about a heroic woman who managed to rescue 15,336 children from Ustaša camps, of which about 12,000 survived the war. However, there are other reports that the Ustaša regime systematically killed tens of thousands of Serbian children during the war in a senseless genocide. Many of these sources are the subject of debate among historians and demographers, and so far, we have not arrived at definitive answers regarding the final number of victims and their age and ethnic composition.

In addition to Serbs, Jews, Roma, communists, and anti-fascists suffered the same fate. All political opponents of the regime were cold-bloodedly imprisoned and killed. Thousands of Croatian anti-fascists and people who held the ideals of Yugoslav unity and togetherness close to their hearts were arrested, imprisoned, and exterminated in death camps.

The total number of Serbian victims of the Croatian fascist regime during World War II cannot be determined with certainty. Figures ranging from seven hundred thousand to over one million victims can be found in Yugoslav sources written in the years following the war. These initial numbers were later contested. More credible domestic and foreign sources and authors suggest that the number of victims was, in fact, lower. Some recent calculations indicate that between 300,000 and 350,000 Serbs were killed, but a comprehensive, individualized list of victims has never been completed.

On the website of the United States Holocaust Memorial Museum, the following estimate appears:

"The Croat authorities murdered between 320,000 and 340,000 ethnic Serb residents of Croatia and Bosnia during the period of Ustaša rule; more than 30,000 Croatian Jews were killed either in Croatia or at Auschwitz-Birkenau."[55]

In the Encyclopædia Britannica, we find the following information:

"The Ustaša planned to eliminate Croatia's Serb minority partly by conversion from Orthodoxy to Catholicism, partly by expulsion, and partly by extermination. As many as 350,000 to 450,000 victims were killed in Ustaša massacres and in the notorious concentration camp at Jasenovac."[56]

Yad Vashem, the Israeli state institution that commemorates the victims and heroes of the Holocaust on its website, has a document titled *Ustasa*. Among other things, it reads:

During their four years in power, the Ustasa carried out a Serb genocide, exterminating over 500,000, expelling 250,000, and forcing another 250,000 to convert to Catholicism. The Ustasa also killed most of Croatia's Jews, 20,000 Gypsies, and many thousands of their political enemies.[57]

Besides Croats, a segment of Bosnian Muslims also participated in the war on the side of the Ustaša and Nazis. The 13th Waffen Mountain Division of the SS *Handschar*, formed in 1943, was the most notorious for its brutality, savagery, and crimes against humanity committed mostly in northeastern Bosnia.

Reflecting on these shocking numbers raises certain questions. According to the cited sources, Croatian fascists and their accomplices killed, expelled, or forcibly converted to Catholicism at least half a million Serb civilians in present-day Croatia and Bosnia and Herzegovina between 1941

---

[55] "Jasenovac." *United States Holocaust Memorial Museum.* Accessed April 9th, 2023. *https://encyclopedia.ushmm.org/content/en/article/jasenovac.*
[56] "World War II." *Encyclopædia Britannica.* Accessed April 9th, 2023. *https://www.britannica.com/place/Croatia/World-War-II.*
[57] "Ustasa.". *Yad Vashem.* Accessed April 9th, 2023. *https://www.yadvashem.org/odot_pdf/Microsoft%20Word%20-%205904.pdf.*

and 1945. How is it that so few people worldwide are aware of these events today? Why does the international community lack knowledge about the genocide committed against Serbs during World War II? Why has this essential viewpoint remained unfamiliar? And yet, this very perspective represents a vital piece for achieving a more comprehensive understanding of the Yugoslav puzzle.

This now-forgotten fact explains one of the main reasons why ethnic Serbs in Croatia and Bosnia and Herzegovina, where they endured genocide during World War II, took up arms in the 1990s to prevent the dissolution of Yugoslavia.

Bosnian Muslim soldiers of the SS Handschar Division read a broshure about "Islam and Judaism", 1943.

They had a profound and historically grounded fear that mass extermination could happen to them again if they were cut off from their homeland.

Ironically, the legitimate fears of Serbs in Croatia and Bosnia and Herzegovina were exploited by the controversial political leadership in Belgrade. These people were used as pawns to achieve the aim of creating a state project which eventually failed. The regime provided false hopes to Croatian Serbs and deceived them. Ultimately, these people experienced mass exodus and expulsion to Serbia.

The Birth of the Resistance Movement in Occupied Yugoslavia

The Royalists

The fascist conquerors were surprised by the speed at which the Yugoslavs established organized resistance to the occupation. Just one month after military defeat, on May 13th, 1941, a general staff colonel, loyal to the state and his oath, placed the remnants of the defeated royal army under his command and declared the formation of the *Yugoslav Army in the Fatherland* (JVuO). His name was Dragoljub Mihailović. This military formation opted for guerrilla warfare and is better known as the *Chetniks*. Mihailović was a nationalist, royalist, and staunch anticommunist. He led the liberation movement in which over 90% of the fighters were ethnic Serbs. Initially, he was considered a hero and immediately received the support of the king and government in London, as well as America. However, the favor of the West turned away from him and his movement, for which he himself would bear a significant part of the responsibility.

General Dragoljub Mihailović, commander of the "Yugoslav Army in the Fatherland", better known as the "Chetniks".

The Communists

During a secret meeting of the Politburo of the Communist Party of Yugoslavia held on July 4th, 1941, in Belgrade, a capable operative of the Comintern, an influential and charismatic person and leader of the Party, made the decision to launch an armed uprising against the fascist occupiers. This man's real name was Josip Broz, but history will remember him as *Tito*, just one of the many names he used during his long illegal party work. After World War II, July 4th would be celebrated in Yugoslavia as one of the most important national holidays, called the Day of the Uprising of the People of Yugoslavia. Whether this is just a coincidence or whether Tito intentionally chose this day to begin the uprising, we will probably never know. But the fact is that July 4th is Independence Day in the United States, dedicated to liberation, revolution, and independence.

After the decision to launch armed resistance against the occupiers, Tito and the Communist Party of Yugoslavia called on all Yugoslavs to join the uprising. The response was great, and partisan units began to form in all parts of the country. In the days and weeks following July 4th, guerrilla warfare with the occupiers began in all parts of Yugoslavia, like a domino effect. This is how the legendary Tito's partisan movement was born. At that time, no one in the world thought that Yugoslav partisans would become the largest liberation movement in all of Europe by the end of the war.

Josip Broz Tito, wartime commander of the Yugoslav Partisans and leader of the communist revolution

The essential difference between the Chetniks and the Partisans was ideological and political. The royalists of Colonel Mihailović wanted to liberate the country and preserve its system as a centralist parliamentary monarchy with the Karadjordjević dynasty at the helm. Tito's partisans wanted the state to transform from a unitary monarchy into a federation of socialist republics with the Communist Party at the helm after liberation. It is clear that armed formations with such opposing goals must sooner or later engage in direct conflict with each other.

It is important to note that the irreconcilable concepts of centrifugal and centripetal political tendencies of the Yugoslavs resurfaced once again. This time, they were not in parliament, but among armed soldiers. The conflict between the two concepts and two irreconcilable ideologies soon escalated into a brutal civil war between the Chetniks and the Partisans, fought in parallel with the struggle against the Nazis and fascists.

The National Liberation Movement of Yugoslavia

In spite of all the challenges mentioned, the concept of Yugoslavia persisted in the hearts of many, even after the country's capitulation. This idea would bring together the South Slavs in a united fight against the occupiers, irrespective of their national identity. The endurance and power of this notion can be attributed to its innate, progressive, and humane nature. It served to unite and inspire people, offering them hope and fortitude. On the other hand, nationalism only fostered divisions and promoted an "us versus them" mentality, whereas the spirit of Yugoslavism encouraged integration.

Not all Croats found themselves on the side of the Ustaša. Although it seemed that in the event of an Axis Powers' victory in the war, the Independent State of Croatia (NDH) would fulfill the centuries-old dream of establishing an independent Croatian state, there were Croats who rejected Ustashism, its ideology, methods, and terror, and turned to anti-fascism. Similarly, many moral and courageous people opposed the quisling regimes that the Germans established in Serbia and Slovenia. To the surprise of the occupiers and their collaborators, peace lasted only a very short time. Just a few weeks had passed since the capitulation, and in the traditionally freedom-loving and rebellious territory of Serbia, two Yugoslav liberation movements were forming: the Chetniks and the Partisans.

Upon receiving the initial news from their homeland, King Peter II and the Yugoslav exile government in London were thrilled with the honorable military conduct of Colonel Dragoljub Mihailović and his organization of resistance against the occupation. He was soon officially appointed Minister of Defense and received various forms of support, as well as a promotion to the rank of general. Such actions by the Yugoslav government led to the recognition of the Chetnik movement by the Allies, Britain, and America.

With a monarchist orientation and Serbian nationalist undertones, the Chetnik movement would eventually succumb to political and ideological disorientation, wavering between abstaining from actions against the Nazis while "waiting for the Allies to arrive," and openly collaborating with the occupiers and quislings. Instead of fighting the occupiers, their focus largely shifted to killing Yugoslavs who held communist ideologies or practiced non-Orthodox faiths.

Tito's Partisan movement was communist and Yugoslav in nature, welcoming people of all faiths and nationalities without distinction. The integrative nature of the Partisan movement, combined with a well-defined political vision, would prove to be its key advantage.

Immediately following the call for an uprising by the Communist Party on July 4th, 1941, the first Partisan detachments were formed. This occurred less than three months after the capitulation, occupation, and disintegration of the country. It seemed that people were eagerly awaiting someone to organize and call them to fight.

A few days before the proclamation, on June 22nd, Croatian Partisans carried out their first act of sabotage near Zagreb by blowing up a railway line. In July and August, significant resistance was offered to the enemy in Serbia, where numerous Partisan units were formed. Good news spread quickly, and Partisan detachments began emerging in other parts of the country. This marked the birth of the People's Liberation Movement (NOP) of Yugoslavia, considered the most successful resistance movement in all of occupied Europe during World War II.

Why did this movement so quickly gain the sympathy of Yugoslavs? There are several reasons for this. First and foremost, one should consider the people's aspirations for freedom. The South Slavs are courageous people, prone to epic stories, heroism, and sacrifice. Their history typically records strong resistance to external pressure, attack, and injustice. The end of World War I brought freedom to all, and new enslavement by foreigners simply was not an option.

On the other hand, people were tired of divisions and disputes and disillusioned with their politicians and religious leaders. The population was resigned due to the way the Kingdom of Yugoslavia had fallen apart as a result of internal quarrels, betrayals, and poor policies.

This situation opened the door for a new paradigm, which was offered by Tito and the Communists. Its backbone was a vision of a new Yugoslavia based on national equality and the ideals of social justice. The proposed doctrine also included granting the status of constituent nations to Macedonians and Montenegrins, who had not held such a status before. As we know, the Kingdom of Yugoslavia recognized only Serbs, Croats, and Slovenes as its constituent nations. The only issue that remained was with the Bosniaks-Muslims, to whom Tito initially did not offer recognition of national status even though they wanted and sought it. However, equality was promised to everyone, including the numerically significant non-Slavic national minorities.

Tito knew how crucial the image of the Partisans would be for the initial success and popularization of the movement. The detachments were multiethnic, with complete interethnic equality and tolerance. Strict rules of ethics and morals were enforced. Initially, there was not much emphasis on the communist revolution. The focus was placed on the fight against the occupier, less on ideology. Over time, however, this would change. The result did not fail to materialize, and soon a strong emotional and ideological commitment of the fighters to the proclaimed vision of a new Yugoslavia became evident. The Partisans were highly disciplined, brave, dedicated, and successful in guerrilla warfare.

And so we come to an important fact. The Germans referred to both the Chetniks and the Partisans equally as "bandits." Soon, they issued a reward of one hundred thousand Reichsmarks in gold to anyone who could help capture or kill Tito or Mihailović. From this, it is clear that the German military command in Serbia initially perceived both movements as equally hostile and dangerous.

Serbs who initially joined the Partisans during the uprising in Serbia clearly did not have a problem with the fact that the leader of the movement, Tito, was a Croat. Therefore, we can conclude that these people were close to the ideas of the political left, or simply to Yugoslavism, and most likely to both. Starting from 1942, when the National Liberation Movement (NOP) shifted the focus of the struggle against the occupiers to Bosnia, we see that many Serbs from the territory of the Independent State of Croatia (NDH) also joined Tito, fleeing from the Ustaša pogroms.

Serbs who sided with General Mihailović were Serbian patriots, predominantly nationalists, and generally closer to the political right. They saw two evils in Tito: he was not only a Croat but also the leader of the communists. As previously mentioned, the

About the Uzice Republic

○ The Republic of Užice, 1941

First liberated territory in Europe during World War II was established by Yugoslav Partisans in cooperation with Chetniks in September 1941. The area was structured as a mini-state called the "Uzice Republic".

Its territory consisted of 15,000-20,000 square kilometers in western Serbia. In Uzice, the city that was the administrative center of the Republic, the newspaper Borba was printed and the pre-war weapons factory was restored. It was the only place in all of occupied Europe where weapons and ammunition were produced to fight against the Axis powers.

The factory still exists, producing ammunition, and proudly bears the wartime name *First Partisan*.

Communist Party was outlawed in the Kingdom of Yugoslavia. Since the king, government, and allies recognized Mihailović's movement at the beginning of the war as the official Yugoslav army in the homeland, this meant that military honor and the oath posed a serious principled obstacle to cooperation with the communists—opponents and destroyers of the monarchy.

Under the pressure of the Allied forces, military cooperation between the Chetniks and Partisans was established at the beginning of the war. However, the irreconcilable political rift soon led to their conflict, civil war, and deep divisions among the Serbs. Serbian Partisans and Serbian Chetniks began shooting at each other as early as the end of 1941. Without a doubt, it is clear that the Serbs wanted to preserve Yugoslavia, but they could not agree on what it would look like after the war. Unfortunately, instead of uniting to fight against the occupiers and collaborators, fratricidal bloodshed occurred, lasting throughout the entire war.

At the beginning of the war, very little was known about Tito, and his identity was merely a subject of speculation. The German offensive at the end of 1941, with significant casualties, crushed the Užice Republic—the first liberated territory in Europe. The remaining Partisan units and the Supreme Headquarters managed to avoid destruction and took refuge in the inaccessible regions of neighboring Bosnia. From that point on, the epicenter of the Partisan movement shifted from Serbia to other areas of Yugoslavia, and this situation would persist almost until the end of the war. History has recorded a steady increase in the number of Parti-

The famous photograph (1943) of the young Partisan Milja Toroman has become a kind of icon of the Yugoslav liberation movement

sans and even stronger and more effective resistance to the enemy. The result was the liberation of new territories, and for the Germans, an unexpectedly significant engagement of troops in occupied Yugoslavia.

Consequently, the Partisan struggle began to attract the attention and sympathy of the Allies. Churchill decided to send his military intelligence officers to Yugoslavia to gather information from the field. Missions were sent to both Tito and General Mihailović. Their goal was to collect accurate information from the Yugoslav battlefield and assess the effectiveness of the resistance movements. Through these missions, as well as some other sources of information, Churchill gradually became aware that the efforts of Tito's Partisans surpassed the results of the Chetniks. The most prominent British officers, who until recently were believed to have exerted a decisive influence on Churchill to withdraw support from General Mihailović and fully turn to Tito, were Fitzroy Maclean, William Deakin, and Randolph Churchill, the only son of the United Kingdom's Prime Minister himself. Their influence is unquestionable. However, the decisive source of information came from the Germans themselves. So, what was this source of information?

In early July 1941, a British team led by mathematician and father of theoretical computer science Alan Turing managed to decode the German communication encryption machine *Enigma*. Although the Nazis believed their flow of information, war reports, and orders were completely secure, the British actually knew everything. According to some estimates, this achievement shortened the duration of the war by about two years and saved around fourteen million lives. However, Britain kept the secret of its information warfare heroes for several more decades.

By combining information from the field, which he received from his intelligence officers, and intercepted German communications, Churchill was able to piece together a very accurate picture. After the war, he stated that Tito and his Partisans were a "much more efficient and reliable ally in the war against Germany." By the fall of 1943, he decided to withdraw support for General Mihailović's monarchists and fully turn to Tito. From then on, the Partisans received significant assistance from the Allies in weapons, food, and equipment.

Although based on intelligence reports, this decision still seems somewhat enigmatic to this day. The Yugoslav king and government were in London and enjoyed British hospitality. The royal family had close and familial ties to the British crown. As expected, they pressured Churchill for Britain to continue supporting the monarchist option and Mihailović. Why did Churchill take a risk with the communists? Why did he turn his back on the young King Peter II and the Yugoslav government in exile? Why wasn't there any pressure applied to the Chetniks to concentrate on battling the Germans, Italians, and Ustašas decisively, rather than engaging in confrontations with the communists and Partisans?

Upon arriving at the Supreme Headquarters of the National Liberation Movement, British intelligence officer and Churchill's envoy Fitzroy Maclean held a conversation with the supreme commander of the Partisans, inquiring about Tito's views on many important issues. At the end of the conversation, probably with some hesitation, he asked whether Yugoslavia would become part of the Soviet Union after the war. Tito's response was a clear signal. In his book of war memories, he recounts the most interesting part of this conversation with Tito:

> "And will your new Yugoslavia be an independent State or part of the Soviet Union?' I asked. He did not answer immediately. Then: 'You must remember,' he said, 'the sacrifices which we are making in this struggle for our independence. Hundreds of thousands of Yugoslavs have suffered torture and death—men, women and children. Vast areas of our countryside have been laid waste. *You need not suppose that we shall lightly cast aside a prize which has been won at such cost.*"[58]

At the Tehran Conference in November 1943, Churchill informed Stalin of his intention to support Tito and the National Liberation Movement. He likely took satisfaction in witnessing the surprise and approval on Stalin's face as Britain committed to supporting the communists in Yugoslavia. However, all indications suggest that the legendary master of political games already knew at that moment that Tito would break ties with the USSR after the war and choose a different path for his country.

Marshal Tito (left) with representatives of the British military mission (1944). Brigadier Fitzroy Maclean stands in the middle.

For the sake of objectivity, it is necessary to look at the prevailing narrative in post-war Yugoslavia about the Partisans as liberators and the Chetniks as traitors and collaborators. History is written by the victors, and things were not black and white. The Partisans had their dark moments, one of the most controversial being in March 1943 when they entered into direct negotiations with the Germans. The negotiations took place during the Battle of Neretva, which was elevated to the level of myth in Yugoslavia, and a super-spectacle film about it was made in 1969 starring American actor Yul Brynner. However, not everything in the film is shown in

---

[58] Fitzroy Maclean, *Eastern Approaches: The Memoirs of the Original British Action Hero*, Penguin, UK, 2009.

accordance with the facts. The goal of the negotiations, conducted at a very high level, was to achieve an unofficial ceasefire that would allow the Partisan units to definitively deal with the Chetniks. The culmination of the negotiations took place in Zagreb on March 23rd and 24th, and the Partisan delegation consisted of Koča Popović, Milovan Djilas, and Vladimir Velebit. After returning from Zagreb, Velebit's surprising words were recorded, which in themselves speak volumes about the essence of the conflict between the Chetniks and Partisans. This conflict was conceptual and ideological, but also reflected the Comintern's stance that Yugoslavia was actually a project of Greater Serbia:

> "With our National Liberation Movement, we strive to create a free Yugoslavia in which all Slavic tribes will have all rights and where the Serbs will not rule alone. Therefore, in the national Chetnik movement, we see our biggest and most dangerous enemy since they aim to create Greater Serbia and push us out. Under such circumstances, we no longer have any reason to fight against the German army or to cause damage to German interests throughout the country, be they military or economic in nature. We only need to be given the opportunity to fight against the Chetniks in order to destroy them."[59]

The scope of these negotiations and the achieved unofficial ceasefire, which is estimated to have lasted about six weeks, was extremely limited but purposeful. It seems that both the Partisans and local German generals were content with a break, but Hitler personally ordered the termination of the negotiations. Taking advantage of the brief easing of German pressure, the Partisans succeeded in their goal of militarily defeating the bulk of Chetnik units in Eastern Herzegovina. This defeat was probably the most significant for the Chetniks during the entire war, and it marked the beginning of their decline.

On the list of crimes of Tito's movement, we must also include the mass killings of civilians at the beginning of the war, in late 1941 and early 1942, in Montenegro and Eastern Herzegovina. Radical leftist elements arbitrarily and brutally killed villagers whom they suspected of belonging to the "class enemy" or the "fifth column" that could join the Chetniks. These were people who did not accept Bolshevik ideology or were often wealthier peasants killed for the sake of plunder.

Far worse and much more massive crimes were committed by the Partisans during the purges of 1944 and 1945 when the killing of "class enemies" or "enemies of the people" continued without trials and with sum-

---

[59] Nikolić, Kosta. *Istorija Ravnogorskog pokreta. Vol. I.* Beograd: ZUNS, 2014, 553.

mary procedures. The communists targeted the upper, middle, and bourgeois classes, intellectuals, wealthier peasants and landowners, businessmen, as well as members of the German and Italian national minorities. After the mass killings, the victims were thrown into numerous pits throughout Yugoslavia, and their locations became a state secret by order of the Ministry of Interior Affairs in May 1945. Like at the beginning of the war, during this wave of senseless "red terror," killings were motivated in many cases by the base self-interest of the then powerful individuals or by denunciations of innocent people for personal gain, for which there is ample evidence.

The number of victims is terrifying. In 2009, the Ministry of Justice of the Republic of Serbia formed a special *Commission for Secret Graves of those killed after September 12th, 1944*[60], which has so far compiled a list of 60,000 victims in Serbia alone, but it is believed that the total number in this republic is around 75,000. For the entire territory of Yugoslavia, there are no accurate data, but according to Serbian historian Srdjan Cvetković[61], the closest estimate, which agrees with newer research of archival materials, has been provided by Swiss historian Michael Portmann. He believes that the number of victims of communist purges in Yugoslavia, up until 1950, is around 180,000. It is sad, tragic, and a warning. May these shocking figures serve as a contribution to a better understanding of the Yugoslav puzzle.

---

[60] Otvorena knjiga. *http://www.otvorenaknjiga.komisija1944.mpravde.gov.rs/cr/*. Accessed April 14th, 2023.
[61] Cvetković, Dr Srdjan. *Represija komunističkog režima u Srbiji na kraju Drugog svetskog rata sa osvrtom na evropsko iskustvo*. In Zbornik radova "1945. Kraj ili novi početak?,"p.66. Beograd: INIS, MŽG, 2016.

THE SECOND YUGOSLAVIA

AVNOJ 1943

Around the same time as the Tehran Conference that laid the foundations for post-war Europe, the historical Second Conference of AVNOJ—
Antifascist Council for the National Liberation of Yugoslavia—was held
on November 29th, 1943, in the small Bosnian town of Jajce. This assembly
was led by Tito and the Communist Party, with the goal of establishing the
foundations for a New Yugoslavia according to the communists' desires.
The essential political transformation entailed the country becoming a
democratic federal union of five nations—Serbs, Croats, Slovenes, Macedonians, and Montenegrins—and six republics—Serbia, Croatia, Slovenia,
Macedonia, Montenegro, and Bosnia and Herzegovina. The possibility to
arrange the state again as a monarchy was rejected, and a decision was
made to ban the king and members of his family from returning to the
country. It was also planned that
AVNOJ's decisions would be confirmed by a nationwide referendum to
be organized after the end of the war.

From a unitary kingdom with administrative regions, Yugoslavia was to
transform into a federation of republics, where the aspirations of Croats
and Slovenes for establishing their own
states would be satisfied by gaining
federal units. It is of great importance
that the decisions of AVNOJ in Jajce in
1943 brought a promise of national
recognition for Macedonians and Montenegrins, so that they, together with
Serbs, Croats, and Slovenes, would
become *constituent* nations of the future Yugoslav Federation. All these
changes, it was believed, would solve

Tito during the AVNOJ assembly,
on November 29th, 1943, when the
groundwork for the New Yugoslavia
was established

the problems manifested in the unhappy kingdom and bring much-desired
internal peace and harmony to all Yugoslavs.

From that moment on, AVNOJ established itself as the de facto decisive
political authority in the country, which would soon be recognized by external factors as well. News of AVNOJ's decisions quickly reverberated
throughout the war-torn country. They sparked hope that Tito's movement
was fighting not only against the Nazis but also for a more just and pros-

perous Yugoslavia. Many saw in these decisions Tito's determined intention to confront the burden of interethnic issues inherited from the kingdom era. Following the described events, the popularity of the national liberation movement grew even more rapidly. Many people joined the Partisans, who would soon become a significant military force.

Almost all researchers of the World War II period agree that 1943 was a turning point. The tide of war suddenly turned against Nazi Germany due to the colossal defeat at Stalingrad. The German attack came too late and was halted by the heroic defense of the Red Army, aided by the harsh Russian winter.

There is also a Serbian contribution to this sequence of events worth mentioning. The beginning and course of *Operation Barbarossa*—the German attack on the Soviet Union—were influenced by Hitler's unplanned assault on Yugoslavia (and Greece) on April 6th, 1941. By massively rejecting the Tripartite Pact with the Axis powers, the Serbs not only complicated Operation Barbarossa but also, through their uprising and resistance in the Partisan and Chetnik movements during 1941 and 1942, engaged far more enemy troops in Yugoslavia than the Germans had ever planned. Undoubtedly, this weakened Germany on the Soviet and other fronts, contributing to its debacle in 1943.

The Military and Political Defeat of General Mihailović

The expansion of the Partisan movement and the support of the Allies led to further wartime successes and an increase in Tito's popularity. At the same time, the Chetniks suffered severe defeats by the Partisans and began openly collaborating with the Germans. After several of Churchill's demands to the Yugoslav government and king to pressure Mihailović to turn his forces against the Germans rather than killing his compatriots, King Peter II eventually dismissed the general and withdrew support by the end of the summer of 1944. A message was broadcast from London, urging all Yugoslavs to "join the People's Liberation Army under the leadership of Marshal Tito." As a result, many Chetnik fighters left their units, and a significant number joined the Partisans in the second half of 1944 and 1945. However, such a move by the young king failed to persuade Tito to change his decision on banning the return of the royal family to the country.

Defeated and abandoned, the leader of the Chetnik movement, General Dragoljub "Draža" Mihailović, hid with a handful of his most loyal followers in Bosnia until 1946, when he was captured by the new Yugoslav authorities and brought to trial. Western countries largely condemned the trial as a biased political process, which was, to a significant extent, true. General Mihailović was found guilty and sentenced to death by firing squad for treason, war crimes, and collaboration with the enemy. The location of his burial remains unknown to this day.

In the United States, this news was received negatively for a reason that

The Trial of General Dragoljub Mihailović.
Belgrade, 1946.

was little known until recently. General Mihailović's fighters successfully participated in the most extensive rescue mission of American airmen in history. During 1944, Allied squadrons took off from Italy to bomb oil fields in Romania, and many planes were hit by German anti-aircraft defenses. Some crashed immediately, while others managed to reach the airspace above Serbia, which was under Chetnik control, despite being damaged. There, the airmen parachuted out, and soldiers and locals from nearby villages took them in, hid, fed, and treated them. Once rescued and refreshed, they were transported by Allied planes from an improvised airfield in the village of Pranjani to Italy to fly again. The total number of evacuated airmen from Chetnik territory was 417, and the operation was codenamed *Halyard*, as described in the book *The Forgotten 500* by Gregory Freeman[62]. As a result, America felt a deep gratitude and disapproved of the Chetnik commander being sentenced to death as a traitor, enemy of the people, and collaborator.

President Truman posthumously awarded General Mihailović the *Legion of Merit* in 1948, but the State Department classified this fact as confidential. America did not want to offend Tito, the side in Yugoslavia to which the Allies had turned after 1943. It was not until 2005 that the deco-

---

[62] Freeman, Gregory A. 2017. *The Forgotten 500: The Untold Story of the Men Who Risked All for the Greatest Rescue Mission of World War II*. New York: Nal Caliber.

ration was officially presented to the general's daughter Gordana Mihailović. His grandson, Vojislav Mihailović, initiated the rehabilitation process for the general before the High Court in Belgrade in 2012. Despite numerous objections and criticisms from both the region and Serbia itself, Dragoljub "Draža" Mihailović was rehabilitated by the court's decision in 2015. The decision was met with approval by a segment of the Serbian public, who see the general as an anti-fascist and anti-communist.

Taking into account all available information, it seems that General Mihailović was unable to successfully cope with the complex historical challenges. He was indecisive and did not act in accordance with the aspirations of the majority of Yugoslavs. He was exclusively focused on defending a unitary and monarchical Yugoslavia. He oscillated between opposing the occupiers and openly collaborating with them. He flirted with the Allies in an attempt to regain their support while simultaneously cooperating with the Germans. He also collaborated with the Ustaša in the fight against the Partisans. He believed that the Communists posed a greater threat to Yugoslavia than the Nazis. He worked towards creating an ethnically pure Serbian territory within

A group of Chetniks pose
with German soldiers

Yugoslavia. His units committed a large number of brutal murders and ethnic cleansing of Bosniaks, Croats, and populations sympathetic to Tito's movement. History has not definitively established the total number of victims, but estimates suggest tens of thousands were killed. They were ruthless towards the Partisans: killing prisoners, the wounded, and medical personnel in field hospitals or refugee camps. Numerous cases of looting and theft committed against completely innocent civilians without any reasonable justification were recorded. There were also instances of mass killings of Serbian populations due to their allegiance to the Partisan movement. The largest in a series of such massacres in several villages near Belgrade took place in the village of Vranić on the night of December 20th/21st, 1943, when sixty-seven civilians were brutally killed, including a six-year-old girl and a one-year-old child who was murdered in its cradle.

Additionally, it is an important fact that as the supreme commander, General Mihailović failed to establish complete military discipline and effective control over all Chetnik units, which often acted independently and without his consent, particularly in Bosnia and Croatia. This further deepened his reputation as an unreliable ally.

220

Unfortunately, it cannot be said that the military actions of the Chetniks had a Yugoslav character despite the official name of the movement as the *Yugoslav Army in the Homeland*. It was a military formation that ideologically operated from the position of the right-wing and the platform of creating an ethnically pure Greater Serbia within a unitary-monarchical Yugoslavia. It often sought to achieve its goals through ethnic cleansing of non-Serbian populations and the physical extermination of political opponents. The Chetniks' fight against the occupiers undoubtedly existed, but it was neither convincing nor unambiguous. For the majority of the time, collaboration with the occupier was present.

The Yugoslav idea is emancipatory and integrative, and according to the prevailing opinion of the time, it is also evolutionary. The Communists understood this well and, by embracing tens of thousands of mainly Serbian victims who were fleeing from the Ustaša pogrom, secured mass support. On the other hand, the political platform of the Chetnik movement contained elements of nationalism and chauvinism and did not reflect the aspirations of the majority of Yugoslav peoples. The Chetnik ideology would be paradoxically invoked once again nearly five decades later. Like an evil spirit from a bottle, it would be revived by the very force that defeated it in World War II. In a disguised form, it would be summoned and used by the communist rulers of Yugoslavia, whose time, after the fall of the Berlin Wall, was rapidly running out.

Tito Assumes Power

The Yugoslav Partisans' guerrilla movement transformed into the People's Liberation Army of Yugoslavia, which, either independently or in collaboration with the Soviet Red Army, managed to liberate most of the country by the close of 1944. As the war came to an end, Marshal Tito commanded approximately 800,000 fighters, making it one of the largest armies in Europe at that time.

Parallel to his military successes, Tito fought for international political recognition of the Yugoslav people's efforts in liberating their country from the occupiers and creating a different state. He enjoyed the support of Britain, the United States, and the USSR, who prioritized the fight against the Nazis over ideology and politics. The Allies recognized that Tito would play a crucial role in post-war Yugoslavia and that the monarchy had lost the support of the people. Winston Churchill exerted immense pressure on the young King Peter II to be cooperative and accept the reality. Indeed, by dismissing General Mihailović and calling on the people to join Tito's army, the king demonstrated flexibility.

Marshal Tito and Winston Churchill in Naples, Italy. August 12th, 1944.

Further efforts of British diplomacy were directed towards the creation of a coalition government consisting of the de facto and de jure representatives: Tito's National Committee for the Liberation of Yugoslavia (NKOJ) and the Yugoslav government in exile. With the king's consent and the support of the Allies, such a government was formed at the end of 1944, and Tito held the majority. In doing so, he not only gained control over the course of future events but also acquired international recognition and legitimacy.

The first post-war Yugoslav elections were held on November 11th, 1945. The main favorite was the People's Front, composed mostly of communists and members of some other movements and parties that supported the partisans. Tito and the Communist Party of Yugoslavia enjoyed strong support from citizens due to their undeniable success in the war against the German occupiers and their supporters. However, Tito's popularity had already reached cult-like proportions at that time. Encouraged by this position, he took the liberty to clearly express his opinion in early 1945 that the multiparty system desired by the West in Yugoslavia would not be allowed:

> "I am not against political parties in principle because democracy also assumes the freedom to express one's principles and ideas. But to create parties for the sake of parties, now when all of us, as one, must direct all our strength towards expelling the occupying forces from our country, when the homeland is leveled to the ground, when we have nothing but our consciousness and our hands (...) we have no time for that now. And here is the people's movement. Everyone is welcome in it, both communists and those who were democrats and radicals, etc., whatever they were called before. This movement is the force, the only force that can now pull our country out of this horror and misery and lead it to complete freedom."

> Prime Minister Josip Broz Tito, January 1945.

Pre-war political parties were re-established and participated in the elections, but they did not achieve significant results. The People's Front won a convincing victory.

However, it must be emphasized that the elections were held in an undemocratic atmosphere, with intimidation of voters and opposition leaders. Voting was conducted by inserting rubber balls into ballot boxes, which produced sound and allowed state security agents to accurately identify people who did not vote for Tito's People's Front. On the other hand, Tito's contribution to the war and the radical political changes he advocated in Yugoslavia gained the support of the majority of voters. People were disappointed with the fruitless politicking of the quarreling pre-war parties, which could not resolve Yugoslav problems, and they wanted to believe that there was something new and better.

After winning more than 85% of the votes, Tito no longer had any obstacles to achieving his political goals. A Constituent Assembly was convened, with a mandate to carry out a fundamental transformation of Yugoslavia. On the second anniversary of the historic session of the Anti-Fascist Council for the National Liberation of Yugoslavia (AVNOJ), on November 29th, 1945, all its decisions were confirmed. The monarchy was formally abolished, and the state was declared a republic. Here is the original text of the decisions:

I

The Democratic Federal Yugoslavia is declared
a people's republic under the name
FEDERAL PEOPLE'S REPUBLIC OF YUGOSLAVIA.
The FEDERAL PEOPLE'S REPUBLIC OF YUGOSLAVIA is a
federal people's state of a republican form, a community of equal
nations that have freely expressed their will to remain united in
Yugoslavia.

II

With this decision, the monarchy in Yugoslavia is finally abolished
on behalf of all the peoples of Yugoslavia, and Peter II Karadjordjević, along with the entire Karadjordjević dynasty, is deprived
of all rights that belonged to him and the Karadjordjević dynasty.

Given in Belgrade,
the capital of the
Federal People's Republic of Yugoslavia
November 29th, 1945

It is important to note that up until the Constitutional Assembly on November 29th, 1945, the country was called the *Democratic Federal Yugoslavia* (DFJ). This name was established by the transitional coalition government. Two months later, on January 31st, 1946, the first constitution of
post-war Yugoslavia was adopted. The state was defined as a federation of
six republics: Serbia, Croatia, Slovenia, Montenegro, Macedonia, and Bosnia and Herzegovina. However, instead of six flames representing the republics, the state coat of arms had only five flames, which merged into
one. This was because the flames did not represent the republics, but rather
the constituent peoples of Yugoslavia: Serbs, Croats, Slovenes, Macedonians, and Montenegrins.

Until 1963, the coat of arms of Yugoslavia had five flames, one for each constituent people. Later, a sixth flame was added to the coat of arms, and its symbolism was aligned with constitutional changes.

Muslims—Bosniaks—still remained unrecognized as a nation, contrary to their feelings and aspirations. The resolution of this group's national question was left for some future time. Gradually, this process began during the 1960s and was definitively legally concluded in 1971. During that period, Muslims (with a capital M—"Muslimani") would be recognized as the sixth Yugoslav nation. After the adoption of the new Constitution in 1963, the redesigned coat of arms of Yugoslavia, with six torches symbolizing six constituent peoples and six united republics, came into use. During the disintegration of Yugoslavia in a bloody civil war, a group of intellectuals and political leaders decided in 1993 to change the name of their nation from Muslims to *Bosniaks*. Today, in 2023, Bosniaks constitute slightly over 50% of the population in Bosnia and Herzegovina, and they also live in significant numbers in Serbia and Montenegro. [63]

---

[63] In Serbo-Croatian language, the names of religious groups are not capitalized, while the names of ethnic groups are. Therefore, the capitalization of the letter "M" in the term "Muslimani" indicates the recognition of a new *ethnicity* that was previously only recognized as a religious group.

The Socialist Yugoslavia (1945–1991)

Reconstruction of the Country
and the Phenomenon of Youth Work Actions (ORA)

"Builder of a New Life"

Tito's anti-fascist movement ushered in a significant transformation for the Yugoslav people. The struggling monarchy, weighed down by internal strife and conflicts, evolved into a nation filled with hope that the new society—emerging from the shadows of the recently concluded war—would promote justice and equality. It seemed that solutions had been found that satisfied the unfulfilled aspirations of many Yugoslavs under the monarchy. The vision of a comprehensive reconstruction and rebuilding of the country, in the spirit of socialism and under the strong leadership of the charismatic war hero Marshal Tito, won the sympathies of a large number of people.

Reconstruction of the war-ravaged country began immediately. However, the turbulent post-war period also brought numerous negative phenomena. Massive nationalization was implemented, accompanied by indiscriminate and brutal repression of political opponents, members of civil society stratum, capitalists, landowners, and clergy, often through summary proceedings. A large number of people had their property, land, honor, dignity, and sometimes even their lives taken away. Unfortunately, the early years of Tito's rule bore too much resemblance to Bolshevism. There were numerous cases of terror, injustice, and arrogant behavior by the new ruling class composed of former partisans and communists who rapidly occupied positions of power and violently seized property from the former elite.

Despite the tragedy that befell tens of thousands of people from the former middle and upper classes with the arrival of the communists, a completely different process was taking place in parallel. A large number of residents selflessly and dedicatedly participated in public works initiated by the new government to rebuild the war-devastated country. During this period, a new phenomenon emerged that would gain immense popularity in socialist Yugoslavia. It was called the "Youth work action" (ORA). Many young people enthusiastically responded to the call of the new authorities to participate in building a brighter future for themselves. The goal of this voluntary work was the reconstruction and development of the economy, infrastructure, sports, cultural and scientific facilities, and sometimes even entire new cities were built. It is estimated that millions of Yugoslavs were part of youth work brigades between 1945 and 1980.

Youth work actions continued even after the initial reconstruction of the

The youth work brigade from Jesenice in Slovenia, during the construction of the sports stadium in the town of Ravne in the region of Slovenian Carinthia (1962).

country. Over time, they increasingly played the role of a powerful instrument of the regime for influencing younger generations. They were considered a potent factor of cohesion and strengthening feelings of love, pride, and belonging to the Yugoslav nation. Therefore, the authorities supported the narrative that it was an honor and a kind of moral duty to participate in work actions. On the other hand, large voluntary public works were an ideal place for young people to meet peers from all over the country, various ethnic groups and traditions, as well as different dialects. Motivated by the vision of a happier future that the regime generously encouraged with propaganda and ideological indoctrination, and carried away by the enthusiasm of youth, thousands of young men and women selflessly built the country with hands calloused from blisters.

It was easy to fall in love with someone who shared the same vision and made the same sacrifice by participating in a work action. Romances were frequent, and an important factor in their popularity. Many love relationships that began during work actions resulted in inter-ethnic marriages. It was believed that generations born from these unions would become the nucleus of a new paradigm—the Yugoslav supranation. What King Alexander had failed to achieve seemed to be succeeding for the communists. In those years, it appeared that many young people were embracing Yugoslavism and were on the path to creating a new nation. Previously rooted in their ethnic affiliation, Serbs, Croats, Slovenes, Macedonians, Muslims, and Montenegrins were now more frequently and more openly entering into inter-ethnic marriages. And what would be the national identity of a child born from a marriage between, for instance, a Serbian father and a Croatian mother? Or a Slovenian father and a Muslim mother? As these children grew up, they would likely identify themselves as Yugoslavs. Youth work actions were frequently referred to as the "forge of brotherhood and unity among the peoples of Yugoslavia."

And that is why this phenomenon played an important role in the constant increase of people who disregarded the previous ethnic-religious paradigm and simply identified as Yugoslavs. The new nation was growing. However, time would show that its numbers would never reach the much-needed critical mass.

Tito-Stalin Conflict and Break With the USSR

In previous sections, we highlighted the fact that, as early as 1943, Tito clearly indicated to British intelligence officer Fitzroy Maclean that Yugoslavia would not easily give up its freedom and would not become part of the Soviet Union. Tito was the only leader of the Eastern Bloc countries who could boast of having liberated his country from the Nazis and fascists primarily on his own, with the help of the Red Army only arriving towards the very end of the war. He acted independently and made decisions without prior consultation with Moscow. Even during the war, there was tension between him and Stalin, but relations between the two countries were maintained at a good level, mostly through the efforts of the Yugoslav side.

Tito was becoming an increasingly powerful political figure and did not hesitate to boldly defend Yugoslavia's interests. As a result of territorial disagreements with neighboring Italy over the city of Trieste, which Yugoslav partisans had liberated from the Nazis and then annexed to Yugoslavia, Tito came into conflict with the West in 1947. Somewhat surprisingly from today's perspective, Stalin did not side with Yugoslavia. Tito remained completely alone but determined not to give in. The resolution came with the agreement on the division of the so-called Free Territory of Trieste between Italy and Yugoslavia in 1954.

Although it was previously believed that the root of the conflict be tween Tito and Stalin was of an ideological nature, today's findings reveal much deeper layers of political and strategic reasons. Tito wanted to revive the centuries-old idea of a Balkan federation. This political project envisaged the unification of Yugoslavia, Albania, and Bulgaria into a single federal state. In an effort to attract Greece to this project, Tito actively supported communist forces during the civil war in that country.

There were many potential benefits that the Balkan federation could bring to the participating countries from a long-term perspective. Yugoslavia would relax territorial disputes with Bulgaria over Macedonia and with Albania over Kosovo. With the eventual inclusion of Greece, a new bloc would be created in the geopolitically highly important area of the Balkans, stretching from the Alps in the West, across the Adriatic, Ionian, and Aegean seas, all the way to the Bosporus and the Black Sea. Of course, Marshal Tito saw himself as the leader of such a federation, and Moscow understood not only that it would not have the final say in it, but that over time, it would likely lose its influence in Bulgaria as well.

It is clear that such a scenario was completely unacceptable to the powerful Stalin. Not only because of the personal conflict he had with the "rebellious" Tito, but also because of the obligations he had undertaken in negotiations with the West regarding the division of spheres of influence in Europe after World War II. At this point, let us recall the very interesting and officially informal "percentages agreement" that Stalin reached with Churchill in October 1944. In this agreement, the division of influence in the countries of Eastern and Southern Europe between the USSR and the Western powers is defined in percentages. On a small piece of paper, Churchill proposed the following ratios of influence to Stalin:

- Romania: 90% Russian, 10% Western
- Greece: 90% Western, 10% Russian
- **Yugoslavia** and Hungary: **50% – 50%**
- Bulgaria: 75% Russian, 25% Western

The outcome of subsequent discussions led to adjustments in the Soviet influence percentages, with Bulgaria and Hungary now set at 80 percent and Romania at 100 percent.

229

It should be noted that Churchill, probably intentionally, did not write "USSR" but "Russia" on the paper. Stalin agreed by "ticking" Churchill's proposal, which can be clearly seen in the upper right corner of the paper.

In accordance with this agreement, 90% of Greece was allocated to the Western sphere of interest, potentially explaining why Stalin did not support Tito's efforts to secure a communist victory in the Greek Civil War and subsequently incorporate Greece into the ambitious Balkan Federation project. At that time, the Soviet Union was likely hesitant to breach the agreement and risk open confrontation with the West. Meanwhile, Tito's clear ambitions and capacity to become a major player in the geopolitically sensitive area raised suspicions among both Moscow and Western power centers.

The West certainly could not

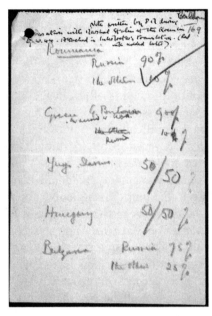

"The Percentages Agreement"

This document, housed in The National Archives, UK, depicts Winston Churchill and Joseph Stalin's division of future spheres of influence in Eastern and Southern Europe between the Western powers and the USSR in October 1944, towards the conclusion of World War II.

look favorably on the possibility of creating such a large bloc that would occupy the entire strategically important Balkan Peninsula under the leadership of the persistent and daring communist Tito. On the other hand, they desired a schism in the Belgrade-Moscow relationship and, of course, had an interest in supporting such a scenario. After all, Tito had hinted at this scenario to the West in 1943 and kept his promise, though again, in his own unpredictable style.

Possibly counting on Western sympathies towards him, Tito decided to work swiftly towards his goal. In Albania, he already had a dominant influence. He met with Bulgarian leader Georgi Dimitrov several times to lay the groundwork for uniting the two countries. These efforts culminated in the signing of a formal document, the so-called Bled Agreement, between Yugoslavia and Bulgaria in 1947, which marked the first step towards creating the Balkan Federation. As expected, the counterstrike did not come from the West.

Towards the end of 1947 and the beginning of 1948, Stalin intensified pressure on Yugoslavia, threatening economic sanctions. With the Cominform Resolution on June 28th, 1948, Yugoslavia was expelled from the organization, accompanied by excommunication and the severing of diplomatic relations, first with the Soviet Union and then with other Eastern Bloc countries. Yugoslavia faced a blockade and severe economic sanctions. The Warsaw Pact dangerously amassed troops near the Yugoslav borders, conducting threatening maneuvers. Soviet media accused Tito and the Communist Party of Yugoslavia of ideological apostasy and other evils. Border incidents in which Yugoslav soldiers lost their lives became a frequent occurrence.

Tito vs. Stalin

Some sources claim that Tito was the only man to stand up to Stalin and survive. It is believed that the Soviets, angered and frustrated by Tito's behavior, attempted to assassinate him twenty-two times. In this context, there is testimony about a letter, now in the NKVD archives, that Tito sent to Stalin in 1950. With a touch of bold humor, Tito writes:

"Comrade Stalin, stop sending your agents to Yugoslavia with the task to kill me. We have already captured seven of your men (...). If this does not stop, I will be forced to send one man to Moscow, and if I do so, there will be no need to send the next one."

(From the book, *The Unknown Stalin*, Roy Medvedev, Zhores Medvedev, NNK International, Belgrade, 2012)

Following the joint action of the USSR and its satellites against Yugoslavia, negotiations on the Balkan Federation came to a halt. Former interlocutors drastically changed their behavior. Bulgaria expressed territorial claims towards Macedonia, and Albania towards Kosovo. A military invasion by Warsaw Pact countries into Yugoslavia was expected at any moment, and the Yugoslav army was on high alert. The situation was further exacerbated by a severe drought in 1950.

Tito turned to the West for support, and the United States was the first to provide assistance through food donations and significant arms deliveries. Britain and France later joined the United States in their efforts to preserve Yugoslavia's independence. The anticipated Soviet intervention never materialized, promp-ting Tito to initiate a brutal purge of pro-Soviet elements—individuals who openly supported the Cominform resolution against Yugoslavia—within the Communist Party, the army, intelligence services, and society at large. These purges resulted in numerous casualties.

Regrettably, the purges also implicated people who had no connections to the Soviets, often due to rampant paranoia or personal vendettas. The regime seized this opportunity to settle scores with various political dissenters. The majority of those arrested were sent to "reeducation" on the barren, rocky Adriatic island of Goli Otok, where they were subjected to brutal treatment until they renounced their pro-Soviet ideas. Tragically, many never returned from the Goli Otok camp.

Yugoslavia became a buffer zone between NATO and the Warsaw Pact, with troops from both blocs stationed along its borders. Tito maintained a neutral course and sought to benefit from the resulting situation. A decade later, he would go even further by dedicating himself to the creation of the Non-Aligned Movement, a broad international initiative aimed at avoiding participation in the bloc-based division of the world. He would serve as its lifelong honorary leader.

Following Stalin's death in 1953, the Soviets changed their tactics. They decided it was in their best interest to reconcile with Tito. Nikita Khrushchev condemned the previous policy, apologized to Yugoslavia, and visited Belgrade officially in 1955. Although diplomatic relations were formally restored and the overall atmosphere somewhat improved, Yugoslavia maintained a noticeable degree of mistrust and restraint toward the USSR at all times.

After Stalin's death, the new leader of the USSR, Nikita Khrushchev, changed course toward Yugoslavia and officially visited in 1955 with an apology and a desire to restore relations between the two countries. During this visit, Marshal Tito was very reserved. The body language of the two statesmen eloquently depicts the dynamic between them.

A careful reader will not miss the connection between Churchill's unexpected decision in 1943 to support the communists instead of the royalists in Yugoslavia, and Tito's subsequent break with Stalin, which occurred just five years later. Given that Tito had clearly indicated to Fitzroy Maclean that he would extricate himself from the Soviet embrace after the war, all signs point to him simply keeping his promise.

But was there more to it? Was Tito inclined to the West and protecting its interests? This bold assumption lacks direct evidence, but we cannot dismiss the possibility that declassifying certain documents in the future may reveal such a surprising truth. However, through indirect observation, one can notice a constant thread in Tito's political actions that could suggest Yugoslavia was a closer friend to the West than the East:

- Rejecting the Tripartite Pact between Yugoslavia and the Axis powers and the military coup involving British intelligence services and Tito's Communist Party of Yugoslavia led to the Nazi attack on Yugoslavia, unplanned German troop engagement, and the delay of the attack on the USSR.
- Britain's denial of support to General Mihailović's royalist Yugoslav Army in the Homeland (JVuO), British backing of Tito and the Partisans, and pressure on the Americans to do the same.
- British pressure on young King Peter II to dismiss Mihailović and call on Yugoslavs to join Tito.
- Tito's post-World War II transformation of Yugoslavia aimed to prevent Serbian domination within the country. The Communist Party labeled Serbs as a hegemonic people and divided them into three republics and two autonomous provinces through a change in the state system. This policy was unofficially called "weak Serbia— strong Yugoslavia." The traditional British stance perceives the Serbs as local hegemons and potential Russian satellites. As such, Tito's policy toward Serbia can be viewed as consistent with broader British (and Western in general) geopolitical efforts to push Russia out of the Balkans, which include attempts to weaken and fragment the Serbs.
- Tito met with Winston Churchill on several occasions. During the war, Churchill's son Randolph stayed at Tito's headquarters, a significant risk due to frequent German attacks. Tito met with Queen Elizabeth II in 1953, shortly after her coronation. The Queen, accompanied by Prince Philip and Princess Anne, visited Tito and Yugoslavia in 1972. Although unprecedented, this visit to a communist country was considered exceptionally warm.

- The West strongly supported Yugoslavia with food, money, weapons, and diplomacy after its split with the USSR.
- From 1963 onwards, there was a noticeable intensification of cooperation between Yugoslavia and the United States. Tito visited John F. Kennedy, and later, cordial visits were exchanged during the presidencies of Nixon, Ford, and Carter.
- One of Tito's last political victories, at the age of 87 and in poor health, came in 1979 when he prevented Fidel Castro's efforts to align the Non-Aligned Movement with its "natural ally—the USSR" during the movement's conference in Cuba.

In any case, it is certain that Josip Broz Tito was a highly intelligent, cunning, unscrupulous, and experienced politician, dictator, and absolutist. Nevertheless, despite the dark stains and significant mistakes, his dictatorship can be said to have had a predominantly benevolent character throughout most of its duration. This fact partly explains why he enjoyed the people's great affection. Tito had the courage to defy Stalin at the height of the USSR's power and then skillfully steer the ship of Yugoslav foreign policy, which brought both the country and himself significant prestige worldwide.

The Unprecedented Visit: Tito's Impact on International Relations

On a breezy afternoon in Britain on March 16th, 1953, an unexpected event unfolded as Josip Broz Tito, Yugoslavia's communist dictator, made

London, March 16th, 1953

a notable arrival. It marked a historic moment as no communist leader had ever set foot in a Western country before. Tito's visit not only initiated warm relations between Britain and Yugoslavia but also signified his departure from the relative safety of Yugoslavia following a dramatic fallout with Soviet leader Joseph Stalin.

Upon his arrival, the Duke of Edinburgh was the first to greet Tito, followed by Prime Minister Winston Churchill and Foreign Secretary Anthony Eden. Though initially considered unnecessary by some at the Foreign Office, royal involvement in the visit was spurred by Buckingham Palace's expression of the Duke's eagerness to personally welcome Tito. This led to an official reception and even a dinner hosted by the royals.

On the following day, March 17th, Tito met with Churchill at 10 Downing Street. During their meeting, Tito emphasized that any potential Soviet attack on Yugoslavia would result in a world war. Initially regarded as a regional concern by the West, Churchill recognized the significance of Tito's suggestion. *He agreed that any Soviet military aggression toward Yugoslavia would prompt full Western intervention on Belgrade's side.* This stance was later embraced in Paris and Washington.[64]

In this manner, Yugoslavia became a "red line" in the geopolitical confrontation between the West and the USSR. The clear message that the world, in the event of a Soviet invasion of Yugoslavia, would find itself in the Third World War, is another contribution to understanding the immense strategic importance of the Balkan Peninsula. Tito's instinct and political brilliance in 1953, prevented Yugoslavia from experiencing the fate of Hungary or Czechoslovakia, averting the loss of the freedom and independence gained during the Second World War through immense sacrifices.

Although the state was preserved at that time, after the fall of the Berlin Wall in 1989, a new geopolitical redistribution of influence between Russia and the West in its territory will follow. The result will be the painful fragmentation and disappearance of Yugoslavia from the historical stage, along with the emergence of new states in its former territory.

---

[64] PREM 11/577 *Report on meeting at 10 Downing Street, March 17th, 1953,* The National Archives, United Kingdom

Did Yugoslavia Enjoy the Favor of the West?

There were indeed clear reasons for the West's support of Yugoslavia, primarily stemming from geopolitical considerations. This support began with the international recognition of the Kingdom of Serbs, Croats, and Slovenes at the Versailles conference, strongly backed by the United States and President Wilson, and continued until the mid-1980s. What motivated the West to maintain a favorable stance towards Yugoslavia?

The strategic significance of Yugoslavia's position in divided Europe during the Cold War. The Warsaw Pact's access to the Mediterranean Sea could be made possible through the territory of neutral Yugoslavia.

The Kingdom of Yugoslavia, under the Karadjordjević dynasty, adopted an explicit anti-Soviet policy and only established diplomatic relations with the USSR in 1940, on the eve of the war. After 1948, Tito's Yugoslavia consistently pursued a course that kept the country outside the Soviet sphere of influence and control. Examining the map of Europe during the Cold War, it is apparent that the Warsaw Pact's access to the Atlantic or the Mediterranean was obstructed in the north by Denmark and Norway, and in the south by Turkey and Greece—all of which were NATO members. The only way for Moscow to gain much-needed access to the warm Adriatic Sea (part of the Mediterranean) and the strategically important Balkans would have been through the accession of non-aligned Yugoslavia to the Eastern bloc or a breakthrough within its territory. Such an outcome in this part of the world would have dealt a severe geopolitical blow to Western interests.

By examining the provided political map, it is clear that the West had an interest in preserving Yugoslavia, while the USSR sought to gain control over it. It can easily be concluded that as long as Yugoslavia remained militarily and politically neutral with respect to the Warsaw Pact, it enjoyed the support of the West. Despite significant pressure, this was indeed the case until the second half of the 1980s, when the endangered and aging communist leadership of Yugoslavia began to lean towards the hardliners in Moscow in an attempt to hold onto power. This geopolitical slide of the country towards the East would consequently lead to a shift in Western policy towards Yugoslavia, providing us an opportunity to gain a more comprehensive understanding of the processes that unfolded during its disintegration.

The Yugoslav Economic Model

In the early 1950s, Yugoslavia demonstrated its ability to achieve significant accomplishments. The country emerged from World War II completely devastated, devoid of any industry, and with a destroyed infrastructure. In these circumstances, it had to face an economic blockade and isolation imposed by the Soviet Union and the entire Eastern Bloc in 1948. The situation was further exacerbated by a severe drought in 1950. The first development plan for the Yugoslav economy was based on the Soviet five-year model and achieved only partial success. The country was electrified, and the construction of industry began. Agricultural land was partly nationalized and partly collectivized. Private ownership of land also existed, but with a limitation of no more than ten hectares per household.

After the break with the USSR, Tito turned to democratizing the economic model. The Soviet doctrine of a planned state economy was gradually abandoned. The introduction of the so-called socialist market economy principles began. Voluntary youth work actions significantly contributed to the country's reconstruction during these initial years.

During the difficult period shortly after the end of the war, marked by Soviet sanctions, political pressures, and military threats, Yugoslav theorists of socialism and communism increasingly distanced themselves from Soviet dogmas. The Yugoslavs wanted to show Stalin that much better could be achieved. The vision was to create an economic-political model that would enable workers to have democratic decision-making rights in managing their enterprises and factories and determining the distribution of income. Thus, the ideas first introduced by the French philosopher and anarchist Proudhon in the 19th century came to life in a unique experiment elevated to the state level. The innovative and hitherto unseen worldwide model of *workers' self-management* was introduced in 1950. Generations of Yugoslav students, including my own, would learn about it as the fairest system in the world.

The fundamental difference compared to the Soviet model of state ownership was that in Yugoslavia, ownership shifted from state hands to the hands of the *society as a whole.* In other words, *all citizens* became owners of the vast majority of their state's assets. According to the creators of the self-management model, workers managed "social property" through the institutions of "socialist democracy." They exercised decision-making rights over their factories and enterprises through so-called "workers' councils" and "assemblies of working people". The management of a company represented an executive body that, in practice, had to implement the guidelines and decisions of the workers, made during workers' council meetings. This division of responsibility did not suit the management personnel, who were, as a rule, exclusively composed of Communist Party members. The ruling oligarchy imposed its will on the workers, which was one of the reasons self-management did not run smoothly in practice.

Another significant weakness of the collective management of enterprises was that, as a rule, the workers were incompetent, or very limited in their ability to manage effectively. From today's perspective, it is clear that a model in which all employees—from unskilled to highly skilled labor—had equal management rights in a company or factory may have been humane, but it was flawed and difficult to sustain. However, vocal thinking in this sense was strongly condemned at the time as a phenomenon contrary to workers' interests and was called "technocracy." The functionality of self-management was further complicated in practice by the fact that ordinary people, after initial enthusiasm, no longer showed great interest in attending long meetings and discussing matters they did not fully understand in order to exercise their management rights. Being a member of a workers' council implied spending many additional hours at work, which came at the expense of family or leisure time.

Many older people from former Yugoslavia still nostalgically remember the fact that no fees were charged for kindergartens and schools. Education was of good quality, accessible to everyone without distinction, and completely free from elementary school to postgraduate studies. The same applied to the healthcare system. The state built an extensive infrastructure of health centers, clinics, and numerous hospitals where everyone had the right to receive medical care. Dental services were also included in the healthcare system, which did not charge patients directly. Additionally, in the widespread network of state pharmacies, all prescribed medications were provided free of charge after a doctor's examination. Of course, all these benefits were only free at first glance. They were financed from state funds, which were filled with money from gross earnings. For the sake of objectivity, it is essential to emphasize that education and healthcare were of higher quality and more accessible back then than they are today, although this fact may surprise many people.

In addition to healthcare and education, the Yugoslav model also included apartment allocations. If you were employed in a society-owned enterprise and did not have resolved housing, you could hope that Yugoslav socialism would accommodate you. According to the ideal scenario, you would receive an apartment without charge, usually after a certain number of years spent waiting on a company or work organization waiting list, along with others who, like you, were waiting for this important issue to be resolved. However, if you were employed in state structures like the military, or the police, you could expect an apartment very quickly.

Unfortunately, in practice, apartment allocations were often burdened with manipulations, favoritism, and other not so honorable occurrences. Although it was not officially a requirement, membership in the League of Communists was a significant advantage that increased the chances of obtaining an apartment. Due to these facts, a considerable number of honest and hardworking people did not receive an apartment at all, or they waited too many years. In numerous cases, people were offered inadequate or temporary solutions. The process of obtaining an apartment was typically associated with uncertainty, latent corruption, and required great patience.

As this topic often causes confusion among audiences outside the former Yugoslavia, especially in the West, it should be emphasized that obtaining an apartment did not involve a mortgage or a multi-year bank loan. If you received one, it would be free of charge, and, as a rule, its size would correspond to the number of members in your household. Officially, the apartment would not be your personal property but rather society property, which in practice meant that you could not sell it. You could exchange it for another, and in that process, a special state service would mediate. However, you could freely use the apartment and even transfer the right to use it to your children. Financing housing construction, as well as education and healthcare, was done through a separate social fund into which all employees contributed a certain percentage of their gross earnings. In this way, everyone built for everyone. These were the well-known universal ideas of socialism modified by the peculiarities of the Yugoslav model. Unfortunately, their implementation was jeopardized by the described weaknesses of human character for which the system did not have an adequate response.

Of course, the described benefits of Yugoslav progressive socialism came at a high cost. The state developed its own agriculture and industry, which mostly met all domestic needs. There was an abundance of goods, food, as well as raw materials that were exported, mostly to Third World countries. A significant foreign currency income came from tourism, which was most developed along the Adriatic coast. Yugoslavia had one of the most beautiful coastlines in the world, with prestigious hotels, resorts, dozens of islands, and pristine beaches. Two international film festivals, in Pula and Belgrade, were regularly attended by world movie stars. Many

Sarajevo '84

In 1984, the Winter Olympic Games were held in Yugoslavia.

241

foreign visitors went to ski resorts in Slovenia, and in 1984, Yugoslavia organized the Winter Olympic Games in Sarajevo.

The M-84 tank, produced in Yugoslavia, is still in service with the Serbian Army and armies of some other countries.

An artistic representation of the fourth-generation fighter jet project, which was prevented by the breakup of Yugoslavia.

However, it is less known that Yugoslavia achieved significant financial income from the production and export of weapons. The country decided to develop a strong domestic military industry to preserve its independence and delicate position as a buffer zone between the two global military blocs. This weaponry began to compete with the weapons of other major players in global markets in terms of quantity and quality during the 1970s and 1980s. In addition to infantry and artillery weapons, Yugoslavia produced missiles, ships, submarines, aircraft, and tanks, which gradually improved over time. Several Arab countries were regular customers. In the last few years before the country's dissolution, the army was working on a project for a new fourth-generation supersonic aircraft, which, if it had taken off, would have been on par with the competition of that time in the world.

According to some opinions, a strong and independent military industry, which was becoming increasingly technologically competitive and had significant exports to other countries, was one of the reasons why some circles in the world wanted the disappearance of Yugoslavia. Although this view is well-founded, it was probably more important for key international actors to see the ideological and political orientations of those who would manage such a large army and accompanying military industry in the changed European circumstances after the fall of the Berlin Wall. This aspect is of utmost importance for understanding the behavior of great powers towards key actors in Yugoslavia during its final crisis and disintegration.

***

The way the Yugoslav socio-political experiment unfolded concerned its creators. Although the statistics showed economic development and GDP growth in the 1950s and 1960s, the first signs of the system's chronic weaknesses were becoming evident. Relatively high unemployment and inflation were constantly present and refused to decrease. The living standard of the population was indeed steadily rising, but so was the overall foreign debt of Yugoslavia.

During the 1960s, the authorities liberalized travel, which triggered a massive departure of the workforce for temporary work abroad, mainly in Germany. Tito wanted to solve several problems with one blow in this way. He opened the country to the West and improved the image of his regime by allowing Yugoslavs to travel freely. Such an opportunity was not available to the residents of Eastern Bloc countries. Internal tensions caused by unemployment were reduced, and a steady inflow of foreign currency was ensured in the country: "gastarbeiters"[65] regularly sent money to their relatives in Yugoslavia, and these remittances played a significant role in the country's overall income.

However, this policy had a serious downside. The most capable men, mostly in their twenties and thirties, were leaving Yugoslavia, often taking entire families after a few years. The outflow of the most productive population had a negative impact on the industry, and the country's defense power was also jeopardized. In addition, Yugoslavs "working temporarily abroad" were targeted by extremist emigration, clerical organizations, and foreign intelligence services. According to some estimates, up to 20% of Yugoslavia's working-age population was abroad during the 1970s. However, in that decade, the highest living standard for Yugoslavs ever was also recorded, with a "golden period" between 1974 and 1977.

The following decade brought problems right from the start. The first shortages appeared, and the national currency was devalued by 30% overnight. Then, deepened issues alternated with unsuccessful attempts by the authorities to get the economy back on track, which mostly only led to taking on new loans and increasing the country's foreign debt. Yugoslavia de facto went bankrupt in 1983 when it could no longer repay its external debt, but this was never announced to the nation. Although well-intentioned, the functioning of the system in practice proved unsustainable.

---

[65] This term was used for temporary workers in West Germany and later expanded to seasonal workers in other Western European countries. In the 1960s and 1970s, the German government organized and implemented a migrant worker program (Ger. *Gastarbeiterprogram*) mainly from Southern Europe and Turkey to solve the problem of labor shortages caused by demographic losses in World War II and rapid economic growth.

Internal economic differences in Yugoslavia between the developed north (Slovenia, Croatia) and the impoverished south (Kosovo, Macedonia, Montenegro) increasingly grew, creating political tensions. Inter-republic solidarity weakened. The wealthier ones resented that they were constantly expected to help the less developed. Even in the economic sphere, a sharp difference was noticed in people's attitude towards work, work ethic, and work habits according to the West-East criterion, that constant fate of Yugoslavia. Areas under Habsburg domination and Germanic culture sharply differed from those under the rule of the Ottoman Empire. These were still two worlds, and changes in the consciousness of the less developed went more slowly than the developed could and wanted to bear, despite goodwill and the constant efforts of the Party. The problem of large inequalities in economic development in Yugoslavia was one of the strong motivators and justifications for the Slovenian and Croatian desire to leave the federation and continue their path as independent states.

Tito's Dilemma

The Second or Socialist Yugoslavia was born out of the joint struggle of the Yugoslavs against fascist occupiers and their local collaborators. In this struggle, as in World War I, the Serbs bore the brunt of the burden. Through communist reform, the state transitioned from a unitary monarchy to a federation comprising six socialist republics. In addition to Serbs, Croats, and Slovenes, Macedonians, Montenegrins, and later, Bosniaks, gained the status of constituent peoples.

In this way, Tito sought to satisfy the emancipatory aspirations of certain peoples that led to secessionism and separatism and to stabilize the state on more optimal foundations. It was believed that the radical transformation of Yugoslavia would establish healthier relationships in the multiethnic nation. Instead of the doctrine of integral Yugoslavism, Tito's redefined Yugoslavia promoted the policy of "brotherhood and unity" among all peoples and national minorities on the basis of equality. It can be assumed that initially, Tito hoped that time would bring a gradual predominance of unity over brotherhood.

Serbs	36,30%
Croats	19,70%
Bosniaks	8,90%
Slovenes	7,80%
Macedonians	6,00%
Montenegrins	2,60%
Yugoslavs	**5,40%**
National minorities	13,30%

Results of the 1981 census in Yugoslavia

He himself was born to a mixed marriage of a Croatian father and a Slovenian mother. After the war, he referred to himself as a Yugoslav; however, he would later lean towards an ethnic definition of his own identity and declare himself a Croat. Those people who identified themselves as Yugoslavs in censuses expressed their readiness to embrace the idea of a supranational identity and rise above narrow ethnic-religious identities. Over time, some outside observers expected the percentage of Yugoslavs to increase and, after several generations, prevail in Yugoslavia, with Yugoslavs naturally evolving into one mixed nation. However, this did not happen.

Many people still maintain that the scenario of forming a unique supranational identity would have been a superior solution, capable of providing the South Slavs with lasting stability and prosperity. According to them, a few more generations, perhaps fifty or a hundred more years, would have been needed for the number of Yugoslavs to prevail, ensuring the survival of the state and rendering ethnic civil war impossible. However, from the multilateral analysis so far, we see that the roots of the problem were much deeper, making this viewpoint somewhat idealistic, albeit well-intentioned.

I often have the opportunity to discuss Yugoslavia with people from various parts of the world. There is one data that surprises them quite a bit, but at the same time opens their eyes. It is the fact that Yugoslavs in Yugoslavia never made up more than a few percent of the population. The maximum was reached in the 1981 census when they made up a modest 5.4%.[66] Probably half of that number consisted of children from interethnic marriages. Thus, the vast majority of the population, a full sixty-three years after the establishment of the state, still firmly identified with their ethnic origins. Clearly, Yugoslavia was not faring well.

After it was believed that radical transformations had eliminated the causes of pre-war tensions, it was logical for socialist Yugoslavia to embark on strengthening the structures of the state. Tito's leadership style, up until the mid-1960s, was firm and centralist. Most power was given to federal institutions, and the mainstay of the country was the *Yugoslav People's Army* (JNA), which guaranteed the territorial integrity of the state. The Army had a constitutionally defined task to defend the integrity of Yugoslavia, both from external and internal enemies. This fact is essential to understanding the behavior of the JNA in the final years of Yugoslavia's demise, and we will discuss it in more detail in the following chapters.

Tito's power grew steadily and reached absolute proportions. He was incredibly popular, an unrivaled leader whose word had a decisive impact on social movements. Although the state had all the necessary institutions, the final say was given by the League of Communists of Yugoslavia (SKJ), with Tito at the helm. I have had the opportunity to hear from Westerners several times that Tito was perceived in their countries as a benevolent dictator. This view is only partially true and can be more significantly applied to the period starting from the mid-1950s. Perhaps under the impression of Tito's long rule, many people in this region still think that benevolent dictatorship is the best solution for state governance, far superior to civil parliamentary democracy. Such thinking is probably most widespread among Serbs and Montenegrins, which partly explains the aforementioned peoples' penchant for absolutists and their corresponding forms of rule. However, this phenomenon will be exploited by some later dictators to come to power and stay there.

---

[66] Feldbauer, Božidar. 1988. *Atlas svijeta*. Zagreb: Leksikografski zavod Miroslav Krleža.

In addition to the Army and the Party, Tito had the loyalty of another important institution in Yugoslavia, which served as a stronghold and executor of Yugoslav political unitarism and centralism. This was the security sector, in which the State Security Administration (UDB) played the most important role—a powerful, ruthless, and well-organized intelligence service. It was skillfully and diligently led by Aleksandar Ranković, Tito's right-hand man and officially the second most important person in the state. Even American sources ranked the Yugoslav security service among the top five best intelligence agencies in the world. Ranković was of Serbian origin and a Yugoslav and communist by conviction. He was a hero of World War II and personally saved Tito's life at least once in 1944. It is quite possible that Tito never had a more loyal friend and ally than Aleksandar Ranković.

Based on the study of stenographic records from the sessions of the top of the League of Communists of Yugoslavia and other documents that have only recently become available, it is evident that the primary conflict between the unitary-centralist and federalist-secessionist conceptions within Yugoslavia unfortunately re-emerged on the surface, intensified, and shook the state already during the 1950s. This was not known to the public. The radical reform, federalization, and the increase in the number of recognized nations, the ideals of socialism and communism, the joint struggle against the occupiers, and the promotion of the policy of brotherhood and unity—all of this failed to calm the aspirations of certain nations to slide towards secession from Yugoslavia. Now, the initial tangled knot, the one that cost King Alexander his life and brought the first Yugoslavia to collapse, came to Tito for unraveling. The great master of politics approached the problem differently than his predecessors. In the early 1960s, *Tito realized that the conflict between the unitarists and secessionists in Yugoslavia could not be resolved by consensus or any compromise.*

He opted for a surgical solution. He had an advantage over his predecessors in the form of a one-party dictatorship and absolute personal power. To preserve the unity of the Party and the state, he decided to completely remove one of these two options from political life. But which one? The unitarists, who promoted a centralized and strong federal state, or the secessionists who demanded the weakening of federal institutions and the strengthening of republics?

It seems that at first, Tito leaned more towards the centralist option, as did his right-hand man, Aleksandar Ranković. This is completely logical. He was an experienced and serious political player who knew very well that weakening the federation would lead to the disintegration of the state, which he did not want. Along with him, the two most significant levers of power in the state—the Yugoslav People's Army and the State Security Administration—were firmly on the same centralist line.

The main political figure on the side of the secessionist forces was Slovenian Edvard Kardelj, the leading political ideologist, a communist theorist, and the author of all Yugoslav constitutions. He will be remembered as the father of the Yugoslav social and economic experiment called "associated labor" and "workers' self-management." However, from my perspective, something else was Kardelj's essential contribution to the disintegration of Yugoslavia. It was his clear criticism of integral Yugoslavism and the affirmation of the Yugoslav supranation. In the late 1950s, he called these "bureaucratic-centralist tendencies" associated with "remnants of Greater Serbian nationalism" in one of his books. It is likely that without a unified nation, Yugoslavia could not survive and last. Was Kardelj very aware of this and deliberately exposed Yugoslavism to his ideological criticism?

Aleksandar Ranković

Edvard Kardelj

Officially, Kardelj advocated for decentralization and the strengthening of republics, and in this, he enjoyed the support of the majority of party cadres from Croatia. In addition to Slovenians and Croats, as expected, the Kosovo Albanians were also uniformly in favor of weakening central authority. Like Ranković, Kardelj was one of Tito's closest friends. They had been friends since before the war, carried out illegal communist activities, were arrested, and imprisoned together.

Kardelj justified his long-standing commitment to the decentralization of Yugoslavia with the key postulate of Marxist philosophy about the necessity of "weakening the state until its complete extinction." In an era intoxicated by Marxism, which put ideology above common sense, this surreal delusion easily found its way to the "understanding" and approval of Party members who were accustomed to uncritically nodding their heads at all directives coming "from above." Assertions that we were "more advanced in Marxism even than the USSR," because we were taking concrete steps for our state to wither away, reached the broad masses through Party members. In this way, Yugoslav secessionism, driven by Slovenian, Croatian, and Kosovar communist cadres and under the guise of Marxist ideals, fought against the centralist concept of a unitary Yugoslavism, which was mainly supported by Serbs. As we can see, the same irreconcilable conflict between the two concepts, rooted in the time before the monarchy's establishment, was now unfolding, but disguised in another ideological attire.

According to today's knowledge, Tito wanted to eliminate Edvard Kardelj and his disguised secessionism on two occasions. The first incident occurred in the late 1950s when, during a state visit to Moscow, Kardelj told the Soviets one thing in separate meetings while Tito said another, which was a serious "foul." The Soviets confidentially informed Tito about this, who was furious and asked Ranković to deal with Kardelj and remove him from politics. However, Ranković refused. Not only did this weaken his position, but this refusal would also influence Tito's stance on what was probably the most significant political game in the Second Yugoslavia.

The conflict between the two concepts culminated in the dramatic session of the expanded composition of the Executive Committee of the Central Committee of the League of Communists of Yugoslavia in March 1962.

The stenogram reveals the drama of Tito's address to the top of his party:

> "What kind of atmosphere is this, comrades? What do I have to convince you of? You see it for yourselves at the meetings of the Federal Executive Council! What discussions are these! It often comes to the point where one wonders: Is our country really capable of holding on, not falling apart? (...) How much blood has been shed for the unity of our peoples, for the unity of our community! And today, all of this is being questioned. The question arises whether this community is mature enough for life or not. There are separatist phenomena. There are statements that make one's mind stop when hearing them."

At that session, Tito offered his resignation. Kardelj immediately said that in that case, Slovenia would ask to leave the Federation. It is certain that before Kardelj, no one in a high position had ever uttered such strong words that meant the de facto death of the joint state. At the end of the session, Edvard Kardelj's political platform was defeated, and the supporters of the "withering of the state" and "strengthening of the republics" lost the battle but not the war. As it happens in communist dictatorships, Kardelj was heading towards an exit from the political arena. The session was closed to the public, and for decades nothing was known about the events that took place there. Yugoslavs had no idea that their state was shaking to its foundations in those days, back in 1962. Many still don't know it today, and the above lines may surprise them.

Tito's words at the end of the session clearly reflect his stance on Yugoslav nationalisms that generate separatism:

> "Republics should not be afraid for national and other interests, because we are also obliged to vigilantly monitor and preserve the achievements of our revolution in the national question. However, we will not allow the national question to be deformed (...) towards the disintegration of our socialist community, because these are two things: decentralization is one thing, and disintegration is the breaking of the socialist community."[67]

Shortly afterward, on May 7th, 1962, Tito appeared at a public rally in Split, Dalmatia, and in front of a hundred thousand people, he criticized social phenomena and accused communists of "inattentiveness." He called for a return to unity and integrity, sending a clear message to everyone about the kind of Yugoslavia he wanted.

After successfully politically defeating the secessionists, Tito demanded from Ranković to remove Kardelj, and if necessary, to arrest him. To his surprise, the principled Ranković refused again, and it would cost him personally. Tito was angry and disappointed. A master of political skill, he knew that Ranković's refusal to remove Kardelj had significantly narrowed his maneuvering space. If Ranković had known that his act would definitely set the course of events in favor of the secessionist political camp, he would probably have acted differently. It is difficult to say how things would have unfolded had Kardelj been arrested and removed from politics in 1962, but it is certain that Yugoslavia would have embarked on a path of strengthening central power and a unified Yugoslav nation. How far it would have come on that path is an entirely different question that can only be pondered.

Following the dramatic session of the Party's top leadership, which was probably one of the most important in the entire history of post-war Yugoslavia, the defeated forces immediately organized themselves well and struck back to save themselves from the looming purge. Highly unusual for the previous methods of political struggle in Yugoslavia, the Slovenes or-

---

[67] Ibid., p.258

ganized public rallies in support of Edvard Kardelj, accusing Tito of having a "personal conflict with the whole of Slovenia."

Immediately afterward, the Communists of Croatia sent a signal that they had sympathics for Kardelj and his political views.

Albanian leaders from Kosovo were also strongly against Ranković, accusing him of his secret services committing terror against Kosovo Albanians in the mid-1950s when an extensive operation to confiscate a large amount of illegal weapons hidden in homes by the population was carried out.

In the Serbian communist leadership, there were a large number of opportunists who looked at Aleksandar Ranković, the deputy president of the Republic, the head of the secret services, and the Party's main personnel officer, with envy. They believed that they would not progress as long as he, as a cadre from Serbia, was so highly positioned everywhere and controlled everything like an all-seeing eye.

Although Aleksandar Ranković was Tito's best man at his wedding to Jovanka Broz, the first lady began to harbor antipathy towards Ranković's beautiful wife after some time, as she significantly surpassed her in education and manners. Jovanka's power, and paranoia along with it, grew over time. Many people close to Tito eventually fell out of her favor. Ranković was no exception. For years, she filled Tito's head with claims that Ranković was eavesdropping on him and secretly preparing a coup.

Considering the wide front of Ranković's enemies, as well as his refusal to remove Kardelj, it suggests that Tito had no choice but to turn against him and the political option he represented. Judging by the statement that he had "thought for almost two years about what to do," it seems that it was not an easy decision for him. This decision would prove to be the most fateful for Yugoslavia in the entire post-war period, as it would direct the country towards a slow and long-lasting disintegration.

Departure of Aleksandar Ranković and the Dismantling of the State Security Administration (UDBA)

In 1963, there were clear signs of a turning point. Tito's concessions to the advocates of decentralization became evident. Edvard Kardelj was fully rehabilitated and returned to the political arena. He was even entrusted with writing the country's new constitution. In it, despite Aleksandar Ranković's opposition, were the first elements of the Marxist ideal of the "withering away of the state."

During the Eighth Congress of the League of Communists of Yugoslavia in 1964, something happened that, to me, was a clear indicator that Yugoslavia would surely disintegrate. The only ideal with any chance of keeping it united was permanently abandoned. The keystone was removed, but it would take thirty years for the entire structure to collapse. Which stone are we talking about?

Threatened by the conflict between secessionists and unitarists, inter-ethnic relations in the state were strained. Slovenes and Croats were on one side, opposing the Serbs on the other end of the political spectrum. Although Tito addressed the issue of improving these relations in his presentation, his conclusion surprisingly revealed the allowance of the possibility that Yugoslavia might dissolve. He specified that the national question should be resolved "on the principle of equality of all nations, based on voluntary association, with the right to secession."

Even more significant is the fact that at this party congress, *Tito officially abandoned the Yugoslav nation*. For the first time, he identified himself as a Croat, not as a Yugoslav. Furthermore, he rejected aspirations for creating a common Yugoslav nation, saying that it appeared "somewhat similar to assimilation and bureaucratic centralization, like unitarism and hegemony."

Evidently, the Croatian-Slovenian narrative about Yugoslavism as a covert Greater Serbian hegemony resurfaced on the political scene, this time promoted by the undisputed, beloved Tito during the communist era. And in Yugoslavia, Tito's word had a strength of a law.

In 1964, the Party Congress officially marked a change of course, rejecting the prevailing state policy of unitarism, centralism, and Yugoslavism. The future of a united nation was sealed—there would be no Yugoslavs. The Yugoslav communists, the leading force in society, definitively gave up on being Yugoslav nationalists. They would mostly become nationalists based on their ethnic affiliation, a phenomenon that would be most felt in the coming decades among Slovenian, Croatian, and Kosovo-Albanian communists.

From that moment on, the state embarked on its own gradual and partially controlled dissolution and disassociation, while the Yugoslav public remained largely unaware. However, suspicions did exist.

Determined to eliminate one of the two opposing currents from political life completely, Tito had another crucial task. With the stage set, a confrontation with Aleksandar Ranković, the strongest advocate of a unitary federation and centralism, was in order. However, along with him, the powerful UDBA—the security service he had led for over two decades—had to fall as well. This was an extremely sensitive issue due to the large number of Service members and their loyalty to Ranković.

The Political Demise of Yugoslavia's Second-in-Command

At the so-called Brioni Plenum of the League of Communists of Yugoslavia, held on July 1st, 1966, far from the public eye, Aleksandar Ranković was accused of abusing the security services. He was charged with wiretapping high-ranking state officials, including Tito himself. However, the investigative team's report itself was controversial and unconvincing. It mentioned microphones in Tito's bedroom that were "not operational," cables leading from the president's residence to a manhole in front of Ranković's nearby house that were "not connected" but "could quickly be put into operation for eavesdropping." In short, no concrete criminal offense was found, but there were "indications."

Visibly downcast and shocked, Ranković, who had endured a minor heart attack the previous day, did not put up much of a defense. He resigned from all public positions, including the vice presidency of the state. Later, he was expelled from the League of Communists. The wiretapping affair was never proven, but his excommunication remained. He lived in complete silence until his death in 1983 when around a hundred thousand people gathered at his funeral. According to one testimony, shortly before the Brioni Plenum, he once again expressed his incredible loyalty to Tito by saying, "Old man, if you need my head, you know I will give it to you." "I need it now," was the response.

Today, it is known that Ranković's dismissal was prepared for several years. Secessionist forces in the state, primarily the Croatian, Slovenian, and Kosovar Party members, were joined by all those who saw the gradual weakening of the federal state as an opportunity for their national or political aspirations. Alongside the greedy politicians who were already burying the aging Tito, the first lady, Jovanka Broz, also joined the hunt for Ranković. Due to her possessiveness, paranoia, desire to control everyone and everything, and ambition to succeed as head of state, she could not bear the close relationship between Tito and Ranković.

These events can be characterized as a kind of coup d'état. In addition to Ranković, several hundred people from the police, military, security structures, and politics were cold-bloodedly purged. Most of them were genuinely committed to the ideals of a united and whole Yugoslavia, and many were willing to lay down their lives in its defense. They were mostly Serbs, but also a significant number of convinced Yugoslavs from other nations.

After the showdown with Aleksandar Ranković and the political vision he represented, rapid and significant consequences followed, leading to the substantial weakening of the federation's institutions and the strengthening of the republics' powers:

- The Federal State Security Administration was immediately disbanded. In its place, independent security departments were formed in the republics, with relatively loose federal coordination. The intelligence service in the Republic of Serbia was halved in personnel and significantly weakened.

- Through constitutional changes between 1968 and 1974, the republics were granted maximum rights, which included the right to self-determination and secession from the federation. Yugoslavia was essentially confederalized. The autonomous provinces of Vojvodina and Kosovo, parts of the Republic of Serbia, were granted rights that almost equated them with the parent republic and all other republics. This solution seriously weakened Serbia, which faced difficulties in functioning due to its two provinces having the right to veto and block any Serbian initiative in institutions at the republic or federal level.

- Administrations in each of the Republics were strengthened by transferring powers previously held by federal institutions to them.

- The military security system was fragmented. The Yugoslav People's Army, until then the only armed force in the state, gained competition. Local standing armies called Territorial Defense (TO) were formed in each republic.

- Decisions in the Yugoslav Assembly could only be made by consensus, as all republics and both Serbian provinces had the right to veto.

- The Presidency of Yugoslavia was introduced in 1971 as a collective head of state to succeed Tito after his death. This body consisted of one representative from each republic, one from each autonomous province, and the president of the Central Committee of the League of Communists of Yugoslavia—a total of nine members. As a form of compensation, Tito was formally declared lifelong president of the Republic. In practice, he gradually withdrew from domestic politics and devoted himself to international activities, mainly related to the Non-Aligned Movement, in which he was a leader. In this way, the secessionists weakened the only remaining federal institution that was still strong and popular in the state—the president of the Republic himself. The aging Tito was a living legend they needed, and none of them would dare to endanger him during his lifetime.

I have long studied this crucial period between the late 1950s and 1966, as it determined the fate of the state in which I would be born a few years later. I sought a satisfactory explanation for Tito's betrayal not only of Ranković but also of the ideals they both fought for during and after the war. It seems likely that he did so out of fear for his own reputation and position, realizing that his position would ultimately be jeopardized. On the other hand, it seems that he wanted to preserve Yugoslavia or extend its life as much as possible. There is a possibility that he even wanted to extinguish the second—secessionist—current at the first favorable opportunity and thus emerge as the winner in the struggle imposed on him. He didn't have to wait long for such an opportunity.

By 1971, secessionism exploded in Croatia in the form of the so-called *Croatian Spring*. The movement was condemned as divisive and anti-state. A political purge followed, in which Tito dismissed the entire Croatian leadership. He did something similar a year later in Serbia, where the liberal leadership advocated for the democratic reform of Yugoslavia's self-governing socialism. Tito's letter was published in the media, suggesting greater Party control over society and a reaffirmation of central authority and federal organs. A meeting with Tito followed, after which the entire Serbian leadership resigned, and loyal Party soldiers were brought in to replace them. In a show of solidarity, Koča Popović, one of Tito's closest associates and comrades since wartime, resigned from all positions, calling the showdown with the Serbian leadership a kind of "palace and state coup."

It seems that Tito, on the one hand, allowed centrifugal forces within the federation as an illusion that he was not against reforms and democratization, and then politically confronted them using his unquestionable authority in the League of Communists. Although in the later years of his life, he always managed to overcome attempts to challenge his absolute power. No one in Yugoslavia was ever up to Tito's level. Seen from another perspective, the elimination of all somewhat capable people from the political scene created another problem. Tito was the "glue" of Yugoslavia. There was no one who could replace him; he was surrounded by mediocrities and party loyalists. So, what could be expected to happen when Tito died?

After the overthrow of Ranković, Edvard Kardelj became the second most influential political figure in Yugoslavia. With prevailing support from Slovenia, Croatia, and Kosovo, he implemented several constitutional changes in the country after 1966, practically transforming Yugoslavia into a loose confederation by 1974. This fact is very little known to a wider audience outside of Yugoslavia.

Kardelj's final legislative document, the 1974 Yugoslav Constitution, has been deemed controversial by many, particularly in Serbia. This legal framework granted the autonomous provinces of Vojvodina and Kosovo within Serbia the power to veto decisions at both the Republic of Serbia and Yugoslav federation levels. Consequently, these provinces essentially achieved a status equal to the republics, with the exception that they lacked the right to secede from either Serbia or Yugoslavia.

Serbia became hostage to its provinces, with frequent blockades in decision-making. Absurdly, the largest nation, most deserving of creating Yugoslavia, no longer had its functional national republic. In addition, about 25% of Serbs in Yugoslavia lived outside the territory of Serbia, mostly in Croatia and Bosnia and Herzegovina. This situation led to frustration and protests. Serbia wanted to break the chains of the unjust constitution. However, all other republics, as well as its own two provinces, actively sabotaged these efforts using their veto power.

As Serbs once, in the kingdom, outvoted other nations and carried out majorization, now this mistake was returning to them like a boomerang. Serbia was mostly outvoted in Yugoslavia after 1974. The nation that made the greatest sacrifice for Yugoslavia in both world wars had found itself in a subordinate status. Did the Serbs deserve such treatment from other Yugoslavs? Were they reduced to the nation with the least rights in the federation by the skillful political maneuvers of other republics? Could this pressure on the most populous nation of Yugoslavia remain without consequences?

The federal units gained nearly all elements of independence and statehood, including the constitutional right to secession. The Yugoslav federation, that shared state of the South Slavs, became inefficient, dysfunctional, and unable to counteract the arbitrary decisions of the republics, and even the autonomous provinces. It turned into a decaying shell, sustained by Tito's strong personality, inertia from previous decades, and a decent living standard fueled by a diverse, albeit stumbling and inefficient economy, whose losses were covered by foreign debt. Serbia was reduced to a powerless member of the community, consistently outvoted or blocked by vetoes. The stage was set for the final phase of Yugoslavia's gradual disintegration.

Yugoslavia's Golden Age of the 1970s: Utopia Strikes Back

Following the victory of secessionist forces in Yugoslavia in the mid-1960s, a fascinating period ensued. The strengthening of republican oligarchies continued, which was interpreted as "democratization of society." The Yugoslav model of "socialist self-management" was developed, expanded, and implemented into all aspects of social and economic life. The country increasingly opened up and turned to the West, mostly in the realms of film, music, and art. Tourism flourished: Yugoslavs freely traveled the world, and the world came to visit them, mainly on the beautiful Adriatic coast. All republics invested in new factories and enterprises, but without a common plan, leading to duplicate capacities without an economic basis. For example, the country had as many as eight steel mills and foundries. Republics

As a "darling of fate," with an exceptional sense for political timing and diplomacy, Tito was the first to understand the potential of Third World countries and harnessed it through the Non-Aligned Movement and the United Nations.

competed with each other in "prestige" and heavily borrowed from foreign creditors. Megalomania and a lack of planned development took their toll. Economists warned of an unsustainable situation, and the federal government was helpless as it no longer had the authority to influence the behavior of the republics.

In fact, the chaotic economic boom was one of the phases in the advancement of disintegration. Republics rapidly built their own infrastructure and capacities in order to be prepared for the collapse of the federation and independent life. This was the real reason for the seemingly unplanned multiplication of capacities in Yugoslavia. Everyone knew that disintegration was a real possibility, though no one was certain whether and when it would happen. However, all were economically "arming" themselves, even those who supported the continuation of the federation, so as not to fall behind others.

Strong investments created many new jobs, and the living standard was comparable to that in some European Community countries. Yugoslavs lived their dream, largely unaware that their country was in a deep crisis and seriously ill. They were happy and proud of their nation. Tito's popularity was immense. He visited numerous countries on his "peace journeys," often on his favorite ship, the *Galeb* ("Seagull"), promoting the "policy of non-alignment" and "active peaceful coexistence" among the world's nations.

A peculiar curiosity was Marshal Tito's love for cinema. He made an effort to watch at least one movie every day. Yugoslavia had a developed

From left to right: Elizabeth Taylor, President Tito, First Lady Jovanka Broz, and Richard Burton at Brioni in 1971.

film industry and hosted two international film festivals each year—one in Belgrade and the other in Pula. Tito adored meeting film stars and frequently invited them to the country.

Richard Burton and Elizabeth Taylor were close friends with the President of Yugoslavia. On several occasions, they spent vacations with him at a villa on the Brioni Archipelago in the northern Adriatic or were guests at his Belgrade residence. He also socialized with Sophia Loren, Orson Welles, Kirk Douglas, and Yul Brynner. In the high-budget Yugoslav war film *Battle of Sutjeska*[68], Richard Burton portrayed Josip Broz Tito. He was paid a million dollars for the role, a record at the time. The film is a true story about the struggle of Yugoslav partisans against the Nazis during World War II and can still be found on Amazon with English subtitles.

President Tito met with President Richard Nixon in The White House
on September 23rd, 1971.

Tito displayed a great love for life and hedonism. He was intelligent, cunning, inscrutable, and unpredictable. Even in his eighth and ninth decades of life, he demonstrated great mastery in political games. Having subdued Yugoslavia, he increasingly turned to the world stage. Starting from the

---

[68] Internet Movie Database. n.d. Accessed April 20th, 2023. URL: *https://www.imdb.com/title/tt0070758/*.

late 1950s, his foreign policy activities were exceptionally numerous. Few 20th-century statesmen could compare to Tito. He was a tireless promoter of Yugoslavia. He met with dozens of world leaders, including Presidents Kennedy, Nixon, Ford, and Carter, Stalin and Khrushchev, three times with Leonid Brezhnev, twice with British Queen Elizabeth II, multiple times with Churchill, Danish Queen Margrethe II, monarchs and prime ministers of Belgium and the Netherlands, leaders of Germany, France, Italy, Portugal, China, India, and many Third World leaders. In his ninth decade of life, between 1970 and 1979, Tito had about 180 meetings with world leaders and participated in several international conferences, in Helsinki, Zambia, and Cuba.

Tito made himself a symbol of hope for a better future for humanity, which many small and impoverished countries, mainly former colonies, wanted to believe in. As a visionary and founder, he became a living legend of the Non-Aligned Movement, which at its peak had about 120 member states. With many of these countries, Yugoslavia had privileged trade relations. Having so many friends, Tito and Yugoslavia became a significant political factor in the United Nations. Without exaggeration, Tito became one of the most influential political figures in the world during the last decade of his life. Therefore, it is no wonder that he enjoyed immense affection from his compatriots at home. Yugoslavs were proud and happy, and only a few foresaw the fate that would befall them after the Marshal's biological end.

On the domestic front, Tito relied on the sole remaining cohesive factor of the Yugoslav federation. Carefully coexisting with secessionists in the republics, he turned to the Army and his loyal generals, to whom he was the supreme commander.

Military personnel enjoyed a privileged status in society. The state continued to invest heavily in weapons production, and Yugoslav military potential became formidable. According to some sources, Yugoslavia was the fourth or fifth military power in Europe. The technological level achieved in weapons production became competitive in the global market. During successful years, military equipment exports reached several billion US dollars, making the defense industry the most significant economic sector in the country alongside tourism.

In a clever attempt to preserve national unity through the military sector and the revenue it generated, Tito diversified the military industry across the republics. For instance, the production process of the highly successful M-84 tank, a source of pride for Yugoslav engineering, took place in five of the six Yugoslav republics. As a result of this policy, no single republic was capable of independently producing complex combat systems: tanks, aircraft, missiles, and many others. Consequently, access to military arsenals and revenue from arms exports under such circumstances presented a strong incentive for the republics to cooperate and remain united.

During the Yugoslav wars in the early 1990s, an intriguing situation arose, as no one could independently assemble the M-84 tank. Amidst the fighting and significant loss of life, Serbian and Croatian leaders Milošević and Tudjman secretly reached an agreement for both sides to jointly assemble a small number of these tanks and deliver them through the Montenegrin port of Bar to Iraq, which had ordered and partially paid for them while Yugoslavia was still intact.

Tito made himself indispensable in the ways described. He outmaneuvered the secessionists politically and played the card of strengthening the military as a cohesive factor. To some extent, he was right. When the actual breakup began, generals of the Yugoslav People's Army (JNA) were the last to accept that it was truly happening. To be fair, the country's constitution mandated that they prevent the breakup and preserve Yugoslavia's territorial integrity. But was there something more? It seems there was. Tito held his last meeting with the top brass of the JNA on December 21st, 1979, in Karadjordjevo. On that occasion, he hinted at his impending biological departure and made it clear to everyone that he fully understood the depth of the crisis in the country. As the supreme commander, he ordered the Army to preserve Yugoslavia, stating that "everything else leads to tragedy and fratricidal war." As usual, Tito was right.

The Army's leadership would attempt to carry out this order a decade later. However, poor judgments, disunity, indecisiveness, political regressiveness, nationalism, and external factors would contribute to the oncemighty army's degradation, fragmentation, and unacceptable instrumentalization during the dissolution of Yugoslavia.

Tito's Death

Marshal Tito's lifestyle always posed a challenge for his doctors. He was a heavy smoker, loved gourmet food, and couldn't resist a glass or two of good whiskey. An extreme hedonist, he knew how to enjoy life. He possessed inexhaustible energy, from which he drew his charisma and enthusiasm for various activities. On one occasion, he told his biographer about how he spent several hours late into the night describing his life to the British queen. She listened very attentively and ultimately expressed her surprise that he had managed to accomplish so much in a single lifetime.

The warnings from his doctors and wife about smoking or diet rarely had a lasting effect. With a smile, Tito would soon resume his usual ways. Concern was heightened because the leader of the Yugoslav state had suffered from diabetes for the last 25 years of his life. This was, of course, one of the most closely guarded state secrets.

The combination of long-standing diabetes and indulgence in tobacco had damaged Tito's blood vessels. Surprisingly, only in the late 80s of his life did complications arise that could seriously threaten his life. Many doctors were concerned about Tito's health. The top of the hierarchy consisted of a council of about ten of the best experts in various specialties, usually chosen from medical faculty professors. However, it happened that a lower-ranking young doctor, Milomir Stanković, assigned to monitor Tito's health daily, measure his blood pressure, and administer insulin, was the first to notice a change in his foot, indicating a blockage in the femoral artery. He immediately reacted, telling the president that a detailed medical examination was urgently needed and informed the main doctors. Tito did not listen to him and thus shortened his life. The events that followed could have been postponed. At that time, a blocked femoral artery was easily treated, but the problem required immediate action.

"It will pass; it's nothing," Tito told the young doctor. When pressed again the next day, Tito said that "there is currently no time for clinics and doctors." They managed to persuade him to receive intravenous therapy, but it had no effect. He was scheduled to attend a celebration for the new year of 1980 and address the nation on that occasion. And he did, visibly weakened in health. Precious time was slipping away. When he was finally hospitalized in early January, the condition of his leg was already so severe that amputation was suggested as the best solution. After hearing the bad news, he refused. "I'm going down in one piece," was his immediate response to the doctors.

They honored his wish. They attempted an arterial bypass, but it was unsuccessful because it was already too late. He received a large amount of medication, but his leg continued to wither and die. Finally, after realizing how bad his leg had become, he accepted his bitter fate and told the doctors to do what needed to be done. A partial amputation of his left leg was performed on January 20th. However, by that time, Tito's body was already poisoned, and his immune system was severely weakened. After an initial improvement in his overall condition and encouraging photographs with his sons, where he smiled, a urinary infection followed by kidney failure occurred. This was followed by pneumonia, difficulty breathing, and heart problems. Doctors connected him to a dialysis machine and artificial lungs. His condition worsened, and internal bleeding occurred. Finally, on February 26th, the president was put into an induced coma from which he never awoke. After more than two months in a coma, during which he survived several crises, the EKG device showed a complete cessation of heart activity on May 4th, 1980, at 3:05 PM. The gathered doctors and nurses stood in complete silence beside the bed, watching the flat line on the monitor for the next ten minutes. Then, Dr. Lalević, an anesthesiologist, turned off the devices. "We stood there for a few more minutes, and then went to write our reports," he wrote in his memoirs.

Almost the Whole World at the Funeral

World leaders at the funeral of President Tito, May 8th, 1980

In early January 1980, in the utmost secrecy, the state leadership of Yugoslavia began to prepare for the possibility of the president's death. A secret meeting was held with the highest leadership of state television, during which they were informed that Tito's health had seriously deteriorated and that a detailed plan in case of death, called Day D + 4, was prepared. It provided that all formalities, processions, and the funeral itself would be completed four days after the president's death. According to his personal wish, Tito would be buried in the House of Flowers, the winter garden within the residence where he loved to spend time and cultivate roses, his favorite flowers.

History records that the funeral of Josip Broz Tito, on May 8th, 1980, was one of the largest ever held in terms of the number of attending delegations. According to data published by the Museum of Yugoslavia in Belgrade, a total of 209 delegations from 127 countries were present.

The arrival of four kings, six princes, thirty-one presidents, twenty-two prime ministers, and forty-seven foreign ministers was recorded. Among the significant world political figures present were Margaret Thatcher, Leonid Brezhnev, Andrei Gromyko, Helmut Schmidt, Kim Il Sung, Hua Guo Feng, Nicolae Ceauşescu, Saddam Hussein, Indira Gandhi, Norwegian King Olav V, Prince Philip from the United Kingdom, Hafez al-Assad, UN Secretary-General Kurt Waldheim, and many others. When U.S. President Jimmy Carter realized that the leaders of all communist countries would attend the funeral, he decided not to go. He may have had an additional reason for abstaining. Namely, Tito's funeral took place just two weeks after the failure of the operation to free American hostages in Iran, codenamed Eagle Claw, when several commandos were killed. Nevertheless, his political opponents at home criticized his decision not to attend. The American delegation was led by Vice President Walter Mondale, and in place of the president, his mother Lillian Gordy Carter attended.

In an interview with the Belgrade newspaper Danas, Mr. Mondale shares his memories:

"At Tito's funeral, which I remember for the incredible presence of world leaders, I walked beside Soviet leader Leonid Brezhnev, and we barely spoke the entire time. For our administration, Tito's funeral held the utmost importance, just as Yugoslavia as a whole did, because they represented a crucial aspect of our relations with the Soviet Union. President Carter did not attend because he did not want to meet the Soviet leader or walk with him in the mournful procession at the Yugoslav leader's funeral. (...) What surprised me, besides the sheer number of people present, was another feeling. It was the first and only time up to that point that I had attended a completely non-religious funeral. Until then, I had always been to funerals that included some religious dimension. At Tito's funeral, everything was secular - from the music to the political speeches that were given."

Yugoslav authorities were somewhat offended by the intense diplomacy taking place on the sidelines of the funeral, thinking that such behavior was inappropriate. On the other hand, Tito's grand exit from the stage was a logical culmination of his decades-long diplomatic activities, which earned him respect in both the East and the West, as well as admiration in Third World countries. Yugoslavs had every reason to be proud of how the world paid its last respects to their president. The country mourned. We who remember know that tears did not flow down our faces only because of sadness. People were shaken by a deep concern, a feeling of vague fear that was difficult to fully articulate or become aware of. We were afraid to say it, but we felt that the good times were just ending. The only remaining factor capable of effectively keeping Yugoslavia together had left the stage. Our instinct told us that a period of painful and lengthy decay and disappearance of the Yugoslav community was beginning. We lied to ourselves and swore by "his path," but deep down we knew things would take a different course. In the collective mourning for Tito, besides sadness, lay a powerless despair for the loss of security. While he was there, people thought, we were safe. I remember well the general anguish and bowed heads that often shook. Quietly, in a half-whisper, people articulated what they felt. Like an echo, the question resounded again and again: "What will happen to us now?"

PREPARATION FOR THE FINALE

After Tito—The Era of the Presidency of the SFR Yugoslavia (1980-1991)

"Even after Tito, there is still Tito" was the slogan used to try to reassure and convince Yugoslavs that nothing had changed after Tito's death. The community would survive if it stayed on "Tito's path"—the political platform devised by the beloved president. While these empty words were persistently repeated through all communication channels, deceiving the general public, Yugoslavia was inevitably sinking into a deeper institutional and economic crisis.

The Presidency of Yugoslavia, as a collective head of state, was far from a substitute for Tito. Its members were selected based on a republic-province principle and rotated in the role of the presiding member every year. None of them had the charisma or ability to emerge as a new leader. In fact, that wasn't even desired. The architects of Yugoslavia's political decentralization during the 1960s and 1970s deliberately planned to prevent the emergence of a new leader after Tito. Constitutional provisions defining the Presidency effectively blocked such a possibility. Thus, this body was a group of experienced communist bureaucrats with great power on paper but no personal charisma. Behind them stood interest groups in the republics that elected them and thus controlled them. These groups used the members of the Presidency as puppets to try to impose their interests on others. Therefore, the real political power lay within the republics. Thus, the most important body in the state, which according to the Constitution governed the country and served as the supreme commander of the armed forces, transformed into an arena for political struggles within the federation.

Imagine a country governed by nine individuals as a collective head of state, all with equal rights. At first glance, a beautiful and democratic idea. But what to think about the efficiency of such a solution? Recall George Orwell and the most famous quote from his renowned work Animal Farm: "All animals are equal, but some animals are more equal than others..." This phenomenon quickly manifested among the members of the Presidency. Confederationists-separatists sought to further weaken federal institutions and sabotage their work, while unitarists-centralists aimed to become "more equal" in the Presidency and prevent the country's disintegration by strengthening federal institutions.

What was officially presented as democratization, decentralization, and federation reform in the early 1970s led to an economic crisis that would last until the very end of Yugoslavia. As part of these reforms, the republics gained the right to independently incur debt abroad without the knowledge or approval of the federal government, which immediately triggered a wave of ambitions for "accelerated development." Suddenly, there was a wave of uncritical borrowing from foreign creditors, which too often was entirely unfounded in economic science and practice. The republics competed over who would build and "prosper" more during this difficult period. We Yugoslavs helplessly watched as incompetent republican oligarchies turned massive borrowed money into unplanned and chaotic development. Some investments proved successful, but all too often, we witnessed phenomena we called "failed investments." These were empty, abandoned hotels in the wrong places without supporting infrastructure, factory complexes producing poor-quality products that did not pass the market test, service companies with low-quality services, lacking knowledge or ideas on how to improve their operations. Due to the Balkan mentality prone to corruption, a significant portion of this money ended up in private pockets. Following the example of some reckless managers, workers, like vultures, tore apart the goods from their factories and enterprises. Only a few were held accountable for misused money or theft, but those were relatively rare cases.

To mitigate this situation and conceal poor state management and deep crises on all levels, the authorities diverted a portion of the borrowed money to raise living standards, which by the mid-1970s approached those of Western European countries. Yugoslavs lived in a utopia. We were happy, carefree, and life was truly beautiful.

Although the Yugoslav social product grew at an annual rate of about 6% at that time, Yugoslavia spent far more than it produced. By 1979, we had a trade and payment deficit measured in billions of dollars, and the country's total debt reached around twenty billion in 1980.

In the year when Tito's death struck us, the unsustainable economic situation led to increased unemployment, a higher rate of young people leaving for temporary work abroad, inflation in the double digits, the first shortages in stores, and a noticeable decline in living standards. Only a month after the president's death, the federal government was forced to devalue the Yugoslav dinar for the first time—by a whole 30%. Devaluations continued periodically until the country's collapse, which, coupled with massive inflation, caused citizens to completely lose faith in the domestic currency and turn to saving in German marks, Swiss francs, or US dollars.

The impotent and disunited political elite of Yugoslavia failed to find a solution to the crisis, and that was no surprise. Primarily, they lacked consensus on whether to stay together or separate, and that was at the core of thc problem. The economic crisis also resulted from significant weaknesses in the model of social self-management. Psychologically speaking, perhaps the greatest mistake of the Yugoslav self-management model was the concept of collective responsibility. Due to this arrangement, there was a sense of security and relaxation that, as a rule, led to a lack of motivation and responsibility at all levels—from ordinary workers to managers, from local politicians to high-ranking officials.

In theory, workers' councils managed enterprises, so no one was individually to blame for business failures. The same applied to cases of poor local community management. It was relatively easy to shift one's personal responsibility to the collective level and escape consequences.

The concept of collective responsibility stemmed from the fact that the most common form of ownership in the socialist self-management model was so-called *society property*—that is, the ownership of society as a whole. We have already discussed this topic in the chapter on the Yugoslav economic model, but we will now look at it from a slightly different perspective. What was state property in the Soviet model, in the Yugoslav model was owned by the society and *not* by the state. Society, that is, all Yugoslavs, owned everything: from factories and enterprises to residential blocks they lived in and hotel complexes where they spent carefree summers on the Adriatic. The idea was that everyone was responsible for everything because everything was ours. Thus, responsibility for failures fell, in solidarity, on society as a whole, instead of on the individuals who caused them.

Such an idealistic model would hypothetically be applicable to a society with an exceptionally high level of consciousness and responsibility, which likely does not exist anywhere in the world at present. Quite predictably, the vast majority of Yugoslavs were not up to the challenge. Unable to understand and identify with the philosophical and ideological foundations of society, many people effectively perceived their ubiquitous property as "someone else's" and "alien," treating it carelessly, often parasitically. Society property was everyone's and no one's, and as such, it became a subject of neglect and plunder.

Yugoslavs aspired to be ideologically exemplary to other nations, especially socialist ones. Some ideologues of the League of Communists of Yugoslavia aimed to put into practice the most advanced socialist and humanist ideas and to surpass the rigid model of the Soviet Union in every respect. However, it turned out that several of the most prominent ideologues were actually pursuing a hidden agenda under the guise of Marxist ideals of the withering away of the state, aimed at the independence of their republics. They knowingly deceived Yugoslavs, and in this fact, I see their enormous responsibility.

The general public believed that we were applying the highest ideals of Marxism in practice and that the "withering away of the state" was a natural and desirable process. We were proud to have advanced further in building society according to Karl Marx's visions than even the USSR, the "cradle of socialism." We saw their model as grey, impoverished, unfree, and inefficient. We feared their tank invasion, knowing that we were an annoyance to them, a thorn in their side. In return, the Soviets were very reluctant to grant travel permits to citizens of the Eastern Bloc to visit Yugoslavia in order to prevent them from seeing how much better life was in our country than in theirs. People there saw Yugoslavia as the West, and their communists regularly accused us of "betraying the ideals" and "selling out to the West." Western tourists perceived Yugoslavia as an "peculiar East" and gladly returned.

Under the spell of grand ideals, persuasive propaganda, and captivating demagogy, Yugoslavs frequently displayed a bold and elegant dance. They possessed the audacity to believe in the visions put forth by their regime, and their spirited performance occasionally inspired other nations. Regrettably, this dance met a somber conclusion, a fate for which Yugoslavs themselves bear substantial responsibility. It is worth noting, however, that the discordant interests of external forces also played a significant role in shaping this tragic outcome.

Unrests in Kosovo, 1981

The prolonged political and economic instability within the Yugoslav federation led to a surge in ethnic nationalism across its regions. Following Tito's departure from the scene, separatism in Yugoslavia did not take long to manifest in a form that would seriously shake the already faltering federation. As early as March 1981, student protests began in Priština—the capital of the Autonomous Province of Kosovo and Metohija—and would soon escalate into mass demonstrations in several local cities. The protests unanimously demanded that the province, which was constitutionally part of Serbia, be granted the status of a new, independent, seventh Yugoslav republic. Understandably, Serbia could not agree to such a partition of its own territory, primarily due to state and national interests as well as historical reasons.

On the other hand, everyone in Yugoslavia knew why Kosovo Albanians, the country's largest national minority, were chanting, "Kosovo—a republic!" According to the 1974 Constitution, only Yugoslav republics had the right to secede from the federation, but not autonomous provinces. If Kosovo became a republic, the path to secession from Yugoslavia would be open. Kosovo would join neighboring Albania, and the local Albanian population would realize their long-held desire for unification with their homeland.

***

At this point, we shall recapitulate what has been said so far and delve deeper into the analysis of the Serbian-Albanian dispute, which has been a source of continuous problems since the time of the Kingdom of Serbia, through the Kingdom of Yugoslavia, and all the way to Tito's socialist Yugoslavia. The destructive impact of the Kosovo Gordian Knot is still painfully felt by both Serbs and Albanians today, in the 21st century, and, unfortunately, a lasting solution to the problem is not yet in sight.

In the Middle Ages, the regions of Kosovo and Metohija were predominantly part of the Serbian kingdom and empire. The 14th century saw the Serbian capital situated in the city of Prizren, within Kosovo, as well as the establishment of the Serbian Orthodox Church's seat in Peć. By the late 14th and mid-15th centuries, Serbia had fallen under Ottoman rule. To facilitate control over the occupied and frequently rebellious Christian Serbs, Ottoman authorities supported and organized the migration of Albanian Muslim populations from the mountainous regions of present-day northern Albania into Kosovo and Metohija. Consequently, Albanians acquired a privileged status, becoming allies of the Ottomans. Concurrently, a repression against Serbs commenced, enduring for centuries. Serbian populations experienced multiple waves of displacement from Kosovo, the most significant of which transpired at the end of the 17th century. It was during this period that intense animosity towards Albanians emerged among Serbs.

As the 19th-century struggle for national liberation unfolded, Serbs launched several uprisings and waged wars against the Ottomans, driving them from the reclaimed national territories. The settled Albanians, perceived as intruders and servants of Ottoman rule, were similarly displaced. During the Balkan Wars of 1912 and 1913, the Kingdom of Serbia liberated Kosovo after several centuries, but also sought to expand its territory into northern Albania in a bid to secure access to the Adriatic Sea. In the process, Serbian troops perpetrated acts of repression and numerous crimes against the Albanian civilian population, as extensively documented earlier in the book. Under pressure from the great powers, Serbia was compelled to withdraw from northern Albania.

Driven by ethnic and religious motivations, as well as their treatment by Serbia, the Albanian population in Kosovo expressed a resolute preference following these events to reside within Albania rather than Serbia. This sentiment marked the inception of an enduring rebellion, whether covert or overt, which continues to the present day. The ultimate goal of this rebellion is the detachment of Kosovo from Serbia and its subsequent annexation to Albania. While Serbia asserts historical claims to the region, Albanians maintain a significant demographic majority.

A myriad of repressive measures against Kosovo Albanians by the Kingdom of Serbia, later the Kingdom of Serbs, Croats, and Slovenes, and eventually Yugoslavia, were documented, including general discrimination, human rights violations, ongoing injustices, and numerous crimes. The state orchestrated the forced displacement of the Albanian population, and concurrently, the colonization of Kosovo by Serb and other Yugoslav populations, primarily Montenegrins and Croats. This policy persisted until the onset of World War II.

The aim of these efforts was to establish a demographic advantage for the Serbian population—disrupted during the Ottoman occupation—and to thwart Albanians' attempts to secede Kosovo and annex it to Albania. However, poorly conceived, shortsighted, and uncivilized measures failed to achieve the anticipated demographic success or resolve the issue in any way. Instead, the divide grew and the problem deepened. During this period, the animosity of Albanians towards Serbs significantly increased.

Following the creation of socialist Yugoslavia in 1945, Kosovo and Metohija were initially designated as a province and later as an autonomous province within the Republic of Serbia. The majority Albanian population was granted extensive rights and the widest local autonomy. Nonetheless, this arrangement did not satisfy the Albanians' strong desire to unite with their homeland in neighboring Albania. Their unwavering separatism and thirst for revenge were directed towards the minority Serbian population in the province, which endured immense pressure for several decades. The pendulum of intolerance and violence swung once more—Serbs started to leave Kosovo, and the Yugoslav authorities remained silent about the situation. The Republic of Serbia was frustrated but powerless to make any changes.

This state of affairs would later play a significant role in the development of Serbian nationalism through the political ascent of Slobodan Milošević.

***

Following the adoption of the controversial 1974 Constitution, Kosovo gained extensive autonomy and veto power in decision-making processes, both within Serbia and at the Yugoslav federal level. Communist officials representing Kosovo's Albanians were generally satisfied with the situation and actively worked to maintain the status quo. The outbreak of demonstrations in 1981 caught them somewhat off guard, and it was not in their interest.

In response to the mass protests by Albanians, the collective head of state—the Presidency of Yugoslavia—assessed that there was an "attempt to undermine the territorial integrity and sovereignty of Yugoslavia" in the province. They decided that the rebellion must be suppressed "by all means". As later decades would confirm, this assessment was entirely accurate. The ultimate goal of the rebellion was to separate Kosovo from Yugoslavia. The military, including armored units, was deployed to the streets, and a state of emergency was imposed. In several instances, armed conflicts arose between the army and police on one side, and the rebellious Albanians on the other. The inept authorities tried to conceal the situation from the global community at all costs, prohibiting reporting for both foreign and domestic journalists. Instead, information was disseminated through official statements, which were rather vague. According to eyewitness accounts, Kosovo's Albanians chanted slogans such as "Kosovo for Kosovars!" "We are Albanians, not Yugoslavs," "Kosovo, a republic!," and "We want united Albanian lands" during those days.

Official reports state that nine people were killed and several dozen wounded in the unrest. Albanian sources, predictably, reported a much higher number of casualties. After the rebellion was quashed, a major purge took place in Kosovo, with some testimonies indicating that as many as several hundred thousand Albanians were subject to police prosecution.

Regrettably, violence only generates more violence. The situation in Kosovo did not improve after these events. Local Albanians felt an even stronger desire to leave Yugoslavia, while their Serbian neighbors grew increasingly fearful that this would indeed happen. Both sides only intensified their resolve—one to leave, the other to prevent them from doing so at all costs. The divide between them continued to widen.

In order to provide the most objective analysis of these complex processes, we should also consider the fact that Albanians fought for Kosovo through high birth rates. Their long-term strategic efforts to achieve the full secession of Kosovo from Serbia and Yugoslavia can be seen through the dramatic population growth. According to data from censuses carried out in Yugoslavia between 1948 and 1991, Kosovar Albanians had the highest birth rate in all of Europe. Over 43 years, their numbers almost tripled: from about 750,000 after World War II to 2,100,000 at the beginning of the 1990s. During the same period, the percentage of Serbs in Kosovo decreased from 23.6% (1948) to just 10% (1991).

Many contemporaries believe that the 1981 demonstrations in Kosovo and their subsequent consequences marked the beginning of the final phase of Yugoslavia's disintegration.

Serbia as a Hostage of the 1974 Constitution

The controversial 1974 Constitution of Yugoslavia marked the final victory of an ideology that, under the guise of lofty ideas of the Yugoslav model of self-managed socialism, promoted absurd decentralization. It turned the country into a loose confederation of willful republics and two autonomous provinces, which frequently used their veto power to block others in anything they disapproved of. Federal institutions struggled to function, and a common economic policy could not be established. Due to vast differences in the levels of economic and cultural development among individual republics, there were completely different interests and priorities. In the wealthiest Slovenia, the level of development was up to seven or eight times higher than in the underdeveloped south: in Kosovo, Montenegro, or Macedonia. The country's indebtedness grew year by year, without a plan and without the possibility of tighter control by the federal government. High inflation and regular devaluations destroyed the population's trust in the domestic currency and institutions. Even the IMF, on several occasions, suggested to the state leadership that the system needed to change towards a market economy and strengthening federal institutions, primarily the federal government, for Yugoslavia to recover.

The only common institution in the country that still mostly functioned well was the Yugoslav People's Army. It served as the "pillar of unity" and the "forge of brotherhood and unity," remaining ideologically faithful to the original principles of the Tito era. Due to the constitutional obligation to protect the sovereignty and territorial integrity of the state from any violent threat from abroad or within, the military leadership sent fairly clear messages to domestic politicians that they would oppose any attempts at secession and disintegration of the country.

The situation in which the country was sliding into disintegration and instability hurt Serbia the most, and for many reasons. The most obvious reason was that, according to the controversial constitution, two autonomous provinces were formed on its territory, over which Serbia no longer had executive authority. To make matters worse, the provinces frequently used their veto power to block Serbia's initiatives to which they formally belonged. At the very least, Serbia was put in a position to be politically blocked whenever it occurred to either of its two provinces.

***

It is certain that everyone else in Yugoslavia at the time failed to understand the extent of Serbia's disappointment and humiliation because of the decline in its status. They either overlooked it or consciously turned a blind eye. Given the importance of this issue, it is essential to examine the situation from a Serbian perspective to understand the feelings of the most populous nation in Yugoslavia at the time. Serbs made unimaginable sacrifices in World War I, fighting to create a common state of South Slavs. They submerged their Kingdom of Serbia into Yugoslavia and soon experienced Croatian and Macedonian separatists assassinating their king and war hero in 1934. They were the most numerous in the ranks of the Partisans and bore the greatest sacrifices in World War II, including the genocide committed against them by Croatian fascists. They accepted Tito, who was a Croat/Slovene, and agreed to the post-war abolition of the monarchy led by the Serbian royal family. With the transformation of the state from a unitary monarchy into a federation, about 30% of Serbs remained outside the borders of their home republic of Serbia. They agreed to that as well. Moreover, for decades they were politically cooperative and loyal to the federation until things reached a breaking point.

Serbs could no longer watch the country they fought for, believed in, and sacrificed for wither away before their eyes, unable to do anything to save it. They were hostages to the constitutionally guaranteed veto power, which political elites in some republics and provinces used to prevent any strengthening of centralism and reinvigoration of the country. Any initiative by Serbia to strengthen the federation or make necessary changes to the constitution to improve its functioning was condemned and labeled as "greater-state tendencies," "greater-state nationalism," "Greater-Serbianism," "suppression of self-management," "Serbian nationalism," and so on.

It seems to me that there is another reason for the Serbian people's hurt in Yugoslavia. As it was described earlier, all nations in the Balkans possess a remarkably strong sense of belonging to their ethnic identity. Facts indicate that many Serbs, entering the Yugoslav community and taking on the greatest responsibility for it, were willing to sacrifice what they held most sacred to the altar of Yugoslavism. Serbs, probably more than any other nation, *were ready to merge* into the newly forming Yugoslav nation.

However, the concept of a single and unified Yugoslav nation was abandoned for good in the early 1960s, and with that, Serbs were essentially let down. A loose confederation of small national states *without a unified nation* was not what they had fought for since the time of King Alexander's unification and integral Yugoslavism, nor were those the ideals that Serbian fighters had died for in Tito's Partisan ranks. Faith and commit-

278

ment to the Yugoslav vision were most widespread among Serbs. After all they had given to Yugoslavia, they had no other choice but to protect, support, and believe that, with time, it would become stronger and more unified. Unfortunately, it turned out they were alone in these intentions. No one else in Yugoslavia followed them, and Serbs felt betrayed.

I am personally glad that in Yugoslavia the Serbs entered into mixed marriages more than anyone else, because the offspring of these unions embraced the Yugoslav identity. Growing up in Belgrade, I was surrounded by many of them, and they enriched my life with their cosmopolitanism. I always found it easiest to connect with them. Genuine Yugoslavs can recognize and sense one another; they possess a breadth of understanding, tolerance, and empathy for their compatriots. They are united by a fully conscious—or perhaps merely intuitive—belief that their vision and commitment to a nation in the making is a courageous, evolutionary, and civilizationally progressive choice. Despite the dissolution of Yugoslavia, it is entirely possible that many of them would still argue today that the Yugoslav concept remains a compelling paradigm—one that could, in some hypothetical future, prove to be the ideal solution for the South Slavs.

All the peoples of Yugoslavia, except for the Serbs, were incompatible with the policy of merging into a single Yugoslav nation. This primarily refers to the Croat and Slovene people due to their centuries-long unrealized aspirations to form their own states. To use a parable: when a young man, mature and ready to face the challenges of an independent life, wants to leave his parents' home, any attempts by the parents to prevent or delay the separation would only meet resistance, anger, condemnation, and accusations, but the separation would inevitably happen. The process of becoming independent is necessary, natural, and evolutionary.

In this, I see the biggest mistake of the Serbian political elite at the moment when they decided to create Yugoslavia. They neither anticipated, understood, nor respected the aspirations for independence of their Croat and Slovene brethren. Encouraged by war victories and prone to militaristic thinking, some circles in Serbia believed that weapons, the army, the police, and a strong state apparatus could solve everything. Events have shown how wrong they were, although, due to the Serbs' propensity for mythomania and a biased view of their own national past, there are still people in Serbia today with identical illusions about the power of a "strong hand." Because of this simple and obvious fact, I advocate the view that *Yugoslavia was doomed to fail from the moment it was formed.* Historical events confirm the correctness of this perspective: from the very beginning of living together, we can see the aspirations of the Serbs to preserve Yugoslavia and those of the Croats and Slovenes to eventually leave it.

To this, we should add the aspirations of Bosniaks and Macedonians to form and affirm their own nations, and then establish national states, as well as Montenegrins' desire to restore their statehood. Yugoslavia served as an ideal incubator for all of them, and in this light, we should consider its deep internal contradiction. In other words, in light of these processes, it becomes clear why the Serbian interest in Yugoslavia was the only one representing integralism, while the interests of all other peoples were directed towards national maturation, emancipation, and ultimate independence.

***

The 1974 Constitution set the stage and provided the legal framework for the disintegration of Yugoslavia into its federal units. Most actors awaited Tito's death to initiate the process of separation and independence.

On the other hand, it should be noted that Serbia had significantly evolved from its initially rigid and dominant stance at the beginning of Yugoslavia, and deserved better treatment. In the last twenty years of Yugoslavia's existence, Serbia attempted to appeal and argue for a change in its unfavorable constitutional status with the other republics. In response, it always faced rejection and accusations of resurrecting Serbian hegemonism. Nothing helped—not the strength of the arguments, nor the sinking of the dysfunctional federation into economic difficulties and debt, nor warnings from international institutions such as the IMF about the necessity of strengthening the federal government and federal institutions. Slovenia, Croatia, and Kosovo were, as a rule, against proposals from Serbia. The secessionists successfully "reined in" Serbia, which, along with the Army, was the only entity that wanted to protect the federation. This inevitably intensified frustration, dissatisfaction, disappointment, and hurt among Serbs. The genie was already quite agitated in the bottle, and internal pressure was mounting. A neutral observer of that time could already conclude with great certainty that the Serbs would not allow themselves to sink along with the ship they had created.

The SANU Memorandum

In 1986, the public was made aware of the "leak" of a controversial and unfinished document drafted by a group of sixteen academics from the Serbian Academy of Sciences and Arts (SANU). Following a call from Ivan Stambolić, then-president of the Presidency of the Socialist Republic of Serbia, for a government discussion on the difficult situation in Kosovo, the Academy established a committee consisting of sixteen prominent aca-

280

demics. This committee was tasked with creating a memorandum that addressed the causes of the economic-political crisis in Yugoslavia and suggested solutions to resolve the issues. In this manner, a portion of the Serbian intellectual elite became involved in the political life of the country by publicly expressing opinions that some met with utmost condemnation, while others viewed as sincere and politically straightforward articulation of what weighed heavily on the hearts of Serbs. The document itself never received internal approval from the Academy's bodies, nor was it ever edited. It was a draft that, in a somewhat peculiar way, ended up in the hands of a journalist from a Belgrade tabloid and was subsequently attacked in its pages. The newspaper did not publish the Memorandum's text, but characterized it as "nationalistic" and "reactionary."

While the work on drafting the Memorandum was ongoing, it was evident that some intelligence circles had gotten hold of the text. The authorities decided to condemn and discredit the document, and remove its authors from political life. Serbian communists competed in criticizing both the Memorandum and the Academy as a whole. Soon after, the League of Communists of Yugoslavia condemned the document, and Slobodan Milošević—then an up-and-coming Belgrade communist—described it as "nothing less than the darkest nationalism."

At first, the West viewed the Memorandum favorably, considering it anti-communist. Later, the narrative that prevailed globally and among a portion of the domestic public—imposed by separatist currents in Yugoslavia—was that the Memorandum was a "political platform on which the Serbian nationalist movement led by Slobodan Milošević later emerged" and that the SANU Memorandum was the "document that initiated the breakup of Yugoslavia."

Did the 1986 SANU Memorandum really initiate the breakup of Yugoslavia?

All the processes and events analyzed thus far clearly demonstrate the depth and decades-long duration of the conflict between secessionists and unitarists in Yugoslavia, easily debunking such a narrative. It is nothing more than a "spin"—propaganda aimed at shifting the sentiment of the global and Yugoslav public in favor of the secessionist bloc. It was a brazen reversal of the thesis, with secessionists attempting to shift responsibility onto the Serbs. Just before the beginning of the final phase of the long-prepared separation, the Serbian people—the only ones who wanted to preserve Yugoslavia—were loudly blamed for everything.

The use of "spin" techniques—propaganda through the non-objective, biased, or entirely inaccurate interpretation of an event, campaign, or document to intentionally manipulate public opinion in favor of the entity launching the "spin"—served secessionists during the final stages of Yugoslavia's disintegration. The unfinished document drafted by a group of Serbian academics can only be seen as the tip of the iceberg and not as any cause for the breakup of Yugoslavia. Such a thesis is naive and absurd. The effort to misuse the Memorandum's text to attribute responsibility for the country's breakup to Serbia is transparent and dishonest. It is pure manipulation and disinformation that has, surprisingly, been uncritically accepted outside of Yugoslavia. The essential reasons for the crisis and the subsequent multi-decade centrifugal processes are detailed in the pages of this book. Yugoslavia dissolved because the majority of its peoples wanted to form national states, opposed by the Serbian people's desire to keep Yugoslavia intact. Unfortunately, both tendencies were influenced by foreign factors, a fact that must not be overlooked.

Examining the content of the document today, more than three decades later, reveals that it accurately predicted future developments in Yugoslavia. The group of academics' efforts were aimed at preserving Yugoslavia and pointing out ways to overcome accumulated problems. Of course, any such intention, at a time when the secessionists finally had the breakup of Yugoslavia within their grasp, was most vehemently and orchestratedly rejected and condemned, with Serbia labeled as wanting to dominate others.

Serbs were not directly breaking up Yugoslavia—on the contrary. However, their persistent efforts to preserve it were an impossible mission. It is abundantly clear that no federation, loose confederation, or even an asymmetric federation, as the last incarnation of the idea of weakening the common state, could satisfy the aspirations of Slovenia, Croatia, and ultimately, Kosovo for their own states. Even if the Serbs had indefinitely agreed to their impossible status within the federation, even if Yugoslavia had been redefined as an asymmetric federation of Slovenia and Croatia on one side and the other republics on the other, it would have still eventually disintegrated. The agony would have only lasted a few more years. In my opinion, this is entirely clear from today's perspective.

However, the thesis reversal remains a problem that still burdens relations between Serbs on one side and Slovenians and Croatians on the other. Accusing the Serbs of motivating others to leave Yugoslavia by their efforts to strengthen and preserve it is, at the very least, an unfair half-truth. We can only hope that responsible leaders will emerge in Slovenia and Croatia on one side, and Serbia on the other, who will be able to call the social processes that occurred in Yugoslavia by their proper name.

It should be emphasized that for today's efforts toward reconciliation, it is essential that the actors recognize their role as proxies in the competition of great powers on the territory of the former Yugoslavia. By the late

1980s, it seems that neither the West nor the USSR had any interest in the continued existence of the South Slav federation.

Did the great powers—as so many times in previous history—intervene and confront each other by instrumentalizing the local small nations: Croats, Slovenians, Bosniaks, and Kosovo Albanians on one side, against the isolated Serbs on the other side?

The Last Guardians of Tito's Yugoslavia— the Yugoslav People's Army and the Counterintelligence Service

"The armed forces of the Socialist Federal Republic of Yugoslavia protect the independence, sovereignty, territorial integrity, and the social system established by this constitution of the Socialist Federal Republic of Yugoslavia."

Constitution of the Socialist Federal Republic of Yugoslavia (1974),
Article 240

Following the death of Josip Broz Tito, the Yugoslav People's Army (JNA) was the only federal institution that firmly adhered to the principles of Titoism. The military's top brass consisted mainly of older generals loyal to Tito's political legacy and the original achievements of the Revolution. It was widely believed that the Organization of the League of Communists in the JNA (OSKJ) was the bastion that gathered the staunchest and most conservative communist core in the country. The OSKJ constituted the ideological backbone of the army and was responsible for its monolithic nature and internal strength.

The de facto confederalization of Yugoslavia, along with the weakening of central authority following the adoption of the 1974 Constitution, greatly troubled the JNA leadership. As the foundation of society and the "forge of brotherhood and unity," the military remained the sole and strongest institution in Yugoslavia that continued to function relatively well. The multiethnic officer corps, raised on the ideals of the People's Liberation Struggle and the communist revolution, seemed to regard the commitment to Yugoslavia—its territorial integrity and unity—as inviolable values. Generally heavily indoctrinated and enjoying a privileged position in society, the officers grew suspicious of the initial signs of pro-Western democratization that tentatively emerged in the mid-1980s.

Perhaps most importantly, the JNA held a constitutionally mandated duty to ensure the preservation of a unified Yugoslavia—a principle enshrined in the solemn oath taken by all members of the armed forces.

Today, it is relatively well-known that Yugoslavia had one of the strongest secret services in the world. Within this complex apparatus, the intelligence structures in the army were exceptionally powerful, well-equipped, and organized. The most renowned among them—the military Counterintelligence Service (KOS)—was held in high esteem. It was often described as a formidable, highly secretive, and dangerous organization that was not to be taken lightly. Established as an independent service in 1946, the KOS was tasked with counterintelligence protection of the army from intelligence and subversive activities, preventing foreign intelligence services from acting against the JNA, and implementing preventive security measures in units. KOS officers had the authority to detain and interrogate individuals suspected of espionage, sabotage, diversions, terrorism, agitation, propaganda, and other acts against the state, the people, or individuals. The head of this service consistently held the position of Assistant Minister of Defense and was required to be part of the top leadership of the League of Communists of Yugoslavia.

Following the ousting of Aleksandar Ranković in 1966 and the political defeat of the centralists, the once-unified civil Federal Security Service was divided into republic-level administrations. As a result, the KOS remained the only cohesive intelligence force that, along with the army to which it belonged, staunchly stood on the ramparts of preserving a unified Yugoslavia. Due to the nature of its work, this service analyzed various scenarios that could arise in the country after Tito's death. From the statements of the highest military officials, we learn that the KOS had assessed that Yugoslavia was inevitably sliding towards disintegration—likely even during Tito's lifetime. Fulfilling its constitutionally defined role, the powerful service devised plans to prevent such a scenario and preserve the country.

Thus, the JNA served as the force in Yugoslav society that sought to preserve the status quo, an important fact for our consideration. This primarily referred to the constitutional order and territorial integrity, positioning the army as the last bastion of the concept of integral Yugoslavism. However, from an ideological perspective, the army held an unsustainable position in the long run, as it firmly opposed any system change that would lead to the democratization of society. By the mid-1980s, Yugoslavia faced severe economic problems, while the atmosphere in Europe began to hint at upcoming changes. At that time, I was quite young, and I vividly remember the aspirations of my generation, which hoped for the fall of communism and democratic changes. In order to suppress the growing sentiment for modernization and transition to multi-party democracy and a market economy across Yugoslavia, the KOS was very active, and its presence was felt. The ideological propaganda activities emanating from the JNA in those years clearly indicated its determination to oppose societal changes.

In the mid-1980s, the Yugoslav intelligence services knew that the end of communism in Europe was approaching, and that the West would increase pressure on the Warsaw Pact countries. However, a different scenario was envisioned for Yugoslavia. In the introduction of a document defining US policy toward Yugoslavia, signed by US President Ronald Reagan on March 14th, 1984, it is stated:

> "...an independent, economically viable, stable, and militarily capable Yugoslavia serves Western and US interests. Yugoslavia is an important obstacle to Soviet expansionism and hegemony in southern Europe. Yugoslavia also serves as a useful reminder to countries in Eastern Europe of the advantages of independence from Moscow and of the benefits of friendly relations with the West."[69]

Furthermore, in the directives, President Reagan proposes activities to pursue "our long-established policy of support for the independence, territorial integrity, and national unity of Yugoslavia." Measures of economic assistance were ordered to overcome economic problems and ensure the continuation of cooperation in the field of supplying Yugoslavia with Western weaponry: "It is in the interest of the United States that Yugoslavia can resist the pressures of the Soviet Union and the Warsaw Pact." The document reveals another important role that Yugoslavia had for the West in the sphere of international relations: "Our policy will continue to be to encourage Yugoslavia to play a moderating role within the Non-Aligned Movement and to counter Cuban and Soviet influence in that organization."

The presented assessments completely confirm all previous conclusions that *Yugoslavia, from its inception until the end of the 1980s, was in political agreement with the geopolitical interests of the West* and enjoyed the benefits of such alignment. However, there was a change in Yugoslavia's course. What could have been the reason for such a change, which would bring hostility from the West and far-reaching consequences?

Hints of what would become an insurmountable obstacle are found in the same document. Reagan instructs the administration to "continue to encourage Yugoslavia's long-term internal liberalization" and "promote

---

[69] National Security Decision Directives. 1984. *NSDD 133: United States Policy towards Yugoslavia*. March 14th.

the trend toward an effective, market-oriented Yugoslav economic structure."

Thus, it becomes entirely evident that America no longer desired Yugoslavia under the leadership of the League of Communists, with a society structured based on the experimental model of socialist self-management. The US wanted a democratic, multi-party, multinational democracy with a market economy. This would mean that the Yugoslav communist leadership had to step down from power, abandon ideals and social privileges—and go into history.

For these people, such a scenario was not an option, and they worked intensively to prevent it. According to the testimony of former Federal Secretary for National Defense, Admiral of the Fleet Branko Mamula, a detailed plan for the Yugoslav People's Army (JNA) to take over power in the country was drawn up in 1986, but was never implemented. However, that same year, the state strategy of "Universal People's Defense" was changed, and for the first time, the JNA was given a mandate to engage in internal matters in Yugoslavia. Mamula actively worked to weaken the republics' territorial defenses and the influence of the republics on the army as a whole, which is why he was criticized in Slovenia and Croatia. In a recent television interview, he expressed his belief that the army should have taken power in the country immediately after Tito's death, thus preventing a bloody civil war.

The Tip of the Iceberg:
The Emergence of Slobodan Milošević

Today, in the secessionist republics of Yugoslavia, it is portrayed that their nationalisms and secessionisms emerged as a reaction to Serbian nationalism. Serbia and Slobodan Milošević are blamed, and it is claimed that "everything began" with him. This thesis has been uncritically accepted, becoming the prevailing narrative worldwide—particularly in the West. However, the evidence thus far unambiguously reveals that the breakup of Yugoslavia was a highly complex process with deep roots extending far into the past. Yugoslavia was unstable from its inception, weathering several crises that nearly led to its demise. I concur with the viewpoint that Milošević served as an ideal excuse for republics seeking to exit Yugoslavia—his presence could hardly have been more ideal. Yet, the thesis that "everything began" with and because of him is easily refuted. A cursory examination of the recent and distant past, thoroughly analyzed in previous chapters, suffices.

Nationalisms and separatist movements in Yugoslavia were ever-present. They existed among all the constituent peoples, as well as national minorities. As for Serbian nationalism, during Tito's Yugoslavia, it was actively suppressed and weaker than other nationalisms; however, this fact remains largely unknown worldwide. Contrary to the propagated narrative portraying Serbs as the destroyers of Yugoslavia, we have demonstrated why they were, in fact, the closest to the ideas of Yugoslavism and sought to preserve the common state. Supporting this argument is the statistical fact that Serbs were most likely to enter mixed marriages with members of other nations. It is crucial to recall that as early as the 1920s, the Comintern characterized Yugoslavia as an "artificial, imperialist creation" and condemned the Serbs—who had created it—as an "oppressive and hegemonic people." Yugoslav communists, a majority of whom were Serbs, accepted the Party's stance and adhered to it for decades. This adherence fostered an imposed sense of collective guilt. I vividly remember how people in Serbia hesitated to declare their nationality, while other nations did so spontaneously and without restraint. To say in Yugoslavia, "I am a Serb" was associated with a suppressed feeling of unease and shame.

Thus, the thesis that Serbian nationalism emerged as a reaction to separatist pressures on Yugoslavia—a state that was of vital interest to the Serbian people—is much more grounded. The brunt of these pressures was directed at the Serbs as a nation and their homeland, the Republic of Serbia.

In other words, the multi-decade separatist and nationalist tendencies in Yugoslavia, ideological disqualifications, the imposition of collective guilt, and the constitutional fragmentation and weakening of the Republic of Serbia provoked a sense of homogenization and nationalism among Serbs as a response to Yugoslavia's slide towards disintegration.

But how and why did the Yugoslav communist oligarchy encourage Serbian nationalism, only to later exploit it for its own interests?

Early Biography

Throughout my whole life, Kosovo has been in the news. I often wonder, will it ever stop? Is the Kosovo issue impossible to resolve? Is it like a Balkan Palestine, whose pendulum of violence and mutual harm eternally swings between Serbs and Albanians? Sacred land for Orthodox Serbs and home to a predominantly Albanian Muslim population over the past few centuries, it has consistently captured the media's attention with virtually no respite since 1981.

On April 24th, 1987, the meteoric rise of Slobodan Milošević's political career began in Kosovo. Twelve years later, that career suffered a catastrophic defeat, leaving devastating consequences for Serbia and the Serbian people as a whole. The climax of this tragic period occurred on June 9th, 1999, when Serbia, under his leadership, de facto lost state sovereignty over Kosovo. Where it began, the ominous cycle closed.

Slobodan Milošević was born on August 20th, 1941, just a few months after Nazi Germany occupied and dismembered Yugoslavia. His parents, father Svetozar and mother Stanislava, were originally from northern Montenegro. Ideologically, the two were quite distant. His mother was a teacher and a convinced communist, while his father taught religious education before the war, and Serbian and Russian languages afterward. Shortly after the war ended,

Stanislava Milošević with sons Borislav and Slobodan (right)

his father left the family and returned to Montenegro. His mother continued to care for the children on her own, looking after her sons, Slobodan and his slightly older brother, Borislav.

During his high school days, Slobodan met Mirjana Marković, the love of his life, a woman who would accompany him every step of the tumultuous journey that destiny had in store for him.

While he was a successful law student at the University of Belgrade, Slobodan learned that his father had committed suicide. A year later, Slobodan's uncle—his mother's brother, Milosav Koljenšić, a major general in the Yugoslav People's Army and a high-ranking counterintelligence officer—also took his own life. Finally, in 1972, Slobodan's mother, Stanislava Milošević, committed suicide as well. Such a tragic sequence of events couldn't help but leave deep emotional scars, a kind of emotional amputation, on the young man. Slobodan found the strength to move forward, finishing his studies with excellent grades. During one year of his studies, he even won a traditional faculty oratory competition. This skill would later prove to be very significant in his political career. Milošević undoubtedly had a talent for igniting the masses with his speeches.

Mirjana "Mira" Marković had a similar family tragedy to Slobodan's. She was born in 1942 as the child of an extramarital affair between pre-war Communist Party member and Partisan Vera Miletić and high-ranking Partisan commander and revolutionary Moma Marković. During the war, Vera stayed in Belgrade with the task of restoring the Party's work and the efforts of the underground fighters who battled against the Nazis. She was discovered and arrested by Special Police agents and subjected to horrific torture, during which she gave up a number of activists. They were all subsequently arrested, tortured, and killed. Vera was executed in a concentration camp in 1944.

Mirjana Marković
(1942–2019),
wife of
Slobodan Milošević

Immediately after Mira's birth, her grandparents—Vera's parents—took care of her. The father merely recognized his paternity, but the care of the girl was left to her maternal grandparents even after the war. A very interesting detail is that a close relative of Mira's mother, Vera, was Davorjanka Paunović, the war secretary and greatest love of Josip Broz Tito.

It is very likely that these family traumas brought Slobodan and Mirjana closer together, forging a strong lifelong bond that began in their high school days and lasted until Slobodan's death in 2006. They got married in 1965 and had two children, Marija and Marko.

People who had personal insight into their relationship mostly agree that it was exceptionally strong, and that Mirjana often had a decisive influence on Slobodan's reasoning. Many contemporaries viewed her as the driving force behind Milošević, believing that her responsibility for the tragic events in Yugoslavia remained hidden, even though it was actually significant.

Slobodan Milošević joined the League of Communists of Yugoslavia at just nineteen years old. He was a committed communist but belonged to a new generation not burdened by the Revolution and the heroic struggle against the superior occupiers during World War II. Milošević's generation of communists was characterized by a modern approach to everything, technocracy, and pragmatism. His early political career was marked by a friendship with Ivan Stambolić, which began during the 1960s. Ivan came from a family whose main exponent, Petar Stambolić, was one of the most powerful people in Serbia and Yugoslavia and part of Tito's inner circle. Ivan and Slobodan became close friends and collaborators. Ivan recognized Slobodan's seriousness and dedication in carrying out party tasks, as well as a certain aggressiveness he sometimes used in internal party conflicts. Milošević succeeded Stambolić in a leadership position at Tehnogas, a successful Belgrade company. In the late 1970s, he moved to the banking sector, where Ivan secured him a position as director of Beobanka, one of the largest banks in Yugoslavia at the time. During his banking career, Slobodan traveled to New York and Paris many times. According to some accounts, he left a positive impression on David Rockefeller, who, after one encounter, said, "This one will go far."

Who Was Really Behind Milošević?

Despite his ambition as a banking official, it was a political career that truly captured his interest, and he decidedly pursued this path in the early 1980s. In 1984, he ascended to the role of president of the Belgrade Communists, and a mere two years later, in May 1986, he was elected as the leader of the League of Communists of Serbia—a position that effectively held the most power in the Republic.

Who supported Milošević in his rise to become the leader of the Serbian communists? Was the decisive influence a long-time friend and mentor, the moderate Ivan Stambolić, who was then the President of the Presidency of Serbia? Milošević would first politically destroy him and, years later, liquidate him. It appears that another, less conspicuous factor likely played a more significant role. It was a conservative communist core at the helm of the Yugoslav People's Army (JNA), leaning towards the ideas of centralism and the politics of a firm hand.

At the moment when Milošević was catapulted into the political orbit, there was a matching of intentions between the vast majority of the staff in the JNA and the Serbian people scattered throughout Yugoslavia. Both parties sought to preserve the state. This alignment of interests between the most powerful force in the country and the biggest nation soon began to yield tangible results.

At the pinnacle of the pyramid, a small circle of individuals held immense power. Those with a decisive influence on the army and security services believed that the energetic Milošević, who advocated for improving the situation in Yugoslavia, would be a better choice than the more moderate and politically spent Stambolić. They expected the skilled speaker and proven Party soldier to strictly follow their instructions and mobilize the masses to achieve the established agenda. In essence, their primary goal was the mere preservation of power and positions. The West introduced changes that were powerfully knocking on Europe's door, and they were acutely aware of this. Nevertheless, they were determined to fight and survive. It is worth noting that these people were also fearful for their own fate. Milošević became their trump card in the unfolding game. But who were these individuals?

According to available information, the most significant person who influenced Milošević's political ascent was retired General of the Army Nikola Ljubičić. At the time of Tito's death, this man was the most powerful in Yugoslavia. Following an impressive wartime and post-war military career, Ljubičić became the highest-ranking officer in the JNA, Tito's right-hand man, and Federal Secretary for National Defense for four terms—from 1967 to 1982. No one held the top position in the JNA longer than Ljubičić. For the next two years, he served as President of the Presidency of Serbia, and from 1984 to 1989, he was Serbia's representative in the Presidency of Yugoslavia. He was the link between Milošević and the retired war generals of the JNA, national heroes, and people who still had a strong influence on younger and active generals. Additionally, Ljubičić had considerable sway over intelligence structures, primarily the KOS.

The orchestrated rise of Milošević to power also involved retired General Petar Gračanin, Chief of the General Staff of the JNA from 1982 to 1985, President of the Presidency of Serbia from 1987 to 1989, and Federal Secretary for Internal Affairs of Yugoslavia from 1989 to 1991. The third significant figure was the Secretary for National Defense of Yugoslavia, Fleet Admiral Branko Mamula, a former Chief of the General Staff of the JNA. He was also close to Tito and enjoyed his trust at one time.

General Nikola Ljubičić
Federal Secretary for National Defense (1967-1982)

These three men were not only at the top of the hierarchy of power due to the positions they held, but also because of the respect they commanded. To understand the ideological profile and value system of Milošević's sponsors, Ljubičić's statement is particularly interesting, in which he expresses his unwavering support for Milošević because he "actively fought against nationalism, liberalism, and all forms of counterrevolution in Belgrade." Those who lived under communism know that the phrase "all forms of counterrevolution" was often used by the authorities to deal with any initiative for the democratization of the system. Thus, the senior communist praised the junior communist, from whom he expected to justify the trust placed in him and maintain a hard line.

It is clear that this was undoubtedly the conservative communist wing with a Bolshevik-centralist-Titoist orientation, which sought to survive the impending democratization of Eastern Europe by using outdated communist dogmas and the military force of the JNA. Neither they nor their political puppet Milošević were nationalists. They were powerholders who saw the West's efforts to tear down the Berlin Wall as an immediate threat—primarily to themselves, and then to the system in which they were the privileged ruling class.

Around this time, the shaping of public opinion began. Through the media, a firm stance was conveyed to the Yugoslav public from the highest level. It was a kind of battle cry and, at the same time, a clear threat directed at all Yugoslav separatists. I remember the moment when I first read it in the daily press. I paused and read it several times. As the agitation within me grew, I thought that a tragedy was looming before us that could no longer be avoided.

> "Yugoslavia was created through a hard struggle in the war, and it would only step down from the historical stage through a struggle, not at some negotiating table."

A few weeks before hospitalization, Tito convened his final meeting with the top JNA officials on December 21ˢᵗ, 1979. During this assembly, he subtly alluded to his mortality, recognizing the severity of the country's crisis. As the supreme commander, he directed the Army to safeguard Yugoslavia, cautioning that any other path would lead to 'tragedy and fratricidal war.' Positioned beside Tito were General of the Army Nikola Ljubičić on his left and Admiral of the Fleet Branko Mamula on his right. Ironically, eight years later, they would facilitate Slobodan Milošević's rise to power.

Operational Implementation of the Plan
to Preserve the Yugoslav Communist Regime

"...There are three great passions: alcohol, gambling, and power. People can somehow recover from the first two, but never from the third. Power is the heaviest vice. Because of it, people kill, die, and lose their humanity. It is irresistible, like a magic stone, for it provides authority. It is the genie from Aladdin's lamp, serving any fool who holds it. Separately, they mean nothing; together, they are the scourge of this world. There is no honest and wise authority, for the desire for power is boundless. Cowards encourage those in power, flatterers embolden them, and thieves support them, so their self-image is always more beautiful than the truth. They consider everyone else foolish because people hide their true opinions, and they claim the right to know everything—and people accept it. No one in power is wise, for even the wise soon lose their judgment, and no one is tolerant, for they hate change. They immediately create eternal laws, eternal principles, and eternal structures, and by tying power to God, they solidify their control."

Meša Selimović,
Yugoslav writer

As expected, the powerful Yugoslav oligarchy did not want to step down. They had a vast apparatus behind them: a large, well-equipped army; a strong intelligence and counterintelligence service with an extensive network of operatives at home and abroad; and a respectable military industry whose revenues reached several billion US dollars annually. The top brass controlled almost all of the media in the country, as well as the League of Communists with hundreds of thousands of members. The hardline wing of the Party was mainly composed of older cadres who could not or would not reform and adapt to the changing times or heed the growing calls for openness and democratization coming from the people. From their perspective, they saw themselves as guardians of the revolution and the state entrusted to them. Giving up power would represent both a defeat and betrayal of their ideals, as well as a loss of social privileges and status.

The tentacles of the communist leaders were everywhere in society, as this enabled totalitarian control. As they began to close ranks against the impending threat from the "imperialist West," it became clear they had a strong foothold in the Serbian Academy of Sciences and Arts, and even in the Serbian Orthodox Church, which found its former oppressors—the communists—more acceptable than the West. Why was this the case? In light of the ongoing struggle between East and West in the Balkans, it is logical to expect the Orthodox Church to react to Western expansionism by seeking protection and support from the most powerful state of Orthodox civilization—Russia.

Thus, this unique sequence of events and historical circumstances led to the creation of an unnatural coalition of interests that included the Yugoslav military leadership, the military-security elite, the hardline wing of the League of Communists, a portion of the Serbian Academy of Sciences and Arts, and a part of the Serbian Orthodox Church. Their common interest was to survive the fall of the Berlin Wall and resist the approaching tsunami of Western democracy. At this critical moment, they abandoned their previous pro-Western geopolitical orientation and turned to conservative military-intelligence-communist circles in Moscow, which faced the same tsunami. This led to a collaboration that opened a front in Yugoslavia against the West, which would intensify over the next decade.

To survive and maintain power, the Yugoslav oligarchy needed four basic things:

1. Territory

Ideally, this was to be the entire Yugoslav state. If that proved impossible, they would settle for a reduced or "abbreviated" version that would welcome anyone who embraced the proclaimed achievements of the communist revolution and the people's liberation struggle: Yugoslavism, brotherhood and unity, socialism, humanism, equality, freedom, and equal rights. Many grand yet empty words were spoken from various sides, all with the aim of mobilizing another crucial factor:

2. Population

This category was intended to include all Serbs, wherever they lived in Yugoslavia. First, those from Serbia, and then Serbs who lived in significant proportions in other republics and provinces: Bosnia and Herzegovina, Croatia, Vojvodina, and Kosovo and Metohija. They would be joined by other nations who wished to continue living in a common state based on the ideological foundations of original Titoism.

3. Funding for the war

To preserve the whole of Yugoslavia or, in a more likely scenario, to forcibly separate the separatists from pro-Yugoslavs, a vast amount of money was needed for war. This was collected in the late 1980s and early 1990s through the brutal plundering of the Serbian people. State loans and "self-contributions" for the "rebirth of Serbia" were issued but never repaid; fraudulent banking pyramid schemes were launched, and people lost their money due to false promises of large profits. The plundering continued with the orchestrated bankruptcy of all banks, where the entire foreign currency savings of the population vanished. The final blow and complete impoverishment occurred during the peak of the Yugoslav wars in the fall of 1993 when the state launched the worst hyperinflation in world history to transfer the little remaining foreign cash held by the population into the hands of the criminalized state apparatus.

4. A populist leader

This person needed to be a proven communist—loyal to the oligarchy's top ranks, a good speaker, and a charismatic politician—who would assert himself as the new leader, becoming the "new Tito" and replacing the lukewarm multi-member Presidency at the head of the state. His primary focus would be on Yugoslavism, but his task would be to gain support from the entire political spectrum under the umbrella of his political agitation, from the far right to the far left. The justification for the "Serbs, Unite!" agenda would be the strengthening of nationalism on the wings of spreading fear of the state and people's immediate endangerment, both from internal and external enemies. This role would be assigned to Slobodan Milošević.

***

The creators of this plan were aware that the Slovenes and Croats were much closer to leaving the federation than staying in it, and the same applied to the Kosovo Albanians. Since the Bosniaks, Macedonians, and Montenegrins were numerically much smaller, the main burden of creating some sort of "third Yugoslavia" was to be carried by the Serbs. It is indisputable that the majority of Serbs wanted the state to survive. However, what the authorities ignored and where their manipulation lies is the fact that the most populous nation also desired a democratic transformation of the country and a market economy.

In order to maintain some kind of state—with them at the helm and an unchanged social system—the rulers employed extensive propaganda to achieve national homogenization of Serbs. However, those who were most intensely exposed to this propaganda were the people I call the "peripheral Serbs."

Who were they?

These are the Serbs who lived in contact with Catholics or Muslims, and in the recent past, were persecuted and killed due to their faith and ethnic background. These individuals comprise the Serbs in Croatia, Bosnia and Herzegovina, and Kosovo. They also include their relatives or descendants who migrated after World War II and resided in Serbia. If I could encapsulate the message sent to them from the highest echelons of the state, the Church, and the Academy, it would declare, "If you allow Yugoslavia to be torn apart, if you are severed from the Serbian homeland as was done during World War II, you will face death once more. Genocide will recur. You will be expelled from your villages and towns, losing everything you possess. We must stand united—one nation, one government, one leader."

On the other hand, there were the "central Serbs"—the majority of whom did not have the traumatic fratricidal experiences of World War II embedded in their family memories. Manipulating them with propaganda and fear proved much more challenging. These individuals actively resisted the regime's dogmatic propaganda, desiring free elections and democracy over war and regressive totalitarianism. As anticipated, they were branded as traitors, cowards, and servants of the West. In response, in the ensuing years, they would amass on the streets of Belgrade and other Serbian cities—demonstrating and singing against the war, supporting the democratic opposition, and shouting at the communist rulers: "Red bandits!"

Of all the "peripheral Serbs," those from Kosovo experienced the most substantial pressure on a national basis. Consequently, the unraveling of the last act of the Yugoslav drama commenced with them.

First Gatherings of Serbs From Kosovo

Today, numerous voices can be heard downplaying the claims that Kosovar Serbs suffered pressure from Albanians after World War II. Personally, I have never been to Kosovo and cannot speak about it firsthand. However, I do remember something. As a child attending elementary school, I spent a lot of time with my grandmother—an exceptionally religious woman who was wholly dedicated to the church. Not only did she adhere to fasting and prayer, but she also frequently organized collections of essential supplies and other necessities for Serbian monasteries. Her small apartment in Belgrade served as a gathering place for both believers who left their offerings for the monasteries and monks and nuns who came to pick up sacks of flour, cardboard boxes filled with sugar, oil, detergents, and other goods from her perpetually overcrowded bedroom. As a playful little boy, I would encounter them almost daily and listen to their conversations. Some of their stories evoked fear, and naturally, I still remember them today. Nun Heruvima was a frequent visitor. On one occasion, I heard her talk about how the sisterhood had hunting rifles they always carried when they went out of the monastery into the forest to gather firewood. This surprised me. Why would nuns need guns? I thought it might be a precaution due to wild animals—wolves and bears that could be in the local mountains. This detail caught my attention, so I listened more closely, especially when she would—with a serious expression—lean towards my grandmother and whisper something to her. My grandmother's reaction to what Mother Heruvima confided in her was a mixture of surprise and disbelief, accompanied by head-shaking and anger permeated by a sense of helplessness. I would pretend to be engrossed in a game on the floor or watching television while actually straining my ears to discern what they were talking about. That's when I heard the words *theft, burglary, fear, rape, Albanians,* and *Kosovo.* I can't say whether Heruvima spoke of these things as something that happened to the monastery's sisterhood or her personally, or whether she recounted incidents she had heard about involving nuns from other Kosovo monasteries. However, I remember the impression that this woman was genuinely afraid.

In the mid-1980s, Serbs mustered the courage to begin gatherings in the towns of Kosovo and Metohija. Until then, public gatherings in Yugoslavia were almost exclusively organized by the regime, mainly on state holidays. Any other gathering was viewed as a threat to the authorities and often ended with police intervention. Serbs in Kosovo and Metohija wanted to gain the attention of officials and voice their grievances about the pressure they endured from separatist-minded Albanians.

Of course, not all Albanians were unpleasant and hostile towards Serbs. Although suspicion existed between the two peoples due to a burdensome history for which both sides shared some responsibility, most people lived in peace, side by side as good neighbors. Among Albanians, a deeply rooted honor code is cherished. It can be said that the Albanian majority generally behaved ethically and fairly towards the Serbian minority. However, incidents and pressures did occur.

When problems became very pronounced, Serbs began to gather and protest, but the local administration—predominantly ethnically Albanian—had no understanding for their appeals or interest in the problems they discussed. To make matters worse, on several occasions, they dispersed the gatherings using police force. Reacting to discrimination by the Kosovo administration, local Serbs decided to organize a protest march to Belgrade and present their problems to the state apparatus in the capital. They wanted someone in Yugoslavia to hear them.

"No one is allowed to beat you!"

However, the communist government at the time feared any form of mass gatherings. The leadership of the League of Communists of Serbia, wishing to prevent the protest march, decided to send someone to Kosovo with the task of calming the situation and addressing the gathered Serbs. The choice fell on Slobodan Milošević, who was then the second man in the party hierarchy but relatively unknown to the broader public.

This event, which can now be called historical, took place on April 24th, 1987, in the town of Kosovo Polje. Most eyewitnesses say that Slobodan did not know what was going to happen. The Serbs had been self-organized and quite desperate for some time, ready to provoke incidents to draw attention to themselves. When they heard that someone from Belgrade would indeed come to address them directly, several thousand people gathered from the town itself and other Kosovo regions with Serbian populations. A meeting of party officials with Serbian representatives was held in the gloomy auditorium of a cultural center that was too small to accommodate everyone. People who heard Milošević's official address were disappointed. It was a million-times-seen, hours-long communist speech full of vague and lukewarm clichés—nothing concrete, nothing that would give Serbs hope that their status would quickly change for the better.

In front of the building, a scuffle between the gathered people and the police—who were trying to prevent them from entering—was taking place at the time. Upon hearing the commotion, Milošević first went out onto the balcony to see what was happening, then stepped outside, passed through the police cordon, and entered the crowd. When people complained to him that the police were beating them, Milošević, shaking his head and visibly agitated, repeatedly uttered the fateful words that would unleash a wave of pent-up Serbian frustration in Yugoslavia and turn him into a national leader:

"No one is allowed to beat you!"

A TV Belgrade crew happened to be there and managed to capture the moment. The police retreated and actually stopped beating people with their batons. For the first time, a high-ranking party official had cast aside the mask of vague party clichés and demagoguery, decisively defending ordinary people. This event resonated in the collective consciousness of all Serbs in Yugoslavia, whose national feelings had been systematically suppressed for far too long. Everyone knew about the pressure Albanians put on Serbs and the repression that occurred, but no one dared to speak about it publicly. Dissatisfaction and powerlessness had been growing for years; the pressure had been mounting, and Milošević's words opened Pandora's box.

The moment when Slobodan Milošević utters:
"No one is allowed to beat you!"

In my deep conviction, that day, Slobodan Milošević realized the power he could gain and exactly how to obtain it. Soon everything would change. He rose above the system that day, and it went smoothly for him. "No one is allowed to beat you" evolved into: "I'm taking control."

Milošević took the Kosovo Polje event and the promise he made there very seriously. He acted quickly. Within a few months, he politically confronted the more moderate faction within the League of Communists of Serbia, accusing them of indecisiveness and hesitation in addressing the accumulated problems of Serbs in Yugoslavia, particularly in Kosovo. Not long after, he removed his mentor and close friend Ivan Stambolić from the position of President of the Presidency of Serbia and established himself as the absolute leader of the Serbian people, both in Serbia and in other parts of Yugoslavia. But it must not be forgotten that Milošević did not act alone; powerful figures from the military and intelligence services stood behind him.

Ivan Stambolić (1936-2000), mentor of Slobodan Milošević

Ivan Stambolić pursued a policy of persistent negotiations with other republics to revise the 1974 constitution and improve Serbia's position. Milošević believed others were deliberately obstructing and sabotaging these talks. As previously demonstrated, he was, unfortunately, entirely correct in this belief. His growing ego, fueled by the erupting emotions of the people who increasingly gathered to hear his speeches, as well as his arrogant temperament, convinced him that the time for soft diplomacy had been exhausted. However, it is quite certain that, especially during the first months of his political ascent, Milošević's main source of self-confidence came from the fact that he had powerful people above and beyond visible political structures supporting him, wanting to see him in a leadership position, and carrying out a preconceived plan.

Such a thing could only happen in a deeply weakened, rotten, and dysfunctional state. The forces that had systematically weakened the state for decades to eventually disassociate their republics were now faced with the consequence: the threat in the form of Slobodan Milošević and the shadowy clique with immense power that stood behind him.

Milošević's Political Tsunami:

Anti-Bureaucratic Revolution and the "Awakening of the People"

Oh Serbia, in three parts, you will be whole again!

Slogan of the anti-bureaucratic revolution

Milošević acted decisively and forcefully, employing fiery speeches and consciously aiming for the total mobilization of Serbs throughout Yugoslavia. The "hard-liners" sought to create a populist tsunami that would primarily unite people with communist-Yugoslav-unitary inclinations, reorganizing the endangered state based on the "original achievements of the national liberation struggle and the communist revolution"—essentially a return to the pre-1962 status. This anachronistic plan, considering the atmosphere in Europe and the balance of power between the USSR and the West at the time, received open support from Moscow. Logically, Moscow likely supported the "revolutionary" scenario in Yugoslavia to slow down the West's progress in Eastern Europe by opening a sort of "front" in the Balkans, reducing the pressure on the disintegrating USSR and buying time to save Russia itself.

The methods used to build the populist wave—intended to flood and transform the joint state—had the unpleasant taste of looming totalitarianism. It began with numerous gatherings and rallies of the "oppressed Serbian people," spilling over from Kosovo first into the rest of Serbia and later into other parts of Yugoslavia with predominantly Serbian populations.

Most newspapers and television stations were fully instrumentalized and used for crudely fueling populism. Propaganda was extremely strong,

301

relying partly on truth and partly on fabricating half-truths and inducing a mythomania to which Serbs were, unfortunately, very prone. Cases of crimes and oppression against Serbs, which indeed occurred in Kosovo over an extended period, were magnified and used to spread fear, anger, and revolt. Former Serbian and most Yugoslav politicians were condemned for their inability and unwillingness to help Serbia, as well as for conspiring against its legitimate interests. They were called bureaucrats who had become alienated not only from the ideals of the communist revolution but also from their own people. To be fair, these qualifications were partly accurate but also deliberately exaggerated. Within just a few months, Serbs were brought into a state of collective hysteria mixed with paranoia as an endangered people surrounded by ancient enemies. The stage for implementing the plan, which Milošević and his newly-formed apparatus of unquestioning followers called the "anti-bureaucratic revolution," was fully prepared.

It is certain that the main stages of the agenda for the events I describe were prepared much earlier, in analyses by Yugoslav security services that developed scenarios for saving the state. The outlines of that plan can be seen quite clearly: to use the "awakening of the people" to seize power and control first within the Republic of Serbia and then in the joint bodies of the Yugoslav federation. Serbs, as the most numerous people living in a large part of Yugoslavia, pro-Yugoslav oriented, with many mixed marriages, and with the largest number of members in the League of Communists of Yugoslavia, were seen as the necessary base for implementing the plan to preserve communist Yugoslavia. Behind it stood the old-guard elite, with Milošević carrying out their vision.

In the first phase of consolidation, it was necessary to bring loyal people to the forefront of the leadership of the autonomous provinces of Vojvodina and Kosovo and Metohija to secure consent for the adoption of a new constitution for the Socialist Republic of Serbia. This would annul the poor solutions imposed on it by the Yugoslav Constitution of 1974, which had made it a dysfunctional hostage to its own provinces.

Simultaneously, there was intensive propaganda and ideological activity through the media and numerous rallies aimed at winning over Yugoslav-oriented Montenegrins, Croats, Slovenes, Macedonians, and Bosniaks who wanted to preserve the common state. Together with the Serbs, all these people would form an absolute majority in the federation, and it could be preserved using political tools from the communist arsenal, such as party congresses or general referendums.

Aged revolutionaries and their descendants rose to defend the achievements of their struggle: communist Yugoslavia and their absolutist power with accompanying privileges. The West brought democratization and the end of communism to Eastern Europe, so it was seen as an immediate threat to losing power. Thus, the endangered USSR, once Yugoslavia's traditional enemy to the east, began to become an ally in their minds based on the principle "the enemy of my enemy is my friend."

I have no doubt that Serbia indeed had a need to change its highest legal act—on which there is broad agreement today among experts. However, the way in which Milošević and the hardline communist core intended to protect the legitimate interests of Serbs and Yugoslavs was anachronistic, regressive, and, as it turned out, entirely unsuccessful, with tragic far-reaching consequences.

Even then, I was aware that the overcrowded regime-organized buses, accompanied by deafening fanfares of the most primitively orchestrated media campaign, sent wherever needed to spread the revolution of "spontaneous awakenings of the people," would unfortunately bring nothing good to my country. Just a few years before these events, Milošević himself was a relatively anonymous but diligent communist apparatchik with a powerful friend, Ivan Stambolić, in a high position. When this ambitious and unscrupulous man carried out a purge within the Central Committee of the League of Communists of Serbia, I knew that his leadership style would bring less capable people to key positions. These were people who, under normal circumstances, would not have made significant progress in political structures nor been appointed to responsible managerial positions in the economy. Party mediocrities, often inferior and frustrated, now sought their chance in obedience to the absolutist-minded Milošević. The leader swiftly assembled a legion of thoughtless, regrettably frequently uneducated individuals who, once they obtained some authority, quickly revealed the darkest aspects of their personalities.

In the second half of 1988, the plan to re-centralize Serbia began to unfold. In the northern autonomous province of Vojvodina—which, due to its 70% Serbian population, was not burdened by secessionism like Kosovo—politicians offered only lukewarm and highly reserved support to Milošević. They were concerned about both their positions and the possibility that Vojvodina's autonomy might be abolished in the future.

To address this, Milošević's regime first sent instrumentalized Kosovo Serbs to the capital of Vojvodina, Novi Sad, to organize a massive rally and inform the majority Serbian population about the "Albanian genocide" they faced in Kosovo. The aim was to stimulate empathy and patriotic feelings among Vojvodina's Serbian population, turning them against the provincial leadership that opposed Milošević. Provincial officials were accused of "autonomism" and "chairmanship"—meaning they prioritized their positions over the plight of Kosovo Serbs. They were asked to consent to constitutional changes in the Serbian Assembly, which would limit the autonomy of the provinces and grant the republic the authority to legally and effectively protect Serbs in Kosovo from Albanian oppression. This all culminated on October 5th and 6th, when demonstrations involving over 150,000 people led to the resignations of the Vojvodina leadership; Milošcvić's trusted individuals were immediately appointed to their positions.

This moment was, in a way, Yugoslavia's Rubicon. Milošević demonstrated his ability to export revolution, and secessionist politicians in other republics took this very seriously. Concern was immediately apparent in Slovenia—a territorially and numerically small republic that had advanced the furthest in Western-style democratization and was waiting for a favorable opportunity to separate and become independent, regardless of the potential domino effect. Like a man bracing for wind gusts, secessionist-oriented oligarchies in other Yugoslav republics hunkered down and began preparations for the final showdown.

In contrast, Serbia embarked on a path to fulfill its interests, led by the wrong man in a key position—supported by powerful people both in the country and abroad with anachronistic aspirations—during the historically significant time following the fall of the Berlin Wall. This man pursued the wrong agenda with the wrong methods, rapidly making enemies within Yugoslavia and beyond, primarily in Europe and the United States. The middle and bourgeois classes, as well as intellectual and artistic circles of Serbian society, were appalled by Milošević. Resistance to everything he did and represented was strongest in Belgrade, but also in other primarily urban areas of Serbia.

The Meeting at Ušće

Belgrade, November 19th, 1988.

In the Soviet Union, Gorbachev's perestroika was underway, and all Eastern Bloc countries were reaching for multi-party elections and democratic reforms. The enormous communist empire was collapsing peacefully. Germans were rushing towards their reunification, which would mark the definitive end of the Cold War, a period of cooperation between Russia and the West, and the complete collapse of communism. The Warsaw Pact was disappearing, and with it, the significant geopolitical reason for Yugoslavia's existence as a neutral buffer zone between two military blocs.

We Yugoslavs were also delighted by these events. We wanted multiparty system, more freedom, a market economy, a better standard of living, world travel, and peace on our continent. A similar mood prevailed in Serbia. Previously, we showed that in Serbia during the 1980s, amidst attempts to maintain the struggling federation and enhance its weakening economy, there were calls for transitioning to a market economy. At that time, "pro-Western" Slovenia and Croatia prevented such an initiative from Serbia, citing ideological reasons, as long as it suited them. It is essential to note that during this period, Serbian public opinion, among all republics, was closest to a market economy and a multi-party system. However, after Milošević and the structures behind him took power, such

305

momentum in Serbian society was effectively thwarted. It is possible that these people saw democratization as too significant a risk and a weakness in their defense against the incoming Western influence.

A year before the fall of the Berlin Wall, the regime organized one of the largest rallies ever held in my country's history. While the world moved in one direction, they were determined to lead us in an entirely different one. In the leading role was Slobodan Milošević, then president of the Presidency of the Central Committee of the League of Communists of Serbia.

Near the confluence of the Sava and Danube rivers lies a vast natural plateau. On November 19th, 1988, from early morning, streams of people flocked to it, brought in for free on private and state buses from Serbia and other parts of Yugoslavia. Radio Television of Serbia and television stations from other republics broadcasted the event live. Several hundred thousand people gathered, hungry for the words and promises that the man they hoped would be their savior, the one who would resolve the crisis in Yugoslavia, would deliver that day at the "Rally of Brotherhood and Unity." And he did not disappoint. On the contrary, the former winner of the speech competition at the Belgrade Faculty of Law, interrupted by applause and ovations, evoked hope, faith, defiance, and pride. They believed in him and wanted to follow him, to fight for what he had convinced them were truth, justice, and the way out of the deep social crisis.

He began the speech in a communist manner, addressing the gathered crowd with "Comrades," and then continued in the spirit of mobilization:

"…such a large rally has not been held in Belgrade since its liberation. The last time this many people gathered on the streets of Belgrade for a grand idea was on October 20th, 1944. Back then, the people on the streets celebrated victory in the war and embarked on an immense battle to rebuild the ravaged country. Just as today, members of all Yugoslav peoples and nationalities stood together—many here today recall how in those days nothing felt difficult, and it seemed as if everything was easy and achievable in the realm of freedom."

Then, at a time when the winds of reform and the imminent collapse of communism were being felt throughout Central and Eastern Europe, he told the gathered Yugoslavs the good news that the revolution was not dead:

"It is true that we have stalled on the road to the society we desired in the revolution, but it is not true that we cannot create that society, that we should abandon that road."

Later in his speech, Milošević adeptly tapped into the feelings of betrayal and hurt experienced by Serbs, stemming from the lack of empathy shown by others in Yugoslavia for their issues. As a solution, he proposed the communist concept of class consciousness and class struggle:

"The solidarity of Yugoslav peoples, especially Yugoslav workers, has always been their most beautiful and strongest characteristic. It has been demonstrated in the assistance we have provided to oppressed peoples, the working class, and even individuals throughout the world. Therefore, it is difficult to explain why this solidarity has been late in manifesting itself to a greater extent, more quickly, and with a greater love when citizens of our own country have been concerned. The long absence of this solidarity for the endless suffering of Serbs and Montenegrins in Kosovo constitutes an unhealing wound on their hearts, as well as on the heart of all Serbia. But it is not a time for sorrow, it is a time for struggle."

In his desire to make everyone aware of the power of the people's energy that he initiated, Milošević says:

"This is a process that cannot be stopped by any force, against which every fear is weak."

Then, speaking about how Serbs can only live in freedom, he further inflames the fighting spirit, issuing a warning to traditional and other potential foreign enemies:

"...and the Turkish and German conquerors know that this nation is winning the battle for freedom. We entered both world wars naked and barefoot with the belief that we were fighting for justice and we won both wars."

Milošević then turns to the recently adopted conclusions of the League of Communists of Yugoslavia regarding the situation in Kosovo. While it is acknowledged that deep problems exist in the province, his rhetoric is intentionally belligerent instead of wise. He recognizes enemies everywhere and convinces those present, as well as the entire Yugoslav public, that an epic battle is inevitable:

"Now we also have unified views of the League of Communists of Yugoslavia on Kosovo, and we will implement them vigorously and to the end. We will win the battle for Kosovo regardless of the obstacles that are being placed before us both inside and outside the country. (...) We will emerge victorious, despite the fact that today, just as before, the enemies of Serbia are uniting against us, both inside and outside the country. We are telling them that we are not fearful at all, that we enter every battle with the intention of winning it, and that we have never waged unjust or unfair battles at the expense of other peoples."

Milošević explains the great significance of Kosovo for Serbia with the following words:

"Let no one be surprised that Serbia rose to its feet last summer because of Kosovo. Kosovo is the very center of its history, its culture, its memory. Every nation has a love that eternally warms its heart, and for Serbia, that is Kosovo. Therefore, Kosovo will remain in Serbia, and this will not be to the detriment of the Albanians."

Then, Milošević emotionally addresses the ethnic Albanians with an emphasis on the traditionally rooted pride and ethical code of this nation:

"I can tell the Albanians in Kosovo that nobody has ever found it difficult to live in Serbia because they were not Serbian.[70] Serbia has always been open to everyone: those with nowhere else to go, to the poor and the rich alike, to the happy and the desperate, to those who were only passing through and to those who wanted to stay.[71] The only people Serbia did not want were evil and bad people, even if they were Serbs. All Albanians in Kosovo who trust other people and respect other people are in their own country. I ask them to unite against the evil and hatred of their chauvinists because they do not only harm Serbs and Montenegrins but also their own Albanian people. They disgrace them in front of the world, shame them in front of their children, and insult their dignity. In this name, I call on Albanians throughout Kosovo to let Albanian mothers and fathers care for the peaceful sleep, calm schooling, and carefree play of Serbian and Montenegrin girls and boys, instead of police and military units, not only because such a division of care is more efficient, but also because it is more hu-

---

[70] Unfortunately, this claim is untrue. Repressive measures were carried out against Albanians in Serbia in the 19th century, then from 1912 to 1941, and again after their uprising in 1981. Repression against Turks and Bulgarians was also documented, up until 1941. In the fall of 1940, the Kingdom of Yugoslavia enacted anti-Jewish laws, and the collaborationist regime of General Nedić actively aided the Holocaust in occupied Serbia during World War II.

[71] In this sentence, Milošević mostly accurately describes the well-known generosity of the Serbian people.

man, more honest, fitting socialism and the ideals that we all in Yugoslavia are fighting for..."

Immediately after these well-phrased and motivating words, Milošević unexpectedly plunges into combative rhetoric, reminding the Yugoslavs of the ideals of the revolution, calling for unity under his leadership, and fighting against Albanian separatists:

"...and we remind the Yugoslav peoples, the working class, the youth, and the communists that half a century ago, Spain was not far away.[72] Many went to its barricades to fight against terror and hatred. Today, terror and hatred run rampant in Kosovo, which is in our Yugoslav land. To fight against the evil in Kosovo, it is not necessary to lay down one's life as once in Spain. It is enough to maintain the oath that we Yugoslavs swore to each other in 1941 that we will, in unity and brotherhood, share everything: both good and bad, victory and injustice, poverty, and build a new and better world."

Towards the end of his speech, Milošević promises reforms in Serbia and an increase in living standards, improvements in the health and education systems, and a flourishing of science and culture. He advocates for the equality of Serbia in relation to other republics of the Yugoslav Federation. Time will soon show that everything happened exactly the opposite of the given promises. In the last few sentences, with a tone that suggested determination to fight for the survival of the communist-Titoist Yugoslavia by all means, he addressed the broadest Yugoslav and global public:

"With this reform, we are moving towards changes that need to occur throughout Yugoslavia. I am confident that all Yugoslav peoples, all citizens of Yugoslavia, will find the strength in the coming months to overcome differences, intolerance, and conflicts, and together, in brotherhood, succeed in preserving, renewing, and developing their country. Tito's Yugoslavia is the achievement of the struggle, work, and love of all Yugoslav peoples and nationalities. (...) Yugoslavia was created in a magnificent revolution by Yugoslav communists, the Yugoslav working class, and the Yugoslav peoples. *It will not expire at the conference table, as its enemies hope. Yugoslavia was acquired through a great struggle and will be defended with a great struggle.*"

---

[72] This is a reference to the Spanish Civil War, in which many Yugoslav leftists participated in the fight against General Franco's regime.

Of the many slogans at the rally, one has remained forever in my memory. It expressed the first and most important point of the communist elite's plan: the formation of a strong populist leader whose political image would draw strength from the enormous reputation that Tito still had in the consciousness of the Yugoslavs.

"Now the people are greatly wondering: who will replace Tito for us? Now it is known who the second Tito is—Slobodan is a noble name."

Anti-Bureaucratic Revolution—Part Two

Montenegro

After addressing the Vojvodina "autonomists", the ignited locomotive of awakened and harnessed popular energy turned to the next target on the agenda—bringing like-minded individuals to power in the Republic of Montenegro. To describe the extremely close ties between Serbs and Montenegrins, who are ethnically nearly identical, a saying was coined in the past about "two eyes in one head"—they see the same and move together.

In this small Yugoslav republic, with only about 600,000 inhabitants, people were, as in Serbia, saddened, worried, and frustrated by the fact that Montenegrins living in Kosovo were also exposed, just like Serbs, to the pressure and terror of Albanian separatists for several decades after World War II. Many Montenegrins made significant contributions to the fight against Nazis and fascists as brave fighters of Tito's partisan movement. Many were committed communists, and even the capital of Montenegro bore the name Titograd ("Tito-city") until the democratic reforms of the 1990s.

In the post-war period, many occupied high positions in the League of Communists or held managerial positions within the state economy. Consequently, many lived and worked in Belgrade with their families. Naturally, Milošević's ideas and plans for resolving the Kosovo and Yugoslav issues by reaffirming the principles of the original communist revolution, and resorting to fighting if necessary, found fertile ground among the traditionally warrior-like and epic-loving Montenegrins. At this point, we must not overlook the fact that "Sloba" himself, as many affectionately called Milošević, was of both paternal and maternal descent from northern Montenegro. However, he declared himself a Serb for the rest of his life, which, to be fair, many Montenegrins still do today.

The coup process began predictably, with the organization of rallies in support of endangered Serbs and Montenegrins in Kosovo. Soon, support for Milošević's policy grew stronger, which the Montenegrin leadership at the time perceived as interference in the internal affairs of their republic and began dispersing demonstrations with police and tear gas. This only made things worse—awakening anger, increasing the number of protesters, and convincing people that the republic leadership was nothing more than a group of alienated bureaucrats who did not hear the voice of their people and did not care about their suffering, but only protected their privileged position. After the largest rally to date, held in Titograd on January 11th, 1989, the old communist leadership resigned, and younger officials—Momir Bulatović, Milo Djukanović, and Svetozar Marović, supporters of Slobodan Milošević—took the lead.

It should be noted that after these events, Mr. Djukanović had been at the forefront of Montenegro's leadership or had led the country independently for over 30 years. Only in 2023, did he lose the presidential election.

Kosovo

In Vojvodina and Montenegro, Milošević astutely anticipated that he could achieve a coup by rallying ethnic Serbs and Montenegrins primarily through populism and solidarity with their compatriots in separatism-ridden Kosovo.

But how could he carry out a coup in a province with an ethnic Albanian majority and leadership that—like those in Slovenia or Croatia—had been harboring aspirations for secession from Yugoslavia for decades? How could he persuade Kosovo to approve consent for such changes to the Serbian Constitution that would reduce Kosovo's autonomy and thus its chances of secession?

Albanians Had Their Plan Too

Over thirty years, the number of Kosovo Albanians nearly tripled. Could such robust population growth be attributed solely to natural increase?

According to many sources, it also involved the illegal migration of hundreds of thousands of Albanians from neighboring Albania to Kosovo, which the renegade leadership of the province facilitated by opening state borders in violation of republic and federal regulations. Serbia was unable to do anything to prevent it.

The official 1961 Yugoslav census indicated 646,000 Albanians and 227,000 Serbs living in Kosovo. Subsequent censuses revealed a dramatic rise in the Albanian population, peaking in the 1991 census. At that time, 1,600,000 Albanians and a mere 194,000 Serbs were recorded. Although the absolute number of Kosovo Serbs decreased by approximately 30,000 during this period, their proportion of the total population in the province plummeted from 23.55% in 1961 to a troubling 9.9% in 1991.

Communist Ideals as a Means of Fighting for the Unification of Serbia

Through the planned demographic dominance of Albanians, Kosovo was sliding towards independence. Milošević chose to halt this process by forcefully reaffirming Titoist ideology and its fundamental values: equality, brotherhood, unity, inter-ethnic tolerance, and communist social order.

Not all Albanians were separatists, nor were all Serbs nationalists. Many honest people had lived together as good neighbors for decades. Among the Kosovo Albanians, there were many communists who kept Tito's portraits in their homes and were proud to belong to the Party and the ideas that formed the foundation of Yugoslavia. In comparison to the lives of Albanians in the neighboring "autistic" Albania under the totalitarian rule of Enver Hoxha, Yugoslav Albanians had it much better, and they knew it. Therefore, many communist cadres in the structures of the Kosovo authorities were against any separatism or the breakup of Yugoslavia in favor of uniting Kosovo with Albania.

The Serbian leadership turned to the so-called "healthy forces" in the League of Communists of Kosovo and quickly achieved ideological unity and understanding with them. This faction was led by Rahman Morina, a man from the police and security structures. But the leader of the Kosovo Communists, Azem Vllasi, was a strong opponent of Milošević and his scenario for limiting autonomy. The conflict between the two factions soon spilled into street demonstrations, a general strike, and the protest of 1,500 Albanian miners in the mine near Pristina, the capital of the province. At that time, Milošević enjoyed certain support from the federal establishment for the stance that order and peace had to be established in Kosovo, and that riots and bloodshed like those that occurred in 1981 had to be prevented.

The Presidency of Yugoslavia, the collective head of state, declared a state of emergency in Kosovo on March 3rd, 1989, and authorized the army to establish order in the province. Within a few weeks, this was done. A large number of people were arrested, including protesters and supporters of Azem Vllasi. Vllasi himself ended up behind bars. I cannot help but notice the anachronistic communist formulation, which was more appropriate for 1949 than for 1989, cited as the reason for Vlasic's arrest: he was accused of "counter-revolutionary activity against Yugoslavia."

Such details speak to the ideological rigidity of the communist wing that took power in Serbia and intended to impose their will on the rest of Yugoslavia.

In an atmosphere of arrests and pressure, the Kosovo Assembly held a session on March 23rd, 1989, where the deputies reluctantly gave their consent to the changes in the republic's constitution. Five days later, on March 28th, 1989, the National Assembly of the Republic of Serbia passed amendments to the constitution, restoring Serbia's constitutional and legal jurisdiction over its entire territory. The so-called "antibureaucratic revolution" was thus successfully completed, without any human casualties. A few days later, Milošević celebrated his victory in Belgrade in the presence of the Chief of the Yugoslav People's Army, General Veljko Kadijević, and the Prime Minister of the Federal Government, Mr. Ante Marković.

Will the Survival of a Communist Island in the Balkans be Allowed?

The New Tito?

Although it is difficult to summarize the personality and intentions of Slobodan Milošević, the impression is that he was a man who almost exclusively wanted to come to power and stay there. Initially, he acted from the positions of a Yugoslav unitarist and then as a Serbian nationalist, using methods that suited him for the purpose of populism and propaganda. However, contemporaries claim that he himself was not a pronounced nationalist. Originally, he was committed to the ideas and methods of communist revolutionary struggle. He gave the impression of a man who, in many ways, wanted to be like Josip Broz Tito. Undoubtedly, he was an absolutist and did not shy away from using any means necessary to

Slobodan Milošević, President of the Central Committee, at the 10th Congress of the League of Communists of Serbia (1986).

achieve his goals. He was charismatic, a tough negotiator, bold, and arrogant. He skillfully manipulated the emotions of the broad masses. Intellectual circles, the civil and middle class, did not accept him nor the ideas he represented, and that's why he often clashed with them. Contemporaries described him as a man of high intelligence and a pragmatist.

However, it is difficult to understand the reasons for Milošević's inability to maintain a healthy grasp on reality during several key moments. How can one explain the fact that, in a time of communist collapse and the transition of Eastern Bloc countries to a market economy and Western-style democracy, Milošević went in the opposite direction? He mobilized the broad masses with the intent to prevent the long-prepared disintegration of Yugoslavia by force if necessary, and did so by returning to the postulates of the communist revolution which would produce him as the new Tito. Is it possible that his political-military-intelligence mentors genuinely convinced him that such a plan was achievable?

Fall of the Berlin Wall

Europe was preparing for a change that had been in the making since the beginning of the Cold War. Behind it stood the most powerful united force in the world, in synergy with hundreds of millions of people who wanted to see the end of communism in their countries. Yugoslavs were no exception. In 1989, few in our country still believed in the future of the socialist self-management model and other dogmatic communist narratives. We, too, longed for democracy and change.

On the evening of November 9th, 1989, the border crossing between communist East Germany and West Germany was opened. The Berlin Wall fell. Thousands of people embraced and shed tears while celebrating the arrival of a new era in which Europe and the world would rapidly and dramatically change. I vividly remember the smiles and hope that filled us in Yugoslavia during those days. Unfortunately, not everyone shared our joy.

The combined military-communist circle led by Milošević had a completely different plan—to oppose the upcoming multi-party system, democratization, and capitalism. *For the first time since 1918, the Yugoslav leadership would turn against the geopolitical interests of the Western world.* Strategically, they would do so at the worst possible moment, when the final phase of the West's forceful political-ideological and military expansion towards Eastern Europe had begun.

They would attempt to preserve their power by force as the rulers of the only socialist country in Europe. *They* would reject democracy, even though the Yugoslavs wanted it. *They* would cling to power, not hesitating to push us into a civil war if necessary. On this path, *they* will betray Yugoslavs and instrumentalize, deceive, cheat, plunder, and drag the Serbs in Yugoslavia along with them into defeat.

In that era, no one could comprehend such an agenda. From the perspective of America and the West, it was inconceivable for the uncompromising communist-military elite to maintain absolute power in strategically significant Yugoslavia, and perhaps in the future, bring Russia to the Adriatic Sea and the Mediterranean. On the contrary, the goal of the West was to force Russia out of Southern and Central Europe, pushing it as far east as they could, while at the same time doing everything possible to weaken and divide it to the maximum extent.

Many Serbs, to this day, have failed to grasp this fundamental truth, due to a lack of understanding of geopolitical trends. This misunderstanding has been exacerbated by the self-serving elite, who have continuously propagated the idea that the West harbors dislike for the Serbs on religious, cultural, and national grounds. It's true that some prejudices exist in the West, stemming largely from the perception of a close civilizational bond between Serbs and Russians. Nevertheless, the West's stance towards Milosevic's regime during the 1990s wasn't triggered by the Russophilia of a segment of the Serbian population, but rather by stark geopolitical interests.

Yes—there was a threat to the Serbian minority in Kosovo. Yes—the Serbs had an interest in preserving the Yugoslav federation for which they sacrificed millions of lives in the First and Second World Wars. Yes— Yugoslavia was the only state project that placed all Serbs, scattered by turbulent history over a large area, under one state roof[73]. Yes—this project was the only one that kept Pandora's box of interethnic boundaries closed, the opening of which would have sparked a fratricidal war among the Yugoslavs.

All of these were clear and indisputable truths. Yet, a large part of the world didn't want to hear them. Why?

The real issue for the West lay with the heavily armed communists and totalitarians in Yugoslavia. These individuals, who draped themselves in militant Yugoslav unitarianism, used disinformation, propaganda, populism, and fear to draw the Serbs—the largest ethnic group—into their political agenda.

Manipulated and entranced, subjected to relentless media brainwashing, the majority of Serbs believed in Milosević's assertions that it was righteous to fight for Yugoslavia by all means. They were convinced that the world would recognize, understand, and support the justice and truth for which the Serbs were striving. This deception exacted a tremendous toll, and its repercussions are still felt today.

Never in the long history of the Serbs has anyone created so many enemies for this nation as swiftly and effectively as the interest group of belligerent communist "old-timers" and their political protege, Slobodan Milosević.

Even if the plan to preserve Yugoslavia by "awakenings of the people," finding "healthy communist forces," dealing with "bureaucratic-separatist elites" in the republics, and reaffirming the communist model of unitary

---

[73] Additionally, it also placed all the other linguistically and genetically closely related Yugoslavs: Croats, Slovenes, Bosniaks, Montenegrins, and Macedonians into one common state.

Yugoslavism from the 1950s had temporarily succeeded, Milosević and the army overlooked one crucial fact.

In 1989, communism in Europe had died.

***

Milošević's plan to preserve Yugoslavia was backed by the generals of the Yugoslav People's Army, staunch communists, and individuals who, according to certain testimonies, pledged to Tito just months before his death that they would uphold Yugoslavia. When viewed from a legal standpoint, it's true that the army was constitutionally bound to safeguard the country's territorial integrity, employing armed force if necessary. This reality partially illuminates why they propelled Milošević into power.

But let's turn our attention to the people themselves, an essential and inescapable factor. Why did so many Serbs choose to place their trust in Milošević and follow his lead?

The emotions and thoughts of the Serbian population across Yugoslavia in those days were focused on history and what they sincerely perceived as the truth:

- that Serbia created Yugoslavia in the First World War by sacrificing 28% of its total population to liberate their South Slavic brethren—Croats, Slovenes, Serbs, and Bosniaks—from Austria-Hungary, while these brothers fought on the enemy's side until the end of the war;
- that Croatian and other Yugoslav separatists brought the country to the brink of collapse in the 1920s and 1930s;
- that Croatian fascists, the Ustašas, in collaboration with Macedonian separatists, with the help of Benito Mussolini, organized and carried out the assassination of Yugoslav King Alexander in 1934;
- that Croatian fascists, with the help of Bosniak fascists, killed, expelled, or forcibly converted to Catholicism hundreds of thousands of Serbs during the Second World War, thereby violently altering the demographic structure in present-day Croatia and Bosnia and Herzegovina;
- and that, in the end, Yugoslavia is again on the brink of collapse in the early 1990s because Slovenia and Croatia want to secede, and they have open political support from powerful Germany.

Fear induced by historical memory was still alive and present, and the demographic statistics were relentless: if Yugoslavia were to disintegrate into constituent republics, about 25% of Serbs would remain outside the borders of Serbia.

In this situation filled with uncertainty and fear, Milošević offered the masses a solution: an uncompromising fight to preserve Yugoslavia with renewed high ideals of social justice, equality, brotherhood, and unity. He offered the Serbs the survival of the Yugoslav dream, an ideal for which their fathers and grandfathers had sacrificed in the past. The sons were now ready to do the same themselves.

But Milošević was lying. His true desire was power alone. The omnipresent feeling of a nation under threat and the desire for the state to endure overpowered the initial inclination towards democratization among the majority of Serbs in Kosovo, Bosnia and Herzegovina, and Croatia. Only the Serbs in the urban areas of Serbia were primarily skeptical or openly opposed to Milošević, enduring immense pressure in the form of accusations of betraying the interests of their own people. As such, many, overwhelmed by the noise of primitive populist rhetoric, fell silent and retreated before the "awakenings" of their own nation.

The Serbian leader's alliance with the Yugoslav military hierarchy was both ideological and pragmatic. The effectiveness of this partnership was showcased in the expulsion of separatists from Kosovo's political elite. This chain of events conveyed an unmistakable message to the leadership in Slovenia and Croatia, which might be paraphrased as: "Embrace communism again and the ideological pillars that underpin our Yugoslav community. If you persist in your separatist tendencies and efforts to fragment Yugoslavia, we—communists and those who cherish Yugoslavia—aided by the army, will confront you. You will be displaced and arrested."

In his bid to assert himself as Yugoslavia's new leader, Milošević drew on Tito's methodology, strategically promoting a variant of militant Yugoslav communist nationalism. This maneuver unfolded during the initial phase of Yugoslavia's ultimate disintegration, painting a vivid portrait of his ambition and tactics.

While I can understand the strong inclination of the Serbian people to preserve Yugoslavia, they, misled and manipulated by a planned, long-term, and intensive propaganda campaign, and following the ideologically retrograde Milošević, took an anti-civilizational direction. Civilization during those years was decidedly against communism and socialism, particularly unwanted in the politically turbulent region of Europe. Milošević's Yugoslavia, with its military-communist orientation, was simply out of the question.

The leader persistently misled his people. Through controlled media, he convinced the Serbs that the entire West has harbored hatred towards them for centuries, and that the only possibility for survival was to form an alliance with the faltering USSR, that is, Russia. In doing so, he effectively extinguished any hope that Western powers and the European Union would have even a hint of sympathy and understanding for Serbian national, political, and territorial interests. These interests were subordinated by the emotionally amputated leader to his own survival in power, which, as he hoped, would be secured by an alliance with Moscow.

***

Consequences of the Anti-Bureaucratic Revolution and Sliding Towards Civil War

At that time, the Presidency of Yugoslavia, the collective head of state, consisted of eight members: one from each of the six republics and one representative from each of the two autonomous provinces within Serbia. After installing loyal individuals in the autonomous provinces of Vojvodina and Kosovo, as well as in the Republic of Montenegro, Milošević secured control over four of the eight votes in the Presidency from mid-1989, effectively preventing Serbia from being outvoted. However, this was a pyrrhic victory.

Inside Yugoslavia, all other republics were seriously concerned about the "awakenings of the people" orchestrated from Belgrade, which sought to retain the existing social order and revert federation relations back to the unitary centralism of the 1950s. For Slovenia and Croatia, which were on the verge of a long-desired peaceful secession, any collaboration with Milošević was out of the question. Proposals coming from the "Serbian bloc" were routinely rejected, which soon led to a stalemate in the Presidency and paved the way for Yugoslavia's further slide towards dissolution.

Today, we can learn about this period from the memoirs of the people who played pivotal roles in it. Primarily, I am thinking of Borisav Jović, the man who was president of the Presidency of Yugoslavia, a close associate of Milošević, and a representative of Serbia in this body. Also, there was General Veljko Kadijević, who held the position of federal secretary for national defense at the time—a man who commanded the Yugoslav People's Army based on the decisions of the Presidency.

From these memoirs, as well as the stenographic records of the Presidency sessions from 1989 to 1991, we observe further actions of the alliance between Slobodan Milošević and the military leadership, which reveal their aspirations. They desired to remain in power and survive the downfall of communism at all costs, even if it meant using armed force. As an illustration, I point out General Kadijević's appeal to the USSR Defense

Minister Yazov, in which he seeks protection in case of Western military intervention in Yugoslavia and requests for weapons delivery. The Russians rejected these demands. In his book of memoirs[74], Borisav Jović recorded Kadijević's words expressing fear of a "counter-revolution" and subsequent anti-communist retaliation: "Anti-socialist forces are threatening retribution, and if we do nothing substantial to prevent their surge, the worst kind of revenge follows—we will hang on lampposts without pardon."

Evidently, these men were in great fear and, regrettably, prepared for anything. Their records reveal the preparation of several scenarios that become increasingly radical over time: they begin with the hope that the threat of military intervention would be enough to scare disobedient republics. Then they advocate for the imposition of a state of emergency in the country, but they do not gain support in the Presidency. They then seriously consider carrying out a military coup. They actively obstruct the federal government's work and infiltrate the federation's monetary system, appropriating an amount of 1.8 billion dollars. After Slovenia and Croatia declared independence in the summer of 1991, they definitively abandon the scenario of Yugoslavia's survival as a whole and consider a political, and if necessary, military solution in which a "shrunken"Yugoslavia would emerge. This would include all the peoples and their territories that chose, via referendum, to stay in the common state. They primarily count on the Serbs in Croatia and Bosnia and Herzegovina, who, at all costs, do not want to be cut-off from Serbia, fearing another pogrom like the one they experienced in the puppet Independent State of Croatia during World War II. In these Serbian areas, political parties are formed, and national councils are elected that declare the desire of the Serbs to remain in Yugoslavia.

From the perspective of the people, these are entirely understandable and expected aspirations. The common state is falling apart, and the past is burdened with betrayed hopes, expectations, traumas, and crimes. The Slovenes and Croats want independence and international recognition, and that is entirely legitimate. The Serbs, scattered along with the Montenegrins in areas and enclaves across a large part of Yugoslavia, wish to preserve the state for which they have made enormous sacrifices, and that too is perfectly fine. But how to reconcile these diametrically opposed interests?

The Serbian argument was that Yugoslavia was created by the unification of the Serbs, Croats, and Slovenes—therefore, three peoples—and so the right of these same peoples to self-determination must be respected during disassociation. According to this opinion, the Serbs had the right to

---

[74] Jović, Borisav. *Poslednji dani SFRJ* [The Last Days of the SFRY]. Politika, Belgrade, 1995, 91-92.

opt for staying in Yugoslavia, just as the Croats and Slovenes gave themselves the right to leave the common state. No one disputed that. The complexity of the situation lay in the fact that the administrative boundaries of the republics did not correspond to ethnic lines. Serbs resided not only in Serbia but also in other republics, with the same being true for Croats, though to a lesser degree. If the international community were to recognize these inter-republic borders—which were merely administrative and essentially invisible during Yugoslavia's existence—as official state borders, a substantial number of Serbs and a noteworthy proportion of Croats would unexpectedly find themselves living in several states rather than in just one—Yugoslavia.

This situation would open the door for a secret agreement between the leaders of Serbia and Croatia on the territorial demarcation of the two peoples, which would largely determine the course of the upcoming war in Bosnia and Herzegovina.

DEATH

Yugoslavia: The Final Years

Commemoration of the 600ᵗʰ Anniversary of the Battle of Kosovo in 1989

On June 28ᵗʰ, 1989, the renowned Battle of Kosovo—a historical event of the greatest significance for Serbs—was marking its six-hundredth anniversary. This battle, seen as the moment of the loss of the Serbian medieval empire, is deeply ingrained in the collective consciousness, symbolizing the holiest ideal of chivalrous self-sacrifice for the homeland. Beyond the willing sacrifice for a higher cause, the Battle of Kosovo also serves as a symbol of freedom and defiance—values, history has shown, that are most highly esteemed by the proud Serbian people. The commemoration of the anniversary of this epic event was an ideal means for magnetizing and mobilizing the widest Serbian masses for the project of a new sacrifice—the salvation of Yugoslavia. An interest group composed of steadfast communists, heads of secret services, army leaders, a part of the Serbian Orthodox Church, and a part of the intelligentsia, led by Milošević in the role of a charismatic leader, decided to demonstrate their power and send a strong political message both to internal opponents and to the world at the most massive rally Yugoslavia had ever seen. Estimates of the number of participants vary, and reach up to a staggering two million. Serbs came to Kosovo from all over Yugoslavia, and many from the diaspora: America, Australia, Canada, Europe... I recall the stirred energy, the collectivism, certain excitement I noticed on people's faces during those days. Even my father, a convinced anti-communist, went to the rally with his close friend. I watched the event on television, which was broadcasting it live. For some reason, people believed in Milošević—it was a phenomenon that swept across wide layers of society. However, the civil intelligentsia in Serbia mainly perceived him as a skillful demagogue. To me, it seemed that behind eloquently phrased populist statements and unquestionable oratory skills, Milošević lacked the genuine power of personal conviction.

Due to the protocol of the time, representatives from almost all other republics, diplomatic corps, academics, as well as the top of the Serbian Orthodox Church were present at the rally. Milošević's speech was relatively moderate. He advocated for the unity of the people and the transformation of Yugoslavia through unity and reforms. He mentioned weaponry only once, and that sentence was immediately seized upon to stoke fear and condemnation in Slovenia and Croatia. That sentence has always since been quoted out of context: "Six centuries later, today, we are once again in battles and facing battles. They are not armed, although such battles are not yet excluded." However, for the sake of objectivity, I quote its continuation: "But no matter what they are, battles cannot be won without determination, courage, and sacrifice. Without these fine qualities that were once present on the field of Kosovo. Our main battle today relates to the achievement of economic, political, cultural, and overall social prosperity. To approach faster and more successfully the civilization in which people will live in the 21st century."

Although many even today refuse to grasp this, there was hardly a scenario that could have saved Yugoslavia. It was simply dying because there was no consensus for its survival, neither among its peoples nor among foreign powers. This death could have been postponed, but not prevented. And as it often happens when death approaches, unfavorable events that announced it began to string together rapidly, like on a film reel. There were multiple catalysts in that final phase of the process, both within Yugoslavia and beyond. Milošević was just one of them, but undoubtedly the most conspicuous.

Already on September 17th, 1989, just three months after the gathering in Kosovo of over a million people disposed towards Yugoslavia and ready to align themselves under Milošević's banner, Slovenia voted amendments to its constitution granting itself the right to secede from Yugoslavia. In November, using police and arrests, it prevented Serbs and Montenegrins from organizing a protest rally "for Yugoslavia" in its capital, Ljubljana, aiming to support the survival of the federation. In doing so, the Slovenes set a decisive barrier against Milošević's tsunami-populism and refused to import the orchestrated revolution.

The Breakup of the League of Communists of Yugoslavia in 1990

At the start of 1990, on January 22nd, the League of Communists of Yugoslavia (LCY) disbanded. It happened during the extraordinary 14th congress of the Party, convened at the initiative of Serbia with the aim of consolidating the leading political force in the country and jointly determining the approach to the crisis in the country. However, instead of ideological unity, the communists publicly split into two irreconcilable factions. One faction, led by Milošević, wanted to preserve the regime and resist the winds of anti-communist changes in Europe. Others, primarily delegates from Slovenia, proposed radical reforms, abandoning communist ideology, and the confederalization of Yugoslavia. Of course, they knew that the first group would find this unacceptable. Formally in protest of being outvoted—decisions were made on the principle of "one man, one vote"—the delegates from Slovenia left the Congress, immediately followed by delegates from Croatia. Many years later, some of them would admit on camera that this departure had been preplanned and their suitcases had already been packed. Sonja Lokar, a Slovenian politician remembered for bursting into tears at the moment of the congress's interruption, gave an emotional depiction of what happened then: "I cried, and it's still hard for me today because the LCY failed to transform into a strong left-wing social democratic party," she said, adding that she cried also because she "felt that her former party comrades would drag the entire Balkans into a fratricidal war."

The First Multi-party Elections in Croatia and Their Immediate Aftermath

In April 1990, Croatia held its first multi-party elections, ushering in a new government after several decades of communist rule. The victory was claimed by the Croatian Democratic Union (HDZ), led by Dr. Franjo Tudjman—a former general of Tito's, later a convicted dissident—who was soon elected as the new president of the republic. However, in the Croatian municipalities where Serbs constituted the majority, the elections were won by the Serbian Democratic Party (SDS). In these territories, Serbs would establish their own national councils. In the summer of 1990, a referendum was organized on the territorial autonomy of Serbs in Croatia.

As the central government in Zagreb attempted to prevent the referendum, Serbs responded with the so-called "Log Revolution"—blocking roads with makeshift barricades of fallen trees and large stones, and setting up checkpoints. This effectively prevented the Croatian police from intervening with the referendum. Today, many in Croatia consider the start date of the "Log Revolution"—August 17th—as the beginning of the armed rebellion of local Serbs. On the other hand, the referendum showed that 97% of Serbs from Croatia voted for territorial and political autonomy, as well as for remaining in Yugoslavia.

Several months after their electoral victory, the new Croatian government, in utmost secrecy, began to engage in the illegal importation of weapons, fortify the police, and initiate the formation and training of special units. The intelligence services of Yugoslavia and Serbia were aware of this and monitored the situation closely. In response, the covert arming of Serbs in Krajina and Eastern Slavonia—regions of Croatia where Serbs were the majority and had expressed a desire for autonomy—followed.

Due to the large-scale genocide that the Croatian fascists—Ustaša committed against Serbs during World War II, an important clause was present in the post-war Croatian constitution, guaranteeing equal status for Serbs and Croats, referred to as *constitutive peoples*:

"The Socialist Republic of Croatia is the national state of the Croatian people, *the state of the Serbian people in Croatia*, and the state of the nationalities living in it."[75]

However, on December 22nd, 1990, the newly elected multi-party Croatian Parliament passed a new constitution in which Serbs lost their constitutive status and became a national minority. The Preamble of this new highest legal act states:

"The Republic of Croatia is established as the national state of the Croatian people and the state of members of those nations and minorities who are its citizens: Serbs, Muslims, Slovenians, Czechs, Slovaks, Italians, Hungarians, Jews and others, who are guaranteed equality with Croatian nationals and the realization of national rights in accordance with the democratic norms of the UN and the countries of the free world."[76]

In the view of the Serbs, the revocation of the constitutive status by Croatia was seen as an attempt to strip them of their entitlement to territorial autonomy and, more crucially, their right to self-determination as a people—a privilege accorded to them under the Yugoslav constitution.

Therefore, the Serbs insisted on their right to continue living, along with everyone else who wished to, in the existing common state of Yugoslavia. Consequently, all territories in Croatia with a Serbian majority held referendums where decisions were made to remain within the confines of Yugoslavia. The closest verbalization of the thoughts of the Serbian people in Croatia during those days would have sounded something like this: "Well, go ahead, Croatian brothers, leave the union if you wish, but we will not go with you. We have our country, and it is called Yugoslavia. You will not forcibly take us with you—we are staying."

---

[75] *Constitution of the Socialist Republic of Croatia.* Chapter I. Narodne novine No. 8, February 22nd, 1974.
[76] *Constitution of the Republic of Croatia,* Chapter I, Narodne novine No. 56/1990, December 22nd, 1990.

Missed Opportunity:
Could There be a Unified Yet Democratic Yugoslavia?

In 1990, circumstances seemed to favor the survival of some form of shared state: the parliament of Bosnia and Herzegovina voted for this republic to remain in Yugoslavia. Initially, the international community also adhered to the Helsinki Act on the inviolability of external state borders and clearly discouraged the aspirations of Slovenia and Croatia for secession. Delegations of the European Community and the President of the United States, George Bush, were still giving strong support to the integrity of Yugoslavia at the end of 1990.

Considering the political developments of the time, it appears the West desired a stable and unified Yugoslavia, which would be swiftly granted access to join the European Economic Community (EEC) and the Western military alliance. This move would have facilitated the rapid and unhindered eastward expansion of the West, seen through the collapse of communist regimes and NATO's enlargement. Consistent with such a policy, the European Community and America were strongly supportive of the federal government and the moderate reformist politician Ante Marković, who was earnestly striving to implement deep-seated economic and industrial reforms. In about six months, he managed to curb an inflation rate of several tens of percent per month to an acceptable level. Marković was an advocate for a market economy, trade liberalization, and a convertible domestic currency. We, as ordinary citizens, recall this period as a few months of sudden prosperity and high living standards. The federal government, under his leadership, was openly pushing for Yugoslavia's accession to the EEC and had begun the enactment of a suite of reformist laws. Marković founded the party Union of Reform Forces of Yugoslavia and became its leader. The plan was for the reformists to triumph in the hypothetical pan-Yugoslav multi-party parliamentary elections. However, these elections never took place. The major players in the Yugoslav crisis did everything in their power to sabotage, defame, and remove Marković from the political landscape.

Ante Marković did not enjoy the support of Slovenia and Croatia as they did not wish for Yugoslavia to remain intact. But why did he not suit Milošević and the Yugoslav People's Army (JNA), who were ostensibly advocating for the preservation of Yugoslavia? The answer is simple. Marković wanted to integrate Yugoslavia into Western structures and abolish the socialist societal order.

Dr. Borisav Jović, at one point a close associate of Milošević and the Serbian representative in the Presidency of Yugoslavia, confirms that for the conspirators, socialism—or rather, the survival of their communist establishment—was far more important than whether Yugoslavia would survive or not. In his diaries, Jović recounts a conversation about Ante Marković held on August 10th, 1990:

> "We spend the whole day on the boat and at sea [on Mljet[77]]—on a trip, Veljko, Sloba, Bogdan [Trifunović] and I with families... The general consensus is that Ante Marković has become unacceptable and unreliable to us. No one doubts anymore that he is a direct exponent of the United States, designated for the overthrow of the system and for the removal of all those who even contemplate socialism... Veljko calls him a 'son of a whore'."[78]

"Veljko" refers to General Veljko Kadijević, Chief of the General Staff of the JNA and Federal Secretary for National Defense, while "Sloba" is Slobodan Milošević.

Prime Minister of the Federal Government, Ante Marković, with members of the government (in the background). Some of them actively sabotaged Marković's pro-Western reformist course.

---

[77] Mljet is an island in Dalmatian region of Croatia, in the Adriatic sea.
[78] Jović, Borisav. *Poslednji dani SFRJ* [The Last Days of the SFRY]. Politika, Beograd, 1995.

330

We find similar views with another key actor. The aforementioned General Veljko Kadijević, the top man in the Army during the years of the country's dissolution, who emigrated to Russia after the Yugoslav wars and lived there until his death in 2014, wrote two books in which he expressed his view of Yugoslavia's breakup. Alongside words of praise for Tito's "genius foreign policy", the general believes that the "only real" period of Yugoslavia's existence was precisely the unitary-centralist one until the beginning of the 1960s when it was a "bridge-connector of two great but very different civilizations", the East and the West.

Although I find some common ground with the aforementioned evaluations, regrettably, there's one with which I cannot concur. Namely, during 1990, Yugoslavia was offered to accept a reform course, followed by membership in the EEC and NATO and a financial injection of several billion dollars. Kadijević, seemingly fearing that he would, as he stated elsewhere, "hang on a lamppost in case of a change of power", speaks of the offered opportunity in his book as a "concept of capitulation", i.e., "a complete surrender to the enemy without a fight".[79]

I remember that at the time, the majority of the people in Serbia were still optimistic about the survival of Yugoslavia, and therefore very favorably inclined towards the support from Europe, America, and most of the world for its integrity and economic reforms. Had the hardline and militant communist wing not consolidated and united in Belgrade, had a reformist course in the people's interest been pursued instead, together with other nations of Eastern and Central Europe, it is entirely possible that the death of Yugoslavia would have been delayed for several more years, or even decades. Its internal relations would still be threatened by separatist movements. However, had a democratic and reformist wave, rather than an anachronistic communist one, been pushed from Belgrade at the time, the West would have been interested in curbing Slovenian and Croatian secession, preserving Yugoslavia as a whole, and annexing it to its bloc of states.

By joining the European democratic wave of the moment, Milošević could have changed the course of events. It is certain that America, then the only superpower and a friend of Serbia since the time of the First World War, would have strongly supported such a turn. In that case, Yugoslavia would likely have survived as a federal or confederal state and become a member of the EU and NATO. The major powers would not have supported the secession of Slovenia and Croatia, and a bloody civil war could have been avoided. The Serbs, through political negotiations, would have achieved substantial autonomy in Croatia and Bosnia and Herze-

---

[79] Kadijević, Veljko. *Protivudar – Moje vidjenje raspada Jugoslavije* [Counterstrike—My View of the Breakup of Yugoslavia]. IP Filip Višnjić, Beograd, 2010.

govina, and the events in Kosovo would have taken a different course. It is possible that there might even have been some corrections to internal borders through political agreements.

Despite the evident prevailing support among Yugoslavs for adopting a reformist, pro-Western course, Milošević and the hardline military-communist wing decided that the old system of government and its protagonists would survive at all costs. "Yugoslavia was created by arms, and by arms it will be defended," they threatened at the time, in fact, telling us how scared they were. Their message was actually, "We came to power by arms, and by arms we will defend ourselves."

By rejecting the offer from the EEC and NATO in 1990 for accelerated admission to these organizations and a financial injection for the faltering economy, the oligarchy in Belgrade started an anachronistic and autistic opposition to the strong reformist and anti-communist historical process in Europe at that time, initiated and implemented by the Western world. Meanwhile, the elites in Slovenia and Croatia continued preparations for secession. An opportunity was consciously missed that could realistically have preserved Yugoslavia through the influence of European powers and the USA. For most of us ordinary Yugoslavs, that moment marks the beginning of years of wars, devastation, suffering, displacement, poverty, and economic backwardness.

The biggest loser will be the Serbian people, who were convinced that they were fighting for their survival, but in fact were fighting for the survival of a totalitarian regime.

Independence Referendum in Slovenia, 1990

In Yugoslavia, it had long been suspected that Slovenia was the closest to deciding to leave the common state. It was felt in the air, recognized through conversations with ordinary people, and it lasted for years. In these final months of Yugoslavia, Slovenia and Croatia coordinated their moves to act unitedly towards the other republics, the rest of the state apparatus, and above all, the military leadership.

Just one day after the adoption of the new Croatian constitution, on December 23rd, 1990, Slovenians held a referendum on independence. Their message was more than clear. Turnout reached almost 90%, and the result was decisive and impressive: around 95% of voters answered affirmatively to the referendum question, "Should the Republic of Slovenia become an independent and sovereign state?" The official results of the Slovenian referendum were announced to the Yugoslav public on December 26th. That's when we found out the day Yugoslavia would formally die—the Slovenian authorities had a legal deadline of up to six months to implement the decision of their people.

The Špegelj Affair—Counterintelligence Service Tapes

Croatia was also sliding towards secession in those days. At the same time, many Yugoslavs were still hoping that the problems in the federation would be overcome through political agreement and that the common state would survive. The international community also continued to express clear support for the integrity of Yugoslavia. Then, a painful awakening occurred.

I vividly remember the shock and public nausea after the secret video footage made by operatives of the Yugoslav Counterintelligence Service was broadcast on state television in prime time on January 24th, 1991. In the material filmed with a hidden camera, Croatian Defense Minister and member of the democratically elected government, Martin Špegelj, speaks about secret arming, smuggling weapons into Croatia, organizing, and executing imminent attacks on border patrol stations and barracks of the Yugoslav federal army. On this occasion, he explains to those present how to deal ruthlessly with soldiers, officers, and their families. Particularly disturbing are the instructions for the instrumentalization of Albanian soldiers for Croatian goals. The Minister uttered the following ominous words at a secret meeting with his associates that took place on October 14th, 1990:

"When it comes to border patrol stations... when it comes to disarming the patrol stations, all of them there will be disarmed. But leave the Albanians with five bullets in their rifles. And lock up the other [soldiers] in the basement and provide food and water... This will not be a war, this will be a civil war in which there is no mercy for anyone. Not for a woman, not for children. Into an apartment, simply — bombs in the family apartment."

The media played this recording for days, which a large part of the Yugoslav public saw. I remember the immense worry I felt then. I was living in Belgrade, far from Croatia, but it was clear to me that after such confirmation of their darkest suspicions, Serbs in Croatia would under no circumstances agree to stay in Croatia if it indeed seceded. I also knew that the Yugoslav People's Army (JNA), ethnically dominantly Serbian, would use this recording to start arming Serbian enclaves in Croatia with the aim of defending these areas from the threatening violent Croatian secession. Besides the fact that the army had a constitutional duty to preserve the territorial integrity of Yugoslavia—which was a vital interest of Serbs from Croatia—there was an ethnic imbalance in its ranks in favor of Serbs due to the simple fact that Serbs were the most numerous nation in the federation. This imbalance was now further disrupted by mass desertion of soldiers and officers who were ethnic Croats and Slovenes. Therefore, it seemed completely certain that there would be joint action by the JNA and Serbs in Croatia.

Around the same time, the mass media under the control of the Belgrade regime orchestrated a stirring of traumas related to Ustaša crimes from the Second World War, sowing fear and panic among Serbs in Croatia: "They will kill and slaughter you again!", "All Croats are Ustaša!"

And so, the Serbs found themselves engulfed in confusing feelings that their life was under threat in Croatia, as it was in 1941. Their legitimate and democratically expressed desires to preserve at least a truncated Yugoslavia through political means were replaced by a survival instinct. Milošević's regime stoked these fears, aiming to expand its influence and control. He calculated that, like Tito, the majority of Serbs would rush to him, fleeing from Croatian or Bosniak pogroms. And, unfortunately, that's exactly what happened.

On the other hand, after the fall of the Berlin Wall, the West was in a hurry to expand to the East, and its politicians didn't have time to think about Serbian traumas from the First and Second World Wars, or how and why the Serbs outside Serbia fell under the influence of a heavily armed communist clique, which was using their feelings in a desperate attempt to save itself from disappearing from the historical scene. For them, the creation of Greater Serbia or a truncated Yugoslavia with a pro-communist system and a totalitarian, autocratic leadership leaning towards Russia was a scenario that simply couldn't be allowed. This fact will greatly determine the future policy of the West towards the Serbian leadership.

This conclusion of mine is also confirmed by Špegelj himself, who speaks of the sudden change in the attitude of the United States after Milošević's victory in the Serbian elections, a few months before the Yugoslav Wars began,

" ...Especially now when that whore has won in Serbia, Milošević. Now the Americans, the day after he won, have offered us all the help. Until then they were all speculating... would they, wouldn't they.. Now they say: a thousand transporters, armored, like these, like those... I don't know. For a hundred thousand soldiers, complete weaponry free of charge."[80]

It remains a question as to why the Yugoslav Federal Army, which was still considerably powerful at that time, did not take action to stop the illegal arms imports into Croatia. Instead, it broadcast to the public the secretly recorded material, effectively spreading fear and carrying out national polarization among the masses. Was it already decided at that time that it was impossible to save Yugoslavia and that war was inevitable?

This controversy was addressed in a 2011 interview by former Federal Secretary for National Defense and Chief of the General Staff of the Yugoslav People's Army (JNA), Admiral Branko Mamula:

"The date of January 25th, 1991, is the day when the definitive destruction of Yugoslavia began; a tragic failure of the JNA with that film about the illegal import of weapons into Croatia. They were making a film instead of preventing that import."

Milošević–Kučan Agreement: Slovenia Can Go!

In support of Admiral Mamula's assessment, the following fact is significant: at the time of the disclosure of the "Špegelj affair," which shocked and frightened the wider Yugoslav public, the Presidents of Slovenia and Serbia, Milošević and Kučan, held a meeting in Belgrade and discussed a modus for Slovenia's unimpeded exit from Yugoslavia.

In the official statement that followed the agreement on a sort of pact "on mutual understanding and cooperation," among other things, it stated: "We have agreed that in resolving the Yugoslav crisis, it is necessary to start from the *right of the people to self-determination*, which must not be limited by anything other than the equal and identical rights of other peoples." Further, it stated: "Slovenia respects the interest of the Serbian people to live in one country," and that any future Yugoslav agreement must respect this interest. On the other hand, the Serbian side guaranteed Slovenia "the unimpeded realization of the Slovenian people's right to their own path."

---

[80] During the trial of Slobodan Milosević before the International Tribunal for Crimes Committed in the former Yugoslavia, in The Hague, the "Špegelj Tapes" were presented as evidence. The aforementioned sentence can be found on page 47,630 of the transcripts, and was read out during the hearing held on January 25th, 2006.

Therefore, the Slovenian and Serbian presidents agreed on January 24th, 1990, on two things very important for a deeper understanding of the course of events:

- that Serbia would not prevent Slovenia from leaving Yugoslavia;
- that Slovenia prioritizes the principle of the right of peoples to self-determination over the principle of respecting the internal republican borders, or the territorial integrity of the Yugoslav republics. This effectively means that the ethnic Serbs in Croatia and Bosnia and Herzegovina received support from Slovenia for the establishment of territorial autonomies that would join the future "shrunken" or third Yugoslavia.

In this development, we see that at that time Milošević had definitely abandoned the plan to preserve a united Yugoslavia based on the principles of socialism and unitarism, to which he had adhered in the early years of his rule. In contrast, he increasingly turned towards a scenario of bringing under one state all the territories of Yugoslavia with a Serbian majority. And for this plan, he secured the support of Slovenia.

However, the military leadership and the federal government, led by reformist Ante Marković, did not want such an outcome. It seems that the Army was disappointed with Milošević's abandonment of a united Yugoslavia. This opened up maneuvering space for a dramatic twist, which, however, did not happen. The President of the Federal Government of Yugoslavia, Ante Marković, asked his Minister of Defense General Veljko Kadijević to arrest the leaders of Serbia and Croatia, Milošević and Tudjman, and to impose a state of emergency in the country. But the general was at the very top of a conspiratorial group with Milošević, working to preserve some kind of undemocratic, pro-communist Yugoslav entity that would seek its footing in the East, in Russia. Therein lay an insurmountable problem between him and the federal government, which enjoyed the support of Europe and the US due to its reformist and democratic stance.

In the coming years, Milošević will outmaneuver those from the military leadership who launched him into political orbit. He will first politically and financially blackmail the Yugoslav People's Army (JNA), and then fully instrumentalize it for his purposes. He will dismiss or pension off many generals. General Kadijević will spend the last years of his life writing memoirs about the disintegration of Yugoslavia in Moscow.

"No One Can Beat You" (except me)—
the Day I Fully Perceived the Cage in Which We Were Trapped

World politics and media, during the period I'm writing about, had a largely simplified, black-and-white perspective towards the events in Yugoslavia. Among the reasons for this were certainly the exceptional complexity of the entire situation, the historical and cultural differences among the main actors, and the Balkan mentality which is distinct and often difficult for other nations to understand. A large number of Serbs still believe that the world does not understand them, and there is some truth in this view. As the Yugoslav crisis unfolded, Western media primarily adopted a simplified narrative where Serbs were largely to blame for everything, while others were their victims. Today, widespread generalizations, simplifications, and prejudices about Serbs are still prevalent worldwide, as part of the media war. One such widespread narrative is that all Serbs strongly supported Slobodan Milošević and his project of "violent creation of Greater Serbia."

However, this prejudice is incorrect. Earlier in the book, it was detailed that those Serbs who felt existentially threatened were drawn to Milošević's strong rhetoric. These were almost all the "peripheral" Serbs from Croatia, Bosnia and Herzegovina, and from Kosovo and Metohija. As shown earlier, their fears were rooted in the horrendous crimes committed against them during the First and Second World Wars. Unfortunately, these justified fears were fanned and amplified by extremely strong propaganda of state and other media under Milošević's control, in order to homogenize the Serbs and to create a pro-communist state project with Serbs as the prevailing nation.

But what about the Serbs in Serbia itself? How did intellectuals, artists, the middle and working classes, and students react? Could their voice be heard—and how—under conditions of media uniformity, condemnation of every different opinion, police bans on gatherings, and the constant hunt by "patriots" for "traitors of national interests"? Did a "normal Serbia" exist at all?

***

It all began in the spring of 1991 with the demand of the opposition parties in the National Assembly for the editors of Radio Television Belgrade to be dismissed due to the scandalously untruthful and biased reporting in favor of the ruling Milošević's political party. It was a disguised Serbian Communist League, which, under the newly introduced multi-party system, simply changed its name to the Socialist Party of Serbia, retaining almost all of its powerful infrastructure: buildings, media, institutions, army, police, enterprises, and money.

The ruling compliant majority in the parliament, in Milošević's manner, smoothly and arrogantly rejected all appeals and demands of the opposition for objective reporting by the national television. In response to institutional ignorance, the Serbian Renewal Movement (SPO), then the strongest opposition party, called for people to gather and peacefully protest in the center of Belgrade on March 9th, 1991. The police, of course, banned the assembly. I remember well the tension in the air and some stirring of the collective spirit that decided to emerge that day.

It seems that both the opposition leaders and the government were surprised by the fact that a hundred thousand people from Belgrade, as well as many other cities in Serbia, gathered at Republic Square. Everything went peacefully and nothing indicated the drama that would follow. Opposition leaders and several independent intellectuals addressed the crowd, interrupted occasionally by applause or chants. And then, suddenly, and without any apparent reason, the police launched a brutal attack. The densely gathered people in the relatively small square were showered with a large amount of tear gas and water cannons. The crowd had nowhere to go. People began to suffocate. There was a stampede, shoving, some falling. The police were beating with batons. Panic, followed by deep contempt and anger. I had no doubt why this was happening. Milošević's absolutist ego could not bear the fact that people ignored his police ban and gathered anyway.

The demonstrators initially began to overturn police vehicles and confront the overpowering force equipped with batons, gas masks, and armored vehicles for riot control. Stunned, opposition leader Vuk Drašković shouted from the balcony of the National Theater, "Charge!", and would later be arrested for these words. A clash with the police ensued that lasted for hours. Cordons, special units, batons, and rubber bullets did not calm the situation. And then blood was shed. First, a police officer lost his life, who, fleeing from demonstrators, fell from a height of five meters and died. Retribution came quickly. About fifteen police officers opened fire on the demonstrators. An eighteen-year-old young man was killed, and several people were injured. After that, the police withdrew and it seemed that the demonstrators had won. Opposition leaders entered parliament and tried to contact Milošević. The enraged crowd systematically shattered almost every window of the Presidency of Serbia building, where Milošević's office was located, with stones. Words that hit the essence of the problem of Serbian society echoed through Belgrade from the throats of thousands: *"Red bandits!"*

Milošević, according to some accounts, took refuge in a secret military underground facility not far from Belgrade and from there monitored the development of events. He asked Borisav Jović, his man in the position of President of the Presidency of Yugoslavia, to send the army to the streets of the capital to quash the demonstrations. Jović called members of the Presidency from other republics by phone and managed to secure votes for such a decision.

That evening, around 8 pm, I watched in disbelief as a long column of tanks of the Yugoslav People's Army, with noise and rumbling, entered the center of Belgrade to protect Slobodan Milošević from the people. Inside me, feelings of anger, helplessness, fear, and determination to not give up alternated. There is no reconciliation with the deprivation of freedom and human dignity. Many thought and felt as I did then.

The tanks did not discourage us. Soon the students took to the streets. The police beat them. The students sat down on the asphalt. The University of Belgrade went on strike, and this example was followed by other universities in the country. Theaters showed solidarity and stopped performing. On the podium, singers, athletes, actors, writers, professors, many prominent and respected people took turns speaking. The Serbian "velvet revolution" was in full swing. In response, the authorities organized a "counter-rally" the next day, March 10th, where they brought supporters by buses from all over Serbia. At this sorrowful rally grotesquely named "For the Defense of the Republic, Freedom, and Democracy", speakers called the students "scoundrels" and "hooligans", and the demonstrators "murderers and fascists". An ominous crescendo arose when one of them, riding a wave of frenzied lynching hysteria, called on the gathered to go to the city center and physically confront the students.

To preserve his power, Milošević clearly demonstrated a ruthless willingness to provoke bloodshed among his own people. Fortunately, it did not happen at that time. Borisav Jović himself, whom Milošević used for the Army's intervention and later, like many other pawns, dismissed and discarded, characterized his boss many years later as follows:

"The main political determinant of Milošević, however, would be political pragmatism. Nothing was stronger in Milošević than the will for power. Principles were not as important to him as political success and maintaining power. He subordinated everything to that."[81]

Time would later show that March 9th, 1991, was the day after which nothing would be the same. Many of us then realized how strong, small,

---

[81] Jović, Borisav. *Knjiga o Miloševiću.* Belgrade: Nikola Pašić, 2001. p.21.

and dark the cage was in which we were imprisoned. Continuous resistance of normal and healthy Serbia against dictatorship and madness would begin, which would not calm down for almost a decade, until the final overthrow of Milošević. Unfortunately, in that decade, many good people would lose their lives.

Military Dictatorship: Yes or No?

The masks have fallen. All of Milošević's assurances that he was fighting for the preservation of Yugoslavia, for the Serbian people in Croatia and Bosnia and Herzegovina, democracy, peace, and political negotiation as an instrument for resolving the crisis in the state and society were false. Cornered, the powerful militant communist oligarchy showed us its true face. The deeply shaken regime sought support in the demonstration of raw military power for its mere survival.

While tanks in Belgrade ominously stood in squares and in front of government buildings, deep underground, the last attempt to preserve a unitary Yugoslavia was taking place.

At the proposal of the General Staff of the Yugoslav People's Army (JNA), a session of the Supreme Command of the Armed Forces of the Socialist Federal Republic of Yugoslavia was scheduled for March 12th. Its members were:

- Members of the Presidency of Yugoslavia, acting as a collective head of state and commander of the armed forces,
- Federal Secretary for National Defense, General Veljko Kadijević, and
- The Chief of the General Staff of the JNA, General Blagoje Adžić.

The representative from Slovenia, Janez Drnovšek, did not travel to Belgrade, fearing he would be arrested. When the remaining members of the Presidency arrived in front of the building where the meeting was to be held, they were loaded onto a military bus and taken to an underground command center, which would house the supreme headquarters in the event of war. The room was very cold, so they were given military cloaks to wrap themselves. The entire course of the meeting was recorded by cameras. Such treatment was undoubtedly meant to exert psychological pressure on the members of the collective head of state. General Kadijević, in a dramatic address, stated that the country was on the brink of civil war and the danger of external military intervention, and that "puppet regimes"

340

would form in the country. He labeled various political movements and separatists in Yugoslavia as Quislings and fascists and stated that "the harsh reality confronts the armed forces with the same enemy as in 1941," presumably referring to Germany's strong support for the secession of Croatia and Slovenia. In this situation, the military leadership proposed a set of measures to the Presidency, the most significant of which were:

- The introduction of a state of emergency throughout the territory of Yugoslavia,
- Raising the army's combat readiness and partial mobilization,
- Disarming and disbanding all paramilitary formations.
- Continuation of political discussions about resolving the crisis and affirming the principle of self-determination of the people: "In republics whose leadership is opting for secession, organize a referendum that will provide every nation with the opportunity for direct and free expression, without any dictate or majoritization."

At the very end, a position is presented that speaks of the possibility of the army changing its political course. Whether this was just false appeasement to the vast majority of people in all republics who desired reforms is hard to say:

"Build the future Yugoslav society as a parliamentary democracy of a multi-party type, without imposing any ideological views or monopolies."

It seems there is no reason to believe that the communists were sincere, as their behavior up to that point and thereafter does not support the above statement.

The Presidency proceeded to vote. The Serbian bloc, which consisted of Serbia, the provinces of Vojvodina, Kosovo and Metohija, and Montenegro, was in favor of introducing a state of emergency and the proposed measures, while Croatia and Macedonia were against it. The representative of Bosnia and Herzegovina, Bogić Bogićević, who was an ethnic Serb, abstained from voting. It was noted that no decision was made. The meeting was adjourned.

After such an outcome of the meeting, General Kadijević secretly traveled to the USSR, and according to some testimonies, the other two generals traveled to Paris and London. They sought support from the world for executing a military coup. However, it was completely lacking. There are certain indications that Kadijević proposed to the Soviet Defense Minister Marshal Yazov a coordinated military coup in both countries to preserve communism and thwart the intentions of the West. However, it appears the Soviets were not prepared for such a move and the plan failed.

***

A new Supreme Command meeting is scheduled for March 14th in the same underground bunker. Now, the representative from Slovenia is also present. After a brief presentation by General Kadijević, they proceed to vote. The proposal is definitively rejected, with a result of 5 to 3. Those against are Slovenia, Croatia, Bosnia and Herzegovina, Macedonia, and the Autonomous Province of Kosovo and Metohija. The ones voting in favor of the military leadership's proposal are Serbia, Montenegro, and the Autonomous Province of Vojvodina.

As a reaction to this outcome, Milošević makes an arrogant and gambling move: he withdraws the representatives of Serbia, Montenegro, AP Vojvodina, and AP Kosovo from the Presidency. He announces that "Serbia no longer recognizes the decisions of the Presidency." In this way, by undermining the Presidency as the Supreme Commander of the armed forces, he tries to create a legal vacuum in which the Yugoslav People's Army (JNA) would have no other choice but to seize power in the country as the only remaining guardian of the constitutional order.

However, the military leadership had already assessed that their independent action, without political consensus in the Presidency, would be doomed to fail, have catastrophic consequences, and cause many human casualties. On the other hand, the generals knew well that without the support of at least one major world power, a military coup had no chance of succeeding. This leads to an unexpected turn, and on March 17th, Kadijević informs Milošević that the army will not independently carry out a military coup. To this, Milošević reacted pragmatically and without any scruples, simply returned his people to the Presidency of Yugoslavia as if nothing had happened.

In his memoir book *Counterstrike*, General Kadijević, speaking about the reasons against a military coup, examines the mechanism by which the Serbian people were, as he says, "entrapped". This is an extremely important quote from the pen of one of the initial members of the interest group for preserving the communist regime in Yugoslavia and confirms the conclusions I have drawn on several occasions in my study of what actually transpired. The Serbs were deceived by propaganda and instrumentalized. Kadijević writes that the only serious politician who demanded a military coup was Slobodan Milošević, but he made such a demand without a fundamental assessment and as pure improvisation, to which he was inclined. Considering the consequences of a possible military coup, the general wonders why the "Serbian people should suffer because the Yugoslav

People's Army wants to forcibly keep other nations in Yugoslavia who do not want to remain in that country".

The Secret Agreement Between Milošević and Tudjman

In March 1991, the first armed conflicts in Croatia began. The local Serbs organized political and territorial autonomy and expressed a firm determination to remain in a truncated Yugoslavia with those territories. In response, Croatia deployed police intervention units to prevent such a scenario and keep them within Croatia—against their will. It was only a matter of time before the first casualties would fall.

Many years later, the Yugoslav public would discover that the war was, to a great extent, prearranged. On March 25th, 1991, the presidents of Serbia and Croatia, Slobodan Milošević and Franjo Tudjman, met in the famous Karadjordjevo hunting grounds, once a favorite retreat of Josip Broz Tito. According to the testimony of the Croatian representative in the Presidency of Yugoslavia, Stjepan Mesić, the meeting took place at his initiative. After one of the numerous agonizing sessions of the Presidency, during a break, he asked the Serbian representative, Borisav Jović, about Serbia's real intentions. Allegedly, Jović told him that "Serbia does not have territorial claims towards Croatia, but it does have them in relation to Bosnia and Herzegovina". Surprised by such a response, Mesić proposed that the presidents meet, come to an agreement on everything, and thus avoid further bloodshed.

We will probably never find out exactly what the two presidents discussed privately during the meeting that lasted several hours. However, a lot can be reconstructed. Upon his return to Zagreb, according to the accounts of his closest associates, Tudjman was noticeably in good spirits. He said that Milošević had offered to divide Bosnia and Herzegovina in such a way that Croatian areas would belong to the future expanded Croatia, Serbian ones to expanded Serbia, and there would be a small territory reserved for Bosniaks in between. It is also claimed that they then agreed on the overthrow of the federal government and its reformist Prime Minister Ante Marković.

After the meeting in Karadjordjevo, another one followed in Tikveš, about which very little is known. However, immediately afterwards, Croatian and Serbian expert commissions were formed, which met in Belgrade and Zagreb and worked on drawing up maps of territorial divisions, but, allegedly, they were unable to reconcile their views.

Statements about this meeting are quite contradictory, ranging from denials of any agreement to complete conviction that the contours of the Yu-

343

goslav Wars—the bloodiest conflicts in Europe since World War II—were drawn there.

Although some Croatian and Serbian historians, politicians, and researchers dismiss the possibility of a concrete agreement having been reached at this meeting, many others believe that is exactly what happened. Some facts are eye-catching. If there was no agreement, why were expert groups formed that dealt with drawing maps, the members of which are known by name and surname?

Even more intriguing are the alleged statements by Borisav Jović that Serbia had no interest in the Serbs in Croatia as early as 1991. This was later spoken about by Josip Manolić, a spy and the Prime Minister of Croatia during the war:

> "Milošević said, 'I'm not interested—even though he stirred up the rebellion of the Serbs in Croatia, despite that, he insisted, 'The question of the Serbs in Croatia is your internal matter. My interest, the interest of Serbia, is the question of the Serbs in Bosnia and Herzegovina.' And he remained consistent with that."

If this is true, it sheds light on the departure of almost the entire Serbian population from Croatia in 1995. Namely, during the Croatian military operation Storm, launched against rebel territories with a Serbian majority, over three days and practically without major combat, around 220,000 Serbs fled from Croatia to the Serbian part of Bosnia and Serbia. Although these events are seen today in Serbian public opinion as ethnic cleansing of Serbs, participants and eyewitnesses have described elements of an organized evacuation during the Serbian exodus from Croatia.

Another example of Milošević and Tudjman's cooperation is the Croatian withdrawal of M-84 tanks from the Vukovar battlefield, their restoration, refurbishment, repainting in the color of desert sand, and export to Kuwait, which was organized and carried out by the Serbian company Jugoimport—SDPR in 1992.

Milošević and Tudjman were the undisputed leaders of two nations at war. How then to explain that from the moment they met, they addressed each other by their personal names and nicknames: "Slobo" and "Franjo," and that throughout the war they had a "hot" phone line through which they could converse at any time? About this phone, Stjepan Mesić, who became the new President of Croatia after Tudjman's death in 1999, gave the following testimony:

> "When I was elected president in 2000, I wanted to call Milošević. My secretaries couldn't connect me, because they said: 'Only Tudjman had that phone number; we don't have it.'. And then I

called the technicians from the Ministry of Internal Affairs who dismantled the phone and took it away."[82]

Journalist Ruža Ćirković, who has been researching for years what really happened at the meeting of the two leaders, expressed in an interview published by Deutsche Welle the opinion that the thesis that there was no agreement suits both Serbia and Croatia at present. Mrs. Ćirković suggests that if there indeed was an agreement, it would mean that the war in Bosnia and Herzegovina could be redefined as an act of aggression by two neighboring countries, rather than being seen as a civil war, which is the prevailing interpretation.

A glimmer of optimism that we will one day learn the truth is provided today (in 2021) by centenarian intelligence officer and former Prime Minister of Croatia, Josip Manolić, in a very interesting statement:

"About [the meeting in] Karadjordjevo, no one will openly talk about it even now. However, I personally think that two or three intelligence services were listening to that conversation and even recorded it. So, we will eventually get to those specific results."

---

[82] Deutsche Welle (online). *Bizarre Friendship Between Tudjman and Milošević.* Accessed June 11th, 2023. Available at: *https://www.dw.com/hr/bizarno-prijateljstvo-tu%C4%91mana-i-milo%C5%A1evi%C4%87a/a-36795210* (in Croatian). https://www.dw.com/hr/bizarno-prijateljstvo-tu%C4%91mana-i-milo%C5%A1evi%C4%87a/a-36795210.

The Definitive Death of Yugoslavia

By mid-1991, the inability of the republic leaders to reach an agreement on anything—brought Yugoslavia to the beginning of a bloody disintegration. Despite all the pleas coming from the European Community, the Soviet Union, and the United States to preserve the country, the Yugoslavs irrationally rushed into chaotic dissolution. U.S. Secretary of State James Baker arrived for a belated visit on June 21st, 1991, advocating for the preservation of Yugoslavia as a democratic federation, providing full support to the federal Prime Minister Ante Marković and his reformists. Western governments were very concerned in those days that the disintegration of Yugoslavia could bring instability to other regions of Europe and awaken dormant antagonisms. Because of this assessment, Slovenia and Croatia were clearly advised that unilateral moves would not be looked upon favorably, but that preference should be given to solutions achieved through the democratic process and in agreement with others. After the visit, frustrated by the depth of divisions and the irrationality of the leaders with whom he spoke, James Baker reported to President Bush that "we (Americans) don't have a dog in that fight."

Powerful America, whose President Woodrow Wilson in 1919 made a crucial contribution to the recognition of newly-formed Yugoslavia at the Versailles Peace Conference, now had its attention elsewhere. The disintegration of the Soviet Union, the unification of Germany, the fall of communism in Europe, and the war in the Middle East were occupying the attention of the world's greatest power. "Yugoslavia no longer enjoyed the geopolitical importance that the United States had given it during the Cold War"[83], was the message American officials conveyed to the Yugoslavs after the disappearance of the Soviet Union.

Washington initially intended to leave this issue to the Europeans, but as it turned out, these expectations would not come to fruition. As events unfolded, it became clear that it was America—through its assertive political and military maneuvers—that would ultimately play the decisive role in terminating the devastating war in Yugoslavia years down the line.

The shift of American attention away from the Balkans created room for other dormant interests to emerge, particularly that of Germany, which viewed not only Slovenia and Croatia but also the rest of the Balkans as within its sphere of influence. One should not overlook the Vatican, which had a potent presence in these two Catholic republics and was ill-disposed

---

[83] Zimmerman, Warren. "Origins of Catastrophe." *Foreign Affairs*, March/April 1995, No. 74, p. 2.

towards the Yugoslav project that would mix Catholics with Muslims and Orthodox Christians. Yet, there was also Russia, which harbored an enduring geopolitical ambition to gain access to the warm Adriatic Sea and, through it, to the Mediterranean. It had tried and failed to sway Yugoslavia into its camp, or to incite internal divisions along the traditional East-West, or Orthodox-Catholic, lines—a tactic at which it had been far more successful.

While Yugoslavia was never a member of the Warsaw Pact, it did sign a military-political agreement in 1953 with Greece and Turkey—NATO members—to mitigate the risk of a Warsaw Pact invasion of the Balkans. Naturally, Yugoslavia enjoyed varying levels of overt American support throughout this period.

The vacuum created by the diminished US interest in the Balkans, amid the looming disintegration of Yugoslavia, immediately awakened Germany's aspirations. Now fortified by reunification, Germany sought, for the first time since 1945, to assert itself as a power to be reckoned with globally. The media and politicians of Europe's most robust economy had already been vocally supporting the leaderships of Slovenia and Croatia in their pursuit of independence, promising recognition regardless of the position of other European allies. Austria's rhetoric mirrored that of Germany. History was repeating itself: on the Balkans, old friendships between Slovenes and Croats with Germans and Austrians were being renewed, much as they had been in both World Wars. I vividly recall conversations with ordinary people in Belgrade during that time. Serbs were convinced they would once again have to face the German enemy, as they had in 1914 or 1941.

Despite the international community's appeals to abstain from unilateral moves, Slovenia and Croatia were relentlessly marching towards realizing a dream. This was a dream harbored since the Middle Ages, and it was finally within their reach. They had been waiting for a suitable opportunity, a favorable confluence of international circumstances that would allow the world to approve the creation of two new national states in the Balkans. Up to that point, the Slovenes had never had a sovereign and independent state, and the Croats had lost their sovereignty in the early 12th century.

As shown in earlier chapters, following the departure of Austro-Hungary from the historical stage, the crafty maneuver of Slovenes and Croats entering the Yugoslav union with Serbs saved them from losing substantial territories that were supposed to belong to Italy and gave them time to nationally consolidate and prepare for their desired independence. The preparations for this grand finale were quiet and persistent, lasting for decades. They saw the Yugoslav state as a necessary transitional solution towards independence, systematically weakening it through decentralization and confederalization. In the years after Tito's death, they practically prepared for the final departure.

And now, at last, Germany was strong, America was looking the other way, the Soviet Union was disintegrating, and communism was dying. In Yugoslavia, the anachronistic, dogmatic communist top brass wanted to survive the fall of the Berlin Wall, sliding towards militarism and Bolshevism, and imposing Slobodan Milošević as their political leader. The situation couldn't have been better.

This was the long-awaited, ideal historical moment.

To the general elation of their people, the parliaments of Slovenia and Croatia unilaterally declared secession from Yugoslavia on June 25th, 1991. This action marked the dissolution of the joint state they had created with the Serbs on December 1st, 1918.

On that day, Yugoslavia died. It had endured for seventy-two years, six months, and twenty-one days.

348

POST MORTEM

Yugoslav Wars of the 1990s:
Balkanization and the Creation of New States

In the Encyclopædia Britannica, we find the following definition of the term Balkanization:

"**Balkanization**, division of a multinational state into smaller ethnically homogeneous entities. The term also is used to refer to ethnic conflict within multiethnic states. It was coined at the end of World War I to describe the ethnic and political fragmentation that followed the breakup of the Ottoman Empire, particularly in the Balkans. (The term Balkanization is today invoked to explain the disintegration of some multiethnic states and their devolution into dictatorship, ethnic cleansing, and civil war.)"

Countless books, studies, and papers have been written, and many films have been made to explain the series of tragic conflicts that, during the 1990s, tore apart the body of an already deceased Yugoslavia. It is certain that in the future there will be more attempts by human intellect to get closer to a more comprehensive understanding of this unusually complex period, as we are still far from achieving a general consensus on what happened.

Perspectives are vastly divergent—often diametrically opposed. The very protagonists of this drama can't even agree on a name for the wars they fought. To some, it was a war for independence; to others, a homeland war. To some, it was a civil war in the former Yugoslavia, while others view it as Greater Serbian aggression. Yet others perceive it as a secessionist armed assault on Yugoslavia. Mischa Glenny, a British author who has made substantial efforts to understand us and depict us in his books, has coined the term "Third Balkan War."

Fortunately, I did not participate in the Yugoslav Wars as a soldier, but I was a witness to these tragic events. Over time, pain and despair, powerlessness and bitterness accumulated within me. Every day, we were exposed to images of violence, dead and injured, bombs and destruction, nationalist madness and people dressed in ominous uniforms resurrected from a time we thought had passed forever.

The pain born in that insane period is still carried by a great number of Yugoslavs today. Recollections awaken sadness for every lost life—for the injured and maimed, for the dishonored women and girls, the traumatized and tortured prisoners of war, for the refugees and displaced and their burnt villages and homes. I strongly empathize with the children born in that tragedy, now adults. I grieve for the generations of youth who were prisoners of madness and darkness, totalitarianism, sanctions, corruption, crime, poverty, and who, at the first opportunity, packed their suitcases and fled the Balkans. I am saddened by the civilizational test that we collectively failed. Sometimes, I feel ashamed for my generation and those older than me because we failed to prevent the madness.

And then the question arises, "Could we have done anything?" Many in the former Yugoslavia then succumbed to collective psychosis and sank into the "us versus them" paradigm. Propaganda was horrific on all sides. Many people protested and demonstrated against the war and militant leaders. There were those like us in every corner of the deceased state. But, truth be told, we were not numerous enough to reach the critical mass that could halt the evil. If dissolution was inevitable, the question remains: could we have done it better, more intelligently, more humanely?

Today, in the countries of the former Yugoslavia, generations of children are coming of age who were born ten or fifteen years after the wars. It's already clear that many of them have been taught to believe that "the others" in their immediate vicinity are bad, dangerous, or less worthy than their own people. This is the future we have left—and are still leaving—to our children. It doesn't take much wisdom to foresee that the dark pages of our history can easily be carried into the years that lie ahead of us.

How Milošević Took the Helm of the JNA

Through covert political agreements between Serbia and Slovenia regarding Slovenia's unimpeded exit from Yugoslavia, and an even more secret agreement with Croatia about the division of Bosnia and Herzegovina, Milošević betrayed and checkmated his erstwhile patrons from the military top brass. The Yugoslav People's Army (JNA) was no longer able to fulfill its constitutional duty to preserve the territorial integrity of the state. Milošević's decision to abandon the course of preserving a united Yugoslavia effectively rendered the Army's purpose meaningless. It had become an army without a state.

The Ten-Day War in Slovenia

The declaration by the Slovenian Parliament about its unilateral secession from Yugoslavia was, highly expectedly, declared null and void on the
same day, June 25th, 1991, by the federal parliament and the federal government in Belgrade. The army and federal police were ordered to establish
control over Yugoslav border crossings in Slovenian territory towards Italy, Austria, and Hungary. This action, often characterized in the media of
secessionist republics for propaganda reasons as an act of "Yugo-Serbian
aggression" towards "democratic Slovenia", was, in fact, very expected. It
is likely that any internationally recognized and sovereign state would have
acted similarly. The Slovenians, on the same day they declared secession,
removed the state symbols of Yugoslavia from border crossings and in-
stalled Slovenian symbols. It is very likely that Spain, for example, would
have reacted identically had Catalonia's secession escalated in such a unilateral way. It is hard to imagine a different scenario if a border state in the
US, like Texas, were to secede unilaterally, remove American flags from
its borders with Mexico overnight, put up different ones, and start appropriating customs revenue.

The sovereignty and territorial integrity of modern states, and the im-
mutability of their borders, are fundamental tenets of the international order established by the UN charters and the Helsinki Accords. Yugoslavia
had the opportunity to disintegrate in a peaceful way, a path foreseen by
the Constitution and likely to be globally accepted. Unfortunately, such a
favorable scenario required internal political agreement, which sadly was
not possible.

Acting in accordance with the orders of the federal government and
Prime Minister Ante Marković, the federal police and the Yugoslav People's Army (JNA) embarked on an operation to reoccupy the Yugoslav
state border on June 26th, 1991, with several thousand personnel. Initially,
they encountered barricades and civilian protests during the passage of
tanks and armored personnel carriers. The following day, the situation
dramatically worsened, and the well-prepared Slovenian Territorial Defense, boasting about 30,000 soldiers, initiated armed resistance.

The military leadership, headed by General Kadijević, was convinced
that a show of force would be sufficient to coerce the Slovenians into re-
tracting their secession decision. However, what unfolded came as a great
surprise to them. Blinded by stubbornness and out of touch with reality,
they failed to understand the intense determination of the Slovenians to
establish their independent and sovereign state for the first time in history.

No pressure exerted by the communistic indoctrinated Yugoslav People's Army on Slovenia stood a chance of success. Slovenians and Croatians were deserting *en masse*, while other recruits from the rest of Yugoslavia were praying they wouldn't have to point their guns at people, and that the drama would end as quickly as possible.

The Yugoslav People's Army (JNA) sent inexperienced eighteen-year-olds, or slightly older, conscripted for mandatory military service and hailing from all across Yugoslavia: Macedonians, Bosniaks, Albanians, Serbs, Montenegrins, to face the Slovenian Territorial Defense composed of adult men. Among these were also a few Croats and Slovenes who had not deserted. I remember my disbelief while watching the dramatic reports from Slovenia on television. I'm sure many of us still remember the frightened face of nineteen-year-old soldier Bahrudin Kaletović, a Bosniak by ethnicity, who, when asked by a TV reporter to explain why there was shooting and dying, said, "As far as I understand, they apparently want to secede, and we're like, not letting them" That day, three of his comrades from the unit, young men aged nineteen and twenty, were killed.

"…they apparently want to secede, and we're like, not letting them".

JNA soldier
Bahrudin Kaletović (age 19)

Despite armed resistance, the JNA managed to occupy almost all border crossings and Brnik airport near Ljubljana by June 27th. But then the tide of the war turned. The Slovenian Territorial Defense attacked JNA columns and barracks across the entire territory of the republic, claiming victory after victory. A large number of armored personnel carriers, several tanks, and two helicopters were destroyed. A vast quantity of weaponry was seized. Sixty-five soldiers and officers were killed on both sides, with the number of wounded estimated at 328. The number of captured JNA soldiers was around 4,700.

While the conflict was raging in Slovenia, a minor drama was unfolding in Belgrade around June 30th. An emergency session of the Presidency of Yugoslavia was convened in its capacity as the supreme commanding body of the armed forces. The Federal Secretary for National Defense, General Veljko Kadijević, informed those present that his concept of limited intervention and show of force in Slovenia had failed. He requested approval for the JNA to launch a full-scale attack, occupy Slovenia, and establish military rule on its territory. To the great surprise of the generals present, the presiding member of the Presidency, Serbia's representative and a close associate of Milošević, Borisav Jović, rejected this initiative, stating that

"Serbia does not support further actions against Slovenia". Considering the previously described agreement between Milošević and the Slovenian President Kučan, it is clear that Milošević adhered to the agreement. One can even take the conclusion a step further. With this move, he saved Slovenia from a military intervention, human casualties, and widespread destruction—a fact that has remained largely unknown to this day.

With the mediation of ministers from the European Community, a ceasefire agreement was signed on July 7th, 1991, setting up a three-month transitional period during which a moratorium on the independence of Slovenia and Croatia would be in place, and the JNA would completely withdraw from Slovenia. During this time, the Slovenians would consolidate their institutions and prepare everything for full international recognition. This recognition came on January 15th, 1992, from the European Community. That same year, Slovenia was admitted to the United Nations. The dream of the Slovenes was realized. For the first time in their history, Slovenia became an internationally recognized sovereign state.

***

The entire Yugoslav public witnessed the disintegration of the army. Soldiers and officers from Slovenia, Croatia, and soon from other republics, began leaving the ranks of the JNA. Only Serbs and Montenegrins remained. Disoriented and ideologically fragmented, the army completely lost its pan-Yugoslav ethnic character and readily fell into the hands of the Serbian leadership and political agenda, led by Slobodan Milošević. Within the now ethnically predominantly Serbian JNA, all those who were not aligned with Milošević's stance were either removed from their positions or marginalized in various ways.

It appears that the generals and old communist cadres misread Slobodan Milošević. He outmaneuvered them, dominated them, and brought the army under his control. Some would later publicly disassociate themselves from him and express regret for the political support they had given him to elevate him to power.

In preparation for the complete monolith of his totalitarian apparatus, Milošević implemented a turnover of the old pro-Yugoslav cadres in the intelligence services and police within Serbia, installing people loyal to himself. Subsequently, all institutions, media, public companies, and financial flows were put under the absolute control of the regime.

What was Milošević's objective? His sole purpose was to retain power, alongside the cosmetically transformed yesteryear communists, members of the military, police, and security services, party affiliates, and other followers motivated by self-interest. To fulfill this plan, they needed territory, people, and money, which they would later seize from their own people.

They already had Serbia; Montenegro was also in the picture. The JNA was now predominantly Serbian-Montenegrin, ideologically cleansed, and brought under their control.

There is another important reason why Milošević supported Slovenia's departure from Yugoslavia that we must not forget in our analysis. Without a Slovenian representative, the number of members of the Presidency would drop from eight to seven, giving the Serbian bloc of four votes a simple majority and the ability to de facto govern this body in a completely legitimate way. This would make Milošević not only the strongest political figure to the rest of Yugoslavia but also the supreme commander of the armed forces.

From Slobodan Milošević's perspective and the faction he represented, there were no remaining obstacles to establishing a "third Yugoslavia," with him as the unequivocal leader. This new federation, he declared, would be made up of "those who love Yugoslavia and opt to remain in it." However, as events unfolded, it became evident that only Serbs, and to a lesser extent, Montenegrins—whose perceptions were clouded and influenced by powerful propaganda—would embrace this vision.

The Aspirations of Serbs Outside the Republic of Serbia: Constitutional Rights Versus Geopolitics

What did the Serbian people in the republics of Croatia and Bosnia and Herzegovina aspire to? They believed that no one had the right to forcibly separate them from their state, Yugoslavia. They possessed Yugoslav passports. This is a strong argument and cannot be overlooked. As an inviolable principle, it was also incorporated into the Constitution of Yugoslavia. The first article unambiguously stipulates that the common state was established through the unification of the Yugoslav *peoples*—not republics— by freely expressed will, starting from "the right of each *people* to self-determination, including the right to secession."[84]

If the Slovenes and Croats wanted to go, their right was unquestionable. But equally unquestionable was the right of Serbs to opt for remaining in Yugoslavia.

However, these two aspirations proved to be irreconcilable and led to war. The reason is simple: the right of peoples to self-determination could not be realized without changing the administrative borders of Croatia and Bosnia and Herzegovina.

---

[84] Constitution of the Socialist Federal Republic of Yugoslavia (1974), Introduction, Basic Principles, Article I.

The Serbian stance was that no one had the right to forcibly drag them against their will from Yugoslavia to some new states. If the Serbs themselves were unwilling to depart from Yugoslavia, what means could possibly coerce them to comply? And on what grounds? Consequently, in regions where Serbs formed the majority, referenda were conducted, and the overwhelming majority chose to remain within Yugoslavia, regardless of its future form and geographical extent.

The internal inter-republic borders in Yugoslavia did not follow an ethnic principle, so the Serbs in Croatia and Bosnia and Herzegovina constituted a minority within these republics, but a majority in the areas where they traditionally lived. They could easily be forced into secession against their will through majority voting within their own republic. When you add to this the collective memory of the genocide during World War II, which was perpetrated against them during the quisling Independent State of Croatia, it becomes clear that these people feared that mass destruction could happen to them again. To make matters even more complicated and tense, serious incidents against Serbs were recorded even after World War II, especially during the "Croatian Spring" period of 1971–1972, when an explosion of Croatian nationalism occurred. Therefore, the majority of the Serbian people firmly believed that in any independent Croatian state they would face discrimination, persecution, and possible physical extermination. Guided by this perception, they believed that their survival was only guaranteed by life in a "shrunken" Yugoslavia, with Serbia as the motherland and with all other nations who wished to live there. The protection of their rights to remain within the boundaries of any kind Yugoslavia could only be provided by the army, which still carried the adjectives "Yugoslav" and "People's" in its name. And so we arrive at a crucial confluence of circumstances and interests that Milošević, I'm sure, counted on.

Since effective control over military power had shifted into the hands of the regime in Belgrade, Serbs from Croatia and Bosnia had no other option but to align with the political program of creating a "shrunken" or "third Yugoslavia." I see this fact as entirely logical and expected. These individuals were simply reliant on Milošević and the Yugoslav People's Army (JNA)—they could hardly make a different choice. However, bombarded with an unprecedented daily indoctrination and propaganda from controlled media, Serbs from Croatia and Bosnia were not able to comprehend the real reason why their efforts would be suppressed and obstructed by the Western world. The regime's propaganda had them convinced that the "West hates them," justifying this with religion, history, or by fabricating conspiracy theories.

However, the primary cause was rooted in the *geopolitical orientation* of Milošević's regime, which, in its desire to endure, actively opposed the efforts of the EEC and the U.S. to democratize Communist Europe and integrate it into NATO. Therefore, Western actions were aimed against the pro-communist, heavily armed establishment in Belgrade, led by the autocratically inclined Milošević—not against the people.

The West did not want individuals who were extending a hand of cooperation to the hardliners in Moscow. At that time, although greatly weakened, Russia was ardently seeking to consolidate and regain its power. Moreover, the possibility that Milošević, through political and military alliance, could bring Russia into the Balkans and the Adriatic via Montenegro became a reality, and the West was resolved to prevent such a development. These are the genuine reasons why the territorial consolidation of Serbs under Milošević's leadership could not have been acceptable to the West. On the contrary, the West endeavored to fragment, divide, and weaken Serbian territories, viewing the Serbs (and Montenegrins) as satellites of Russia. The alliance of Milošević and Russia threatened the key geopolitical and strategic interests of the West in the Balkans and the Mediterranean. Russia, driven by its own interests, fostered pro-Russian sentiments among the Serbs and sought to present itself as their protector against the West. On the other hand, the West aided Russia in this endeavor by subjecting the Serbs to strong political, media, and military pressure, without making any efforts to pursue a more far-sighted policy towards this ancient, proud, and state-building European nation.

Thus, the Serbs became collateral damage in this geopolitical confrontation between the West and Russia, and consequently, the Western world did not wish to heed their needs, aspirations, historical or political rights.

However, this truth was never openly and simply explained to the Serbs. They, as proxies of the regime, collectively sank along with Milošević who—quite predictably—lost his battle with the West.

Formation of the Federal Republic of Yugoslavia – FR Yugoslavia

To understand the various perspectives of the main actors in the Yugoslav crisis, a good source of information is the diary kept by Borisav Jović, the Serbian member of the Yugoslav Presidency, who has been cited earlier. In mid-October 1990, a dramatic session of this body was held, during which Slovenia and Croatia signaled their intention to leave the federation. Macedonia and Bosnia and Herzegovina took the position that they would remain in Yugoslavia only if Slovenia and Croatia also stayed. Kosovo wanted to be separated from Serbia and declared a new republic within the federation. Immediately after that, it would have pursued a path towards secession. Serbia and Montenegro wanted either a federal Yugoslavia, which would be constitutionally reformed towards centralization, or a re-definition of borders; specifically, the division of territories of those republics that wanted to secede, based on ethnic principles.

What a multitude of opposing and conflicting aspirations. It was clear that the chances for Yugoslavia's survival were very slim.

Since apparently no republic outside the Serbian-Montenegrin bloc wanted a centralized Yugoslavia, especially not with Milošević at the helm, Belgrade was left to prepare an agenda in which territories with a Serbian majority from other republics would be annexed to Serbia and Montenegro. To assess the legitimacy of such a policy, it is significant to determine how many Serbs were actually in other republics by examining statistical data. The last census in Yugoslavia was conducted under chaotic conditions in 1991 when the country was already falling apart, but its results were largely accepted on all sides.

In Bosnia and Herzegovina, there were 31.21%, or 1,366,104 Serbs, and in Croatia, 12.16%, or 581,663.

Looking from another angle, we can establish that in the rest of Yugoslavia, outside of Serbia, there were 2,080,000 Serbs, or approximately 25% of their total number which amounted to 8,526,872.

This leads us to the following conclusion: in the event that Yugoslavia disintegrates into its constituent republics and the world recognizes them as new states, 25% of Serbs would involuntarily:

a. be left without their state of Yugoslavia, into which they had invested the Kingdom of Serbia and for which they had made the greatest sacrifices in World War I and II,

b. become citizens of some new small states where they would have the status of a national minority, and in some of them (Croatia, Bosnia and Herzegovina), they had experienced mass extermination or genocide in the past, and

c. be cut off from the rest of the Serbs and Serbia.

For these reasons, the homogenization of the Serbs was expected and logical. To say that it happened because of Milošević, that he "incited the

Federal Republic of Yugoslavia (1992-2003) and Serbia and Montenegro (2003-2006)

OO · Republic of Serbia

O · autonomous provinces (Vojvodina and Kosovo)

O · Central Serbia (under direct jurisdiction of the government of Serbia)

O · Republic of Montenegro

Map of the Federal Republic of Yugoslavia, later
State Union of Serbia and Montenegro.

Serbs," is to confuse cause and effect. They would have homogenized and resisted their own fragmentation even without him. It is likely that many other peoples around the world would have reacted in the same way if they had found themselves in such a position. However, it leads to the conclusion that the Serbs would probably be much better off today had someone with much greater human and democratic capacities emerged instead of Milošević during those years.

The United States wanted to leave the resolution of the dispute in Yugoslavia to its partners from the European Economic Community. In 1991, Europeans established the Conference on Yugoslavia and appointed one of the most experienced British politicians, former foreign secretary, defense minister, and NATO general secretary Lord Peter Carrington as its head. With the need to first resolve key legal issues that the Yugoslavs could not

360

agree upon, an Arbitration Commission was established, composed of the presidents of five European constitutional courts, led by Robert Badinter from France. This expert body provided a set of conclusions that would guide the EEC in its policy toward the states that would emerge from the ruins of former Yugoslavia. Some opinions of the Badinter Commission would be in direct opposition to the aspirations of the Serbian people, but generally in line with the aspirations of all others.

In response to Lord Carrington's question: "Does the Serb population in Croatia and Bosnia and Herzegovina, being one of the constituent peoples of Yugoslavia, have the right to self-determination?", it was clarified that "the Serb population in Bosnia and Herzegovina and Croatia possess all the rights associated with *minorities and ethnic groups...*". Furthermore, the Commission asserted that the borders between the republics "cannot be altered, except through a freely reached consensus". Understandably, these positions taken by the EEC left the Serbs greatly disappointed, instilling in them a belief that they were being subjected to significant injustice. However, they struggled to comprehend the geopolitical dimensions of their situation.

The process of homogenization and unification—essentially, the strengthening of the Serbs—was deemed undesirable in the West due to the pro-Eastern bias of the regime that was leading them and representing their interests before the international community. This was further complicated by the prevailing Western perception of Serbs as "little Russians", a viewpoint influenced by the traditional Russophilia among a sizable portion of Serbs.

Could there have been an alternative course of action at that time? Let's examine the case of Bosnia and Herzegovina.

The expectation of the European Economic Community (EEC) that the ethnic Serbs, who accounted for 31.21% of the total population, would immediately renounce their Yugoslav passports and accept a "minority and ethnic group" status appears highly unrealistic. This perception is further strengthened by several facts:

- Bosnia and Herzegovina's strong Ottoman legacy
- The Bosniaks, the largest population group, are predominantly Muslim
- Their leader, Alija Izetbegović, was convicted in Yugoslavia for holding views closely aligned with Islamic fundamentalism
- The Bosniaks advocate for a centralized internal structure of the republic

Such a scenario would inevitably lead to the marginalization of national minorities in future decision-making processes. Given their traumatic historical experiences, the Serbs simply could not consent to such a loss of their status.

In accordance with the conclusions of the Arbitration Commission, Lord Carrington, on October 18th, 1991, offered recognition by the EEC to all Yugoslav republics within the confines of their existing inter-republic borders. All republics agreed except Serbia. Later, only Montenegro changed its opinion under pressure from Belgrade. Milošević justified the refusal by arguing that the proposed solution deprived the Serbian people of their right to self-determination, as they had chosen to continue living together in Yugoslavia rather than being fragmented among several independent republics. Serbia believed then—and this has not changed to this day—that the international community exhibited double standards by recognizing the right to self-determination for all Yugoslav peoples except the Serbs.

Under the given circumstances, Serbia and Montenegro chose to continue with the already paved path toward creating the "Third Yugoslavia." For the sake of historical and legal continuity, the decision was made in the Federal Council of the Socialist Federal Republic of Yugoslavia, in which only representatives from Serbia and Montenegro were present. On April 27th, 1992, the Federal Republic of Yugoslavia—FRY—was established.

The introductory provisions of the new state's constitution stated:

"The Federal Republic of Yugoslavia is composed of the Republic of Serbia and the Republic of Montenegro as member republics."
"Other republics may join the Federal Republic of Yugoslavia in accordance with this constitution."

Which other republics were in question? Slovenia, Croatia, and Macedonia had already declared their independence. The only remaining one was Bosnia and Herzegovina, with which unsuccessful negotiations took place regarding its accession to the union. There was also the contentious Republic of Serbian Krajina, a self-proclaimed republic of Croatian Serbs. In the event of definitive failure in negotiations with Bosnia and Herzegovina, it was widely anticipated that a Bosnian Serb republic would be established, with the intention of seeking membership in the FRY.

Therefore, Milošević's "Third Yugoslavia" project could hardly be assigned a Yugoslav (South Slavic) character, except in name. It would be a state of Serbs from Serbia, Bosnia and Herzegovina, and Croatia, and Montenegrins, who are also of Serbian origin. In other words, the Federal Republic of Yugoslavia would be a state of only the Serbian people across their entire ethnic territory. It would most closely resemble the extended or "Greater" Serbia envisioned by the provisions of the London Treaty of

1915. Comparing these two historical moments, one significant geopolitical difference emerges. King Alexander Karadjordjević and the Serbs had crucial support from the U.S. and France at the end of World War I and were oriented towards the West. Slobodan Milošević had open support from no one in the world, except Belarus, Iran, and North Korea. Even official Moscow was reserved. At that time Russia was in a partnership with the West and had to publicly refrain from fully supporting Belgrade.

However, observing the later development of events indicates the deep and substantive presence of both Russia and the West in the processes of the Yugoslav breakup. This complex relationship has continued into later times and is clearly felt to this day, most notably in Bosnia and Herzegovina, Serbia, Kosovo, Montenegro, and to some extent, North Macedonia.

It seems logical and quite likely that Milošević's regime's insistence on keeping the country's name "Yugoslavia" was motivated by the homogenization and instrumentalization of Serbs and Montenegrins, whose ancestors had made enormous sacrifices in two world wars to first create and then defend that state. "We will preserve Yugoslavia—the country for which your fathers and grandfathers fought. Yugoslavia will not disappear!" was the key message, then strongly presented to the public from the highest place.

The Federal Republic of Yugoslavia was not admitted to the UN as the successor to the previous Yugoslavia, despite Milošević's insistence. It would only be admitted to the world organization after his overthrow. Stubbornness and arrogance, as well as inconsistent behavior in international relations, made Milošević an undesirable interlocutor. Domestically, the FRY was sinking into crime, corruption, and the degradation of cultural, moral, and human values. International sanctions and blockades would soon follow due to military and financial support to the Serbs in Croatia and Bosnia and Herzegovina. Russia would agree with the sanctions—there would be no veto in the UN Security Council. The FRY was labeled as the main culprit for the war in Bosnia and Herzegovina, and a punitive economic war began against it by practically the entire world. The year was 1992. The course and outcome of such massive pressure were quite predictable. A sanitary cordon was formed around the country, and life within it became very, very difficult.

Despite all the difficulties, life in Serbia was still much better than for the hundreds of thousands of people in Croatia and Bosnia and Herzegovina, who were caught in the whirlwind of the bloodiest and most brutal conflict in Europe after 1945.

War would come to us as well, but not until seven years later.

The War in Croatia

Although animosity between the two peoples had existed for centuries and was caused by belonging to rival branches of Christianity, it became more pronounced with the settlement of Serbs in the Austrian Military Frontier in the 16th century. From the chronological perspective, the last escalation of relations between Croats and Serbs in Croatia began in 1990 after the first post-communist multi-party elections. The political program of the victorious Croatian Democratic Union (HDZ) led by Franjo Tudjman consisted of undisguised ambitions to leave Yugoslavia and establish an independent Croatia, and its political leaders used pronounced nationalist rhetoric in their public addresses.

Burdened by distrust and fear that were deeply rooted in their collective memory, primarily due to the genocide they suffered in the Independent State of Croatia during World War II, coupled with the unending animosity of Croats in the post-war decades, the Serbs in Croatia largely cast their votes for the Serbian Democratic Party (SDS), their political representative. Its program envisaged staying in Yugoslavia and closer ties with Serbia. The SDS won in all municipalities where Serbs were the majority. Roughly speaking, this accounted for about 30% of the territory of Croatia, which was still just one of the six republics within Yugoslavia.

Territories of the self-proclaimed Republic of Serbian Krajina (RSK) within the borders of Croatia (in red color).

After Croatia declared its secession, around mid-1991, there were attacks by newly formed Croatian units on the Yugoslav People's Army (JNA) barracks. The aim was to force the federal army to leave Croatia while also seizing its weaponry. Quite expectedly, the army defended itself and there were casualties. The Croats viewed these events as natural steps towards full independence, whereas the local Serbs perceived them as an armed attack on Yugoslavia and its legitimate army.

As a political response to Croatia's slide towards secession, the Croatian Serbs formed the Republic of Serbian Krajina (RSK), an unrecognized state that existed from 1991 to 1995. It mostly encompassed territories of the former Habsburg Military Frontier, to which Serbs had migrated from the 16th to the 19th centuries, as detailed in the chapter *South Slavs between the Ottomans and the Habsburgs*. As its ultimate goal, and in line with the referendum-determined will of the people, the RSK declared its intention to unite with the Federal Republic of Yugoslavia.

Between 1991 and mid-1992, ignoble conflicts were recorded in the Dubrovnik theater of war. From within the UNESCO-protected cultural heritage zone, Croatian forces engaged the ships of the Yugoslav Navy, which retaliated with fire and later a siege of the city—this included shelling and ground operations involving not only the Yugoslav People's Army (JNA) but also units of Montenegro's Territorial Defense.

By the end of 1991, the Battle of Vukovar concluded—a city on the Danube in the far east of Croatia, bordering Serbia. The population of this city, located within the self-proclaimed Republic of Serbian Krajina, consisted of both Croatian and Serbian residents living together. The three-month battle between Croatian military and police forces on one side, and JNA units in cooperation with local armed Serbs on the other, resulted in several thousand deaths on both sides and grim images of a devastated city. Although the JNA captured Vukovar, it was a Pyrrhic victory.

The world was appalled by reports from old Dubrovnik and Vukovar, which Croatia extensively media exploited to its advantage. The war around Dubrovnik caused significant material damage, unacceptable shelling of the city's historical center in December 1991, and after the warring sides had signed a ceasefire plan. About 350 human lives were lost on both sides, and about 15,000 Croats fled from the war-affected area.

Due to the use of force against world cultural heritage, the JNA and Milošević, and consequently all Serbs, experienced severe condemnations from the international community and a loss of reputation and credibility. In Serbia today, few remember the fact, obscured by state propaganda, that as a reaction to the bombing of Dubrovnik—and with significant lobbying by emigrants and friends of Croatia in the USA—even 104 Nobel laureates, gathered at the initiative of biochemist and peace activist Linus Pauling, signed an Appeal for Peace in Croatia in which the "war of the Yugoslav Army against Croatia" is condemned. This appeal was published on a full page of The New York Times on January 14th, 1992. Never before or since has such a mobilization of world Nobel laureates for a political goal occurred. The next day, January 15th, 1992, at the initiative of Germany, all twelve members of the European Community and eight other countries recognized Croatia as an independent state within its Yugoslav administrative borders.

Croatia achieved its long-cherished dream. As an expression of gratitude to Germany for its tremendous support, Croatian musicians composed and performed the song "Danke Deutschland" in the main square of Zagreb.

From the temporal distance of about thirty years, it is significant to examine Germany's role in recognizing Slovenia and Croatia, and ultimately in the final disintegration of Yugoslavia. Relatively little is known about this in the global public, even though it is extremely important for forming a complete picture. Mr. Horst Grabert, advisor to Chancellor Willy Brandt for Eastern and Southern Europe and Ambassador of West Germany to Belgrade between 1979 and 1984, provided a very precise description of this:

> "The interest of Germany is to demonstrate its own increased political weight to the world and to establish new power relations in the first European crisis after German reunification."[85]

Viewed from the angle of geopolitics, however, the long-standing German interest in making a breakthrough to the warm seas of the Adriatic and thus the Mediterranean through a strong influence in Croatia is also noticeable.

In Belgrade, Milošević's television portrayed Germany as once again dismantling Yugoslavia, just like in 1941, with the assistance of "Croatian traitors."

In the aftermath of the Dubrovnik fiasco and the Pyrrhic victory in Vukovar, a global outcry arose in unison, condemning Milošević and the Yugoslav People's Army (JNA). It was around this time that an enduring stigma began to take shape within the international community, branding the Serbian people as collectively barbarous. Truth be told, there was an unusual detail amidst all this. Seen from the sidelines, the JNA's conduct seemed peculiarly inconsistent. They advanced, conquered, inflicted destruction, caused human casualties, and invited the world's condemnation, only to subsequently retreat. I distinctly recall the deep-seated frustration and discussions among ordinary people, as well as those who had served as soldiers. They spoke of their inability to understand the puzzling "advance-retreat" logic of JNA warfare. "We press forward and seize [land, cities, villages...], incurring losses," they would express, "only to suddenly receive an order from above to pull back to previous positions." The term "from above" pertained to a political decision issued from the pinnacle of the machinery that reached as high as Milošević himself. It is likely that covert agreements between Tudjman and Milošević, as well as pressures

---

[85] *Deutsche Welle*, January 28th, 1992.

from foreign powers, significantly influenced this seemingly illogical command of the army.

For the sake of objectivity, it must be said that within Serbia, numerous and vehement voices of opposition to the war resonated, particularly in Belgrade. However, these were drowned out by the regime's fevered war propaganda. Vuk Drašković, the leader of the then most prominent opposition party, urged the soldiers of the JNA to "take up their rifles and flee," and later wrote that "Vukovar was the Hiroshima of Serbian and Croatian madness." Among artists, intellectuals, and rock musicians, there were numerous instances of anti-war engagement. From the vantage point of contemporaries and witnesses to numerous events, it seemed that Western media—partly in the service of political interests, partly in an attempt to portray very complex events to their audience—were creating a simplified, black-and-white depiction of the Yugoslav conflicts. In this narrative, the Serbs were assigned the role of the aggressors, and all others that of the victims. Serbs were described using terms that carry a widely accepted negative connotation in the West, such as communism, Bolshevism, nationalism, chauvinism, Eastern (pro-Russian) and Orthodox orientation, totalitarianism, primitivism, Orientalism, non-Europeanness, and so on. The impression was that this generalization aimed to portray Serbs as culturally, morally, and civilizationally inferior and incompatible with Europe.

The imposed narrative deliberately overlooked the anti-war efforts among Serbs or the media attention given to those Serbian demands that were legitimate under international law. This was simply too intricate for both comprehension and war reporting. Most critically, portraying Serbs in a positive light did not align with the West's geopolitical interests. Regrettably, it can be observed that biased, and at times wholly inaccurate reporting to the detriment of Serbs was part of an orchestrated information war, the repercussions of which linger to this day. From such media treatment of a nation as a whole springs long-lasting harm that manifests both in the West—where the perception of Serbs remains more negative than positive— and among the Serbs themselves, who, having been rejected by the West, harbor profound mistrust. In the long term, such a policy proved advantageous to Russia, which, under the ensuing circumstances, found it considerably easier to promote Russophilia and bolster its influence.

***

The army indeed retreated towards Serbia by mid-1992, but they largely funneled weapons to the Serbs in Croatia, enabling them to defend their territories against Croatia's "forcible secession" and to fight for remaining in Yugoslavia "with all others who desire so."

By the end of 1991, the international community was actively involved in preventing further bloodshed, and with considerable success. Serving as the special envoy of the UN Secretary-General, former US Secretary of State Cyrus Vance proposed a peace plan, which led to the cessation of hostilities and creation of protected zones inhabited by Serbs, within which United Nations Protection Forces (UNPROFOR) would be dispatched. The agreement was signed by Slobodan Milošević on behalf of Serbia, General Kadijević on behalf of the JNA, and Franjo Tudjman on behalf of Croatia on November 23rd, 1991, in Geneva. A subsequent 'Implementation Agreement' between the JNA and the Croatian Ministry of Defense had to be signed, which largely brought the conflicts to a halt over the next few years. The agreement established so-called UNPA zones (United Nations Protected Area), wherein the Serbs and Croats were separated by international peacekeeping forces.

After this, there were no major conflicts between the Republic of Serbian Krajina (RSK) and Croatia until the summer of 1995. Then, this unrecognized Serbian republic rapidly vanished in the Croatian military and police operations known as Operation Flash and Operation Storm. In just a few days, and under the threat of Croatian firepower, the vast majority of Serbs—around 220,000—fled Croatia in endless columns and sought refuge in Bosnia and Serbia. The speed at which the RSK collapsed militarily, the lack of assistance from Bosnian Serbs, the absence of reaction from Serbia and Milošević, as well as the well-organized reception of the fleeing populace—are all indicators that support the hypothesis that "Milošević sold out Krajina," as was quietly and confidentially whispered from ear to ear at the time. That was my impression too as I watched what was unfolding on TV.

Only many years later, with the emergence of testimony on the secret negotiations between Milošević and Tudjman in 1991 and their continuously open phone line, did this thesis seem entirely plausible. How could such a turn of events occur in zones under the protection of UN peacekeeping forces? Why did the war in neighboring Bosnia and Herzegovina also come to an end soon after? These questions pave the way for further investigation into how an agreement between the Yugoslav warlords and the international community, led by the United States, was achieved behind the scenes to bring a general end to the hostilities.

Two diametrically opposed views and corresponding narratives have formed about the war in Croatia from 1991 to 1995, persisting to this very day. The Croats argue that Belgrade "instigated" the Serbs in Croatia to carry out a "Greater Serbian aggression." Hence, they perceive their war as defensive, referring to it as the Homeland War. And to some extent, they're right—Milošević indeed instrumentalized the Serbs in Croatia for the interests of his state project.

On the other hand, the Serbs believe that their constitutional right to national self-determination was denied in Croatia, implying that Croatia, by using force, intended to draw Serbian regions into secession, contrary to the Serbian desire to remain within Yugoslavia. Therefore, Serbs perceive the war in Croatia as an aggression on Yugoslavia and on themselves as a people. They believe that they were expelled from their homes, villages, and cities by the majority Croats and had to continue their lives in neighboring countries or in the diaspora.[86]

A column of Serbian refugees is leaving Croatia during the "Operation Storm" (August 1995).

However, there's a significant flaw in the Croatian narrative that Milošević "instigated the Serbs in Krajina" to carry out a "Greater Serbian aggression on Croatia." It lies in the refusal to confront the whole truth. The truth is that the Serbs from the region of Croatia *feared the Croats many years before Milošević's rise to power.*

Under the given circumstances, what could the Serbs in Croatia do? Whom could they turn to? Whose protection should they seek? The answer is self-evident. Their inclination toward Yugoslavia, the Yugoslav People's Army (JNA), or Serbia wasn't primarily motivated by ideology or nationalism, but by existential fear based on previous historical experience with Croats. They rallied around Milošević because he promised them safety and protection under the umbrella of a truncated Yugoslavia.

His colossal historical responsibility lies in the fact that he continually infused false hope into the Croatian Serbs and *consciously deceived them.* The fate of these people was determined as early as March 1991, when a secret agreement between Milošević and Tudjman took place. According to testimonies, Milošević then renounced the Croatian Serbs in exchange for territory under Croat control in Bosanska Posavina[87]. From the course

---

[86] There's a certain similarity with the situation faced by the Scots after Brexit. Even though they didn't want it, Scotland was drawn into secession from the EU as part of the UK. In this case, the English, as the most populous group, made the decision for everyone in the kingdom, including the much less numerous Scots. Had the Scots responded to Brexit with an internal referendum for "remaining in the EU" and then declared Scotland's secession from the UK, the similarity with the actions of the Serbs in Croatia would have been even more pronounced.

[87] A region in northern Bosnia, situated in the valley of the River Sava.

of the war, it can be inferred that the JNA knew nothing about this agreement, nor did the Serbs who saw the JNA as the guarantor of their survival. Supporting this concept of a "negotiated war" between the two presidents are not only the "forward-backward" behavior of the JNA due to illogical "top-down" withdrawal orders after advancements, but also a statement by the Croatian leader Franjo Tudjman. Addressing the gathered crowds on the central square in Zagreb at the peak of the war on March 24th, 1992, he explicitly stated:

"There wouldn't have been a war, if Croatia had not desired one. But we assessed that this was the only way to achieve independence."

This blatantly public admission by the Croatian leader that Croatia wanted war, however, went largely unnoticed by Western media. This fact also neatly fits into a broader geopolitical context and the information war against Milošević and the Yugoslav People's Army (JNA), which enjoyed Russia's favor and sought political and military alliance with it.

By shrewdly planning steps toward achieving independence, Croatia accurately assessed that by waging war against the pro-communist JNA and the absolutist Milošević—who was backed by Russia—it would gain the sympathy and support of the West. Croatia's involvement in the war aligned with the geopolitical interests of the US and the EEC (European Economic Community). If this was the case, then the "desired war," in the words of the Croatian president, should not be solely portrayed as an "attack by Yugoslavia and Milošević on Croatia," but it should also be acknowledged that it was an armed struggle by the Croats to secede from Yugoslavia. Croatia, therefore, tactfully and successfully used the war to gain the world's favor and change the stance of key powers, which initially were explicitly against secession and in favor of preserving the integrity of Yugoslavia. In the end, Croatia utilized the war to significantly reduce the percentage of its Serbian population during and after Operations Flash and Storm in 1995.

One of the key pieces of evidence in the trials before the International Court in The Hague, which demonstrated the intent of the Croatian state to expel the Serbian population, is the so-called Brioni transcripts. These are the transcripts of a conversation from a meeting that President Franjo Tudjman held with his highest-ranking generals and closest associates just before Operation Storm, on the island of Brioni on July 31st, 1995. In a crucial sentence, Tudjman says, "To inflict such blows that the Serbs will effectively vanish. That is, what we don't immediately seize must surrender within a few days."[88]

Two years after Operation Storm and the end of the war in Croatia (1997), an article was published in The New York Times titled "Croats Moving Into Homes of Serbs," which begins with the following sentence: "The Croatian government has quietly confiscated tens of thousands of homes that once belonged to ethnic Serbs who were expelled from southern Croatia and has implemented a program to settle ethnic Croats from Bosnia and Serbia into the confiscated property, say humanitarian workers and diplomats." The article goes on to say: "The campaign appears to crush any hope that more than 350,000 exiled and displaced Croatian Serbs will be able to return home, as called for in the Bosnian peace accords negotiated in November 1995 in Dayton, Ohio. And Western diplomats say it has raised questions about Croatia's aspirations to join the European Union."[89]

The figures also support the thesis that Croatia consciously and deliberately reduced the number of Serbs. Just before the war, according to the 1991 census, 581,663 Serbs, or 12.16%, lived in Croatia. Twenty years later, in 2011, the official Croatian census recorded 186,633 Serbs living in the republic, making up 4.36% of the population—a decrease of nearly 400,000 people. According to the 2021 census, the number of Serbs in Croatia was 123,892, accounting for just 3.2% of the total population.

Croatia and Serbia have both filed lawsuits against each other before the International Court of Justice (ICJ) for genocide. Although both sides had high hopes of winning their arguments, on February 3rd, 2015, the court ruled that "neither Serbia nor Croatia provided sufficient evidence that either party committed genocide", dismissing both claims.

For the sake of reconciliation in the region, it may be time to stop laying all the blame for the war in Croatia on Croatian Serbs and Milošević. While it's undeniable that they bear a significant share of responsibility, there's also responsibility on the Croatian side, as well as with foreign powers whose involvement was significant.

It seems more equitable to say that the breakup of Yugoslavia triggered a war within the administrative borders of Croatia over disputed municipalities where Serbs made up a significant ethnic majority. The Croats pursued the legitimate fulfillment of a thousand-year-old dream of reestablishing a sovereign Croatian state, invoking the constitutional right to secession of republics. Ethnic Serbs invoked the constitutional right to self-determination of peoples, expressing their wish not to live in an independ-

---

[88] The International Criminal Tribunal for the Former Yugoslavia, Case No. IT-06-90-A, September, 2011.
[89] Hedges, Chris. "Croatia Resetting Its People In Houses Seized From Serbs." *The New York Times*, May 14th, 1997.

ent Croatia, but to remain in Yugoslavia. In my view, it's undeniable that both nations had strong arguments for their positions. I regret that the actors dominating the historical stage, both domestically and internationally, lacked the visionary and statesmanlike capacity to direct political processes towards a historical Croatian-Serbian agreement on coexistence. Such an agreement would have closed many old pages and opened a new chapter in Serbian-Croatian relations.

According to the opinions of many experts and researchers, this very relationship is crucial for stability in the Western Balkans region.

The War in Bosnia and Herzegovina

Bosnia and Herzegovina was distinct from the other republics of Yugoslavia. Among its three peoples—Serbs, Croats, and Bosniaks—none held an absolute majority. Consequently, it could not be a nation-state; instead, the constitution defined the republic as an "equal community of three constituent peoples—Muslims, Serbs, and Croats." To briefly recall what was previously outlined: the Muslim population was recognized as a distinct people or ethnic group in the Socialist Federal Republic of Yugoslavia (SFRY) in the early 1970s. The name of the people was changed to "Bosniaks" by a declaration adopted by the Second Bosniak Congress in 1993.

Many individuals in the rest of Yugoslavia perceived Bosnia and Herzegovina as the place where the Yugoslav idea and nation had advanced the furthest. At its core, Bosnia and Herzegovina was a heterogeneous blend of religions, cultures, and peoples. In support of this viewpoint is the fact that more than a quarter of marriages were mixed interethnic unions. This republic also had the highest percentage of inhabitants who identified as Yugoslavs. Ultimately, the shots fired by Yugoslav nationalist Gavrilo Princip at Archduke Franz Ferdinand of Austria-Hungary in 1914 in Sarajevo set in motion a series of events that would lead to the creation of Yugoslavia just a few years later.

An examination of the ethnic map of Bosnia and Herzegovina following the last pre-war census in 1991 reveals an exceptional intermingling of the three peoples' enclaves, in a so-called "leopard skin" pattern. In Yugoslavia, there was a prevailing belief that war among the amiable, hospitable, and cheerful inhabitants of Bosnia and Herzegovina was simply inconceivable. They were like a lifeline to us ordinary folks, who in those ominous months leading up to the war sought solace in baseless optimism, earnestly believing that our country would not disintegrate and that "Yuga"[90] would endure. "Anything, anything, but there cannot be war in Bosnia; it is impossible," we reassured each other, refusing to see the blood-red clouds looming on the horizon. Notably, even the geographical center of Yugoslavia, its symbolic "heart," was situated a mere fifteen kilometers from the capital city of Sarajevo.

And then "impossible" turned into the most brutal and terrifying war on European soil since World War II, claiming over a hundred thousand lives and causing immense destruction, ethnic cleansings, concentration camps,

---

[90] Slang nickname for the name of the country Yugoslavia, commonly used in everyday speech.

massacres, systematic rapes, and a widespread civilizational decline of involved peoples and leaders.

In the complicated Bosnian Knot, everything was entangled: the aspirations of Serbia and Croatia to divide Bosnia and Herzegovina and annex territories populated by their respective people, in contrast to the Muslim-Bosniaks' desire to maintain it as a unitary state where they would be the majority. Once again, for who knows how many times, the opposing interests of the Islamic, Western-Christian, and Eastern-Orthodox civilizations collided. Before our eyes, a proxy war began between the advancing West and the faltering East for a new geopolitical redistribution, where everyone played their part: the Serbs, Croats, Bosniaks, Serbia and Croatia, Germany, France, Italy, Britain, the European Economic Community, Turkey, and of course, Russia and the United States.

The eternal subplot in the analysis that this book deals with, the cyclical centuries-old conflict between Eastern and Western civilizations, manifested itself in its most extreme form in the late 20th century in the Balkans—a relatively small area that, with its rich ethnic, religious, and cultural-historical diversity, reminds me of Lebanon. The last episode of this confrontation, manifested as a seventy-year long clash between centripetal and centrifugal forces in Yugoslavia, would reach its tragic crescendo in the Bosnian War.

***

The wave of multi-party elections in the Yugoslav republics reached Bosnia and Herzegovina (BiH) at the end of 1990. As was the case elsewhere, parties with a distinctly nationalistic agenda achieved resounding victories. Ordinary people felt that democracy might ultimately prevail. The new government was formed according to a pre-arranged national "key": the president of the Presidency of BiH became a representative of the most numerous ethnic group—the Bosniak people—with Alija Izetbegović at the helm. The position of the president of the parliament was assumed by a Serb, while a Croat took on the role of prime minister.

However, in line with a behind-the-scenes agreement already made by the leaders of Serbia and Croatia regarding the division of BiH, both the Serbian and Croatian communities set to establishing their autonomous regions where they constituted an ethnic majority. The Croatian regions aspired to join Croatia, while the Serbian regions aimed to remain in Milošević's "truncated" Yugoslavia. It was unclear what fate the Bosniaks had been allotted in this arrangement, but I distinctly recall both sides claiming them through propaganda, trying to draw them to their side. In response, the Bosniaks pursued the maximalist goal of preserving the integrity of BiH, where they were already the majority. Their higher birth rate compared to the other two ethnic groups played in their favor, as they saw their demographic potential as securing their future. Additionally, unlike the Serbs or Croats, the Bosniaks did not have neighboring countries to join. BiH was the only homeland they had.

The European Economic Community (EEC) wanted to recognize Bosnia and Herzegovina (BiH), but respecting the conclusions of the Badinter Commission, it demanded that a referendum on independence be held in this republic, as had been previously done in Slovenia and Croatia. As expected, the political representatives of the Serbs opposed this resolution, striving for the entirety of BiH to remain in Yugoslavia. Bosniaks and Croats desired the independence of the republic, so they voted for the holding of a referendum, against the will of the Serbs. This action breached a key protective mechanism whereby significant decisions had to be made by consensus among all three constituent peoples. The referendum was held in a highly tense atmosphere on February 29th and March 1st, 1992, with a complete boycott by the Serbs.

When the results were announced, a major dispute immediately ensued. The Serbian side declared the referendum unsuccessful since less than two-thirds of eligible voters participated, which was a condition for success stipulated by the constitutional provisions. Interestingly, this fact was not disputed by the Bosniak side either. According to their official data, 63.7% of the population voted. Of that number, a staggering 99.7% opted for independence. This unanimous outcome in the official results raised high suspicions among some researchers, considering the large number of citizens in BiH with a Yugoslav orientation who were expected to vote against independence and for staying of this republic within Yugoslavia.

Despite such a serious issue that arose from the disregard of the mechanism that required consensus of all three peoples and the absence of a two-thirds majority in the referendum, the representative of the Muslim, i.e., Bosniak people, and the chairman of the Presidency of Bosnia and Herzegovina, Alija Izetbegović, officially declared the independence of the Republic of Bosnia and Herzegovina on March 3rd, 1992.

Somewhat later, the Parliament of BiH, in the absence of Serbian representatives, ratified this decision. The manner in which the referendum was conducted and independence declared became a sort of Bosnian Rubicon. Armed incidents with casualties began during the voting and continued in the following days with the erection of barricades, territorial positioning, and the first significant armed conflicts. Within a month, the flames of war spread throughout the whole republic.

Driven primarily by geopolitical interests, the international community decided to swiftly recognize the controversial referendum as a valid expression of the will of the citizens of Bosnia and Herzegovina (BiH), despite the absence of participation by the Serbs—one of the three constituent peoples. The reason for this is once again evident, simple, and rooted in geopolitics. The Western 'No pasarán!' directed at Milošević should be seen as delivering the final, lethal blows to the dying communist establishment in Europe. Regrettably, the West, and subsequently the vast majority of the rest of the world, would equate the entire Serbian population in the former Yugoslavia with Milošević. The Serbs would not be given the opportunity to territorially unite into a larger state entity through the right of self-determination. Powerful nations would be unresponsive to the historical and national interests of the Serbs due to fears that their leadership could bring Russia into the Balkans and the Adriatic. From the perspective of geopolitical movements along the West-Russia axis, it can be said that falling under Milošević's leadership was the greatest historical mistake the Serbs made in the entire 20th century, as an immensely high price was paid. This came in the form of territorial fragmentation and loss, expulsion, economic and cultural regression, material destruction, and most tragically, numerous human casualties.

The European Economic Community (EEC) recognized the independence of BiH on April 6th, 1992. A day later, the United States followed suit, simultaneously recognizing Slovenia and Croatia as well. The General Assembly of the United Nations (UN) admitted all three republics into its membership by acclamation on May 22nd, 1992. The remaining Yugoslav republic, Macedonia, which had not experienced armed conflicts, was admitted into the world organization only on April 8th, 1993, due to a dispute with Greece over its name. This dispute was resolved only in 2018 when the prime ministers of the two countries agreed on the name North Macedonia. Milošević's Federal Republic of Yugoslavia, composed of Serbia and Montenegro, thus found itself isolated and condemned by nearly the entire world.

After international recognition, the interethnic war in Bosnia and Herzegovina (BiH) escalated. By then, three factions had clearly formed:

1. Bosniak, loyal to the Republic of Bosnia and Herzegovina, whose name reflects the Bosniaks' political and military goal for BiH to be a unitary state.

2. Croatian, loyal to the self-proclaimed autonomous region of the *Croatian Republic of Herceg-Bosna* and Croatia.

3. Serbian, or "Yugoslav," loyal to the self-proclaimed *Republika Srpska* and the Federal Republic of Yugoslavia, i.e., Serbia and Montenegro.

What followed was a war of all against all: Serbs killed Bosniaks and Croats, Croats killed Serbs and Bosniaks, and Bosniaks initially fought against both, and even for a time among themselves. Towards the end of the war, with the help of the United States, they reconciled with the Croats and together waged war against the Serbs.

Milošević and the Yugoslav People's Army (JNA) supported the creation of the Army of Republika Srpska (VRS) in every way. All JNA officers originating from BiH were expected to become part of the VRS, which the vast majority did. The JNA left them with complete weaponry before its withdrawal to the Federal Republic of Yugoslavia. Later during the war, aid in money and ammunition flowed despite international prohibition, resulting in Milošević's state being placed under a UN embargo and subjected to international economic sanctions.

Croatia supported the Croats in Herceg-Bosna in the same way that Milošević supported the Serbs but did not face consequences for it. Initially, Croatia also supported the Bosniak side so that they could together better resist the more powerful Serbs, but this support soon ceased and turned into a bloody Croat-Bosniak war that raged during 1993 and 1994. The world mainly remembers the destruction of the 16th-century Old Bridge in Mostar, which was on UNESCO's World Heritage list, from this episode. It was predominantly believed that Croatian forces were responsible for this vandalism, although the Croatian side denied this and claimed that the Bosniaks themselves had destroyed the bridge and blamed the Croats to gain the sympathy of the international community.

The Bosniak side had it the hardest. After 1993, they were fighting alone, both against the Serbs and the Croats, under the conditions of the UN's embargo on the delivery of arms to all warring factions. The Bosniaks received assistance primarily from Muslim countries that sought to supply them with weapons through secret channels. There are reports that Pakistan's intelligence service successfully participated in this, and with the help of Saudi Arabia, facilitated the arrival of Mujahideen who fought on the Bosniak side. There were also strong voices in the US advocating for the lifting of the embargo and providing aid to the Bosnian Muslims. Two such resolutions were passed in Congress, but President Clinton vetoed both due to opposition from partners: the United Kingdom, France, and other NATO countries, as well as Russia. However, according to a report presented later in Congress, it appears that the US gave a "green light" for the smuggling of Iranian weapons to the Bosniaks through Croatia.[91]

---

[91] US Congress House Report 105-804, *Investigation Into Iranian Arms Shipments to Bosnia,* (October 9th, 1998).

Dutch professor Cees Wiebes delved even further in his research. In his book "Intelligence and the War in Bosnia 1992–1995,"[92] he claimed that there was cooperation between the Pentagon and radical Islamist groups from the Middle East with the objective of covertly assisting the Bosnian Muslims. Interestingly, the US later found itself compelled to wage a "war on terror" against some of these groups. Over several years, Professor Wiebes had complete access to the archives of the Dutch intelligence service, from which he learned, among other things, how Iran and Turkey, with financial assistance from Saudi Arabia, violated the UN embargo by flying personnel and weaponry into Bosnia. However, in an intelligence document that emphasizes the "close connection of the US" with this air bridge, there are also mentions of mysterious black C-130 Hercules aircraft, which are used by the US military.

On the other hand, Professor Richard J. Aldrich from the University of Nottingham pointed to intelligence activity that was taking place in favor of the Serbs. In an article published in The Guardian on April 22nd, 2002, he states:

"Meanwhile, the secret services of Ukraine, Greece and Israel were busy arming the Bosnian Serbs. Mossad was especially active and concluded a deal with the Bosnian Serbs at Pale involving a substantial supply of artillery shells and mortar bombs. In return they secured safe passage for the Jewish population out of the besieged town of Sarajevo. Subsequently, the remaining population [of the city] was perplexed to find that unexploded mortar bombs landing in Sarajevo [from Serbian positions] sometimes had Hebrew markings."[93]

Throughout three and a half years, despite international community's peace efforts, an embargo—which was violated—the involvement of UN peacekeeping troops (UNPROFOR), alongside rejected peace plans and failed ceasefires, the three warring factions in Bosnia brutally cleansed territories from the other two ethnic groups that they claimed as historically or ethnically theirs. Violent relocations and persecutions were carried out, with warlords transforming the rugged and "colorful" ethnic map of Bosnia into three ethnically clean territorial entities.

For the first time since World War II, concentration camps emerged in Europe. Both the Croats and Bosniaks had them, but the Serbs had the

---

[92] Wiebes, Cees. *Intelligence and the War in Bosnia: 1992–1995.* Publisher: LIT Verlag, 2003.

[93] Aldrich, Richard J. *America used Islamists to arm the Bosnian Muslims.* The Guardian, April 22nd, 2002. Accessed June 21st, 2023.
[https://www.theguardian.com/world/2002/apr/22/warcrimes.comment].

most. Inhumane treatment of prisoners, torture, killings, starvation, and humiliation occurred on all sides. Thousands, possibly tens of thousands of women, became victims of systematic rape. According to findings by the International Criminal Tribunal for the former Yugoslavia, Bosniak women were the most numerous victims of rape.

The central part of Sarajevo, controlled by Muslim forces, was under a three-and-a-half-year siege, with artillery and sniper fire from Serb forces on surrounding hills and mountains. Thus, the entire city, with shortages of food, water, and electricity, and under the daily threat of death, became a symbol of the Bosnian tragedy, the madness, and civilian suffering. During the war, over sixty massacres occurred, the largest and most infamous being in Srebrenica in July 1995, when Serb forces, in an act of mass murder, killed thousands of Bosniak men aged fourteen and upwards.

In early 1994, the battlefield on all sides, both in Bosnia and in Croatia, had significantly stabilized. The Serbs held approximately 65% of the territory in Bosnia and Herzegovina and about one-third of the territory in Croatia under their control. Bosnian Croats controlled around 16% of Bosnia and Herzegovina's territory, while the Bosniaks held only about 20%, including the capital city, Sarajevo.

Around this time, a shift in the war initiated by a strong multilateral initiative from the US began, which eventually led to the long-awaited peace agreement.

Chronology of the Turning Point

- In February 1994, the Washington Agreement was signed, establishing peace between the Bosnian Croats and Bosniaks and agreeing on a constitutional framework for their joint entity named the Federation of Bosnia and Herzegovina. This entity is essentially a federation of cantons, which are largely ethnically "pure" regions—only two of them have a relatively evenly mixed Muslim and Croat population. On this occasion, a confederation between the Republic of Croatia and the Federation of BiH was even agreed upon, but it never came to fruition. One Croat official later remarked that this was merely a lure meant to entice the Bosnian Croats into agreeing with the deal.

- Throughout 1994, the world's major powers—the United States, the United Kingdom, France, Germany, and Russia—representing both the West and East—worked intensively on drafting a peace plan based on dividing BiH into two entities: the Serbian—Republika Srpska, which would be allocated 49% of the territory, and the Bosniak-Croat—Federation of BiH, which would be given 51%.

- Tensions and disagreements between Milošević and the leaders of the Serbs in Croatia and Bosnia were evident as early as 1993. These culminated when the Federal Republic of Yugoslavia imposed com prehensive sanctions on Republika Srpska in 1993 to temper the stubbornness and insubordination of its leadership, headed by Radovan Karadžić. The enforcement of these Serbo-Serbian sanctions was overseen by UN troops. Over time, the sanctions weakened the military capabilities of both self-proclaimed Serbian republics. The distancing from Milošević likely arose due to the realization that his regime's main priority had become maintaining power in a sanction-weary Serbia, rather than protecting the Croatian and Bosnian Serbs at all costs. On the other hand, the Serbian leadership in Republika Srpska and the Republic of Serbian Krajina demonstrated significant obstinacy and consistently rejected all peace plans proposed by the international community, which ultimately led to military action by NATO, with the approval of the UN Security Council, to weaken their military potential.

- The combined forces of Bosniaks and Croats, with logistical and other support from the United States and NATO, began to achieve military victories against the Serb forces in BiH, reducing the territory they controlled.

- On May 1st, 1995, Croatia conducted a military-police operation named "Flash" with the aim of taking over the Serbian enclave of Western Slavonia, which was a UN-protected zone, known as "Sector West". This area was part of the self-proclaimed Republic of Serbian Krajina (RSK) in Croatia. In less than two days, around 18,000 Serbs fled from the enclave to Republika Srpska in Bosnia and the Federal Republic of Yugoslavia, resulting in the almost complete removal of their ethnic presence in the area. Likely in an attempt to deter Croatia from attacking other Serbian areas, the President of the Republic of Serbian Krajina, Milan Martić, ordered indiscriminate shelling of the Croatian capital, Zagreb, and several other towns, resulting in civilian casualties. Martić was later convicted of war crimes by the International Tribunal in The Hague. No one stepped in to assist the Croatian Serbs from UN protected zone of Western Slavonia—not Milošević in Belgrade, nor the Bosnian Serbs, nor the international community. The lack of aid further suggested that there was indeed a secret agreement between Milošević and Tudjman in which the Serbs in Croatia were sacrificed for other objectives.

- Emboldened by the lack of concrete international reaction and an easy military victory against the forces of the Republic of Serbian Krajina,

Croatia conducted another operation from 4th to 7th of August, known as "Storm," against most of the territory of the Republic of Serbian Krajina. This operation targeted UN-protected zones "North" and "South". The Serbs put up little resistance against the numerically superior and better-equipped Croatian military and police forces, in what appeared to be a staged series of events. Almost the entire population of the protected zones, estimated between 200,000 and 220,000 people, fled these areas retreating toward the Federal Republic of Yugoslavia through territories controlled by Bosnian Serbs. Croatian forces committed crimes against the remaining civilians and attacked and bombed columns of refugees. The number of killed on the Serbian side was around 2,000. Following Croatia's military success, there was systematic demolition, looting, and burning of thousands of Serbian homes, with the intention of preventing the return of Serbs in the future. According to one source, as many as 20,000 homes were affected, though estimates on the total number of destroyed buildings vary widely. Relatively few Serbs returned to this area after the end of the war.

- In July 1995, members of the Army of Republika Srpska killed thousands[94] Bosniaks in the UN-protected zone of Srebrenica, leading to strong condemnation around the world and a determination to end the war and force the Serbs to negotiate.

- On August 28th, 1995, Markale marketplace in Sarajevo was bombed with five mortar shells, killing 43 civilians and wounding 75. UNPROFOR accused Serbian forces of the attack. The Serbs denied this and accused Muslim forces of staging the sacrifice of Sarajevo civilians to provoke a Western military intervention in their favor. Horrific images were broadcast worldwide. As an immediate response, two days later, NATO began a campaign of air strikes aimed at weakening the military power of Republika Srpska, called Operation Deliberate Force. Approximately 3,500 sorties were flown and 338 Serbian targets were attacked. The campaign ended with the withdrawal of Serbian artillery around Sarajevo and the lifting of the siege after three and a half years.

- At the same time, a joint Bosniak-Croatian operation called Maestral was underway in Western Bosnia, further reducing the territory under the control of the Army of Republika Srpska. This led to a new wave of refugees which, according to Serbian sources, numbered around

---

[94] Estimates of the number of Bosniaks killed by Serbian forces in Srebrenica vary significantly depending on the source. The most commonly mentioned figure is around 8,200 victims, predominantly men aged 14 and above.

125,000 people. The Serbs were suffering defeat after defeat and there was a danger of Republika Srpska disappearing and the possible involvement of the Federal Republic of Yugoslavia in the war. However, somewhat unexpectedly, high politics came into play. Western powers halted the Croat-Bosniak offensive by issuing an ultimatum demanding that all actions against the Serbs cease. This indicated the existence of an agreement among the great powers regarding the cessation of the war in BiH and Croatia and the division of territories, about which very little is still known.

- After intensive shuttle diplomacy throughout September and October 1995, key negotiations began that would lead to the signing of the "General Framework Agreement for Peace in Bosnia and Herzegovina," better known as the Dayton Peace Agreement. From the 1st to 21st of November, at the Wright-Patterson Air Force Base in Dayton, Ohio, there were tough, often very dramatic negotiations among the three warring parties. The heads of the delegations were Alija Izetbegović, representing the Bosniaks, Croatian President Franjo Tudjman representing the Bosnian Croats, and the President of the Federal Republic of Yugoslavia Slobodan Milošević representing the Bosnian Serbs. The conference was chaired by the United States Secretary of State Warren Christopher, and the chief negotiator was Richard Holbrooke, assisted by EU representative Carl Bildt and Russia's Igor Ivanov. In the Dayton Agreement, all three sides agreed to the formation of a sovereign state of Bosnia and Herzegovina consisting of two entities: Republika Srpska (49% of the territory) and the Federation of BiH (51% of the territory). Croatia and the Federal Republic of Yugoslavia committed themselves to be guarantors of the territorial integrity of Bosnia and Herzegovina, effectively renouncing territorial aspirations towards BiH, i.e. the creation of a "Greater Croatia" and "Greater Serbia." The formal signing of the full agreed-upon agreement took place in Paris on December 14th, 1995, in the presence of US President Bill Clinton, Russian Prime Minister Viktor Chernomyrdin, EU representative Felipe González, UK Prime Minister John Major, German Chancellor Helmut Kohl, and the host, French President Jacques Chirac.

Official signing of the peace agreement that ended
the war in Bosnia and Herzegovina. Paris, December 14th, 1995

Territorial organization of Bosnia and Herzegovina
established by the Dayton Agreement in 1995.

Casualties

The war in Bosnia and Herzegovina ultimately claimed fewer lives than had been feared for years. Immediately after the end of the armed conflict, speculation in both domestic and global public discourse suggested figures ranging from approximately 250,000 to 300,000 dead and missing. As expected, the conflicting parties tended to inflate the casualty figures. As years passed, these numbers in official statements gradually decreased.

The first comprehensive research was published in 2007 by the Sarajevo Center for Research and Documentation under the title "The Bosnian Book of the Dead." This document received its second and final revision in 2012. It specified that the total number of dead and missing citizens of Bosnia and Herzegovina was 101,040. Of this total, 62,013 were Bosniaks (61.4%), 24,953 were Serbs (24.7%), and 8,403 were Croats (8.3%). Additionally, there were approximately 5,100 individuals listed as dead or missing, for whom no ethnic affiliation was determined.

The prosecution of The Hague Tribunal conducted its own investigation and, in 2010, announced relatively similar results. According to them, around 104,000 people had perished. This report indicated a slightly higher number of Bosniak casualties (68,101) and a slightly lower number of Serb casualties (22,779). However, in 2017, the War Research Center of the Republic of Srpska announced that they had compiled a list of names of deceased Serbs, totaling 29,070 individuals. Therefore, considering all cited sources, it appears that the total number of casualties in the Bosnian war did not exceed 110,000.

Lawsuits and Trials

Bosnia and Herzegovina filed a lawsuit against the Federal Republic of Yugoslavia, and Serbia as its legal successor, before the International Court of Justice for genocide across its entire territory. In a judgment issued in 2007, the court concluded that Serbia had not committed nor participated in genocide, and thus did not bear direct responsibility for the crimes committed by the Army of the Republika Srpska. The court's opinion was that only in the case of the Srebrenica massacre were there elements of genocide, but not in other areas of Bosnia and Herzegovina. On the other hand, the court did find Serbia guilty of violating the Convention on Genocide because it "did not do all within its power to prevent genocide" and did not punish or extradite the perpetrators to the International Court.

However, by the end of 2011, Serbia fulfilled this obligation by locating, arresting, and extraditing all remaining suspects to The Hague Tribunal, including the wartime commander of the Republika Srpska Army, General Ratko Mladić, as well as the political leader of the Bosnian Serbs, Radovan Karadžić.

The International Criminal Tribunal for the former Yugoslavia convicted dozens of individuals for war crimes, crimes against humanity, breaches of the laws and customs of war, and genocide, due to the war in Bosnia and Herzegovina. The majority of those convicted were Serbs, followed by Croats, and several Bosniaks were also prosecuted. The court either implicitly or explicitly found Serbia and Croatia to be involved in the war. Even though the war contains many elements that define it as a civil war, there are reasons to characterize it as an international conflict as well. The responsibility for this lies with Slobodan Milošević and Franjo Tudjman, due to their agreements on the division of Bosnia and Herzegovina and their later active support of the Serbian and Croatian factions in the conflict, as well as influencing their political decisions and military actions. However, the influence of foreign states on the conflicts in the former Yugoslavia, their involvement, and potential responsibility, largely remained outside the focus of this court.

Radovan Karadžić

Wartime president of the Republika Srpska and the supreme commander of the Army of the Republika Srpska. In 2019, the International Criminal Tribunal for the Former Yugoslavia sentenced him to life imprisonment for genocide, crimes against humanity, and violations of the laws and customs of war.

Jadranko Prlić

The Prime Minister of the Croatian Republic of Herzeg-Bosnia and the military commander of the Croatian Defense Council (HVO). In 2017, the International Criminal Tribunal for the Former Yugoslavia sentenced him to twenty-five years in prison for crimes against the Bosniak population.

Differing Perspectives on the Nature
of the War Crime in Srebrenica

The United Nations General Assembly adopted the *Convention on the Prevention and Punishment of the Crime of Genocide* on December 9th, 1948, and Yugoslavia was among the signatory states. This international treaty defines genocide as acts committed "with intent to destroy, in whole or in part, a national, ethnical, racial or religious group, as such." It further specifies that these acts can include "killing members of the group, causing serious bodily or mental harm to members of the group, deliberately inflicting on the group conditions of life calculated to bring about its physical destruction in whole or in part, imposing measures intended to prevent births within the group," and "forcibly transferring children of the group to another group."

Drawing on the above definitions, the International Criminal Tribunal for the Former Yugoslavia and the International Court of Justice have characterized the Srebrenica massacre as an act of genocide in which around 8,300 people were killed. However, there are several disputes regarding these findings. The disputes relate both to the total number of victims and the characterization of this undeniable war crime as genocide. A commonly highlighted counterargument is the fact that the Serbian forces separated women, children, and the elderly and evacuated them from the besieged enclave before they began killing thousands of captive men—including minors, boys as young as thirteen or fourteen years old.

Efraim Zuroff—famed Israeli Nazi hunter and Director of the Simon Wiesenthal Center—believes that the events in Srebrenica cannot be described as genocide and that comparisons to the Holocaust are "absurd" and "dangerous." He was quoted as saying, "I would have wished for the Nazis to have spared Jewish women and children ahead of their bloody onslaught, rather than killing them, but as we know, that did not happen. Neither Rwanda nor the Holocaust are the same, even though the crimes that occurred in Rwanda are much more akin to the Holocaust than what happened in Srebrenica. But, again, it's not the same. Primarily, neither Rwanda nor Srebrenica were industrial-scale mass killings as was perpetrated in the Holocaust."[95]

A similar viewpoint was expressed by Yehuda Bauer, an Israeli Holocaust expert, who thinks what happened in Srebrenica was a "mass mur-

---

[95] Zuroff, Efraim. "Srebrenica se nikako ne može porediti sa holokaustom." (in Serbian). Politika. Accessed July 2nd, 2023. *https://www.politika.rs/sr/clanak/330671/Efraim-Zurof-Srebrenica-se-nikako-ne-moze-porediti-sa-holokaustom*

der," but not genocide. He found no evidence that Serbian forces intended to exterminate Bosniaks either entirely or partially.

Canadian General Lewis Wharton MacKenzie, who commanded the international UNPROFOR forces during the war, believes the official number of murdered men has been quadrupled, and someone intending to commit genocide would start by killing women, which was not the case here. The number of victims is also disputed by the Srebrenica Research Group, led by American Professor Edward S. Herman. They argue that the events in Srebrenica were labeled as genocide for propaganda-political reasons.

Similar doubts were raised by Carlos Branco, a UN military observer during the war and a Portuguese general, in his books and memoirs. Canadian professor and genocide expert William Schabas considers the events in Srebrenica and elsewhere in Bosnia to be ethnic cleansing, but not genocide.[96]

Such opinions fuel a culture of doubt regarding the prevailing version of the Srebrenica tragedy within Serbian society. This culture largely revolves around the narrative that behind the "genocide" definition, established by court rulings of two international tribunals, lies a continuation of geopolitical pressure on Serbs with the aim of further weakening and fragmenting the territories they inhabit. It is speculated that certain circles wish to abolish Republika Srpska by declaring it an "entity born out of genocide," whereas the real reason lies in the fact that the Serbian entity opposes Bosnia and Herzegovina's entry into NATO, contrary to the will of the Bosniak-Croat entity.

On the other hand, among Serbs, there is a painful memory of the genocide committed against them by the Ustaša and Nazis during World War II. Every attempt by the West to impose the label of a "genocidal people" on them is perceived as cynicism and a grave insult. However, it should also be mentioned that during Milošević's regime, which had total control over the media, the informing of Serbs about the Bosnian war was highly propagandistic and manipulative. It was biased, unobjective, filtered, and often false. Similar tendencies continued afterward.

To this day, the average Serb is only partially aware of the dark chapters of Serbian history written in their name during the 1990s. The wider audience has still not been officially provided with truthful and unembellished information on the war events. The discomfort of confronting crimes is often cushioned by the counter-argument, "but they also committed crimes against us." According to public opinion surveys conducted twenty-five years after the Srebrenica tragedy, about two-thirds of people in Serbia

---

[96] William Schabas, *Genocide in International Law: The Crime of Crimes*. Cambridge University Press, 2000, pp. 175–201.

believe that a severe crime occurred in Srebrenica, but not genocide, which causes strong disapproval and condemnation from the Bosniak community throughout the region.

However, this tragedy should also be viewed from a less noticeable perspective. The strengthening of internal bonds and a sense of identity within a nation is sometimes crucially contributed to by experiences of collective suffering. Just as Auschwitz is a symbol for the Jews, Jasenovac holds a similar significance for the Serbs. For the Bosniaks, Srebrenica has become such a symbol. They will continue to nurture and preserve its memory for generations to come. It has become a unifying symbol and a source of inner strength.

A "NO" to a Muslim State in Europe?

Was there a reluctance in Europe to allow the creation of a unitary Bosnia and Herzegovina where Muslims would be the majority and have the final say? There are certain indications pointing in that direction.

Taylor Branch, a close friend of President Bill Clinton, a journalist, and a Pulitzer Prize winner, authored an intriguing book[97] where he describes his confidential conversations with the president. In one conversation, Clinton talked about the war in Bosnia and Herzegovina and the opposition of key European allies to lifting the arms embargo, which the Bosniak side was requesting in order to arm itself and somewhat equally oppose the more powerful Serb and Croat forces. To the president's surprise, the allies told him that an independent Bosnia and Herzegovina would be "unnatural" as the only Muslim state in Europe. French President Mitterrand used the term "does not belong," while British officials spoke of a "painful but realistic restoration of Christian Europe."

That there was concern in key European countries about arming Bosnian Muslims is also suggested by a study conducted by the International Centre for the Study of Radicalization and Political Violence (ICSR). The study presents the thesis that radical Islam in Britain grew due to fear caused by deliberate procrastination, even a lack of desire by the country to oppose the pogrom of moderate Bosnian Muslims. According to the author[98], British Islamists pointed out the fact that the targets of ethnic cleansing in Bosnia were "well-integrated European Muslims, blond-haired and blue-eyed," which convinced them that Muslims were not safe in Europe,

---

[97] Branch, Taylor. *The Clinton Tapes: Wrestling History with the President*. Simon & Schuster, 2009.
[98] Bronitsky, Jonathan. *British foreign policy and Bosnia: The rise of Islamism in Britain, 1992–1995.* ICSR, 2010.

that they had to rely only on themselves, and that "only a caliphate could guarantee them security." He cites the conclusion of Jane Sharp from King's College London that "policy-makers in Whitehall wanted Serbia and its proxies in Bosnia to prevail." In support of this thesis, figures of casualties that emerged after the war are telling: significantly more Bosniak Muslims were killed compared to Bosnian Serbs and Croats.

Traumas from the distant past, the collective unconscious, and the war in Bosnia and Herzegovina

In the early nineties of the last century, Belgrade was flooded with different people, strangers to me. They gave the impression of dangerous individuals, who could easily exhibit brutality and aggression. Being near them was uncomfortable because it seemed that incidents could easily occur. A huge number of people were going out on the streets, to bars, and cafes armed, and shootouts were part of our daily lives for several years. At first, I thought they were Serb refugees from war-torn areas. Some indeed were. But it took me time to realize that most of them were actually my fellow citizens, untouched by the war, from whose consciousness something foreign, dark, and extremely dangerous was surfacing. The ghosts of the past were suddenly breaking into the present from the collective national subconscious, through transformed individuals.

This caught my attention. People were changing overnight. A neighbor, who was peaceful and dear until yesterday, would suddenly, with troubled emotions and narrowed consciousness, express hatred towards members of other Yugoslav nations or religions. As a rule, he would communicate his beliefs, fear, anger, and condemnations, mentioning long-past events in which he did not participate because they happened before his birth. Some dark force was surfacing into reality, taking over many people, like a matrix program in the eponymous movie.

War rhetoric rolled over the population like heavy waves. Deliberate and calculated, primitive and populist propaganda assailed us from all media. Nationalism and chauvinism manifested themselves either openly or poorly camouflaged as an aggressive "patriotism" that saw enemies in everyone else. Pejorative terms began to be widely used for our former Yugoslav compatriots. All Croats became "Ustaša." In neighboring Croatia, it was the same—propaganda and populism, with the external enemy being labeled as the "Serbian aggressor." The term "Chetniks" or "Yugo-Chetniks" was used for people from Serbia. Serbs and Croats, when they wanted to insult each other, would immediately start calling each other

"Ustaša" and "Chetniks." This was seen countless times, and in my opinion, it was disheartening and pathetic.

However, the term that Serbs began to use for Bosniaks, formerly referred to as Muslims, opened my eyes. I had a sudden insight that one awakened spirit from the bottle was very, very old. That term was: *Turks*.

This word concealed everything. In the moment of insight, I was flooded with a memory of the "collective unconscious", a concept introduced by Swiss psychiatrist and psychoanalyst Carl Gustav Jung (1875–1961), and things suddenly made sense. The traumas of a nation can't disappear, but they can be suppressed. Once asleep, they can lie dormant for decades, sometimes centuries. They become the collective painful content of the subconscious of that nation, which gets restimulated under certain circumstances. Then they burst to the surface with all the force of suppressed emotions, manifesting themselves through individuals who relive this trauma.

The attempt of Muslims, with the help of Croats, to create a unitary Bosnia by outvoting the Serbs in the independence referendum restimulated Serbian traumas from the Ottoman and Ustaša periods, during which they experienced catastrophic sufferings.

We all know that Bosnian Muslims are not Turks. Hidden within this derogatory term lies contempt and hatred, whose historical reasons are shrouded in thick layers of forgetfulness, but the emotions remained. Before my eyes, the mechanism that Jung described became clear as day: the centuries-old suppressed collective traumas of the Serbs were penetrating the individual subconscious. Which traumas am I referring to? A sequence of key events is described in detail in the chapters titled "The Tragic Fate of the Serb Bogomils" and "The Ethnogenesis of the Bosniaks," so I will only provide a brief recap here.

The roots of Serbian contempt and hatred toward today's Bosniaks began with religious conflicts involving the Serb Bogomils that lasted from the 12th to the 14th century, initially within the Serbian state, and later in the Bosnian state. From the 15th century, this hatred acquired a new layer. With the arrival of the Ottoman Empire in Bosnia, the persecuted "heretics" and "apostates" known as Bogomils—in the eyes of the Serbs—became traitors who "turned Turk," that is, converted to Islam and formed the modern Bosniak nation.

Within the word "Turks" echoed centuries of Serbian pain and despair accumulated during the harsh Ottoman occupation. A desire for revenge flared: for all the victims, persecutions, oppressions, and rapes; for the demolition of churches and monasteries; for disenfranchisement, hopelessness, and the loss of statehood. The true culprits of this centuries-long Serbian suffering—the Ottoman Turks—though defeated on the battlefield in the 19th and 20th centuries, were far away and largely escaped Serbian retribution. Thus, it happened that all the re-stimulated misery and anger were directed towards the "Turks"—the Bosniaks. In 1992, they were perceived as a threat to forcibly place the Serbs under the green flag of Islam again. To be fair, such a perception of the Bosniak goal among the Serbs persists to this day.

From the perspective presented, one can conclude that the most intense and tragic conflict in the Bosnian War, between the Serbs and Bosniaks, was the latest episode in a cyclical spiral of violence that began eight centuries ago with a brutal internal Serbian, Orthodox-Bogomil religious clash. Taking the current situation in Bosnia and Herzegovina into account, sadly, there is no reason for optimism that the episode of 1992–1995 will be the last. I wish I were wrong in this assessment.

Ivo Andrić, the only Yugoslav Nobel laureate, originally from Bosnia, wrote the following words that support the conclusion about the subconscious dimension of the last war there:

"Bosnia is a land of hatred and fear (…) For, the fatal characteristic of this hatred is that the Bosnian man is not aware of the hatred that lives within him, he shies away from analyzing it, and hates anyone who tries to do so. Yet, the fact remains: in Bosnia and Herzegovina there are more people who are ready, in bouts of unconscious hatred, on various occasions and under various pretexts, to kill or be killed, than in other Slavic and non-Slavic countries that are much larger in population and area.

Yugoslav Nobel laureate Ivo Andrić (1892-1975)

(…)

And just as the soil in which we live transforms—under the influence of atmospheric moisture and heat—into our bodies and gives them color and appearance, and determines the character and direction of our way of life and our actions, so too does the immense, subterranean, and invisible hatred upon which the Bosnian man lives enter unnoticed and indirectly into all his, even the best, actions.

(…)

Perhaps in Bosnia, one should admonish people to guard themselves at every step, in every thought and in every, even the most exalted, feeling against hatred—innate, unconscious, endemic hatred. For this backward and impoverished land, where two different faiths live closely together, would need four times more love, mutual understanding, and tolerance than other countries. But in Bosnia, on the contrary, misunderstanding, which occasionally turns into open hatred, is almost a general characteristic of the inhabitants. The chasms between the various faiths are so deep that only hatred manages sometimes to cross them."[99]

General Ratko Mladić, the Chief of the General Staff of the Army of Republika Srpska, just before the horrific war crime that forces under his command committed in the Bosniak enclave of Srebrenica, uttered a few sentences to the camera that most vividly illustrate his detachment from reality. Mladić's consciousness was anchored in a distant past that shaped his actions in the present. In Srebrenica, in July 1995, there was an explosive surfacing of centuries-long suppressed Serbian trauma from the Ottoman era. This pent-up energy would manifest itself through the General, who had the levers of power in his hands. I quote his words:

"Here we are, on July 11th, 1995, in Serbian Srebrenica. On the eve of yet another great Serbian holiday, we give this town to the Serbian people as a gift. After the Uprising against the Dahije[100], finally, the moment has come to, *take revenge on the Turks* in this region."[101]

Viewed from another angle, let's ask ourselves where the Bosniaks' desire to create a unitary pro-Islamic and pro-Turkish Bosnia in modern times could stem from? The answer once again emerges from historical memory. Only the Ottoman Empire allowed Slavic converts to Islam to live safely and peacefully, protecting them from attacks by their Orthodox and Catholic brethren.

In conclusion, without taking into account the influence of traumas stored in the collective unconscious of ethnic groups, it is not possible to fully understand the war in Bosnia and Herzegovina from 1992–1995, nor the current relations in the republic. On the other hand, understanding the magnitude, depth, and age of the Bosnian stage can help key factors in international politics to, in cooperation with the local peoples, create a more effective and long-term peace policy toward the region.

---

[99] Andrić, Ivo. "Pismo iz 1920. godine." [A Letter From 1920]. In *Nove pripovetke*, published by Kultura, Beograd, 1946.

[100] The initial phase of the First Serbian Uprising (1804) began with the "Uprising against the Dahije." Dahijas were renegade Janissary officers who in 1801 seized power in the territories that are now central Serbia, imposed brutal treatment on Serbs, and rebelled against the Ottoman sultan.

[101] The footage is available on YouTube: *https://www.youtube.com/watch?v=2uCS19lznuw*, accessed on 04.07.2023. (quote at 12:00/14:39)

What Was Life Like in Slobodan Milošević's "Shrunken" Yugoslavia?

Today, there is relatively little awareness globally about how severely Milošević's regime harmed the population of Serbia. Moreover, it is not widely known that for almost an entire decade, citizens persistently resisted Milošević until a mass revolution led to his removal from power on October 5th, 2000.

I had my first encounter with tear gas on March 9th, 1991, when tens of thousands of people took to the streets to protest against the regime and state-controlled media. In response, Milošević employed a brutal police intervention, using tear gas, water cannons, and deploying tanks on the streets of Belgrade. From that day until Milošević's final departure in 2000, I was a part of numerous anti-war and anti-regime protests that sometimes lasted for days, sometimes weeks, and even months.

Manipulation by Continuity

I would like to reiterate my stance here that the factual death of Yugoslavia occurred on June 25th, 1991. On that day, two out of the three peoples that had formed it in 1918—the Slovenes and Croats—declared the independence of their federal units. Their example was quickly followed by all the others. Milošević in Serbia, and his loyal leadership in Montenegro, found themselves alone.

Then came this play with continuity. The persistent labeling of the two remaining republics as "Yugoslavia," even though the state had completely lost its pan-Yugoslav character and was displaying an increasingly pronounced Serbian nationalism. "Nothing has changed," they were telling us. "We will preserve the country for which our fathers and grandfathers gave their lives in two world wars."

But what was the purpose behind promoting this untruthful narrative? It turns out that it was part of a well-crafted strategy by the former communist establishment to retain power. By pretending we were still in Yugoslavia, the regime created political and overall confusion among the population. Through a deliberate refusal to accept the disintegration of the common state and by appropriating everything associated with it, even though it was already dead, Milošević adeptly managed to gather under his wing — under the pretext of state endangerment — a broad cross-section of the Serbian populace. The proclaimed narrative was readily embraced by Serbs from Croatia and Bosnia and Herzegovina, concerned about their survival if they were to be cut off from Serbia. Domestically, Milošević was accepted by people spanning from left to right ideological beliefs; he was the hope and the promised leader who understood the emotions and aspirations of the people.

The pro-communist establishment's effort to achieve pan-Serbian homogenization was astutely observed by author Olivera Milosavljević in 2002: "...when his star shone brightly, everyone was 'for' Milošević: communists because of his communism, nationalists because of nationalism, Titoists because of Titoism, anti-Titoists because of anti-Titoism, democrats because of democratism, atheists because of atheism, monarchists and religious individuals because of the return to tradition..."[102]

Volunteers and Mobilization

The onset of the implementation of Slobodan Milošević's plan, in conjunction with military and intelligence structures, to integrate territories populated by Serbs in other republics into the Federal Republic of Yugoslavia—i.e., Serbia and Montenegro—began to cast its sinister influence on our lives in 1991. I remember the relentless war-mongering rhetoric of state-controlled media. I remember a political landscape with a plethora of parties, ranging from the extreme left to the extreme right, which had been created by the secret service in 1990 as a semblance of democracy and a way to gain control over the vast majority of the electorate. The leaders of these puppet political parties primarily advocated for the "preservation of Yugoslavia", albeit through different means. Those on the left sought to maintain a communist status quo and use the Yugoslav People's Army (JNA) as the "legitimate army of Yugoslavia" to "defend and protect the people who wished to remain in Yugoslavia" from the "violent secession of separatist republics." Meanwhile, the right-wingers harbored the idea of "defending the Serbian people from a new genocide" by assembling volunteers who would be transported to Serbian communities outside Serbia.

Even back then, the term "national communism" entered my consciousness for the first time, and to this day I haven't found a better word to describe my perception of Milošević's political course.

I remember the massive manipulation of the guilt complex. Propaganda imposed the stigma of being a traitor on anyone who refused to fall in line under Milošević's banner. This was mainly among the thoughtful individu-

---

[102] Milosavljević, Olivera. "Izbor ili nametanje tradicije." *Republika*, no. 281 (March 2002): 17-30.

394

als from urban areas, those slightly better educated and of middle economic status. They were the first to be targeted by the regime for being ineligible.

Among the volunteers who flocked to Belgrade from all over Serbia, there were many who believed that their action was highly patriotic and in the interest of protecting the people. However, there were also those whose wild and evil nature was drawn out by the scent of war. Both were sent by the authorities for swift military training, provided with weapons and gear, and dispatched to the front lines as paramilitary units. The number of volunteers and recruits who had to report for mandatory military service in the JNA during those months probably wasn't sufficient, so mobilization of the reserve forces was initiated. It mainly took place at night. The military police would knock on your door and by the next morning, you could already be somewhere on the battlefield.

There were also raids taking place in cafes, bars, and nightclubs, where some people were taken to war after being identified. Due to these occurrences, many people hid at friends' or relatives' homes, briefly and discretely visiting their own apartments during the day. I remember employing the strategy of simply not opening the door to anyone and being vigilant not to make any noise. Another widespread phenomenon was fleeing the country. According to data published by the immigration authorities of Western countries, as well as by the Yugoslav government, between 90,000 and 150,000 people fled to avoid mobilization by 1993. According to NIN, a well-known Belgrade weekly, surveys showed that more than half of the military conscripts between the ages of 18 and 36, despite intense state propaganda, were opposed to the war policies. I also recall the persistent gatherings of parents of mobilized young men in front of the JNA General Staff building, demanding that their sons not be sent anywhere outside of Serbia. In the heated parliamentary debates of that time, there were reports of massive problems and "desertion," and that in Belgrade, military authorities were only able to mobilize about 15% of military conscripts.

However, all the while, the authorities were assuring both the domestic public and the international community that "FR Yugoslavia is not at war." Indeed, war was never formally declared on Croatia or Bosnia and Herzegovina, and the mobilization of volunteers and movements of the JNA troops were justified as defending the endangered Serbian population in these republics, which considered itself a part of Yugoslavia. There was a degree of truth to this. However, this truth was exploited to achieve war and political goals—it was magnified and distorted for the purpose of implementing the plan of "all Serbs in one state."

Paradoxically, the very clique led by Milošević, through its behavior, destroyed every chance for the realization of such a plan. Despite lacking the support of the EU and NATO due to its previously described pro-Russian geopolitical and ideological orientation, it still had the potential to achieve much more. Instead of playing by international rules and conventions, the communist militant establishment allowed itself to slide into arrogance, numerous violations of the laws and customs of war, and war crimes. The Serbian people, as a nation and collective, would pay the highest price. They would remain territorially fragmented and with a very poor image in the world—an image associated with Milošević, Karadžić, and Mladić.

Media in the Service of State Propaganda

One of the main pillars of Milošević's regime was state-controlled media. Strict control was exercised over them, using methods directly inherited from the communist era. In an attempt to maintain a semblance of democracy in the eyes of the world, a small number of independent electronic media outlets were tolerated, but their visibility was strictly limited. When necessary, TV and radio stations, as well as print media, were forcibly shut down; equipment was confiscated, transmitters dismantled, and journalists arrested or even assassinated.

French professor Renaud de La Brosse, at the request of the Prosecution of the International Criminal Tribunal for the former Yugoslavia, compiled a report on the instrumentalization of media in Milošević's Serbia. Among other things, the document contains the following description, which, based on personal memory, I can confirm is entirely accurate:

"In Serbia, Slobodan Milošević consciously used and controlled the media to impose the leitmotif of nationalist propaganda in order to justify, in the eyes of the citizens, the creation of a state within whose borders all Serbs would live, as well as to strengthen his own power. For the propaganda disseminated through print and audiovisual media to achieve full efficacy, Milošević personally ensured control over public information outlets, limited the freedom of speech of existing independent media—by crippling them in every way possible from informing citizens—and vigilantly ensured that journalists adhered to the official line and embraced the ideas and programs of the government: in short, that they respected the imposed discipline."

From the books and diaries of the previously quoted Borisav Jović, much was revealed about what was really happening behind the scenes during those tumultuous years. Jović writes about Milošević's approach to the media:

"For years, he devoted the most attention to means of information, especially television. He personally selected the chief editors of newspapers and news programs, and especially the directors of radio and television stations. In this field, perhaps more than anywhere else, he maintained direct control over all editors who "fed" the public with news, comments, and information. He was deeply convinced that citizens formed their views on the political situation based on what was served to them, not according to their actual material and political positions. What was not published did not happen — that was Milošević's motto."

It is certain that the degree and malice of the propaganda that the Serbs were exposed to over a long period are comparable to those implemented in some of the most totalitarian regimes of the 20th century. I still remember the state television's reporting of the massacre of "41 Serbian babies slaughtered by Croatian Ustašas in Vukovar." This news was first reported, then retracted by Reuters, as well as by a Serbian doctor from the field. However, this didn't prevent the regime from brutally brainwashing us with this news for days afterwards. The induced anti-Croatian hysteria was evident. Perhaps a worse example is when a bishop of the Serbian Orthodox Church appeared on television holding a small, darkened human skull in his hand. He claimed it belonged to a Serbian child whom the Croats had snatched from its mother's arms, slaughtered in front of her, and then burned and buried the body. The story was never confirmed, but there is a photograph of that same church dignitary from the Croatian war zone in 1991 holding a machine gun and standing next to a tank with several Serbian volunteers posing on it.

There are many such examples throughout the entire period of Milošević's rule from 1987 to 2000. The same pattern of multilateral hypnotizing of the population unfolded during the wars in Croatia, Bosnia, and Kosovo. It is therefore unsurprising that the following example, found in the report of the French professor cited earlier, was documented: a young Serbian woman in uniform, a mother of two children, when asked by Radio Television of Serbia about the reasons that led her to volunteer and go fight in Vukovar, explained, "Well, when I watch television, I see what is happening," and added, "it is worth sacrificing one's life for our Serbia...."

Plundering the People

War is expensive, but for some, it can be very profitable. A lot of money is needed to wage war. It becomes especially difficult if the entire world imposes economic sanctions and an embargo to hinder you. Milošević's private state found itself in a serious problem. To access funds, the authorities in Belgrade turned to their own people. First, a "Loan for the Economic Revival of Serbia" was announced, and the population was called upon to voluntarily invest money in the country's recovery. Through the media, it was portrayed as an act of pure patriotism, and company managements were instructed, through party channels, to pressure employees into collective participation. As a result, like everyone else in the company I was employed by, I was forced to give money to Milošević against my will. We received nicely printed bonds with the promise that the state would repay us one day—a promise that, of course, was never fulfilled.

However, it turned out that the money collected was not enough for the authorities. So, it happened that one morning, the media outlets reported that all foreign currency savings in banks were "frozen" until further notice by a government decision. No withdrawals were allowed. That was it. Our savings simply vanished. I remember the despair of the people who lost access to the funds they had been saving their entire lives for old age. Was that the end of it? No, they didn't stop there.

The government knew that Yugoslavs did not have much trust in banks. In Yugoslavia, high inflation persisted due to the economic and financial crisis that had begun in the latter half of the 1970s. The government devalued the domestic currency relatively frequently. For this reason, most of the population converted their Yugoslav dinars into stable Western currencies and kept the money in their homes. The criminal regime estimated that there were several billion dollars that needed to be somehow snatched from the people. This leads us to the dark episode of creating the quasi-state banks Jugoskandik and Dafiment, which, from mid to late 1992, promised gullible depositors huge monthly interest rates (up to 160%) and rapid enrichment. The owners of these two "banks" were constantly featured on screens and front pages of state media, talking about their "business successes," "investments," and "foreign partners." There was even a claim that the deposits were insured by the British Lloyd's, which was a sheer lie. Ordinary people were shown who had become rich in a month by investing in these "banks."

In reality, this was a pyramid scheme scam that was devised and organized from the top of the state. According to records found years later in the basement of the National Bank of Serbia, this was a secret operation led by Milošević himself, along with a few close associates, including the governor of the National Bank. The liquidity of these pseudo-banks was maintained with printed dinars pumped into them by the National Bank in order to snatch hard currency from the people. After six months of media-orchestrated euphoria about the profitability of investing money in this scam, when it was estimated that there was not much more foreign curren-cy remaining among the people, both "banks" went bankrupt and their owners were arrested to quell the rage of the plundered masses.

The civilized world has no memory of such a shameless state-led plun-der of its own citizens. However, even this episode was not the end of Mi-lošević's "creativity" in this regard. He was a banker by profession, and the worst trial was yet before us. Although high inflation, exceeding 100% an-nually, had already been present since 1990, what happened in the second half of 1993 was unprecedented.

In an attempt to extract even the little remaining foreign currency from the people, the government launched a deliberate and controlled hyperin-flation by printing huge quantities of worthless money. In the peak of this madness, a phase which most people in the world cannot even fathom, the exchange rate of the dinar against the German mark dropped several times a day. Prices doubled every sixteen hours. At the height of hyperinflation, the government issued a 500,000,000,000 (five hundred billion) dinar banknote, which made it into the Guinness Book of Records. In-flation that year reached about 20,000%. I remember in October 1993, receiving my salary for the previous month packed in two plastic bags full of bundles of money. My intention was to spend the entire amount on food as soon as I left work. However, a few hours later, the value of my earnings had fallen by about 50%. I was able to buy one loaf of bread and ten eggs with a month's salary. The real value of those two bags full of banknotes was about two German marks. What was the solution? How to survive? The state forced you to dip into the little remaining hard currency you had saved at home. Of course, until supplies last.

The Yugoslav five hundred billion dinar banknote was issued at the end of 1993.

I can never forget the moment when I sat and looked at my last one hundred German mark banknote. I was considering whether to spend it on food or education. I chose the latter, and it turned out to be a decision that

399

would most positively change my life in the long run. This education set in motion events that led, among other things, to the writing of this book.

How did Milošević's criminalized state organize the executioners in this phase of plunder? Near markets and shops, individuals of dubious appearance stood, who were "exchanging currency." Their hands and pockets were full of bundles of hyperinflationary banknotes. At these "exchangers," you would trade a minimal amount of German marks for dinars, and with that money, you would rush to the market to spend it as quickly as possible on bare necessities. Because if you waited, the value of the dinar would melt away within hours. How did this network of street currency exchangers come into existence? Who was supplying them with inflationary banknotes from the National Bank's primary emission every day? To whom did they hand over the foreign currency at the end of the day? The answer is crystal clear. They all worked for the state, for a small commission, and that's how they too managed to survive.

One significant virtue of Tito's Yugoslavia was reflected in the fact that it managed to create and nurture a numerous and prosperous middle class. However, in the second half of 1993, the middle class in Serbia was decimated and almost vanished. During those months, you could see impoverished intellectuals, retired professors, or artists rummaging through garbage bins with immeasurable shame, despair, and defeat in their eyes, looking for something that could be eaten or sold at the market. Suicides among this population were frequent. The civic middle class of Serbia never supported Milošević, and he dealt with them in the recognizable manner of a communist dictator. It was a sort of purge conducted through economic exhaustion. These individuals were not accustomed to "getting by" on the edge of the law, to "deal in currency" or engage in smuggling goods. Moreover, such business "opportunities" were mostly offered to ethnic Serb refugees from Croatia and Bosnia, as well as to domestic sympathizers of the government. Admittedly, many other "ordinary" people joined them out of sheer necessity for survival. Many children of middle-class members were mobilized and sent to battlefields in Croatia and Bosnia. Children of workers were also mobilized, but the call to go to the battlefield largely bypassed the elite's children. Unfortunately, at the same time, the children of some politicians and intellectuals close to the government were being educated at prestigious universities in the West.

Consequently, a large number of young people fled the country during those years and never returned. The authorities were quite pleased with this, as Milošević did not want them, knowing that they were not and would never be his supporters.

Life Under Embargo and Sanctions

Thus plundered and humiliated, we lived under strict sanctions imposed on the regime—and on all of us—by the UN Security Council. Stores were almost empty. Occasionally, bread, milk, oil, or flour would appear, which you would know if you saw a long line in front of the store. Quantities were limited and purchases were made with ration coupons. There were many people involved in smuggling groceries of dubious quality from neighboring countries. At the markets, you could buy diapers, soap, canned goods, cigarettes, and even chocolate if you could afford it. For years, fuel was not available at gas stations; instead, we bought smuggled gasoline and diesel from bottles or cans on the street. Besides being prohibitively expensive, this fuel often contained water that smugglers and resellers added to make more profit. Severe engine breakdowns were a common occurrence, and repair options were minimal.

Between 1993 and 1995, we lived with constant electricity restrictions. We had to adapt to such a reality. Cities were divided into groups, and the blackout schedule "by groups" was announced through the media. The blackouts lasted for four hours, sometimes longer, and this happened every day. The only concessions were around holidays, such as New Year's, when they "rewarded" us with no blackouts. Heating in the cities was very poor or nonexistent, and due to the restrictions, you couldn't warm up much using electric power. So, we mostly froze during the winter. In villages and smaller towns, it was somewhat better since people there heated their homes with wood or coal.

Between 1993 and 1995, we lived with constant electricity restrictions. We had to adapt to this harsh reality. Cities were divided into groups, and the media announced a disconnection schedule "by groups." The power cuts lasted for four hours, sometimes even longer, and this happened every day. The only exceptions were during holidays, such as around New Year's, when we were "rewarded" with no power cuts. Heating in the cities was very poor or non-existent, and due to the power restrictions, you couldn't rely much on electric heating. Therefore, we mainly froze during winter. In the countryside and smaller towns, the situation was somewhat better as people there heated their homes with wood or coal.

The healthcare system was devastated. Hospitals lacked the most basic medical supplies: medicines, antibiotics, bandages, sheets, blankets, or pillows. Even syringes for injections. The little they had was reserved for severely ill patients or the privileged. If you needed medical treatment, you had to obtain medicines and everything else on the black market or through a contact whose phone number, often handwritten on a small piece of paper, would be discreetly passed to you.

After the end of the wars in Croatia and Bosnia in 1995, we were overwhelmed by a massive wave of refugees. About 250,000 Serbs, mainly from Croatia, arrived in just a few days. As a society, we were so impoverished and exhausted that we could offer little to these people. It was yet another episode of deepening general despair and poverty. However, there were many shining examples of human solidarity even under such circumstances. The integration of refugees into Serbian society, which totaled over half a million after all the wars, was a painful and lengthy process. Today, almost thirty years later, it is still not fully completed. However, the end of the Bosnian war gave us a brief respite of about two years. Then came a new, graver ordeal, harder than all the previous ones.

***

The process of Western civilization's economic, ideological, and military "advancement towards the East," whose execution phase began in 1989 with the fall of the Berlin Wall, was in full swing by the late 1990s. Communist regimes had vanished from Russia and the former USSR countries, as well as from the rest of the European continent. The war in the former Yugoslavia had subsided. The Cold War seemed to have been replaced by an era of cooperation between superpowers. Many countries in Central and Eastern Europe were undergoing democratic transition; some had already become members of the European Union, while others embarked on the demanding journey of joining the family of united European nations. Almost all the former Warsaw Pact countries aspired to NATO membership.

In Serbia and Montenegro, which still officially referred to themselves as the "Federal Republic of Yugoslavia," the situation stood in stark contrast to these European trends. Milošević's authoritarian and repressive establishment continued to fiercely resist the changes brought by the winds from the West. It was an oasis of totalitarianism clothed in a cloak of apparent democracy. The regime rejected the possibility of joining the EU and NATO, and instead, exerted efforts to establish closer political and military ties with Russia, Belarus, China, Libya, Iran, North Korea, and a few other countries. Such geopolitical aspirations in the late 1990s were supported by Russia but were deemed unacceptable by practically all other countries in Europe and America. It was only a matter of time before Milošević's regime would find itself under new pressure from the West. The agenda of pushing back Russian influence to the north and east was well underway, and it was not conceivable for the West to allow a regime in the sensitive Balkans region that sought close ties with the East and resisted the new European and world order.

Serbs, known for their loyalty and commitment to preserving tradition, have long held a deep-rooted Russophilia. This sentiment is derived from the shared history, Orthodox faith, and Slavic origins. In the collective consciousness of Serbs, Russia stands as a stalwart "big brother" in the east, sought during times of immense distress when no other protector seemed evident. Throughout the annals of history, Russia has primarily extended diplomatic support while occasionally providing military aid. Notably, Serbs cherish the memories of Russian assistance, particularly during their arduous liberation wars against the Ottomans and the alliances forged in both world wars.

The Western pressure on Milošević's establishment during the Yugoslav wars, which inevitably spilled over onto the Serbian population as a whole, was perceived among Serbs as a great injustice, the reasons for which, regrettably, were not sufficiently understood. In an attempt to divert attention from the true cause of Western pressure—which lay in the affiliation with Russia—the regime often attributed Western policies to a "hatred toward Serbians" or to conspiracy theories that sought to prove an international plot against the Serbs, typically involving the Vatican and Germany. Even today, very few people in Serbia understand that the Serbs are but one piece in a complex chess game played by major powers.

For several decades, a multi-layered operation has been underway, through which the West aims to push back Russian presence and influence in the Balkans and elsewhere in Europe, promoting a new order based on globalism and the military power of NATO. Traditional Serbian Russophilia only contributed to the creation of a black-and-white narrative in Western societies, painting Serbs as "little Russians" whose unification and empowerment should not be permitted.

On the other hand, constant pressure from the West instilled a sense of national vulnerability and insecurity among the Serbs. A logical consequence was the awakening of an age-old historical reflex to seek salvation from Russia. Paradoxically, it was primarily America that pushed the Serbs into Russia's embrace far more than during Tito's Yugoslavia—which maintained a clear distance from the USSR. During the 'stick and carrot' policy throughout the Yugoslav crisis, the Serbs were generally offered the stick, while other Yugoslavs typically received the carrot.

By consistently lumping all Serbs and Milošević's regime together, communication was severed with a nation that, throughout its history, demonstrated significant democratic and nation-building potential, and with whom the U.S. once shared extraordinary relations. Unlike other ex-communist nations of Eastern Europe that embraced U.S. leadership during their democratic transition, the opposite effect was created among the Serbs. Milošević managed to profit from this paradox for a long time. In his efforts to preserve his power, he exploited the negative emotions of the people, induced by Western pressures, stifling the democratization of society and intensively advocating for closer ties with Russia and its allies.

This course of action would experience an unprecedented new blow from the West by the end of the 1990s—eloquently underscoring the strategic and geopolitical significance of the territories inhabited by the Serbs.

Kosovo War

Even though in the months following the signing of the Dayton Agreement, the West was calling Milošević a "factor of stability," things would soon start moving in an unfavorable direction. The united force that at the time held a considerable geopolitical advantage over Russia wanted to confront the unacceptable regime in Belgrade. The biggest vulnerability of the Federal Republic of Yugoslavia was the unresolved issue of relations between the Albanians and Serbs in Kosovo, which has been eroding every Serbian state since the 19th century. Milošević's political ascent began in Kosovo, and it was precisely there that his political journey would experience its most significant defeat—with profoundly severe and far-reaching consequences for the Serbian nation as a whole.

During the 1990s, ethnic Albanians in the Autonomous Province of Kosovo and Metohija—which was its official and full name—were actively developing their parallel institutions. They self-proclaimed a "Republic of Kosovo" and boycotted the census as well as all elections organized by the Republic of Serbia. At the beginning of the decade, they formed the Kosovo Liberation Army (KLA), a guerrilla paramilitary organization whose aim was to achieve the separation of Kosovo from the rest of Serbia through armed struggle. However, changing international borders is a difficult feat without international support, and the Albanians knew this well. They rightly assessed that Milošević had severely weakened Serbia's position and credibility during his decade-long rule, and that the Yugoslav state, consisting only of Serbia and Montenegro, wouldn't survive. They realized that the time had come to engage in the final battle for the realization of their dream of breaking away from Serbia and uniting with other members of the Albanian nation. They enthusiastically sought allies in the United States and NATO.

And so it happened that, following the tried-and-true principle of "the enemy of my enemy is my friend," NATO began to provide military support to the Kosovo Liberation Army and political backing for the self-determination of Kosovo's Albanians and their secession from Serbia.[103]

The KLA's initial attacks, mostly targeted against Serbian police forces in Kosovo, began in 1996, but did not escalate into larger-scale conflicts until the spring of 1998. Although the United States had previously labeled the KLA as a terrorist group, a shift in American policy was evident around this time. After an operation by Serbian anti-terrorist units against the KLA on March 5th, 1998, in which, in addition to armed men, twenty-eight civilians were killed, U.S. Secretary of State Madeleine Albright declared that "this crisis is not an internal affair of the FR Yugoslavia."

The Serbian side continuously tried to convince the world that an Albanian project of unification was underway in Kosovo, aiming to create an Albanian state that would encompass all territories inhabited by Albanians. They argued that since these territories were not only in Serbia but also in North Macedonia, Greece, and Montenegro, a lack of international reaction would lead to the destabilization of the recently pacified Balkans. As expected, no one wanted to listen to Milošević or the Serbian arguments, and this was part of the information war that had been relentlessly waged against his state and regime since the early 1990s. However, KLA leaders themselves confirmed the Serbian claims.

In his book, "Liberating Kosovo: Coercive Diplomacy and U.S. Intervention,"[104] author David Phillips quotes the words of KLA commander Sulejman Selimi:

"There is de facto Albanian nation. The tragedy is that European powers after World War I decided to divide that nation between several Balkan states. We are now fighting to unify the nation, to liberate all Albanians, including those in Macedonia, Montenegro, and other parts of Serbia. We are not just a liberation army for Kosovo".

KLA spokesperson, Jakup Krasniqi, publicly stated in an interview with Germany's *Der Spiegel* that the "goal of the KLA is the unification of all areas inhabited by Albanians."[105]

However, Milošević's regime—an ideological and political threat to the establishment of a new order in Europe—had to be removed. It appears

---

[103] In Serbia, even twenty years later (2021), this fact continues to be cited as an example of double standards: "Why did the West support the Albanians' desire to secede Kosovo from Serbia while opposing the Catalans' desire to secede from Spain or the Crimean Russians' desire to secede from Ukraine?"

[104] Phillips, David L. *Liberating Kosovo: Coercive Diplomacy and U.S. Intervention.* Belfer Center for Science and International Affairs, 2012, p. 69.

[105] "Interview with Jakup Krasniqi." *Der Spiegel*, no. 28/1998, pp. 122-123.

that for the West, this was the first geopolitical priority in the Balkans. John Norris, a high-ranking diplomat in the Clinton administration, clearly speaks about this:

> NATO's large membership and consensus style may cause endless headaches for military planners, but it is also why joining NATO is appealing to nations across central and eastern Europe. Nations from Albania to Ukraine want in the western club. The gravitational pull of the community of Western democracies highlights why Milosevic's Yugoslavia had become such an anachronism. As nations throughout the region sought to reform their economies, mitigate ethnic tensions, and broaden civil society, Belgrade seemed to delight in continually moving in the opposite direction. It is small wonder NATO and Yugoslavia ended up on a collision course. It was Yugoslavia's resistance to the broader trends of political and economic reform—not the plight of the Kosovar Albanians—that best explains NATO's war. Milosevic had been a burr in the side of the transatlantic community for so long that the United States felt that he would only respond to military pressure. Slobodan Milosevic's repeated transgressions ran directly counter to the vision of a Europe "whole and free," and challenged the very value of NATO's continued existence.[106]

Norris was the Communications Director for U.S. Deputy Secretary of State Strobe Talbott and was involved in diplomatic activities related to the Kosovo War. The very title of his book, "Collision Course: NATO, Russia, and Kosovo," eloquently confirms that the fundamental dynamism behind the Kosovo processes—as well as earlier ones related to the breakup of Yugoslavia—was the redistribution of spheres of influence between NATO and a weakened Russia, during which the small nations of the Balkans played the role of proxies. I hope that over time, there will be a broader understanding of this simple truth among the general public in Serbia.

During 1998, a war between the police and military forces of the Federal Republic of Yugoslavia and the KLA in Kosovo was escalating, and the West was intensively preparing for military intervention against the regime in Belgrade, justifying it with humanitarian reasons and ethnic cleansing. Air strikes could have occurred as early as October 1998, but they were averted at the last moment by an agreement between Milošević and American diplomat Richard Holbrooke. They agreed to a ceasefire, the arrival of

---

[106] Norris, John. *Collision Course: NATO, Russia, and Kosovo*. Greenwood Publishing Group, 2005.

the Kosovo Verification Mission (KVM), OSCE observers, and the with-drawal of the army and police to their barracks.

However, the KLA used the ceasefire to regain territories from which it had been pushed out. A new escalation of the conflict occurred, and im mense pressure was put on Milošević to reach a political agreement for Kosovo during peace negotiations at the Rambouillet Château near Paris. U.S. Secretary of State Madeleine Albright said, "if the Albanians do not sign (the final document) and Serbs do so, we (USA) will revoke their fi-nancial assistance. If the opposite happens, we will bomb Yugoslavia."[107]

After initial successes in the negotiations, there was a stalemate. The reason was obvious. The proposed plan involved a NATO administration in Kosovo, the entry of 30,000 NATO soldiers into the province to main-tain order, the unhindered right of passage for NATO troops throughout Yugoslavia, and immunity for NATO and its agents from Yugoslav laws. To make matters worse, the plan envisaged a "democratic expression" of the Kosovo population, which was over 90% Albanian, about the final po-litical status of the province in the foreseeable future. The outcome of such a referendum was very easy to predict. No state could accept such a severe breach of sovereignty, and many authors share the belief that the West in-tentionally set impossible conditions for Milošević.

On March 18th, 1999, the Albanian, American, and British delegations signed an agreement that was, however, rejected by the Yugoslav and Rus-sian delegations.

Interestingly, less than a month later, on April 14th, 1999, President Clinton met with representatives of the Serbian community in the US. Dur-ing this meeting, he remarked that the negotiations had "gone too far" in trying to enable a referendum on Kosovo's independence for Albanians. Furthermore, he admitted that he "probably would not have signed the Rambouillet agreement draft if he were in Milošević's shoes."[108]

The nature of the Rambouillet negotiations was also assessed by the In-ternational Criminal Tribunal for the former Yugoslavia in The Hague, an institution that many in Serbia perceive as biased and anti-Serbian. How-ever, in a 2009 verdict, it can be read that the failure of the Rambouillet negotiations was also due to the fact that "international negotiators did not have an entirely balanced approach towards the positions of the interested parties and tended to favor Kosovo Albanians."

---

[107] *David vs. Goliath: NATO War against Yugoslavia and Its Implications.* Edited by Nebojša Vuković. Belgrade: Institute of International Politics and Economics, Faculty of Security Studies, 2019, p. 142.
[108] From the testimony of Obrad Kesić, a participant in the mentioned meeting, before the International Criminal Tribunal for the former Yugoslavia in 2007.

Another interesting viewpoint was expressed by Raju G.C. Thomas, a professor of international relations from the US. According to him, even if Yugoslavia had signed the Rambouillet document, it would have been invalid. Article 52 of the 1980 Vienna Convention stipulates that an agreement forced under the threat of use of force is not valid. However, it seems that in the case of Yugoslavia, the message was clear: "If you don't sign, you will be bombed."

NATO Attack on the Federal Republic of Yugoslavia

It was March 22nd, 1999. American diplomat Richard Holbrooke paid a visit to Milošević in a last-ditch attempt to avoid war. After the meeting, he stated that "no substantial progress was made." The following day, on March 23rd, Javier Solana, the Secretary General of NATO, issued an order to attack the Federal Republic of Yugoslavia. Local media relayed the message of Momir Bulatović, the Prime Minister of the federal government, about the immediate threat of war. The official name of the military operation was "Operation Allied Force," while in the US it was referred to as "Noble Anvil." This was set to be a war full of precedents.

By that point, almost all foreigners had already left the Federal Republic of Yugoslavia. Most of the embassies had been evacuated. Despite clear signals that things were headed in a very bad direction, people displayed disbelief and hope that something might still occur at the last minute.

Around half-past seven in the evening on March 24th, the media reported that planes had taken off from Italy. The first air raid sirens could be heard. In the hallway of the building, I could hear the excited chatter of neighbors. I also stepped out of my apartment. An older lady, a member of the middle class with anti-communist beliefs, was speaking anxiously: "This isn't happening, this is Milošević's propaganda and lies, he wants to make us quarrel with the West, the Americans won't bomb us, we were their allies in both world wars." A gentleman from the corner apartment replied resignedly: "Nonsense, they want to destroy us because we're Orthodox. But you'll see, Russia will help us." We all descended into the atomic shelter built in the basement of the building back in the 1960s. Some residents were already there, bringing blankets, pillows, water, and food. One woman was visibly panicking—I was told she had psychiatric issues.

I went back up to my apartment on the top floor of the building. From the west-facing window, I could see a large part of Belgrade. In the distance, I noticed ominous flashing and heard detonations. The night sky was streaked with hundreds of sparks created by the anti-air defense of the Yugoslav Army. I couldn't hear the planes. I grabbed my camera and started taking pictures.

A mix of fear, anger, and disappointment stirred within me. Milošević had consumed ten years of my life. I spent countless days amidst tens of thousands of other people in street protests against his rule. We didn't want wars—quite the opposite. We wanted our country to be "normal," its politics mundane. We simply wished for our Serbia to be a part of the democratic and civilized world. And now, that democratic world was dropping bombs on us. "If I receive a call for mobilization, I will join the defense of the country," I thought.

That call never came.

Yevgeny Primakov, Russian Prime Minister was on that day en route for an official visit to the United States. While his plane was over the Atlantic, US Vice President Al Gore informed him by phone of NATO's commencement of air strikes on Yugoslavia. In protest, Primakov canceled the visit and ordered the plane to turn back over the ocean and return to Moscow.

"This is a strike against the entire international community," said Russian President Boris Yeltsin. "This is a very serious step, and to undertake it without the consent of the UN Security Council is more than incomprehensible." In protest, Russia withdrew from the NATO Partnership for Peace program and pulled its representative from the Alliance's headquarters in Brussels. The Russian peacekeeping contingent in Bosnia ceased obeying NATO's joint command.

After the collapse of the USSR and the Warsaw Pact, the global structure established after World War II became too restrictive for America. The only remaining superpower was discontented with the limitations imposed by decision-making within the UN Security Council and sent a powerful message that it, along with its NATO allies, was potent enough to bypass it without consequences. The intervention against the Federal Republic of Yugoslavia demonstrated this new balance of power. The world's greatest power sought a unipolar world organized around the concepts of liberal capitalism and globalization.

The highest legal act of NATO—the North Atlantic Treaty—foresees the use of military force in only two cases: if requested by the UN Security Council, or if one of the member states is attacked. However, there was no decision from the Security Council—China and Russia were against it. On the other hand, the Federal Republic of Yugoslavia had not attacked any NATO member state. Neither of the two conditions for initiating military action was met. And yet, the bombing occurred. The action was not legal either under international law or according to the internal rules of the

Western military alliance. These are the main reasons why, in Serbia, it is consistently referred to as the "NATO aggression" to this day.

Opinions in the West about this issue are divided. Those justifying the military intervention say it was "illegal but legitimate" because it stopped ethnic cleansing and potential genocide in Kosovo. Some Western media and officials spoke of "100,000 missing Albanians in Kosovo," alluding to a disaster of enormous proportions. However, subsequent findings would show that the drastic increase in casualties and refugees only occurred after NATO's intervention had begun.

The 2000 German documentary "It All Started with a Lie"[109] shows that Germany's Minister of Defense, Rudolf Scharping, deceived the public with false reports of a massive humanitarian catastrophe in Kosovo, thus justifying the necessity of NATO's intervention. The film features a statement by German General Heinz Loquai, who was part of the OSCE's observation mission on the ground, that the humanitarian catastrophe—which would have given legitimacy to Germany's participation under international law—did not exist in Kosovo before NATO's military intervention. Another official in the film denied that a humanitarian catastrophe could have been a reason for NATO's attack on the Federal Republic of Yugoslavia. This was Norma Brown, an American diplomat in the OSCE, who in the film says:

> "There was no humanitarian crisis until NATO began to bomb. Though the truth is, there were serious humanitarian needs. There were a lot of people who were out of their homes because of fighting. But the pattern that had been developing was one of the population leaving villages while the anti-KLA operation was being performed by the authorities, and then there were people gradually moving back to their villages. The reality is that everyone knew there would be a humanitarian crisis of massive proportions if NATO bombed. It was discussed in NATO, it was discussed in the OSCE, it was discussed in our mission, it was discussed among the general population".

Judging by these testimonies, the true reasons for NATO's engagement did not, therefore, lie in a humanitarian catastrophe. It only unfolded on a large scale after the attack on Yugoslavia had begun.

However, another intriguing question arises: did Western planners anticipate that the Yugoslav President would make such poor decisions that, as we'll see, would ultimately play into their favor?

---

[109] Werth, Mathias and Jo Angerer. *Es begann mit einer Lüge*. 2000. Produced by WDR Fernsehen.

***

During the initial days, NATO targeted exclusively military and police facilities. However, they soon started to bomb bridges, oil refineries, chemical plants, and factories. Cluster bombs, later prohibited by war conventions, started falling. Then, even more distressing news arrived: the attacks were using ammunition with depleted uranium; there were many civilian casualties, including children, the television reported. The attacks occurred every night, and less frequently during the day. The passing of time was marked by the sounding of sirens announcing incoming air raids. Power would occasionally go out, and sometimes even the water supply. People started gathering on Belgrade's bridges, risking their bare lives to prevent their destruction. Several thousand individuals would go to the bridges where concerts and other events were held. Journalists, reporters from world media, couldn't believe what was happening.

Eventually, NATO did not bomb the bridges in Belgrade.

I vividly remember the cafés and clubs where people would spend the night under candlelight, as the lights had to be turned off due to the air raids. I recall the masses of young people going out every night, bonding and falling in love with an unusual intensity. It seems as if the very principle of life, endangered by the bombs, was putting extra energy into itself. I know of several babies conceived during those harsh times.

Several days after the beginning of the bombing, on March 27th, the anti-aircraft defense downed the American stealth aircraft F-117A. This is the first and so far only confirmed loss of an aircraft with stealth technology. The pilot, Darrell Patrick Dale Zelko, a veteran of the Gulf War, was rescued a few hours later and remained unharmed. After the war, he met several times with Zoltan Dani, the commander of the Yugoslav anti-aircraft defense unit that downed him. Their encounters took place in the USA and Serbia, and a documentary about them titled "The Second Meeting" was filmed in 2013.[110]

During those days, at the beginning of April 1999, NATO was celebrating a significant anniversary—fifty years of existence. The day before the anniversary, their planes brought down the Petrovaradin bridge over the Danube in Novi Sad, the country's second-largest city. Since then, a widespread belief in Serbia holds that the bombing campaign was rushed in order to magnify the celebration.

Reports of civilian casualties were coming in more and more frequently. Passenger buses were burning, with dozens of civilians losing their lives in them. There was a horrifying footage of a train crossing a bridge just as

[110] Mirković, Željko, dir. *The Second Meeting.* 2013. IMDb, *www.imdb.com/title/tt2558556/.*

a projectile hits it. Again, dozens of casualties. Then, even Kosovo Albanians were killed. NATO mistakenly attacked their refugee column. The Alliance's spokesperson referred to civilian casualties as "collateral damage". In Serbia, they responded to such an attitude as "callous cynicism".

One of Belgrade's landmarks, the 205-meter-high television tower that we used to joyfully spot when returning from a long car journey or vacation, or when our parents took us as children to view the city from a bird's-eye perspective, vanished on the night of April 29th. The next day, police, government, and military buildings in the very center of Belgrade were bombed. A powerful explosion took the lives of young men waiting at a traffic light in a car in front of the Army General Staff building. In the second wave of attacks on the same buildings, firefighters and already arrived photojournalists were injured.

The bombing of the Radio Television of Serbia building on April 23rd, in which sixteen workers were killed, is one of the most controversial attacks. Several journalist associations around the world condemned the attack, believing that Serbian television could not have been a legitimate military target. Some went a step further and called the attack an act of terrorism. The director of the television station, Dragoljub Milanović, who failed to evacuate the building despite receiving information to do so, served a ten-year prison sentence for this act.

The Chinese embassy in Belgrade was bombed on May 8th. Three diplomats were killed. NATO's spokesperson, with a significant apology, announced that there had been a mistake due to "outdated maps." No one believed him. In Beijing, enraged masses attacked US diplomatic missions. More than twenty years later, on the site of its former embassy in Belgrade, Beijing has built a Chinese cultural center.

The end of May was marked by continued pressure on Milošević. The West had expected him to give in much earlier, but when that did not happen, they turned to so-called graphite bombs. Their use causes short circuits in power lines and energy facilities, so we no longer had electricity. And when there is no electricity, the water supply soon cuts off. We made water reserves and lived by candlelight and kerosene lamps.

What did Milošević Attempt?

A document from the police top brass, dated February 16th, 1999, that surfaced during Slobodan Milošević's trial before the Hague Tribunal, states the following:

"With the Pristina Corps [of the Yugoslav Army] a plan is being finalized... for a broad operation during the period between potential air strikes and the entry of ground forces."

So, the Serbian state leadership anticipated that a ground military intervention by NATO would follow the air strikes, and this fact largely explains the steps that Milošević would take. In the case of an invasion of Yugoslavia, it was estimated that the ethnic Albanians in Kosovo would massively side with the aggressor. Analyzing events after the start of NATO's intervention, it seems that the military strategists in Belgrade were creating defense plans that, in addition to military actions against the KLA, also envisaged a significant reduction in the number of Albanians overall. In this way, the chances of defense in the case of a ground invasion by Western allies would be strengthened.

Milošević's regime would attempt to change the demographic structure in Kosovo by expelling the Albanian population from the province, especially those who had settled illegally from neighboring Albania since 1974. To remind, the Constitution of the SFR Yugoslavia from 1974 granted broad autonomy to the province of Kosovo and Metohija. Local (ethnic Albanian) authorities abused this autonomy by allowing a large number of Albanians from neighboring Albania to settle, thereby changing the demographic structure to the detriment of the Serbs.

On the other hand, the Albanians' resistance against Serbian state institutions in Kosovo had escalated into a mass enlistment of able-bodied Albanian men into the Kosovo Liberation Army (KLA). It was, therefore, a widespread uprising that the Belgrade authorities tried to downplay by informing domestic and global public opinion about fighting with "armed groups of terrorists."

After the joint attack initiated on March 24th, 1999, in which NATO operated from the air and the KLA on the ground, Milošević and the generals of the army and police of Yugoslavia launched a high-intensity counteroffensive in Kosovo. In his testimony before the Hague Tribunal, Milošević confirmed that they had launched a counter-offensive: "We had to engage in uncompromising combat against terrorism in Kosovo because it was clearly evident that the terrorists were NATO's ground forces."

However, fighting against armed Albanians is one thing, and ethnic cleansing and crimes against civilians are something entirely different. Trials before foreign and domestic courts have shown that Serbian forces perpetrated persecution of Albanian civilians, looting and destruction of their villages, as well as confiscation of personal documents, all with the aim of preventing their return to Kosovo. There was widespread intimidation, beatings, and summary executions. It often happened that attacks on KLA strongholds were carried out by random and intensive artillery fire, which killed not only armed Albanians but also civilians who were not involved in armed conflicts, including women and children. Instances of Serbian armed forces members raping Albanian women were recorded. A large number of mosques were destroyed or severely damaged.

According to data from the UN High Commissioner for Refugees (UNHCR), about 170,000 Albanians had fled from Kosovo to neighboring countries or Western Europe before the start of NATO's intervention. Then, the situation dramatically worsened. The Commissioner recorded a total of 862,979 refugees by the end of the war, which lasted two and a half months.

During the trial of Slobodan Milošević before the Hague Tribunal, one of the witnesses was Police General Obrad Stevanović. In his war diary, a page from May 1999 reads, "left the country: 900,000," which approximately matches the number of refugees that the UNHCR reported later.

After the cessation of hostilities and the arrival of international forces, the vast majority of Albanian refugees returned to Kosovo.

The renowned Serbian writer Dobrica Ćosić, whose influence on Slobodan Milošević's policy-making is undisputed, felt remorse during those days for the tragedy to which he himself had contributed through his political actions. In his book of memoirs from the 1999–2000 period, we find these words of Ćosić's:

"Svetozar Stijović, a linguist from Peć and a great patriot, relayed to me the tale of his cousin from Peć who had just arrived from Metohija. Our military and police have driven all the Albanians from Peć and Dečani; the Albanian part of the city across the Bistrica (river) has been burned and destroyed... This man from Peć asserts that indeed, the majority of Shiptars[111] have been driven out and have fled Kosovo due to the actions of our military, police,

---

[111] The Slavicized form of the original Albanian ethnonym *Shqiptar*, used by the members of the Albanian people to refer to themselves. Although it was officially used in Yugoslavia after World War II, over time it acquired offensive connotations as it does not sound correct and offends Albanians. It was withdrawn from official use in 1968. Today, it is considered a politically incorrect term.

and volunteers. The majority that remains is in Priština. I cannot understand this expulsion of the Shiptars; I consider this decision insane, fatal, anti-Serbian. If it really is an order from the Supreme Command and the supreme commander, then they should be tried in Belgrade for war crimes and genocide against the Albanian people. Will we end our fight for the defense of the 'holy Serbian land' with the ethnic cleansing of Kosovo and Metohija? This national disgrace, this collective crime of the Serbian army negates the ethos of the Serbian people and ranks it among barbaric nations like the Germans, Americans, Croatians, Muslims, Asians... How will we continue our historical existence with this collective guilt? What will literature, culture, spirit, and morality of the Serbian people be like after this war?"[112]

***

The Kosovo Liberation Army (KLA) also committed crimes. They targeted mostly Serbs, and then Roma, who seemed to have sided with Serbian forces during the war. Victims also included Albanians loyal to Serbia or those who collaborated with Serbian authorities in any way. During 1998, a large number of kidnappings and killings took place, often involving innocent civilians. There is a list of around ten

Destroyed Serbian church of the Holy Trinity in the village of Petrić, Kosovo.

massacres committed by the KLA during 1998 and 1999, in which about a thousand people were killed. It is estimated that about three hundred thousand Serbs and non-Albanians left Kosovo during the war and in the months following it.

The Serbian public was shaken about ten years later by news about Serb civilians who were taken to the so-called "Yellow House" in Albania, where their organs were extracted and sold on the black market. The first person to speak about this was Carla Del Ponte, the former Chief Prosecutor of the International Criminal Tribunal for the former Yugoslavia (ICTY). The Tribunal then conducted an investigation, which found medical equipment and traces of blood around the house.

---

[112] Ćosić, Dobrica. *Vreme zmija – Piščevi zapisi 1999–2000*. (title translated: "Time of Serpents – Writer's Notes 1999-2000.") Službeni glasnik, Beograd. 2008, p. 98.

At the request of the Council of Europe, Swiss prosecutor Dick Marty prepared a report in which he stated that he had come across "credible indications" of illegal trade in human organs. According to French television station France24, the UN knew about this problem from the testimonies of British soldiers within the international forces. However, the aforementioned investigations did not lead to indictments due to a lack of witnesses willing to testify and insufficient evidence.

Edward Tawil, a Canadian expert on minority rights, determined in a 2009 report[113] that 155 Serbian Christian churches and monasteries were destroyed in Kosovo between the end of the war and 2004. In addition, many monuments to Serbian notable personalities or those associated with the victory over fascism were destroyed. There were also many cases of desecration or destruction of Serbian cemeteries.

When the war ended and international forces and administration entered Kosovo, numerous acts of revenge were committed against the remaining Serbs, including expulsion, property damage, beatings, and killings.

***

At the beginning of June, faster than I had expected, the war with NATO ended. The West, together with Russia, exerted pressure on Milošević, and that was the end of the game. The peace proposal was brought to Belgrade by Finnish diplomat Martti Ahtisaari and Russian President's envoy Viktor Chernomyrdin. Milošević asked Ahtisaari what needed to be done for the bombing to stop, to which he offered a paper and said, "This is the best offer you can get." Chernomyrdin consistently sided with Ahtisaari. The peace proposal entailed the entry of NATO forces into Kosovo under the UN mandate, the withdrawal of Serbian military and police forces, international administration, keeping Kosovo within the FR Yugoslavia with the widest autonomy, and a prohibition on a referendum on the province's independence for at least three years. Surprisingly, it was a better proposal than the one offered in Rambouillet. Milošević agreed, and the National Assembly of the Republic of Serbia formally approved the plan at a session that almost resulted in a fight between deputies. Then the military Kumanovo agreement was signed, which stopped the bombing on June 10th, 1999, after 78 days. We breathed a sigh of relief and celebrated in the streets. Then Milošević appeared on TV and said, "We defeated NATO!"

The final episode in Milošević's political tenure—his "victory" over NATO—brought Serbia human casualties, massive material destruction measured in tens of billions of dollars, a devastated economy, an impover-

---

[113] Tawil, Edward. *Property Rights in Kosovo: A Haunting Legacy of a Society in Transition.* International Center for Transitional Justice, February 2009, p. 14.

ished, exhausted, and humiliated people, the worst reputation of Serbs in history, an embargo, sanctions, and the effective loss of control over the "holy Serbian land" of Kosovo.

However, during the bombing, the people's anger towards Milošević was largely redirected towards NATO forces. This significant fact would greatly determine Serbia's later attitude towards Euro-Atlantic integrations.

After the signing of the Military-Technical Agreement in Kumanovo, the Yugoslav army and Serbian police withdrew from Kosovo with such an amount of undamaged equipment that it considerably surprised foreign media correspondents. Although NATO initially announced relatively large numbers of destroyed tanks and other combat equipment, it later turned out that the real losses of Serbian forces were much smaller and that soldiers and officers had proven to be well-trained and skillful professionals. Many creative tactics were used in combat, including the use of plastic and wooden models of planes and tanks, old tanks from World War II, decoys, hiding, camouflage, and fake "radar" emissions using microwave ovens.

United Nations Security Council Resolution 1244 on Kosovo

This internationally legally binding document was adopted on June 10th, 1999. It envisaged international military and civil presence in Kosovo, namely the establishment of the United Nations Interim Administration Mission in Kosovo (UNMIK). The resolution was passed in accordance with the Ahtisaari-Chernomyrdin peace plan, which Slobodan Milošević accepted in Belgrade two days earlier—with fourteen votes "in favor" and China abstaining, still angry about the bombing of its embassy in Belgrade.

The main provisions of the Resolution called for a cessation of violence and repression in Kosovo by the Federal Republic of Yugoslavia, the withdrawal of the army and police, as well as the disarmament and dissolution of the Kosovo Liberation Army and other armed ethnic Albanian formations. The province was placed under the temporary administration of the UN, with the KFOR peacekeeping forces, led by NATO, responsible for security. The creation of temporary local self-governance institutions was allowed, and it was anticipated that political discussions would be held until a final status of Kosovo would be decided upon by a new resolution in the UN Security Council.

The document called for the "ensuring of a safe and unimpeded return of all refugees and displaced persons" and the "establishment of conditions for a peaceful and normal life for all inhabitants of Kosovo."

Referring to the Helsinki Final Act in its text, Resolution 1244 clearly expressed the commitment of all member states to the "sovereignty and territorial integrity of the Federal Republic of Yugoslavia and other states of the region" in several places. According to the Constitution of the Federal Republic of Yugoslavia, Kosovo and Metohija is an autonomous province within the Republic of Serbia. The Republic of Serbia is internationally recognized as the legal successor of the Federal Republic of Yugoslavia. However, a large part of the international community would later change its stance on sovereignty and territorial integrity and support Kosovo's secession from Serbia.

Declaration of Independence of Kosovo 2008 and Its Consequences

In an effort to fulfill the undeniable desire for self-determination expressed by the Kosovo Albanians, the Kosovo parliament, operating outside the legal framework and mandate provided by Resolution 1244, adopted the Declaration of Independence of Kosovo on February 17th, 2008.

Serbia, as expected, rejected this decision, arguing that it violated its territorial integrity guaranteed by international law and Resolution 1244. What followed was a renewed global polarization along the East-West axis. A large number of Western countries immediately recognized Kosovo as an independent state, while Eastern and Third World countries mostly expressed opposition to the unilaterally declared independence. As of mid-2023, when I write this, the world is divided on the status of Kosovo in roughly a 50%:50% proportion.

Some of the countries that do not recognize Kosovo include the Vatican, Russia, China, India, Argentina, Brazil, Mexico, Chile, the Philippines, Indonesia, Mongolia, Iraq, Iran, Lebanon, Spain, Greece, Ukraine, Romania, Slovakia, and Cyprus.

The self-proclaimed independence of Kosovo, which reaffirmed the principle of self-determination, was welcomed in Basque Country and Catalonia, among other territories wishing to secede from their parent nations. The Central Tibetan Administration in exile, led by the Dalai Lama, also extended its support, stating that "If Kosovo has a right to independence, then Tibet has every right to become an independent nation, and Tibetans have the complete right to self-determination."

Russian President Putin compared Kosovo to Crimea, accusing the international community of applying double standards. In an interview with the German newspaper Bild, he stated, "If Kosovars have a right to self-determination, why shouldn't the people of Crimea have the same right? I would say: everyone should comply with uniform international rules and not change them from time to time at their discretion."

The West does not accept the assessment of double standards. According to them, the territorial inviolability of states remains a principle to be adhered to. However, they consider Kosovo a "special case" because Serbia violated the human rights of the local population and consequently lost its rights to govern the province.

Upon evaluating all the perspectives presented, it appears that the 'Kosovo knot' is an extremely complex issue, containing certain precedents and the potential to set off global processes in various directions. I pay tribute to the political wisdom of my ancestors that I quoted in the initial chapters of this book. To remind, they had warned as far back as the 1970s that a "third world war could break out in Kosovo."

Is a resolution to the Kosovo issue on the horizon? Apart from the long-awaited historical agreement between Serbs and Albanians, which we have been waiting for over a century, it will also require the consensus of all global powers, but only when favorable conditions are met. However, it is uncertain when such a historic opportunity will arise.

Victims of the War in Kosovo

Given the duration and intensity of the conflict, the number of internally displaced and refugees, all the warring parties, including the world's largest allied military force, our expectations were that the number of casualties in the Kosovo war would be substantial—tens or even hundreds of thousands. In the months leading up to NATO's airstrikes, and during the final phase of the war, some media outlets and global officials accused Milošević's regime of a "new genocide" and hundreds of thousands of Albanian deaths, ethnic cleansing, and a humanitarian disaster. They deemed intervention absolutely necessary and justified. According to data published later, however, such an apocalyptic scenario did not materialize in reality.

After the war, Serbian media and officials provided rough estimates of the number of casualties. They typically spoke of "thousands of dead soldiers and civilians," but to this day, no Serbian state institution has released official figures. Researchers, including myself, hope that this will eventually occur due to the exceptional historical significance of the topic.

The task of tallying the casualties was undertaken by the Humanitarian Law Center in Serbia and Kosovo. This non-governmental organization does not enjoy a good reputation in Serbia, as it is often accused of anti-Serbian views. Since it's the only comprehensive study we have available, I will share the data published by these two organizations here.[114] The result of their work, after processing 31,600 documents, is a list of victims by name, released in 2014. The list contains the following data:

The total number of dead and missing during the Kosovo war, over a three-year period (1.1.1998 – 31.12.2000), is **13,535**.

Civilian casualties:

- 8,676 Albanians
- 1,196 Serbs
- 445 Roma and members of other nationalities

Casualties among members of armed formations:

---

[114] The results are available on the Internet at the following address: *kosovo-memorybook.org*

420

- 2,131 Albanians
- 1,084 members of the Yugoslav Army and Serbian Ministry of Internal Affairs[115]
- 3 members of KFOR

Although significant, the number of casualties in the Kosovo war is much smaller than initially feared, and ten times lower than some of the figures circulated by various global media outlets and officials. A similar pattern occurred in the Bosnian war, where it turned out that the final number of victims was about three times less than the initial figures that circulated in the international public.

Due to these and other inaccuracies in reporting on the Kosovo and other Yugoslav wars, it is a widespread belief in Serbia that not only was a military war waged against it, but also a propaganda war. The aim was to convince public opinion—most significantly in Western countries—to support an unprecedented military intervention that did not have a consensus in the UN Security Council, and to make numerous political decisions that were detrimental to Serbian interests. Serbs were publicly condemned, though many allegations against them later proved to be false or exaggerated. The negative image created about the Serbs during this time is still felt today and is slowly giving way to a more realistic picture based on known facts.

The biased reporting from major global media outlets, such as CNN and the BBC, is still leveraged by factions in Serbia that lean towards Russia and the East and oppose Serbia's entry into the EU and NATO. These groups talk about an unforgivable, deliberate, and calculated demonization of the entire Serbian nation by the West, which they claim spanned all the Yugoslav wars, not just the final, Kosovo war. Advocates of this narrative are reluctant to discuss crimes committed by Serbs, instead they redirect public attention to the crimes of Albanians, Croats, and Bosniaks. They argue that Milosevic's main sin was, in fact, his persistent opposition to globalization, the West, or the new world order.

Due to all that has been presented, it seems essential to add truth to the list of casualties of the Kosovo war. All interested parties have transgressed against it many times since the very beginning.

---

[115] According to the information obtained by FHP (Fond za humanitarno pravo - Humanitarian Law Center), as a result of the NATO airstrikes (March 24th, 1999 - June 10th, 1999), 274 members of the Yugoslav Army and Serbian police were killed. The remaining 810 members of government forces were killed in battles with the KLA (Kosovo Liberation Army) and other armed Albanian formations.

Less-Known Geopolitical Curiosities Related to the Kosovo War

Who Will Arrive in Kosovo First—NATO or Russia?

The Russian battalion from the peacekeeping forces in Bosnia was the first to arrive in Kosovo via Serbia, taking control of the Priština airport. Russia had a plan to deploy several thousand soldiers by IL-76 aircraft and establish their own sector in the northern part of the province. The plan was thwarted when Hungary, Romania, and Bulgaria, at the intervention of the West, denied the Russian transport aircraft the right to fly over their territories. NATO's Supreme Commander General Wesley Clark ordered British and French troops to forcibly take over the airport from Russian soldiers. British General Mike Jackson opposed the order, telling Clark, "I'm not going to start the Third World War because of you." Despite Clark's insistence, a direct confrontation with the Russians did not occur thanks to an order that came directly from the British Ministry of Defense. Clark was later asked to withdraw from his position in NATO earlier than planned, and Jackson, whom soldiers called Darth Vader, was honored and appointed as the Commander-in-Chief of the land forces of the United Kingdom.

In May 2003, Russian President Putin decided to withdraw all Russian Federation peacekeeping troops from the territory of the former Yugoslavia. This action was explained as Russia's refusal to be a "smokescreen while Western countries partition Serbia and seize Kosovo". However, it seems that Russia's motives were grounded in a longer-term policy. In 2014, the Russian Federation annexed the Crimea peninsula from Ukraine, and on several occasions in public statements, justified its actions by drawing parallels with the actions of the West in Kosovo.

Camp Bondsteel

Immediately following the end of the war in 1999, construction began on the largest U.S. military base in the Balkans, capable of housing over seven thousand soldiers. It's located in eastern Kosovo, near the town of Uroševac—or Ferizaj in Albanian. The base was named Bondsteel, after James Bondsteel, a Vietnam War veteran and Medal of Honor recipient. Today, the base is the main

The U.S. military base "Bondsteel" in eastern Kosovo

NATO headquarters for the KFOR Multinational Battle Group East. There is not a lot of information available about this military facility. What is known is that the base spans an area of approximately four square kilometers and already had fifty-two helipads as of 1999. It was visited by President George Bush in 2001 and Vice President Joe Biden in 2009. In 2018, the commander of the base was Colonel Nick Ducich, an American of Serbian descent.

The Federal Republic of Yugoslavia (FRY) and Serbia Desired NATO Membership

Beginning in 1996, Milošević was attempting to secure NATO membership for both the Federal Republic of Yugoslavia (FRY) and Serbia. His closest associates—Milan Milutinović, the former Prime Minister of the FRY and President of Serbia; Momir Bulatović, another past Prime Minister of the FRY; and Nikola Šainović, the former Prime Minister of Serbia and Vice President of the FRY—discussed this in multiple interviews. According to their statements, the proposal was extended to the U.S. several times from 1996 onwards, lastly during the negotiations in Rambouillet. Milošević proposed that the FRY join NATO, with the condition that Kosovo would remain part of Serbia in return. Concessions on mineral resources were also offered, alongside consent to establish Western military bases in Kosovo and throughout the FRY territory.

However, the U.S. rejected this initiative.

Bulatović thinks the reason lay in a broader agenda: "They needed that war," while Milutinović is more specific: "The idea was already in the talks with Holbrooke[116] in 1996, to go directly into NATO, not through the Partnership for Peace program, because I thought that in that context, many things would go differently. And they did, even up to 1998. It failed because it clearly didn't fit into a concept that was being prepared for other purposes. We wanted to avoid any conflict at all costs and resolve things differently."

America's rejection of the FRY's entry into NATO is a very interesting, even intriguing question. The decision to go to war instead—certainly opens up space for deeper exploration of geopolitical, strategic, and other interests that influenced the events in the Balkans. It seems that there were several reasons why the FRY was not admitted to the Western military alliance.

At first glance, the NATO airstrikes on the FRY, bypassing a UN Security Council decision, took advantage of a time of Russian weakness to send a strong message about the newly established primacy of the U.S. and NATO in the world. It is also clear that Milošević was politically and ideologically unacceptable and set a bad example for other countries that NATO sought to influence. The cause might lie in a broader agreement between Russia and the West about the division of influence among Balkan peoples. From this perspective, Russia traditionally exerts influence among Serbs, and the U.S., since the mid-1990s, holds significant sway among Kosovar Albanians.

So, one might reasonably consider this hypothesis: Milošević's offer for the FRY, along with Kosovo, to join NATO—with consent for the construction of military bases across its entire territory—was declined by the U.S. because a decision had already been made for a different scenario. The military presence of NATO in Kosovo, where Albanians make up a significant majority, would be achieved through another process in which airstrikes against the FRY would play a key role. If such a hypothesis is true, then the Federal Republic of Yugoslavia was divided along ethnic lines between two spheres: Serbs remained in the zone of Russian influence, while Albanians came into the sphere of American influence.

The idea that Milošević was too late with his initiative is supported by statements from several witnesses, including Milutinović and Šainović. They speak of how U.S. officials typically responded to repeated offers for the FRY to join NATO by saying, "that is not the topic now" and "the train has already left the station."

Therefore, it is essential to consider the following question: why did Milošević—who initially aspired to a political and military alliance between the Federal Republic of Yugoslavia and Serbia with Russia and Bel-

---

[116] Richard Holbrooke (1941-2010), an American diplomat and author, served as the special envoy for the Balkans under President Bill Clinton of the United States.

arus—begin attempting to reverse the course of events and switch sides starting from 1996? Did he already have knowledge then that Russia would relatively easily surrender Kosovo to the West due to other interests? Did Milošević, in the nick of time, attempt to extricate himself from Russia's embrace, preserve Serbia's integrity, and save himself by jumping onto the Western bandwagon? It's possible. But the West did not trust Milošević. He was politically spent and—as would soon become apparent—his time was rapidly running out.

Milošević's Departure:
The Serbian Democratic Revolution

Starting from 1991 and lasting until 2000, protests against Milošević's regime were constant, initiated by supporters of opposition parties as well as self-organized students, professors, artists, and a multitude of ordinary people expressing profound objections to the general degradation of society. The University of Belgrade repeatedly went on strike. In short, the broadest front against Milošević's absolutism and the disastrous policies he implemented consisted of democratically-minded Serbia. This primarily included the civic layers of society from urban areas. These people are typically characterized by tolerance and political passivity. They often abstain from voting, and only participate in protests when the situation is extremely concerning or life has become unbearable.

And during Milošević's rule, the conditions were indeed concerning, unacceptable, and unbearable. Impoverished and humiliated, democratic Serbia persistently and stoically endured the challenges posed by the regime for an entire decade. Sometimes the demonstrations lasted days or weeks, sometimes months. Often in the rain or snow. Day after day, every day. Most of these were protest marches through the streets of Belgrade and other major Serbian cities. During the broadcast of the central news program on state television, protesters would blow whistles or bang pots, creating an enormous racket. Regime-controlled media portrayed the protests as "destructive" or "traitorous" and drastically downplayed the number of participants in their reports, leading people to fight their lies with noise.

When protests swelled to tens of thousands, the regime would usually orchestrate street conflicts with the aid of its supporters (a "counter-rally") to justify the use of police cordons and special units to break up demonstrations. Beatings and arrests were frequent. Two assassination attempts were made on opposition leader Vuk Drašković. Ivan Stambolić, the former president of the Presidency of Serbia and Milošević's first political mentor and patron—who assisted his rise to power in 1987—was kidnapped and killed a month before the year 2000 presidential elections, ordered by the very top of the state. The reason? Rumors circulated that he could be the joint opposition's counter-candidate. Milošević assessed that Stambolić could potentially defeat him, and that was enough to order his elimination. This political assassination was carried out by members of the Special Operations Unit of the Serbian State Security Service. In a subsequent court proceeding, they were sentenced to a total of 137 years in prison.

Research suggested that Milošević could easily lose an election if the opposition was united and if the inexperienced Serbian opposition figures were guided on how to win an election. The West took on this role, but only after the disastrous actions of the regime in the previous decade had aided in achieving its main strategic objectives. A broader perspective on the course of events suggests that Milošević's disastrous policies and unfavorable character traits were useful in facilitating NATO's expansion into the Balkans and Central Europe.

When the time for change had ripened, the opposition and groups of young activists were provided ample logistical, marketing, and financial aid from the West—mainly through non-governmental organizations, the most significant of which was "Otpor" ("Resistance"). The pivotal presidential election was held on September 24th, in an atmosphere of broad support for opposition candidate Vojislav Koštunica. It seemed that everything would proceed smoothly and democratically. The opposition declared a narrow victory right in the first round. However, the state election commission announced that the opposition candidate had obtained 2% less than the necessary 50% of votes required for victory, thereby ordering a second round of elections.

This sequence of events ignited an unparalleled revolt in Serbia, leading to massive public demonstrations in all major cities. The citizens yearned for change, and there was a palpable sense in the air that a critical turning point had been reached. Facilities began to cease operation—power plants, factories, schools, universities. Serbia was effectively paralyzed. The number of protesters grew day by day. The critical mass would be reached on October 5th, 2000, when between five hundred thousand and a million people took to the streets of Belgrade to depose Slobodan Milošević.

***

I returned to Belgrade from my honeymoon in Greece on the evening of October 4th. Even the beauty of the island where we stayed couldn't completely distract us from following the events back home. We simply couldn't remain indifferent. The next morning, we went to the protests. My mother wanted to join as well. We parked our car near the Faculty of Mechanical Engineering and walked about a mile to the Parliament and Presidency—where the epicenter of the events was located. We encounter many people we know, and my chest swells with pride at the sheer number of us. I couldn't estimate the crowd's size, but it was several times larger than any protest I had participated in before.

As far as my gaze reaches, in all directions and towards every side street leading to the spacious square where I am, I see rivers of people arriving. It was magnificent, and I felt optimistic that something positive was about to happen. The crowd incessantly chanted, "He's finished!" I noticed a police helicopter in the sky. From the direction of the Radio Television of Serbia building, people are running, and there is commotion. People broke

Protesters in front of the Parliament building of the Federal Republic of Yugoslavia, during the October 5th Revolution.

through the police cordon and stormed the Assembly building. A stampede and surges of hundreds of thousands of people began—it was getting dangerous. Suddenly, tear gas was thrown at us from somewhere. We started to retreat along the boulevard toward the St. Mark's Church. I saw overturned, burning police cars. We moved with the crowd towards the church, but got caught in the intense clash between the police and demonstrators trying to take over the detested regime's Radio Television of Serbia building, which we dubbed "TV Bastille." The tear gas was so thick that we had trouble breathing. Not far from us, police and citizens were fighting. We tried to take cover. More tear gas. We ran as far away from the toxic gas cloud as possible. I lost my sight and began to choke—we held hands. We ran into a building, climbed the stairs as far from the entrance as possible, and exhausted and blinded, sat down on the steps. Gradually, we began to breathe more normally. Our eyes were red and swollen. After half an hour, we decided to rejoin the crowd. Some people were saying that the Television station had been taken over and the Assembly building was burning. We soon saw it for ourselves. Surprisingly, I didn't see many police officers.

Suddenly, from the direction of Takovska Street, a column of unmarked military Humvees[117] appears armed with heavy machine guns. A few uniformed individuals, who I couldn't discern as either military or police, stood on the rear platforms of these ominous-looking green and black vehicles. "If they start firing," I think, "there will be hundreds of casualties." The column stops. We look at them, and they look at us—a prolonged moment of uncertainty. Unexpectedly, the soldiers start laughing, removing their gas masks, and waving at the people. Drawn closer, I join a few others in climbing onto their vehicle to greet them. I am swept up in the emotions and euphoria: "Are they on our side?" I notice that these men bear no insignia on their uniforms. Holding onto the Humvee's railing, I naively ask them, "Who are you, guys?" They laugh. One looks at me and says, "We are the 'Written Off'"[118] On the vehicle floor, I spot about twenty hand grenades. I probably failed to hide my astonished expression, as it seems one of them noticed what I saw. I look at him, and he looks away. I think to myself: "They brought bombs against the crowd—who in their right mind would order that?" . I descend from the vehicle, offering them a few more supportive words, like "bravo guys!" A thought appears: "Am I insane for climbing onto these Humvees?"

In an instant, I realize that the end has come. It was the turning point. The power of the state had ceased to obey Milošević. The people around me come to the same realization—they are euphoric, filled with immense joy and relief. The system is collapsing before my eyes. I see 'regular' policemen, slightly scared, exchanging greetings with the same people they were fighting just moments ago. People are hugging them and patting them on the back in encouragement. The policemen are handing out their gas masks, presumably as souvenirs.

Only later did I find out that the heavily-armed, intimidating guys in the Humvees were members of the Unit for Special Operations (JSO), the most dangerous armed formation birthed by Milošević's regime, mainly composed of veterans from the wars in Croatia and Bosnia.

∗∗∗

The uncertainty lasted until the following day, October 6th, when the Russian Minister of Foreign Affairs, Igor Ivanov, unexpectedly appeared in Belgrade. He first met with the newly elected President Vojislav Koštunica, and then with Milošević. News agencies RIA and Interfax quoted Ivanov saying that he had "congratulated Koštunica on his election victory

---

[117] The High Mobility Multipurpose Wheeled Vehicle (HMMWV), colloquially known as the "Humvee."

[118] *Written Off* (1974), original title: "Otpisani" is a cult Yugoslav film and television series that depicts young guerrilla fighters in occupied Belgrade during World War II.

on behalf of President Putin." That same day, Interfax also conveyed the words of Russian Prime Minister Mikhail Kasyanov, who stated that the issue of asylum for Yugoslav President Milošević "has not been raised and is not being discussed." Kasyanov further added, "we are a long way from looking at the question in that way."[119]

The message was quite clear. The Russians let Milošević go down the drain. A few hours later, he appeared noticeably resigned on television, conceded defeat, and stated that he would "devote himself to his family and grandchildren."

He miscalculated. The majority of the remainder of his life would be spent in Scheveningen, in the detention unit of The Hague Tribunal, where he would be tried for war crimes committed during the Yugoslav wars. Remaining true to his principles until the end, he defended himself independently in court. He did not live to see the verdict. He died of a heart attack on March 11th, 2006, at the age of sixty-five.

Around two and a half months later, on June 3rd, 2006, his state project, the "shrunken" Yugoslavia, met its definitive end. Montenegro left the union with Serbia and went its own way.

Serbia was left alone, with a young and unstable democracy, burdened with the unresolved issue of Kosovo, in the process of slow and painstaking recovery from the devastating decade of Milošević's rule.

Today, more than two decades after Milošević's exit from the scene, attempts to objectively assess the consequences of his era continue. Despite the prevailing negative sentiment, there are opinions that Milošević successfully represented the interests of Bosnian Serbs during the Dayton Peace Negotiations, and that the establishment of the Republic of Srpska within Bosnia and Herzegovina is his greatest achievement of historical importance. However, the analysis indicates that Milošević could not have achieved this result on his own—it came about with the significant support of Russia and the consent of the West, as part of a broader agreement between these two powers on the redistribution of influence in the territories of the former Yugoslavia.

Post-Yugoslav Reconciliation

The Yugoslav Wars resulted in the creation of six independent and internationally recognized states, and one (Kosovo) that is still attempting to achieve this status. Following the bloody, prolonged, and deeply traumatic

---

[119] *Radio Free Europe/Radio Liberty.* "Serbia: The Fall Of Milošević." RFE/RL, October 6th, 2000. *https://www.rferl.org/a/1142255.html.* Accessed: July 14th, 2023.

disintegration of our homeland, we began to heal our own wounds and learn what it means to be alone and independent. The path of each state demonstrated peculiarities different from those of the others. It has been noted that former Yugoslavs carefully observe one another across fences— now state borders—monitoring the development of events among their recent compatriots. The Yugoslav cultural space continues to thrive, and this is not unexpected. In fact, it functions rather well, primarily in the realms of music, television, film, and theater. While it might surprise foreigners, many people from this region, despite everything that happened, still harbor sympathies and love for their ex-Yugoslav neighbors. I have personally witnessed this phenomenon several times, which usually manifests more readily in far-off places and more often among younger people.

I recall socializing in 2010 with a group of young men and women from the former Yugoslavia who worked on a Royal Caribbean cruise ship. Excellent professionals, they enthusiastically told me how they "stick together, as one," speak "our" language, and sing hits from Yugoslav pop and rock artists arm-in-arm during moments of relaxation. When I asked why they got along so well, cared for, and loved each other here, in the middle of the Pacific, but argue and divide back in the Balkans, I received a seemingly illogical answer that anyone from the former Yugoslavia would understand: "Well, over there—it's something else!"

Does this mean that the Balkan soil, the matrix in which the interests of world powers and religions are constantly clashing, represents the fate of the South Slavs? If displaced in a completely different environment, will they naturally exhibit cohesion due to their pronounced genetic and linguistic similarity? In my opinion—yes. And this is one of the key reasons why the Yugoslav idea still flickers and lives in some people.

But is it possible for reconciliation to occur at home, on the stormy Balkan crossroads?

Mutual Apologies

The process of reconciliation between Serbia, Croatia, and Bosnia and Herzegovina is ongoing, but unfortunately, it is progressing at a much slower pace than many had hoped. The wounds and traumas are deep and severe, with millions of displaced and uprooted people, many of whom have lost their loved ones. Nationalism, often falsely labeled as patriotism, is present on all sides. To some extent, such feelings compensate for the immense discomfort and fear of confronting responsibility. On the other hand, political elites often resort to invoking the ghosts of the past with sharper rhetoric. Populism, a "hard stance", and nationalistic rhetoric towards neighbors usually surface ahead of elections, for the sake of political points. In this way, painful memories of war are exploited, and people are re-traumatized. Negative feelings are dumped on generations of young people born after the wars. However, there are also bright examples and steps in the right direction.

During a meeting with the President of Croatia, Mesić, in Belgrade in 2003, the President of the State Union of Serbia and Montenegro, Svetozar Marović, said, "I want to apologize for all the harm that any citizen of Montenegro and Serbia has done, or caused, or committed to anyone in Croatia." Responding to Marović's gesture, Mesić went a step further, offering an apology to the Serbs for crimes committed in the distant past, referring to the crimes of the Ustaša: "I take this opportunity to accept this symbolic apology, and I, for my part, can say that I apologize to all those who have been hurt or harmed by citizens of Croatia, at any time and anywhere, misusing or acting against the law, or abusing their position. I say, at any time, anywhere."

The Presidents of Serbia and the State Union of Serbia and Montenegro, Tadić and Marović, apologized in Bosnia in 2004 and 2006. Tadić issued an apology to Croatia in 2007, and in 2010, the Croatian and Serbian presidents visited the monument to Croatian victims in Vukovar and exchanged apologies on behalf of their nations. In April 2010, the Croatian President Ivo Josipović said in the Parliament of Bosnia and Herzegovina that "he deeply regrets that the Republic of Croatia, through its policy in the 90s of the last century, contributed to the suffering of people and the divisions that still trouble us today."

On March 31st, 2010, the National Assembly of the Republic of Serbia passed a *Declaration of Condemnation of the Srebrenica Massacre*, in which it "strongly condemns the crime committed against the Bosniak population in Srebrenica in July 1995, in a manner determined by the judgment of the International Court of Justice." The document further condemns "all social and political processes and phenomena that have led to the formation of an awareness that the realization of one's national goals can be achieved through the use of armed force and physical violence against members of other nations and religions" and expresses "condolences and apologies to the families of the victims because not everything was done to prevent this tragedy."

This is the first and only condemnation at the parliamentary level to date. Although the final paragraph of the Declaration expresses hope "that the highest authorities of other states from the territory of the former Yugoslavia will condemn in this manner the crimes committed against members of the Serbian people…", this has not yet happened.

In an interview with Bosnian television BHT, in April 2013, the President of Serbia, Tomislav Nikolić, offered strong words of apology: "I kneel and ask for forgiveness for Serbia for the crime that was committed in Srebrenica. I apologize for the crimes that any individual from our people committed in the name of our state and our people."

Regrettably, apologies from political leaders to their neighbors have generally sparked heated debates in their home environments, condemnation from radical elements, and the loss of political points. Although these gestures are highly commendable, they have not been accompanied by informational and educational actions aimed at the broadest layers of the population. In a word, the political elites have never dared to mobilize ordinary people towards genuine reconciliation and forgiveness. Internal political reasons still prevent them from doing so today, as well as the unavoidable interests of external powers in the Balkans.

The International Criminal Tribunal
for the Former Yugoslavia (ICTY)

Established by United Nations Security Council Resolution No. 827 in 1993, this ad hoc court is located in The Hague, the Netherlands, which is why it is commonly referred to as the Hague Tribunal. It has indicted 161 individuals for crimes committed between 1991 and 2001 against members of various ethnic groups in Croatia, Bosnia and Herzegovina, Serbia, Kosovo, and the Former Yugoslav Republic of Macedonia. Among those prosecuted are people in the highest positions—heads of state, leaders of self-proclaimed republics, prime ministers, ministers and politicians, as well as numerous military and police leaders from the highest ranks to individuals of lower ranks. During 2021, investigative proceedings were ongoing for crimes committed by the KLA in Kosovo. Towards the end of 2020, the first indictments were raised against the highest leaders of Kosovo Albanians, including the President himself.

The majority of those prosecuted and convicted are Serbs, but judgments have also been handed down to Croats, Bosniaks, and Kosovo Albanians for crimes committed against Serbs and members of other nationalities. An important aspect of the International Court's work is the termination of the untouchable status of people in high positions, thereby sending a powerful message to leaders in future world conflicts. Quite rightly, the emphasis has been placed on individual guilt, thus protecting nations from the label of collective responsibility.

The Tribunal's website states the following: "The International Court has contributed to the undisputed establishment of historical facts, fighting against the denial of truth and helping communities confront their recent past."

In the states of the former Yugoslavia, there are very divided opinions on whether the Hague Tribunal has contributed to or hindered reconciliation in the region. Its supporters are mainly found in the circles of the international community and believe that it has absolutely justified its role. However, this court is very poorly accepted where it was most important—among the main actors of the Yugoslav wars. Political elites bear a large part of the responsibility for this fact. However, there is also responsibility on the side of the Tribunal. Surveys have shown that a majority of Serbs and Croats challenge the integrity and impartiality of the court due to certain acquittals or reduced sentences that have caused strong reactions in these republics.

In Croatia, for example, they are very dissatisfied with the acquittal of Serbian General Perišić, who was the Chief of the General Staff of the Yugoslav Army during the war, or the reduction of the sentence for Lieutenant Colonel Šljivančanin for crimes in Vukovar.

Resistance is strongest in Serbia, even though public opinion generally accepts the knowledge that Serbs committed the largest number of crimes during the Yugoslav wars. In that republic, there is a widespread view that the Tribunal discredited itself with certain decisions that demonstrated bias against Serbs or the state of Serbia. This primarily refers to the process against Croatian generals Gotovina and Markač for crimes against Serb civilians in Operation Storm. They were initially sentenced to twenty-four and eighteen years in prison, respectively, and then acquitted a year later. Two high-ranking judges, Pokar and Agius, publicly opposed the overturning of verdicts and expressed their deep disagreement.

A similar sentiment is held in Serbia towards the case against the KLA leader Ramush Haradinaj, who was charged with crimes in Kosovo and then acquitted, as well as the absence of indictments for the trafficking of human organs of captive Serbs during the Kosovo war. In both instances, the court cited a lack of evidence as the official reason, a point which is disputed in Serbia.

Dr. David Harland, an immediate witness of the war events in Bosnia and Herzegovina and the Executive Director of the Centre for Humanitarian Dialogue in Geneva, also believes that the court has found it easier to convict Serbian crimes than the crimes of Croats, Bosniaks, or Kosovo Albanians, who are "friends of the West". In his article "Selective Justice for the Balkans"[120], published in The New York Times in 2012, he wrote:

---

[120] Harland, David. "Selective Justice for the Balkans." *The New York Times*, December 7th, 2012. Accessed July 15th, 2023.
https://www.nytimes.com/2012/12/08/opinion/global/selective-justice-for-the-balkans.html.

Too bad if you were a Serb victim of any crime in the former Yugoslavia. More Serbs were displaced—ethnically cleansed—by the wars in the Balkans than any other community. And more Serbs remain ethnically displaced to this day. Almost no one has been held to account, and it appears that no one will be.

The United Nations war crimes tribunal in The Hague has acquitted Ramush Haradinaj, Kosovo's former prime minister, of war crimes. Last month, it acquitted on appeal the generals who led Croatia to victory over the Serbs.

Altogether, almost all of the West's friends have been acquitted; almost all of the Serbs have been found guilty. These results do not reflect the balance of crimes committed on the ground...

...I have no sympathy with the Serbs who have been convicted. On the contrary. I lived through the siege of Sarajevo. I served as a witness for the prosecution in the cases against the former Serbian president, Slobodan Milosevic, the wartime leader of the Bosnian Serbs, Radovan Karadzic, and, most recently, the Bosnian Serb military commander, Ratko Mladic, who is accused of ordering the massacre at Srebrenica.

The Serbs committed many of the war's worst crimes, but were not at all alone, and it is not right, or useful, for them to carry the sole responsibility. Convicting only Serbs simply doesn't make sense in terms of justice, in terms of reality, or in terms of politics...

... What has happened at the tribunal is far from justice, and will be interpreted by observers in the Balkans and beyond as the continuation of war by legal means—with the United States, Germany and other Western powers on one side, and the Serbs on the other.

This will amplify the worst political instincts of the peoples of the former Yugoslavia: the persecution complex of the Serbs; the triumphalism of the Croats; the sense of victimization of the Bosnian Muslims; the vindication of the Kosovar Albanian quest for racial purity. Each of these traits has some basis in truth, and each has been exaggerated and manipulated by politicians on all sides.

Nothing in life is completely black or completely white— it always comes down to shades of gray. The same applies to the Hague Tribunal. It's certain that there have been some errors or inconsistencies in its work, as well as compromises influenced by high-level politics. However, it's undeniable that this international court has given a voice to an enormous number of victims of all nationalities, established many facts, and, to some degree, delivered justice. It has indeed helped Yugoslavs to "confront their recent past," but it has become clear that the readiness of elites to truly lead their people down this path was mostly lacking.

Could it have been done better? Absolutely. Did the UN Security Council make a mistake by establishing the Hague Tribunal? It seems not. A step has been made towards elevating international humanitarian law to a higher level, a development that can have a positive impact on the participants and course of future wars.

Reconciliation of Serbia and the West

Since 2009, high-ranking officials of the United States and NATO, such as Joseph Biden, then Vice President of the United States, and Secretary-General of the Alliance Jens Stoltenberg, have expressed regret for civilian casualties during the NATO bombing of the Federal Republic of Yugoslavia in 1999 and offered condolences to the families of the victims. The latest in a series of apologies to Serbia from the West came from diplomatic representatives of France, Germany, the Netherlands, Norway, Italy, Canada, the United Kingdom, and the United States on the 20th anniversary of the NATO bombing in 2019, by laying wreaths at the monument to the fallen. In their statement, they said they "remember March 24th as the day when diplomacy failed" and expressed "regret for civilian casualties during the events of 1999."

However, very few Serbian citizens are aware of such gestures by Western countries. They receive very little media attention and are largely ignored. In contrast, anti-NATO and anti-Western propaganda is very prevalent in the media. The traumas that the Alliance inflicted on the Serbs, which are, unfortunately, not minor, are continuously revived in the public discourse, thus maintaining a high level of restimulation. From personal experience, I testify that the NATO bombing was a horrific experience in which, according to data published by the Humanitarian Law Center in 2014, 754 people of all nationalities lost their lives—454 civilians and 300 members of the armed forces.[121]

On the other hand, it is important to note that in the First and Second World Wars, at least 1,800,000 Serbs perished, and, for example, the German Luftwaffe killed at least five times more Serbian civilians during a

---

[121] According to the records of the Humanitarian Law Center (HLC) and HLC Kosovo, a total of 754 people lost their lives in the NATO attacks, including 454 civilians and 300 members of the armed forces. Among the civilians, there were 207 ethnic Serbs and Montenegrins, 219 ethnic Albanians, 14 Roma, and 14 members of other ethnic groups. In total, 274 members of the Yugoslav Army/Ministry of Internal Affairs (VJ/MUP) died, along with 26 members of the Kosovo Liberation Army (KLA). Source: *https://www.hlc-rdc.org/?cat=266*. Accessed on May 11th, 2021.

single day of bombing on April 6th, 1941, than NATO did throughout the 78-day campaign. Nevertheless, the tragic events of 1999 were a kind of precedent that shocked and deeply wounded the Serbs, resulting in a strong animosity towards the NATO alliance. Thus, today in Serbia, the memory of the NATO bombing is mostly overshadowed by memories of other, incomparably greater human losses and material destruction that occurred earlier in the 20th century.

In the creation and fostering of negative Serbian sentiment towards NATO, analysts see Russia's involvement, which pursues its interest in keeping Serbia committed to the proclaimed course of military neutrality, and also ensuring Bosnia and Herzegovina remains outside of NATO. While this is undoubtedly in Russia's interest, such lobbying creates obstacles to the reconciliation process in the region. A new knot has been tied in Bosnia and Herzegovina, where there is no consensus on security policy. The Croat and Bosniak peoples desire NATO membership, but the Serbian entity—Republika Srpska denies consent. Thus, the Serbs have once again cast themselves in the role of proxies of Russia, while everyone else are friends, or rather, proxies of the West. The situation on the ground is such that Serbia and BiH are, as of 2021, completely surrounded by NATO. All other former Yugoslav states, as well as all neighboring countries, are members of the Western military alliance. Is such a position in Serbian interest? Historical experience says it is not, but it is justified by Russia's blocking of Kosovo in international bodies and organizations. In this way, Russia maintains Serbia's formal territorial integrity in the UN Security Council, and this is its key lever of power for exerting influence over the Serbs. If Serbia were to join NATO, it is believed, Russia's "nyet" for full membership of Kosovo in the UN could be withdrawn.

In Serbian public discourse, the fact that Serbia has very close cooperation with NATO and has signed agreements that give it a status only one step lower than full membership is relatively little exposed. Time will tell which way the competition between the West and Russia in the Balkans will break. In this game, Serbia has willingly positioned itself between a hammer and an anvil, trying to arrive at a favorable "package solution" that would benefit its interests in Kosovo and Bosnia and Herzegovina through a "sitting on two chairs" policy. In the context of such "package" political maneuvering, if there is a shared desire among the involved parties to attain a mutually beneficial outcome (win-win scenario), it is not implausible to envision Serbia opting to increase its proximity to NATO as it progresses towards full membership in the European Union.

General, Historical Reconciliation?

Sustainable reconciliation in the Balkans has so far been impossible due to the ceaseless clash of powerful political interests, which this book discusses from its opening pages. The inhabitants of the Balkans have largely been instrumentalized by the forces striving to realize these interests. The integrative spirit, abandonment of tribalism, and transcendence of religion—three likely most significant virtues of the Yugoslav idea—have shown the path towards changing the paradigm and overcoming this challenging situation. Although it seemed—during the first two decades of Tito's era—that things were moving in the right direction, it turned out that neither internal factors nor foreign ones had an interest in the materialization of the Yugoslav idea into a strong and unified Yugoslav super-nation. For a complex and comprehensive process of reconciliation among the peoples of the former Yugoslavia, the political will of their leaders is necessary. They do not express this, both due to internal reasons and the influence of external interests with which they align. Nationalistic rhetoric and the creation of "external enemies"—a strategy steeped in tradition—are employed to distract from poor governance or corruption scandals. Given the ongoing influence of external factors, a renowned rock musician from the former Yugoslavia once said, "The international community must enable us to reconcile; it needs to leave the Balkans." His viewpoint is well-intentioned, but regrettably naive. The international community has been clashing in the Balkans practically since the Roman Empire was divided into East and West. There's no basis in historical observation to suggest that the rivalry of the great powers in this strategically and geopolitically important area will simply cease on its own. However, the fact that all Balkan countries are either members of the European Union or on their way to becoming members offers a reason for moderate optimism.

The process of general reconciliation could begin by educating the South Slavic peoples about the strategic and geopolitical significance of the region in which they live, and the mechanisms that make them proxies in the games of powerful forces. The more they know about this, the harder it will be for them to accept the imposed role. In this endeavor, expert circles should play a crucial role.

Parallel to education, efforts toward deep and comprehensive reconciliation—which must include forgiveness in its initial phase—are necessary. The formerly warring peoples of the ex-Yugoslavia are often overly informed about the crimes committed against them by members of other nations during the tragic wars and conflicts of the past. However, there is a

437

significant lack of awareness in the opposite direction—understanding the crimes their own people have committed against others. The adoption of joint declarations about past events by Serbian, Croatian, Bosniak, Kosovar, and other Yugoslav scholars would be of invaluable significance. Such initiatives have begun to timidly emerge. This collective endeavor by scholars and professionals would create the precondition for the commencement of the forgiveness process, a step without which reconciliation is impossible.

People's traumas cannot be suppressed; they do not vanish with the passage of time, nor do they "fade," as many might believe. Traumas delve into the collective unconscious, where they lie in wait, explosively surfacing when the right historical conditions present themselves. We saw this phenomenon manifest in the Bosnian War, but it can also be seen elsewhere around the world. A notable example is the enduring tensions that suppressed traumas from the time of the American Civil War still generate in that society more than a century and a half later.

The resolution of trauma can only occur if the once conflicting groups turn to sincerely experiencing the pain they have inflicted on others. Such an approach is implemented in German education, here is an example:

At the start of the lesson, the teacher tells the children how in 1937, special police broke into an old man's apartment in the neighborhood, ordered him to come with them, and gave him a mere fifteen minutes to pack his belongings. Then, the teacher places a small old suitcase on the desk. The children are asked to compile a list of things they would put into the suitcase they are observing, as if they were in the shoes of this gentleman. The pupils object and struggle. When the allotted time expires, the teacher explains that the neighbor was called Lieberman and that he was taken to a concentration camp where his suitcase items were confiscated and he was killed for being Jewish.

In other words, any true reconciliation should start from us, not from our "enemies". Definitely not from the logic present among traumatized Yugoslavs, which roughly translates to: "Let them apologize to us first, then we'll see". In the case of the former Yugoslavia, a winning strategy would imply that Serbs, Croats, Bosniaks, and Kosovo Albanians should first sincerely confront their own sins committed against the "enemies" at any time, and relive those traumas by empathizing with them, as in the German example. Only then would the conditions gradually be created for mutual forgiveness, leading naturally to reconciliation.

Another indispensable factor that must be incorporated into the process of broad reconciliation involves the return of all displaced and expelled individuals, without exception, on all sides. This must happen with the active and sincere participation of all states of the former Yugoslavia. The violent demographic changes that occurred during the Yugoslav wars need to be reversed. The return of all displaced and expelled individuals must be ensured, and in specific cases where this is not possible, suitable compensation should be provided. In addition, all victims, on all sides, must be objectively accounted for, and the lists must be made publicly available. There needs to be a more concerted effort towards reaffirming the values of civil society and embracing diversity across the entire war-torn region.

In conclusion, words of apology from officials, though significant, cannot alone lead to the reconciliation for which they ostensibly advocate. We need a more comprehensive and profound approach, some courage, and a genuine desire from all sides. Only through this can we collectively heal, restore mutual respect and solidarity, and achieve a level of cooperation similar to that shared by the Scandinavian nations today.

Another prerequisite for healing processes that could lead to widespread reconciliation and progress is undoubtedly the assurance of peace in the Balkans. This could be achieved through a collective security policy adopted by all states. In the near future, NATO—already incorporating all Balkan countries except Serbia and Bosnia and Herzegovina[122]—seems to be a realistic solution for such a scenario. This means that we currently have a situation that constitutes a historical precedent, a phenomenon that hasn't been seen in this region since the time of the unified Roman Empire.

From Slovenia in the west to Turkey in the east, and from the Sava and Danube in the north to Greece in the south, almost all are part of the same military alliance and are contractually obligated not to wage war against each other. Therefore, only a global conflict of substantial magnitude could trigger turbulence in the traditionally volatile Balkans at this point, not local wars, which have been the case for centuries. Is NATO on the path to effectively dismantling the "powder keg of Europe", as the Balkans is often referred to? If the current situation can endure the test of time, it is quite plausible that a period of stability could foster economic and cultural development in the Balkan states, which has been disrupted by frequent conflicts in the past. This is undoubtedly an exciting possibility with exceptional potential.

However, it's a fact that the historical reconciliation of the former Yugoslav nations does not align with certain state, economic, military or religious interests. Yet, it's perhaps in this very fact that additional motivation to strive toward reconciliation should be found. Achieving such reconciliation would undoubtedly create a qualitatively different balance of forces that perpetually sweep across the strategic crossroads of the Balkans.

---

[122] Author's note: as of the time of writing, 2024, they remain militarily neutral.

INSTEAD OF
CONCLUSION

Was Yugoslavia a Mistake?

On this issue, intense debates are held across the entire former Yugo-slav region and beyond, among researchers worldwide. It's impossible to provide a clear-cut and definitive answer; instead, there are various schools of thought characterized by different perspectives. It is noticeable that the tone of today's discussions still bears a strong echo of the wars of the 1990s. The prevailing view in post-Yugoslav societies today is that Yugo-slavia was a significant mistake. However, deeper analysis reveals that matters are neither simple nor black-and-white.

In Serbia, the perspective that the creation of Yugoslavia was the "greatest Serbian delusion of the 20th century" is pronounced. There's a widespread belief that Serbs were betrayed, tricked, and deceived in that state—implying that Yugoslavia served as a transitional solution for other nations, to the detriment of the Serbs. King Alexander and other politicians are blamed for not exploiting the momentum of Serbian victories in World War I and reaching for a Greater Serbia, which may have been within grasp thanks to the allies' will expressed in the Treaty of London of 1915. The Serbs laid their Kingdom of Serbia on the altar of Yugoslavia, believ-ing they were making the historically most appropriate decision under the given circumstances.

They opted for the creation of Yugoslavia with the intention of resolv-ing the most vital national interest—integrating the territorially scattered Serbian people. However, the result was highly unfavorable for them. The Serbs entered Yugoslavia fragmented and ultimately exited it fragmented, failing to achieve national and territorial integration. They endured massive casualties in both world wars, fighting for the unification and survival of Yugoslavia. In the years of its dissolution, they gained a negative reputa-tion attempting to forcibly preserve it, led by ideologically anachronistic leadership. By aligning with Moscow and the East, Milošević and the Yu-goslav People's Army stood in opposition to the geopolitical and strategic interests of the West, which was experiencing the pinnacle of its military and political dominance on a global scale during that era. So far, a high price has been paid for such policies at the expense of Serbian national, territorial, and historically grounded interests. Serbia emerged from the Yugoslav wars weakened and facing the difficult issue of Kosovo, but it established special relations with the Republic of Srpska in Bosnia and Herzegovina. Considering all of the aforementioned factors, it is completely understandable that the prevailing view in Serbia leans towards the belief that Yugoslavia was a mistake.

***

The impression is that the Croats always felt confined in Yugoslavia. Their animosity towards the South Slavic state project is even more pronounced, but the reasons for it are diametrically opposed to the Serbian perspective. Most often, it is argued that the Croats were subjected to Serbian hegemony.

The Croat people were at the forefront of centrifugal tendencies. During the kingdom era, these manifested as secessionism, while during the socialist Yugoslavia period, they emerged as aspirations for decentralization and the strengthening of federalism. Ultimately, these aspirations evolved into advocacy for the state to transform from a federation into an "asymmetric federation" of Croatia and Slovenia on one hand, and all other states on the other, or even to be reorganized as a pure confederation.

Croatia is the only one among all the states of former Yugoslavia that has incorporated a ban on unification with other South Slavic peoples into its highest legal act. In the Croatian constitution, in Article 135, Paragraph 2, it states:

> "It is forbidden to initiate the procedure of associating the Republic of Croatia with other states in which the association would or could lead to the renewal of Yugoslav state unity, or some Balkan state union in any form".

However, such an exclusive and negative stance is at odds with apparent historical gains. In 1918, thanks to the Serbs, the Croatian people managed to preserve Dalmatia from Italy. Later, they were the only ones in the Kingdom of Yugoslavia to gain special status—the autonomous Banovina of Croatia—in 1939.

Despite the existence of the fascist Independent State of Croatia, with its genocidal policies towards Serbs, Jews, Roma, and political opponents, as well as its historical and military defeat, these transgressions proceeded without severe consequences.

Following World War II, the Socialist Republic of Croatia was established as an equal federal unit within the Socialist Federal Republic of Yugoslavia. Furthermore, the Socialist Republic of Croatia territorially expanded to include Istria and part of Dalmatia, thereby achieving the historical integration of Croats in areas that were previously part of Italy. The undisputed leader and lifelong head of the Yugoslav state, Marshal Tito, was a Croat. Several Yugoslav constitutional changes after 1962 gradually strengthened the sovereignty of the republics while weakening the jurisdiction of the federation—all were enacted either at the initiative of or with the consent of Croatian politicians. These were the steps in which the Croat people completed the formation of their sovereign nation and state. This process was finalized by exiting Yugoslavia in 1991, with the support of Germany, and gaining full membership in the UN in 1992.

One consequence of the war from 1991 to 1995 was the national homogenization of the Croats, which necessitated a distancing from the Yugoslav idea. Additionally, this conflict resulted in ethnic and ideological uniformity in Croatia as at least 220,000 Croatian Serbs—loyal supporters of the Yugoslav idea and state—fled from it in 1995.

If the representatives of the Croatian people in 1918 had not decided, together with the Slovenes, to enter into a Yugoslav union with the Serbs, it is very likely that the current outcome for them would not have been as favorable, but rather much more modest. Croatia would have occupied significantly less territory, and according to some opinions, might have even been divided between Italy, Austria, and Hungary. Of course, these are speculations, and one can't definitively ascertain what would have truly happened, but it seems that entering the Yugoslav union was then in the highest national interest of the Croats. Therefore, I hope that in future times, when the echo of the recent wars finally subsides, we'll see an evolution towards a more comprehensive, realistic, and sincere perception of the Yugoslav state in Croatian public.

***

The Slovenes, as the smallest of the three founding nations of Yugoslavia, had the greatest interest in joining it. They lived divided in several regions within Austria and Italy, and their primary national idea was to create a unified Slovenia as an entity within a larger state. It was only towards the end of the existence of Austria-Hungary that they took up arms and, with crucial assistance from Serbian troops, liberated themselves from the Austrians at the end of World War I. However, the other half of what is now Slovenia had already been occupied by the Italians under the provisions of the secret Treaty of London. That likely would have remained the case if Yugoslav unification had not come into play, with the military and political support of the Serbian leadership. I remember the response given by former Slovenian dissident, prominent politician, and Foreign Minister Dimitrij Rupel to a Radio Free Europe journalist: "But, excuse me, if Slovenia did not enter Yugoslavia in 1918, it would not exist today as a nation-state, would it?" the journalist asked. "That is correct," Rupel replied succinctly.[123]

By joining the Kingdom of Serbs, Croats, and Slovenes, the Slovenes were able to preserve and unify their territories and people, avoiding assimilation. They became one of the three equal peoples founding the new state, and soon had a significant role in its governance. Concurrently, the maturation of the Slovene nation and strengthening of their national identity proceeded. Throughout this process, there was noticeable Slovenian concern about losing their language and culture—essentially, their readiness for political, but not cultural, unity with others. This stance remained unchanged until the end, significantly influencing Slovenian nationalism in the later phases of Yugoslavia.

Although Slovenia saw the resolution to their national question within the confines of Yugoslavia in the first decades after World War II, their vision of its internal arrangement was entirely different from what suited the Serbs. Similar to the Croats, the Slovenes could only accept Yugoslavia as a loose federation or confederation of independent national states.

Starting from the mid-1980s, Slovenia began democratization through alternative culture, youth political activism, civil society, and resistance to the dogmas of dying socialism. Slovenes desired multiparty democracy and inclusion in the sweeping changes blowing strongly across Europe. Expectedly, Slovenia did not see itself in an undemocratic Yugoslavia dominated by Milošević and old-school generals leaning towards Russia, so they put up a strong resistance.

With a successful operation to break away from Yugoslavia, together with Croatia and backed by Germany and Austria, the Slovenes achieved sovereign, independent statehood for the first time in their history. They became a full UN member in 1992, and later joined the EU and NATO. Their joy and patriotism manifested in economic successes and the management of their small country, adorned with untouched nature, abundant forests, blue-green lakes, and the snow-covered peaks of the Julian Alps. Slovenia has been ranked among the cleanest countries in the world multiple times in recent years.

Was Yugoslavia a mistake for the Slovenes? Certainly not, quite the opposite. The aforementioned Slovenian politician Mr. Rupel said about this: "I think we need to be very careful and fair here. Yugoslavia helped the Slovenes. Honestly, I believe that in Yugoslavia, we were able to create many things that we couldn't have otherwise."[124]

---

[123] Interview: "Rupel: Slovenci su bili kao na studentskoj ekskurziji u Jugoslaviji" (Rupel: Slovenes Were Like on a School Trip in Yugoslavia), *Radio Free Europe*, series "Sto godina Jugoslavije" (One Hundred Years of Yugoslavia), November 12th, 2018.
[124] Ibid.

***

The Macedonians also made gigantic strides during the existence of Yugoslavia, achieving similar gains to the Slovenes. From being an unrecognized people in the region of Southern or Old Serbia at the start of the 20th century, to becoming an equal federal unit as the Socialist Republic of Macedonia in Tito's Yugoslavia and having their status as a people recognized, all the way to a peaceful exit from the common state and international recognition. After resolving the dispute with Greece over its name, today's Macedonian people has its own national state, a member of the UN and NATO, under the name of the Republic of North Macedonia.

***

The Bosniaks made significant progress towards nation-building within Yugoslavia. Initially, they were treated as Serbs of Muslim faith, but their persistent fight for recognition and acknowledgment of their distinctiveness resulted in achieving the status of a separate ethnic group—first under the name "Muslims" in the early 1970s, and later as "Bosniaks". The dissolution of Yugoslavia and the tragic war in Bosnia and Herzegovina, in which they were the greatest victims, did not yield them a national state or separate republic as this was prevented by high-level politics. However, they are one of the three equal constituent peoples in Bosnia and Herzegovina and have an entity they share with the Bosnian Croats. The Bosniaks rightly cherished Tito's Yugoslavia, as it granted them emancipation and equality.

***

Montenegro has completely restored its statehood, which, like Serbia, it incorporated into the Kingdom of Serbs, Croats, and Slovenes in 1918. Today, this state is home to just over 600,000 inhabitants, and those who identify as ethnic Montenegrins make up only about half of that number. Although they are genetically, ethnically, and religiously almost identical to the Serbs, they enjoyed the status of a full-fledged people and a separate federal unit in Tito's Yugoslavia. In the post-war period, Montenegro was economically behind other, more developed republics, but it benefited from development funds. It succeeded in building tourist and transportation infrastructure, as well as emancipating and modernizing its society. After the catastrophic earthquake that struck it in 1979, Montenegro enjoyed a decade of solidary aid from all over Yugoslavia.

Montenegrin cadres were highly represented in the army, security sector, and leadership positions in Yugoslav enterprises. They remained loyal to Serbia in the post-Yugoslav project, but in the end, the desire for life in an independent and sovereign state prevailed among Montenegrins too, which was realized in 2006. This status naturally further strengthens Montenegrin national feelings and differentiation from the Serbs. It is highly likely that in the future, the tendency to fully consolidate the formation of a nation through the struggle for the recognition of the Montenegrin Orthodox Church[125] by other Orthodox churches will continue to be evident. Today, in 2023, Montenegro is on the path to full membership in the EU and is a member of NATO.

---

[125] This process has been unfolding for decades in North Macedonia, where the Macedonian Orthodox Church (MOC) existed unrecognized for a long time because the Orthodox world recognized the jurisdiction of the Serbian Orthodox Church (SOC) in North Macedonia. However, the SOC decided to recognize the autocephaly (independence) of the MOC recently, in May 2022. On the other hand, the SOC strongly opposes recognizing the autocephaly of the Montenegrin Orthodox Church.

The Incurable Wound of Primary Conflict

Before the creation of Yugoslavia, I perceive the South Slavs as individual ethnic entities, akin to atoms, that would eventually combine to
form a more intricate structure—a molecule. The post-World War I political circumstances provided an ideal environment for this transformative
process to take place.

The Yugoslav dream inspired many individuals to embark on a noble
and audacious endeavor of creating a new nation and state. Over a significant period of time, a tremendous amount of positive energy was invested
in forming and preserving the 'molecule' that symbolized the Yugoslav nation. Hundreds of thousands of lives were lost in two world wars in pursuit
of Yugoslav ideals. Generations of people dedicated their best efforts to
rebuild and construct their shared homeland, ensuring its growth and development.

How great was the energy invested by many generations? Can we
roughly measure it? Perhaps. One of the fundamental laws of physics says,
"Energy cannot be created or destroyed; it can only change the form of its
existence." Let's apply this as a basis for the following perspective: when
the partially formed, still loose molecule of the Yugoslav nation was violently broken down into ethnic atoms, a huge amount of energy exploded
in the form of a brutal fratricidal war. If the process of creating a nation
involved the addition of positive and integrative aspirations over several
decades, then the death of that nation brought self-destruction on the same
scale. There was a sudden release of energy through hatred and anger,
tragedy and war, which shocked the world, as well as us Yugoslavs. After
the complete disintegration of the molecule, only atoms remained on the
stage. Today, all Yugoslavs live in their independent and small atom-states.

Among all the South Slavs, there were sympathizers of the idea of Yugoslav unification. Initially, these were mostly intellectuals and artists,
people with liberal views, avant-gardists, idealists, and romantics. Many of
them clearly saw the practical advantages of unification: why should we
remain divided and fragmented, mostly on a religious basis, as before?
Why should we continue to be easy prey for powerful neighbors? Overcoming historical and religious divisions and uniting into a new, strong,
and powerful South Slav nation that we could be proud of—this seemed to
these people a logical and natural line of thought. All together—it means
much more strength, a larger territory, a larger market, lasting stability, a
better economy, diversity, cultural richness... In short, in the eyes of its
supporters, the Yugoslav state was a grand, evolutionary, emancipatory,

and logical idea for which they were ready to sacrifice. Emotionally and wholeheartedly, in a way that only the Balkan Slavs know how.

However, we have shown that from the beginning of the 20th century, two diametrically opposed goals are clearly observed among the peoples who will form Yugoslavia. These largely arise from the different levels of development of the constituent peoples and, consequently, opposing aspirations. Past events, as well as looking from today's perspective, show that this primary conflict was impossible to avoid. In simplest terms, the "Yugoslavia project" had an internal rift from its earliest days, manifested through simultaneous centrifugal and centripetal tendencies of its peoples. The Serbs and Croats found themselves on different sides of the front line. The rest tried to find their interest in this confrontation, and it determined which side they would lean toward.

Yugoslav unitarianism and Yugoslav secessionism coexisted even before the state was born. We observe them during World War I in disagreements between the Serbian government and the Yugoslav Committee about the future structure of the state, and even much earlier in discussions of intellectuals and politicians who sincerely wanted to create Yugoslavia. After its creation, the unitarian concept prevailed, bringing with it an ideological environment for the gradual creation of a new nation through the doctrine of Integral Yugoslavism. However, as a response and a kind of counterweight, secessionism appeared on the political stage practically immediately.

The creation of a unified nation was crucial for the success of the Yugoslav project. However, this did not happen, resulting in slim chances for the state's long-term survival. The transformation of the Serbs, Croats, Slovenes, and all others into Yugoslavs was a significant challenge. It demanded that nations, who had always defined their identity through a sense of ethnic belonging, now embrace a new national and state project and tie their identity to it.

The progression towards an integral supra-nation had the potential to yield significant gains, with the most crucial one being the elimination of centuries-long conflicts among the South Slavs, which had been fueled by their role as proxies for big powers. This would lead to extended periods of internal stability, economic strengthening, and cultural development. However, this kind of quantum leap demanded a high price: the gradual and conscious allowance of ethnic blending within the framework of "one nation with three names." Time has shown that none of the South Slavic nations—except partially the Serbs—were ready to pay this price. The concept of blending peoples, which succeeded in America—did not succeed in the Balkans.

For a nation to be adequately prepared for unification on more complex levels, such as a federation or union, it first needs to achieve its own statehood independently and live that collective experience over a sufficiently long period until it reaches overall national maturity. This is the ideal scenario. Only then is a nation ready to sacrifice part of its sovereignty in favor of association with others and the gains that come with it. At the time of unification, only the Serbs already had a duration in a fully formed state. Therefore, their development logically moved towards consolidation by including other South Slavic nations and, of course, ethnic Serbs from Austria-Hungary. The Serbs, as a nation, were more prepared for integration. Such a starting point gave them a completely different perspective compared to other Yugoslavs.

Following this line of thinking, it can be concluded that the vast majority of Croats and Slovenes were not ready for a 'marriage' with the Serbs and the acceptance of the Yugoslav paradigm because these peoples had not previously established their modern national states. Although many of them felt sympathies towards the ideals of Yugoslavism, the achievement of a national-based, internationally recognized state was their priority goal. This is natural, expected, and quite clear. In this light, it is obvious why, from the earliest years of its existence, most Croats and Slovenes perceived Yugoslavia as a transitional solution—a necessary station on the path to achieving full national and state sovereignty, waiting for a favorable historical moment.

And yet, many Serbian advocates of the unitary concept mostly refused to see and understand the aspirations of the Croats and Slovenes in the right way. Sweeping things 'under the rug' is never a good strategy. Suppressed problems eventually resurface, as was demonstrated in Yugoslavia, in a very unpleasant way.

The fundamental Yugoslav misunderstanding was brilliantly described by Serbian historian Predrag Marković, saying:

"Generations of Serbs believed that Yugoslavs would become a unified nation, at least in a multicultural, American way. What seemed to Serbs like a fraternal embrace, often felt like suffocation to others".

The 'clamp' of the Serbian unitary concept, although motivated by strengthening the state and unity of the Yugoslavs, paradoxically, enhanced the nationalisms of other peoples and accelerated the process of their independence. For them, Yugoslavia was a temporary "safe house", where they were building, strengthening and affirming their identity and attributes of statehood.

The Gordian knot of constant conflict between unitarists and secession-ists drained the life force of Yugoslavia from its birth to its ultimate death. If our reasoning up to this point is correct, it leads us to a sad and sobering conclusion:

Yugoslavia never had a chance to survive. Although it was a valu-able idea, most Yugoslavs were not ready for it.

The preponderance of desires to create ethnically based national states clearly explains why Yugoslav nationalism never prevailed in Yugoslavia. The Yugoslav project failed in the most important thing—to create Yugo-slavs, and therefore its end was inevitable.

Remaining faithful to observation from different perspectives, we can conclude that Yugoslavia served as a kind of incubator for small and frag-mented South Slavic peoples. It provided them with protection and enabled gradual growth in political, economic, and cultural terms until they were ripe for the final phase of rounding off national identity through the crea-tion of independent states.

In this light, it is clearly seen that the disintegration of Yugoslavia was a completely logical and expected process, which produced new states and nations and brought emancipation and sovereignty to peoples who have never had them before. If we recall what the initial position of the op-pressed, occupied, and fragmented South Slavs was before the First World War, we must conclude that this is an excellent result achieved in less than eighty years. It is fair and necessary to note that it would have been com-pletely absent without the Serbs, and that only for them the ultimate out-come is significantly more unfavorable than the position they had at the beginning.

The future, however, may bring a new turnaround. After several dec-ades during which all Yugoslav peoples will mature in their sovereign states, the evolutionary and integrative idea of Yugoslavism can become relevant again in appropriate historical circumstances. If that happens, there is a basis to expect that integration would then rest on healthier and completely different foundations.

Utopia or Inspiration?

When it emerged a few centuries ago, the Yugoslav idea was far ahead of its time; progressive, evolutionary, and emancipatory, it managed to evolve into a state, persist through great trials, and—in dying—give birth to new states and nations.

Is there a perspective, then, thoroughly soaked in contemplative thought, that could ever deem this idea a utopia?

Born in the place where the border between the eastern and western world was formed in antiquity, it unexpectedly grew into a bridge that connected them. Defiant with wisdom, not with a sword, it inspired tribes and peoples across the Balkans and beyond. In this legacy lies its enduring beauty and the reason why it refuses to consign itself to oblivion.

Bibliography

Andrić, Ivo. *Nove pripovetke* ["New Stories"], short story "Pismo iz 1920. godine" ["A Letter from 1920"]. Belgrade: Kultura, 1946.

Aldrich, Richard J. "America used Islamists to arm the Bosnian Muslims." *The Guardian*, April 22nd, 2002.

Bogetić, Dragan. *Tito i ustavno-pravno regulisanje nacionalnog pitanja u Jugoslaviji. Period centralizovanog upravljanja federacijom 1945-1965* ["Tito and the Constitutional-Legal Regulation of the National Question in Yugoslavia. The Period of Centralized Management of the Federation 1945-1965"]. Belgrade: Institute for Contemporary History, 2009.

Bogićević, Vojislav. *Sarajevski atentat* ["The Sarajevo Assassination"]. Sarajevo: State Archive of the Republic of BiH, 1954.

Branch, Taylor. *The Clinton Tapes: Wrestling History with the President.* Simon & Schuster, 2009.

Bronitsky, Johathan. *British foreign policy and Bosnia: The rise of Islamism in Britain, 1992–1995.* ICSR, 2010.

Brzezinski, Zbignew. *The Grand Chessboard: American Primacy and Its Geostrategic Imperatives.* New York: Basic Books, 1997.

Carnegie Endowment for International Peace, Division of Intercourse and Education. *Report of the International Commission to inquire into the Causes and Conduct of the Balkan Wars*, Pub. No. 4. Washington D.C.: 1914.

Chomsky, Noam. *Yugoslavia: Peace, War, and Dissolution.* Edited by Davor Džalto. Oakland: PM Press, 2018.

Cvetković, Srdjan. *Represija komunističkog režima u Srbiji na kraju Drugog svetskog rata sa osvrtom na evropsko iskustvo* ["Repression of the Communist Regime in Serbia at the End of World War II with Reference to European Experience"]. In *Zbornik radova „1945. Kraj ili novi početak?"* [Collection of papers: "1945. The End or a New Beginning?"]. Belgrade: Institute for Recent History of Serbia, Museum of Genocide Victims, 2016.

Ćosić, Dobrica. *Vreme zmija – Piščevi zapisi 1999–2000* ["Time of Snakes - Writer's Notes 1999–2000"]. Belgrade: Official Gazette, 2008.

Der Spiegel. "Interview with Jakup Krasniqi," no. 28 (1998).

Deutsche Welle. "Bizarno prijateljstvo Tudjmana i Miloševića" [Bizarre Friendship between Tudjman and Milošević]. Website article.

Encyclopedia Britannica. Article: "Croatia - World War II." Online edition.

Feldbauer, Božidar. *Atlas svijeta* ["World Atlas"]. Zagreb: Miroslav Krleža Lexicographic Institute, 1988.

Farnam, Ruth Stanley. *A Nation at Bay: What an American Woman Saw and Did in Suffering Serbia.* Bobbs-Merrill, USA, 1918.

Freeman, Gregory A. *The Forgotten 500.* Penguin Publishing Group, USA, 2008.

Fromkin, David. *Europe's Last Summer: Why the World Went to War in 1914.* New York: Random House, 2004.

Hebblethwaite, Peter. *Paul VI, the First Modern Pope*. Harper Collins Religious, 1993.

Hedges, Chris. "Croatia Resettling Its People In Houses Seized From Serbs." *The New York Times*, May 14th, 1997.

Hrvatska enciklopedija, vol. 7 [Croatian Encyclopedia, vol. 7]. Zagreb: Miroslav Krleža Lexicographic Institute, 2005.

Hrvatski službeni list Narodne novine [Official Gazette of Croatia "Narodne novine"], July 7th, 1941.

Imamović, Mustafa. *Historija Bošnjaka* ["History of the Bosniaks"]. Sarajevo: BZK "Preporod", 1997.

Jović, Borisav. *Knjiga o Miloševiću* ["Book about Milošević"]. Belgrade: Nikola Pašić, 2001.

Jović, Borisav. *Poslednji dani SFRJ* ["The Last Days of SFRY"]. Belgrade: Politika, 1995.

Kadijević, Veljko. *Protivudar—Moje vidjenje raspada Jugoslavije* ["Counterstrike—My View of the Disintegration of Yugoslavia"]. Belgrade: IP Filip Višnjić, 2010.

Kjellén, Rudolf. *Staten som livsform* ["The State as a Life Form"]. Stockholm, 1916.

Komisija za utvrdjivanje ratnih zločina okupatora i njihovih pomagača u Srbiji 1941-1944. *Otvorena Knjiga* [Commission for Determining War Crimes of the Occupiers and Their Collaborators in Serbia 1941-1944. "Open Book"]. Online edition.

Krizman, Bogdan. *Pavelić izmedju Hitlera i Musolinija* ["Pavelić between Hitler and Mussolini"]. Zagreb, 1980.

Krizman, Bogdan. *Ustaše i 3. Reich*, ["Ustashas and the Third Reich"] Volumes 1-2. Zagreb: Globus, 1983.

Mackinder, Halford John. "The Geographical Pivot of History." *The Geographical Journal* Vol. 23, No. 4, Apr. 1904. The Royal Geographical Society, UK.

Maclean, Fitzroy. *Eastern Approaches: The Memoirs of the Original British Action Hero*. UK: Penguin, 2009.

Mahan, Alfred Thayer. *The Influence of Sea Power upon History, 1660–1783*. Boston: Little, Brown and Company, 1890.

Mackinder, Halford. *Demokratski ideali i stvarnost* ["Democratic Ideals and Reality"]. Belgrade: Metaphysica, 2009.

Marjanović D., Fornarino S., Montagna S., et al. "The peopling of modern Bosnia-Herzegovina: Y-chromosome haplogroups in the three main ethnic groups." *Annals of Human Genetics*, 69 (Pt.6), 2005.

Medvedev, Roy, Medvedev, Zhores. *Nepoznati Staljin* ["Unknown Stalin"]. Belgrade: NNK International, 2012.

Miklošič, Franc. *Monumenta serbica spectantia historiam Serbiae, Bosnae, Ragusii*. Vienna, 1858.

Milosavljević, Olivera. "Izbor ili nametanje tradicije" ["Choice or Imposition of Tradition"]. *Republika*, no. 281. Belgrade, March 2002.

National Security Decision Directives. NSDD 133: *United States Policy towards Yugoslavia*, 3/14/1984.

Nenezić, Zoran. *Masoni u Jugoslaviji* ["Masons in Yugoslavia"]. Belgrade: National Book, 1984.

Nikolić, Kosta. 2014. *Istorija Ravnogorskog pokreta* [History of the Ravna Gora Movement]. Vol. I. Belgrade: Zavod za udžbenike i nastavna sredstva [Institute for Textbooks and Teaching Aids].

Nikolić, Kosta, Petrović, Vladimir, eds. *Od mira do rata, dokumenta Predsedništva SFRJ* ["From Peace to War, Documents of the Presidency of the SFRY"], Vol. I (January – March 1991). Belgrade: Institute for Contemporary History, Fund for Humanitarian Law, 2011.

Norris, John. *Collision Course: NATO, Russia, and Kosovo* / foreword by Strobe Talbott. Praeger, 2005.

Novine Novi list, June 3rd, 1941. Rijeka, Independent State of Croatia.

Phillips, David L. *Liberating Kosovo: Coercive Diplomacy and U.S. Intervention*. Belfer Center for Science and International Affairs, 2012.

Piljak, Milan. "Brionski plenum 1966. godine — pokušaj istoriografskog tumačenja dogadjaja" ["Brioni Plenum 1966 - an Attempt at Historical Interpretation of the Event"]. *Tokovi istorije* 1/2010. Belgrade: Institute for Recent History of Serbia.

Rudolf, Davorin. "*Jugoslavija: Unitarna država ili federacija. Povijesne težnje srpskoga i hrvatskog naroda – jedan od uzroka raspada Jugoslavije*" ["Yugoslavia: A Unitary State or Federation. Historical Aspirations of the Serbian and Croatian Peoples—One of the Causes of the Breakup of Yugoslavia"]. *Zbornik Radova Pravnog Fakulteta u Splitu* 46, no. 2 (2009).

Rokai, Petar, Zoltan Djere, Tibor Pal, Aleksandar Kasaš. *Istorija Madjara* ["History of the Hungarians"]. Belgrade: IP CLIO, 2002.

Rupel, Dimitrij. "Rupel: Slovenci su bili kao na studentskoj ekskurziji u Jugoslaviji" ["Rupel: Slovenes were like on a student excursion in Yugoslavia"]. Interview by *Radio Slobodna Evropa* [Radio Free Europe], November 12th, 2018.

Sandes, Flora. *An English Woman-Sergeant in the Serbian Army*. London: Hodder & Stoughton, 1916.

Sandes, Flora. *The Autobiography of a Woman Soldier: A Brief Record of Adventure with the Serbian Army 1916–1919*. London: H. F. & G. Witherby, 1927.

Schabas, William. *Genocide in International Law: The Crime of Crimes*. Cambridge: Cambridge University Press, 2000.

Selimović, Meša. *Tvrdjava* ["The Fortress"]. Belgrade: Marso, 2009.

Seton Watson, R.W., Young A. "Jugoslavia and Croatia." *Journal of Royal Institute of International Affairs* 8, no. 2 (1929).

Stanković, Dj. *Sto govora Nikole Pašića – Veština govorništva državnika, knj. 1* ["Hundred Speeches of Nikola Pašić – The Skill of Statesmanship Oratory", Vol. 1]. Belgrade: RAD, 2007.

Uebersichts-Tafeln zur Statistik der österreichischen Monarchie: besonderer Abdruck des X. und XI. Heftes der „Statistischen Mittheilungen", 1850. [Statistical Reports of the Austrian Monarchy for the year 1850.]

Šlaus, M, et al. "Craniometric relationships among medieval Central European populations: implications for Croat migration and expansion." *CMJ* 45, no. 4 (2004).

Tawil, Edward. *Property Rights in Kosovo: a Haunting Legacy of a Society in Transition*. New York: International Center for Transitional Justice, 2009.

Tesla, Nikola. "A Tribute to King Alexander." *The New York Times*, October 21st, 1934.

The International Criminal Tribunal for the Former Yugoslavia. Case No. IT-06-90-A. The Hague, September 2011.

United States Holocaust Memorial Museum. "Jasenovac." Official Website.

US Congress House. Report 105-804: *Investigation Into Iranian Arms Shipments to Bosnia*, October 9th, 1998.

"Ustav Republike Hrvatske" ["Constitution of the Republic of Croatia"]. *Narodne novine*, no. 56 (December 22th, 1990).

"Ustav Socijalističke Republike Hrvatske" ["Constitution of the Socialist Republic of Croatia"]. *Narodne novine*, no. 8 (February 22nd, 1974).

"Ustav Socijalističke Federativne Republike Jugoslavije" ["Constitution of the Socialist Federative Republic of Yugoslavia"]. *Official Gazette SFRJ*, Belgrade, 1974.

Valiani, Leo. *The End of Austria-Hungary*. New York: Alfred A. Knopf, 1973.

Velikonja, Mitja. *Religious Separation and Political Intolerance in Bosnia-Herzegovina*. College Station, Texas: Texas A&M University Press, 2003.

Vuković, Nebojša, ed. *David vs. Goliath: NATO War against Yugoslavia and Its Implications*. Belgrade: Institute for International Politics and Economy, Faculty for Security Studies, 2019, p. 142.

Vuković, Slobodan. 2008. "Paradigma prijatelj-neprijatelj: model antisrpske propagande '90-ih" [The Friend-Enemy Paradigm: The Model of Anti-Serbian Propaganda in the '90s]. *Sociološki pregled* 42, no. 3.

Werth, Mathias, and Jo Angerer. 2000. *Es begann mit einer Lüge* [It Started with a Lie]. Documentary film. WDR Fernsehen.

Wiebes, Cees. 2003. *Intelligence and the War in Bosnia: 1992–1995*. Berlin: LIT Verlag.

Zečević, Miodrag, ed. 1998. *Početak kraja SFRJ, Stenogram i drugi prateći dokumenti proširene sednice Izvršnog komiteta CK SKJ održane 14-16. marta 1962* [The Beginning of the End of SFRY, Transcript and Other Accompanying Documents of the Extended Session of the Executive Committee of CK SKJ Held on March 14th-16th, 1962]. Archive of Yugoslavia, Belgrade.

Zimmerman, Warren. 1995. "Origins of Catastrophe." *Foreign Affairs*, March/April.

Zupan, Andrej, et al. 2013. "The Paternal Perspective of the Slovenian Population and Its Relationship with Other Populations." *Annals of Human Biology* 40, no. 6.

Zuroff, Efraim. 2015. "Srebrenica se nikako ne može porediti sa holokaustom" [Srebrenica Can in No Way Be Compared with the Holocaust]. *Politika*, June 18th. Belgrade.

Image Credits

Page 23: Image edited. Original image: "The topography of the Balkan Peninsula, as defined by the Danube-Sava-Kupa line." by user Captain Blood~commonswiki on Wikimedia Commons (CC BY 3.0).

Page 30: "Geopolitical conceptualization of the world according to Heartland and Rimland doctrines". Nicolas Spykman. Source: Macedonian Academy of Sciences and Arts. By user Македонец on Wikimedia Commons (CC BY-SA 4.0).

Page 43: Image edited. Original image: "The origin and dispersion of the Slavs in the 5-10th centuries" by user Fphilibert from fr.wiki and user:Limulus on Wikimedia Commons (CC BY-SA 3.0).

Page 45: Image cropped. Original file: "Krisztus megkoronázza VII. Konsztantinosz Porphürogennétoszt, elefántcsont, 945". By Wooofer on Wikimedia Commons (CC BY-SA 4.0).

Page 48: Image cropped. Original file: "Historical Map of Europe at the death of Charles the Great, 814..jpg" by user MiG174 on Wikimedia Commons (CC BY-SA 4.0).

Page 51. Image cropped. Photo of the The Šopot inscription, near Benkovac, mentioning Duke Branimir, who was recognised by Pope John VIII as the ruler of Croatia (reigned until his death in 892), while Croatia was recognised as an independent state. Source: https://croatia.eu/index.php?view=article&lang=2&id=20.

Page 53: File: "Borders of the Historical Habsburgian Lands in the Republic of Slovenia.svg" by user DancingPhilosopher on Wikimedia Commons (CC BY-SA 3.0).

Page 57: Image "Stefan Nemanja". Source: Fotomagacin (http://www.antikvarne-knjige.com/fotomagacin/).

Page 60: File: "Coat of arms of the Kingdom of Serbia (medieval).svg" by user ХЕРАЛДИКА СССС on Wikimedia Commons (CC BY-SA 4.0)

Page 60: Image cropped. Original file: "Denaro of Domenico Gattilusio.jpg" by user Classical Numismatic Group, Inc on Wikimedia Commons (CC BY-SA 2.5).

Page 77: Map "Balkans in 1815" by user Mladifilozof on Wikimedia Commons (CC BY 3.0)

Page 78: Image edited. Original map: "Military Frontier Province Between the Habsburg and Ottoman Empires, ca. 1600-1800". In *Yugoslavia, 2: History, Peoples and Administration*. London: Admiralty, Naval Intelligence Division, 1944, pp. 20.

Page 82: Photo of Nikola Tesla taken by American artist Napoleon Sarony circa 1893. Public domain.

Page 83: Image "Vožd Djordje Petrović Karadjordje". Source: Fotomagacin (http://www.antikvarne-knjige.com/fotomagacin/).

Page 84: Image "Knez Miloš Obrenović". Source: Fotomagacin (http://www.antikvarne-knjige.com/fotomagacin/).

Page 85: Image edited. Original map: "Europe 1878. Historical map of the political situation after the Congress of Berlin and the territorial and political rearrangement of the Balkan Peninsula" by user Alexander Altenhof on Wikimedia Commons (CC BY-SA 4.0).

Page 109: *"Portret Petra I Karadjordjevića"* [Portrait of Petar I Karadjordjević], Creator: Sima Žikić, 1912, Pencil drawing, courtesy of Zavičajni muzej Knjaževac [Knjaževac Local Museum] on Wikimedia Commons (CC BY-SA 3.0).

Page 121: Map edited. Original map: "Evropski vojni savezi 1915. godine" [European Military Alliances of 1915]. by user Historicair (derivative work: Augusta 89. File:Map Europe alliances 1914-fr.svg) on Wikimedia Commons (CC BY-SA 3.0).

Page 129: Illustration "Serbian and American Flags Waving Together above the White House". Source: U.S. Embassy in Serbia website.

Page 140: Image "Nikola Pašić". Source: Fotomagacin (http://www.antikvarne-knjige.com/fotomagacin/).

Page 156: Divisional General Petar Živković with participants of the Masonic Congress, Belgrade, September 1926. The photograph was taken in front of the Royal Guard House in Topčider. (photographed by Aleksandar Simić, Museum of Yugoslavia).

Page 205: Image "Josip Broz Tito in Bihać in 1942". Source: Marxists Internet Archive on Wikimedia Commons.

Page 209: Image "Kozarčanka" [Woman from Kozara]. Photo taken in 1943 by Georgije-Žorž Vladimirovič Skrigin (1910—1997). The subject of the portrait is a young Yugoslav Partisan, Milja Toroman.

Page 211: Marshal Tito with British officers, island of Vis, 1944. In the middle is Fitzroy Maclean. (Photograph from the album presented to Marshal Tito by the editors of "Life" magazine, Museum of Yugoslavia).

Page 226: "Builder of a New Life." (Photograph from the Photo Album of the construction of the Brčko-Banovići railway presented to Marshal Tito by the builders, Museum of Yugoslavia).

Page 230: "The Percentages Agreement." Printscreen from a video. Image credit: The National Archives, UK.

Page 232: The visit of the Soviet delegation to Yugoslavia: the first visit of the delegation members to President Tito, Belgrade, May 26th, 1955. In the picture are Tito and Nikita Khrushchev. (Photo service KPR, Museum of Yugoslavia).

Page 235 and back cover page: Visit of President Tito to Great Britain: reception at Westminster Pier, London, March 16th, 1953. Beside Tito is Prince Philip, in the background Winston Churchill. (Photo service KPR, Museum of Yugoslavia).

Page 237: File: "Cold war europe military alliances map en.png" by user San Jose on Wikimedia Commons (CC BY-SA 3.0).

Page 258: Visit of Richard Burton and Elizabeth Taylor to President Tito and Jovanka Broz, Vanga, Brioni, August 3rd, 1971. (Photo service KPR, Museum of Yugoslavia).

Page 259: Visit of President Tito to the USA: Meeting with President Nixon at the White House, Washington, October 28th, 1971. (Photo Service KPR, Photographer: Aleksandar Stojanović, Museum of Yugoslavia).

Page 264: Funeral of President Tito: Paying respects in front of the House of Flowers, Belgrade, May 8th, 1980. Around the coffin are the president's aides-de-camp, while in the background, there is a grandstand with statesmen from around the world. (Photo Service KPR, Museum of Yugoslavia).

Page 292: File: "Nikola Ljubicic General Armije.jpg" by user Ljubicic on Wikimedia Commons (CC BY-SA 3.0).

Page 293: Reception of the Yugoslav People's Army delegation by President Tito and a joint seated lunch, Karadjordjevo, December 21st, 1979. General of the Army Nikola Ljubičić sits to the left of President Tito, and Admiral Branko Mamula is seated to the right. (Photo Service KPR, Museum of Yugoslavia).

Page 300: Slobodan Milošević in Kosovo Polje on April 24th, 1987. Youtube/printscreen. Footage by Radio-Television Belgrade.

Page 300: Ivan Stambolić, May 1986. Photo by Stevan Kragujević (with the permission of his daughter, Tanja Kragujević).

Page 305: Rally of "Brotherhood and Unity" (also known as the Ušće Rally), Belgrade, November 19th, 1988. (Photo by Stevan Kragujević, Museum of Yugoslavia).

Page 314: Slobodan Milošević at the 10th Congress of the League of Communists of Serbia, Belgrade, May 26-28, 1986. (photographed by Stevan Kragujević, Museum of Yugoslavia)

Page 330: Prime Minister Ante Marković with members of his Cabinet on the day of the elections in the Federal Assembly, Belgrade, March 16th, 1989. (Photo by Stevan Kragujević, Museum of Yugoslavia)

Page 354: Young JNA soldier Bahrudin Kaletović during 10-day war in Slovenia. Footage by TV YUTEL on June 27th, 1991.

Page 364: File: "Map of Republika Srpska Krajina.png" on Wikimedia Commons (CC BY-SA 3.0).

Page 385: File: "Jadranko Prlić 2017.jpg". Source: UN International Criminal Tribunal for the former Yugoslavia's photostream/Flickr on Wikimedia Commons (CC BY-SA 2.0).

Page 385: File: "RadovanKaradzicICTY.jpg". Source: UN International Criminal Tribunal for the former Yugoslavia's photostream/Flickr on Wikimedia Commons (CC BY-SA 2.0).

Page 391: File: "S. Kragujevic, Ivo Andric, 1961.jpg". Photo by Stevan Kragujević (with the permission of his daughter, Tanja Kragujević).

Page 416: File: "Intolerance.jpg" by Flickr user marietta amarcord on Wikimedia Commons (CC BY-SA 2.0).

Page 465: Author's photograph by Nebojša Babić, https://orange.rs

Author's Note

It's been a true pleasure to share this exploration of Yugoslavia's fascinating yet profoundly complex history with you. As you've delved into the story, you've discovered a captivating tapestry woven with triumphs and struggles that offers an eye-opening perspective into 20th-century Europe.

Your voice is important. Did Yugoslavia offer a glimpse of a utopian future, or does its legacy serve as a guidepost for a better understanding of ongoing geopolitical competitions and provide insights for a brighter path forward? Please share your honest thoughts by leaving an authentic review on Amazon.

(Scan the QR code below to access the review page for
Yugoslavia: Utopia or Inspiration? on Amazon.)

Every review helps others make informed choices about their next read and contributes to the ongoing conversation about Yugoslavia's lasting impact.

Thank you again for joining me on this journey.

Warmly,

Srdjan Ristić

About the Author

Srdjan Ristić was born in Belgrade, the 'crossroads of worlds'—where myriad civilizations have intersected since time immemorial. He descends from families whose ethnic, religious, and cultural diversity significantly influenced his interest in neutrally observing the complex historical, political, and sociological processes characteristic of the tumultuous Balkans and the region of the former Yugoslavia.

With a professional background in tourism, Ristić's work took him to corners of the globe, where he deepened his understanding of world history, art, culture, and politics. He engaged in numerous fascinating encounters and opinion exchanges with people from all continents, of varied origins, skin colors, education levels, and professions. This experience allowed him to better appreciate the place and role of his homeland, its people, and its neighbors in the global context. For three decades, Ristić has immersed himself in the study of Yugoslavia, unraveling the complexities of its vibrant, yet tumultuous history.

Throughout the years, Ristić has shared his knowledge widely as a guest lecturer, crafting lectures in both English and Serbian that delve into the cultural, historical, and political legacies of the Balkans, Yugoslavia, and Serbia. In addition to these educational endeavors, he has built enduring relationships with state institutions, companies, and embassies, representing Belgrade and Serbia to a range of state, economic, and scientific delegations, the diplomatic corps, media, and numerous influential individuals.

Srdjan Ristić's *Yugoslavia: Utopia or Inspiration?* represents the pinnacle of his research and dedication to the Yugoslav phenomenon. It navigates the labyrinthine complexity of former Yugoslavia's history with skill and illuminates readers with its profound analysis. The book not only tells the riveting tale of a nation's rise and fall but also presents a multitude of perspectives, adding layers of depth and meaning to the historical narrative. Through its multidimensional and unbiased exploration, it enriches readers' understanding of the intricate dynamics that shaped Yugoslavia, making it an invaluable addition to both scholarly and popular literature on the subject.

Printed in Great Britain
by Amazon

47501380R10258